Eva Perón

Significant Figures in World History

Charles Darwin: A Reference Guide to His Life and Works,
by J. David Archibald, 2019.

Leonardo da Vinci: A Reference Guide to His Life and Works,
by Allison Lee Palmer, 2019.

Michelangelo: A Reference Guide to His Life and Works,
by Lilian H. Zirpolo, 2020.

Robert E. Lee: A Reference Guide to His Life and Works,
by James I. Robertson Jr., 2019.

John F. Kennedy: A Reference Guide to His Life and Works,
by Ian James Bickerton, 2019.

Florence Nightingale: A Reference Guide to Her Life and Works,
by Lynn McDonald, 2019.

Napoléon Bonaparte: A Reference Guide to His Life and Works,
by Joshua Meeks, 2019.

Nelson Mandela: A Reference Guide to His Life and Works,
by Aran S. MacKinnon, 2020.

Winston Churchill: A Reference Guide to His Life and Works,
by Christopher Catherwood, 2020.

Catherine the Great: A Reference Guide to Her Life and Works,
by Alexander Kamenskii, 2020.

Golda Meir: A Reference Guide to Her Life and Works,
by Meron Medzini, 2020.

Karl Marx: A Reference Guide to His Life and Works,
by Frank Elwell, Brian Andrews, and Kenneth S. Hicks, 2020.

Eva Perón: A Reference Guide to Her Life and Works,
by María Belén Rabadán Vega and Mirna Vohnsen, 2021.

Eva Perón

A Reference Guide to Her Life and Works

María Belén Rabadán Vega
and Mirna Vohnsen

ROWMAN & LITTLEFIELD
Lanham • Boulder • New York • London

Published by Rowman & Littlefield
An imprint of The Rowman & Littlefield Publishing Group, Inc.
4501 Forbes Boulevard, Suite 200, Lanham, Maryland 20706
www.rowman.com

86-90 Paul Street, London EC2A 4NE, United Kingdom

Copyright © 2021 by María Belén Rabadán Vega and Mirna Vohnsen

All rights reserved. No part of this book may be reproduced in any form or by any electronic or mechanical means, including information storage and retrieval systems, without written permission from the publisher, except by a reviewer who may quote passages in a review.

British Library Cataloguing in Publication Information Available

Library of Congress Cataloging-in-Publication Data

Names: Belén Rabadán Vega, María, 1980– author. | Vohnsen, Mirna, author.
Title: Eva Perón : a reference guide to her life and works / María Belén Rabadán Vega and Mirna Vohnsen.
Description: Lanham : Rowman & Littlefield, [2021] | Series: Significant figures in world history | Includes bibliographical references, filmography, and index. | Summary: "Eva Perón: A Reference Guide to Her Life and Work captures Evita's eventful life, her works, and her legacy. The volume features a chronology, an introduction, a bibliography, and a cross-reference dictionary section that includes entries on people, places, and events related to her"—Provided by publisher.
Identifiers: LCCN 2021011755 (print) | LCCN 2021011756 (ebook) | ISBN 9781538139127 (cloth) | ISBN 9781538197615 (paper) | ISBN 9781538139134 (epub)
Subjects: LCSH: Perón, Eva, 1919–1952—Bibliography. | Presidents' spouses—Argentina—Biography.
Classification: LCC F2849.P37 B44 2021 (print) | LCC F2849.P37 (ebook) | DDC 982.06/2092 [B]—dc23
LC record available at https://lccn.loc.gov/2021011755
LC ebook record available at https://lccn.loc.gov/2021011756

Contents

Preface — vii

Acronyms and Abbreviations — ix

Map of Argentina — xi

Chronology — xiii

Introduction — 1

ENTRIES A–Z — 9

Bibliography — 153

Filmography — 167

Index — 171

About the Authors — 187

Preface

No Latin American woman has ever elicited such extreme feelings of love and hate, either in life or death, as Eva Perón (1919–1952). She was an actress of humble origins who fell in love with and married the soon-to-be president of Argentina, Juan Domingo Perón. Evita, as she was fondly known, became the most influential and powerful woman in the history of Argentina. Adored by the masses and loathed by the bourgeoisie, Evita polarized Argentine society. While her devoted *descamisados* or working-class people revered her as a saint, a benefactress, and a heroine, her opponents judged her as a social climber, a prostitute, and a lowlife. Not even her death could put an end to the mixed feelings she aroused during her lifetime, and Evita remains, to this day, a deeply controversial figure both in her native Argentina and abroad.

Despite her flaws, there is no denying that she was a woman who crossed borders and overcame gender barriers. At the age of 15, she left her provincial hometown and her family to try her luck in the capital city of Buenos Aires. There she became a radio actress and eventually managed to secure a few small film roles. Her life changed drastically when a massive earthquake in western Argentina brought her and Perón together. Not only did she move in with Perón shortly after having met him, she was also present at his meetings and accompanied him to official events. The Argentine establishment was shocked by the brazenness of her behavior. Evita was only 26 when she became the first lady of Argentina but soon showed that she was a far cry from her predecessors. Contesting the hitherto ceremonial role of the first lady, she became actively involved in politics and set up her own foundation to help the disadvantaged classes of Argentina. She never held an official position in government, but this was not an impediment to carrying out her work; on the contrary, she was unstoppable. She paid an official visit to Europe, helped women in Argentina win the right to vote, aspired to be the vice president of the country, and created her own political party. Despite her short life—she died of cervical cancer aged 33—Evita had changed Argentine society forever.

Although she passed away almost 70 years ago, Evita's image continues to thrive. Far from making her vanish from the shared public memory, the anti-Peronist campaign set up by the military government that toppled Perón in 1955, in tandem with the subsequent disappearance of her body, which had been embalmed immediately after her death, accentuated her iconic quasi-religious status. During the 1960s and 1970s, the image of Evita was used by guerrilla groups in Argentina as a symbol of liberation and political change. Former Argentine president Cristina Fernández de Kirchner eulogized and promoted Evita on every possible occasion. Renewed interest in Evita abroad was fueled by Tim Rice and Andrew Lloyd Webber's rock opera *Evita*. This successful musical was followed by the publication of Tomás Eloy Martínez's bestselling novel *Santa Evita* in 1995, which further increased international interest in Evita. A year later, Alan Parker's film *Evita*, starring the

American singer Madonna, cemented Evita's transnational iconic image.

Our goal with this volume is to capture Evita's short eventful life, her works, and her legacy. The book begins with a chronology that identifies the main events in Evita's life, including her childhood, her acting career, her trip to Europe, her political life, her illness, and her death, as well as more recent events that have kept her memory alive. The introduction offers a brief account of her life. The dictionary section lists entries on people, places, and events in Evita's life and beyond, even if they were tangentially related to her. Entries on recent Argentine history and politics are also featured in this book, which reveals the extent of Evita's legacy. To facilitate the location of information, we have provided extensive cross-references in this section. The bibliography offers a list of works by and about Evita. The final section of the volume is a filmography that includes the films in which Evita appeared as well as the TV series and movies that have been made about her.

As Argentines, women, and researchers in Argentine culture, we were thrilled and honored when Jon Woronoff asked us to work on this project. We are extremely thankful to him and the entire team at Rowman & Littlefield for giving us this opportunity and being so supportive throughout the process. Writing about Evita has taught us not only about her and our country of origin but also about the huge influence she still exerts on Argentine society. When we embarked on this project, little did we know that months into it we would be facing the global COVID-19 pandemic. Its impact was felt on our personal lives and our research. Archives, libraries, and other institutions that we needed to access have now been closed for months, and a research trip to Argentina was canceled. As a result, gathering information for this project turned out to be challenging.

We would like to extend a special thank-you to David Barnwell and Alan Smyth for reading part of the manuscript and providing perceptive suggestions and constructive feedback. We wish to thank María Mercedes Di Benedetto for sharing her knowledge with us. We are also extremely thankful to our families, as this project would not have been possible without their support.

María Belén Rabadán Vega
Maynooth University
Mirna Vohnsen
Technological University Dublin

Acronyms and Abbreviations

AAA	Asociación Argentina de Actores (Argentine Actors' Association)
ARA	Asociación Radial Argentina (Argentine Radio Association)
CGT	Confederación General del Trabajo (General Confederation of Labor)
FPV	Frente Para la Victoria (Front for Victory)
FREJULI	Frente Justicialista de Liberación (Justicialist Liberation Front)
FREJUPO	Frente Justicialista de Unidad Popular (Justicialist Front of Popular Unity)
GOU	Grupo de Oficiales Unidos (United Officers Group)
INIHEP	Instituto Nacional de Investigaciones Históricas Eva Perón (Eva Perón National Institute of Historical Research)
JP	Juventud Peronista (Peronist Youth)
PJ	Partido Justicialista (Justicialist Party)
PL	Partido Laborista (Labor Party)
PP	Partido Peronista (Peronist Party)
PPF	Partido Peronista Femenino (Peronist Women's Party)
UCR	Unión Cívica Radical (Radical Civic Union)
UES	Unión de Estudiantes Secundarios (Secondary School Students' Union)

Map of Argentina

Chronology

This chronology provides key information and facts about Evita together with related historical events. Several sources were explored to create this timeline, prime among these being biographies, scholarly articles, and other publications on Evita and Peronism. In addition, data was collected from press articles and authoritative webpages, such as evitaperon.org.

The task of uncovering Evita and details about her life has always been challenging for scholars given the relative shortage of trustworthy sources available. Scholar Alberto Ciria reflected on this issue when he stated that the tendency to take sources at face value without critical appraisal is a problem that constantly plagues researchers of Evita, Juan Domingo Perón, and Peronism. We were also affected by this issue, as the compilation process revealed source discrepancies, especially in accounting for details on the early years of Evita's life and her artistic side. We opted for carrying out a comparative analysis of different publications, both academic and nonacademic, on Evita and Peronism. Through this laborious task, we wanted to ensure that the information provided here had been corroborated by at least two of the consulted sources. Accordingly, the chronology that follows outlines information shared by most of these sources.

1919 **7 May:** Eva María Ibarguren (hereafter Evita), the fifth of five children, is born on Estancia La Unión in General Viamonte County, Buenos Aires Province, Argentina, to Juan Duarte and Juana Ibarguren, an unmarried couple. **21 November:** Evita is baptized at Our Lady of the Pillar Church in Los Toldos, General Viamonte County.

1920 **January–May:** Juan Duarte abandons Juana Ibarguren and her children and moves back to Chivilcoy, Buenos Aires Province, where he has a wife and children. Juana and her children settle in a modest house by the railroad in the town of Los Toldos, General Viamonte County, Buenos Aires Province. Evita is known as "Chola."

1926 **January:** Evita's father dies in a car accident. Evita together with her mother and siblings attends Juan Duarte's funeral in Chivilcoy.

1927 **March:** Starts attending primary school in Los Toldos.

1929 Repeats second grade due to her poor attendance.

1930 **January–June:** Evita and her family move to Junín, Buenos Aires Province. **August:** Attends Catalina Larralt de Estrugamou School.

1933 **December:** Finishes her primary education.

1934 **28–29 April:** Reportedly makes her radio debut at Radio La Nación. **28 April:** Mentioned in Junín's newspaper *El Amigo del Pueblo*. **1 October:** Recites the poem "¿Adónde van los muertos?" (Where Do the Dead Go?) at Radio Cultura in Buenos Aires.

CHRONOLOGY

1935 January: Moves to Buenos Aires to pursue an artistic career. **28 March:** Makes her stage debut in the play *La señora de los Pérez* (Mrs. Pérez) at the Comedia Theater. The theater company performing this play, the Compañía Argentina de Comedias, is managed by actor José Franco and director Joaquín de Vedia. The leading actress is José Franco's daughter Eva Franco. Evita works with this theater company until January 1936. **29 March:** *Crítica* reviews *La señora de los Pérez* and mentions Evita. **30 March:** *El Amigo del Pueblo* publishes a short article about Evita's career in Buenos Aires. **April:** Starts working at Radio París. **19 June:** Evita is part of the cast of the play *Cada casa es un mundo* (Every Home Is a Different World), which is performed at the Comedia Theater. **6 July:** Evita's first solo photograph is published in *Sintonía*. **November:** Has several small walk-on roles in the play *Madame Sans-Gêne*, performed at the Cómico Theater.

1936 2 January: Premiere of the play *La dama, el caballero y el ladrón* (The Lady, the Gentleman, and the Thief) at the Cómico Theater. Plays the role of Miss Wade. **February:** Evita is allegedly part of the cast of a *sainete* by Alberto Vaccareza, *La fiesta de Juan Manuel* (Juan Manuel's Party), performed at the Sociedad Rural Argentina in Buenos Aires, an association of some of the country's biggest farmers and landowners. **May:** Joins the theater company of Pepita Muñoz, José Franco, and Eloy Álvarez. Their debut play, *Miente y serás feliz* (Lie and You Will Be Happy), opens at the Odeón Theater in Rosario, Santa Fe Province, on 22 May. **11 June:** Performs in the play *El beso mortal* (The Mortal Kiss) at the Odeón Theater. **26 July:** Evita's portrait is published by *La Capital* newspaper. **30 July:** Makes her debut in Mendoza, the capital of the eponymous Argentine province, in the play *Baturros y más baturros* (Nothing but Stubborn People) at the Municipal Theater. **December:** Joins Pablo Suero Siero's theater company in *Las inocentes* (*The Children's Hour*) at the Corrientes Theater in Buenos Aires.

1937 14–20 January: Travels abroad for the first time with Suero Siero's theater company. They perform at the 18 July Theater in Montevideo, Uruguay. **5 March:** Takes part in the play *La nueva colonia* (The New Colony) at the Politeama Theater in Buenos Aires. The theater company performing this play is managed by the distinguished theater writer and director Armando Discépolo. **Spring:** Reportedly begins working at Radio Porteña in a *radioteatro* series titled *Los caminos de la historia* (The Paths of History). **June:** Evita is reportedly part of the cast of the *radioteatro* or serial radio drama *La vengadora* (The Avenger) at Radio Belgrano. **August–October:** Begins working at Radio Mitre and Radio Belgrano, where she acts in several *radioteatros* performed by the theater company Compañía Remembranzas. **4 August:** Premiere of film *¡Segundos afuera!* (Seconds Out!), in which Evita has a bit part. **November:** Joins the theater company of Leonor Rinaldi and Francisco Charmiello. Lands a small part in the play *No hay suegra como la mía* (There Is No Mother-in-Law Like Mine), performed by this company at the Liceo Theater in Buenos Aires.

1938 March: Joins the theater company of Pierina Dealessi, the Compañía Argentina de Espectáculos Cómicos, and continues working with this company during 1938. Performs in several plays, including *El cura de Santa Clara* (Santa Clara's Priest) and *Una noche en Viena* (A Night in Vienna). **17 March:** Performs in the play *La gruta de la fortuna* (The Grotto of Fortune) at the Liceo Theater. **Spring:** Reportedly starts working as a model with the advertising agency Linter Publicidad. **Summer:** Allegedly secures a two-month contract with Juan Guereño Rodríguez, manufacturer of the popular Radical soap. **19 October:** Evita's first interview is published in *Sintonía* magazine.

1939 January: Becomes a member of the Asociación Argentina de Actores (Argentine Actors' Association). Joins Camila Quiroga's theater company. **5 January:** Performs with Camila Quiroga's theater company in the play *Mercado de amor en Argelia* (Market of Love in Algeria) at the Astral Theater in Buenos Aires. **22 April:** *Antena* magazine publishes Evita's portrait. **May:** Leads together with Pascual Pellicciotta the theater company Compañía de Teatro del Aire, which is hired by Radio Prieto and Radio Mitre to broadcast a series of *radioteatros* starting on 1 May. Has her first starring radio role in *Los jazmines del 80* (The Jasmines of 1880), the first *radioteatro* in the series sponsored by Radical soap. **20 May:** Evita lands her first cover for *Antena* magazine. **25 October:** Appears on the cover of *Sintonía* magazine. **13 December:** Graces the cover of *Damas y Damitas* magazine.

1940 **20 January:** Attends her sister Blanca's civil wedding in Junín. In the afternoon, the whole family travels to Luján, Buenos Aires Province, to celebrate the religious ceremony, which takes place at the Basilica of Our Lady of Luján. **24 January:** Appears on the cover of *Guión* magazine. **April:** Evita and Juan Piñeyro are the hosts of the show *Aquí siempre pasa algo* (There Is Always Something Going on Here), broadcast by Radio Prieto. The Compañía de Teatro del Aire, headed by Evita, starts performing 30 episodes of *La carga de los valientes* (Only the Valiant) at Radio Argentina. **3 April:** Appears on the cover of *Mundo Argentino* magazine. **12 June:** Premiere of the film *La carga de los valientes*, in which Evita has a supporting role. **July:** Joins Leopoldo and Tomás Simari's theater company in *¡Llegaron parientes de España!* (Our Family from Spain Is Here!), which opens at the Smart Theater in Buenos Aires on 20 July. Attends several public events, including a party to celebrate the recovery of Tomás Simari, who was in a serious car accident, and a party in honor of Radio Argentina's artistic director, Roberto Gil. **18 July:** Features in an article in *Cine Argentino* magazine. **August:** Continues working with the Simari brothers in two plays: *Corazón de manteca* (Heart of Butter) and *¡La plata hay que repartirla!* (Money Should Be Spread Around!) at the Smart Theater in Buenos Aires. **September:** Attends the premiere of the film *El inglés de los güesos* (The Englishman of the Bones). **22 October:** Attends the premiere of the film *Amor* (Love) and is photographed with other artists. The picture is published in *Guión* magazine on 30 October. **14 and 28 November:** Evita together with other actresses appears in *Cine Argentino* magazine articles.

1941 **Summer/Autumn:** Secures an exclusive five-year contract with Guereño Rodríguez. The first sponsored radio program by Radical soap is allegedly *La hora de las sorpresas* (The Hour of Surprises), hosted by Radio Argentina. **19 March:** Release of the film *El más infeliz del pueblo* (The Unhappiest Man in Town), in which she plays a small role. **27 March:** Appears on the cover of *Cine Argentino* magazine with soccer player Bernardo Gandulla. **13 November:** *Cine Argentino* publishes photographs of a visit paid by Evita and other actresses to the River Plate soccer team, winner of the 1941 national league title. **11 December:** Travels to Junín to visit her firstborn nephew. **24 December:** *Ondanía* magazine publishes a photo of Evita alongside a short article outlining her plans for the following year.

1942 **January:** Performs with the theater company Compañía Juvenil de Radioteatro at Radio Argentina. **March:** Premiere of the film *Una novia en apuros* (A Bride in Trouble), in which Evita plays a lesser role. **May:** The theater company Compañía Juvenil de Radioteatro moves from Radio Argentina to Radio El Mundo and joins the Compañía Candilejas. Becomes Radio El Mundo leading actress and performs in a series of *radioteatros*, including *Una promesa de amor* (A Promise of Love), *Infortunio* (Misfortune), *El rostro y el aullido del lobo* (The Face and the Howl of the Wolf), *Mi amor nace en ti* (My Love Is Born in You), and *La otra cara de la máscara* (The Other Side of the Mask). **10 June:** Appears in an article in *Sintonía* magazine. **July:** Reportedly joins the theater company Compañía Romances del Pueblo, headed by Atilano Ortega Sanz, at Radio Mitre and becomes the leading actress in the *radioteatro* *La calandria ciega* (The Blind Calandra Lark). **September–December:** Tours the country with Ortega Sanz's theater company.

1943 **January–September:** Takes a hiatus from work, and thus her appearances in publications are minimal. Reasons for her taking a break are not clear. **March–April:** Allegedly secures a six-month contract with Linter Publicidad. Evita is sponsored by Linter Publicidad to perform at Radio Belgrano. **3 August:** Becomes one of the founders of the Asociación Radial Argentina (Argentine Radio Association) or ARA. **October:** Starts dramatizing the lives of famous women in history in a radio series titled *Heroínas de la historia* (Heroines in History) at Radio Belgrano.

1944 **6 January:** Evita and other members of the ARA have an audience with Secretary of Labor and Social Welfare Colonel Juan Domingo Perón. **19–22 January:** An earthquake strikes San Juan Province on 15 January, leaving 10,000 people dead and more than 12,000 injured. Walks the streets of Buenos Aires with other actors and actresses collecting money to aid the victims of the San Juan earthquake. Officially meets Perón at the end of the fund-raising events at the Luna Park Stadium in Buenos Aires. Evita and Perón start a romantic relationship. **Late January–early February:** Perón visits Evita at Radio Belgrano. **5 February:** *Radiolandia* magazine publishes the first picture of Evita and Perón together at Radio Belgrano. **March–May:** Signs a 12-month contract with Radio Belgrano. Her salary is one of the best in the radio industry. Also secures a contract with Estudios San Miguel to appear in a supporting role in *La cabalgata del circo* (Circus Cavalcade). **April–May:** Meets costume designer Francisco Vicente Jamandreu, the creator of Evita's famous *tailleur*. Moves in with Perón, who lives on Arenales Street, Buenos Aires. In the same year, they move to two adjacent apartments on Posadas Street, Buenos Aires. **17 May:** Named president of the ARA. This labor union requests official recognition from the government to become the only union that can represent radio workers in the country. **1 June:** Appears on the cover of *Antena* magazine. **3 June:** Graces the cover of *Radiolandia* magazine. **17 June:** Has a starring role at Radio Belgrano and Radio del Estado in *Hacia un futuro mejor* (Toward a Better Future), a propaganda radio series supporting Perón's political policies. **July:** Reportedly stars in the *radioteatro El pasado regresa* (The Past Returns) at Radio Belgrano. **7 July:** Lands the cover of *Ondanía* magazine. **September:** Due to health issues and a hectic schedule, takes a few days off work. **2 September:** *Radiolandia* magazine publishes an interview with Evita. **21 September:** Evita lands the cover of *Antena* magazine. **October:** Secures a three-film contract with Estudios San Miguel. In addition to performing in *Hacia un futuro mejor* and *Heroínas de la historia*, takes part in *En el valle hay una sombra* (There Is a Shadow in the Valley), a mystery *radioteatro* broadcast daily on Radio Belgrano. **22 November:** Like many other artists, Evita takes part in a special program at Radio Belgrano to celebrate St. Cecilia's Day. **December:** Evita appears in a Christmas Eve special program with actor Narciso Ibáñez Menta at Radio Belgrano. **14 December:** *Antena* magazine publishes an article on the opening of Jamandreu's new atelier. Evita and other guests are photographed together with the designer. **23 December:** Appears in a two-page article in *Radiolandia* magazine.

1945 **January:** Continues working at Radio Belgrano in *Heroínas de la historia*, *Hacia un futuro mejor*, and in the *radioteatro Tempestad* (Storm). **6 January:** Evita, Perón, and Domingo Alfredo Mercante distribute toys among children to celebrate the biblical Magi festivity. **15 February:** Appears on the cover of *Antena* magazine, which shows Evita donning the same outfit she wore for the 9 July 1944 gala function at the Colón Theater. **March–September:** Stars in the film *La pródiga* (The Prodigal Woman). **30 May:** Release of the film *La cabalgata del circo* at the Grand Palace Cinema in Buenos Aires. Has dyed her hair blonde for her role in this film. **9 July:** Attends a gala function with Perón at the Colón Theater in Buenos Aires to celebrate the Argentine Independence Day. **22 October:** Marries Perón at a civil ceremony in Junín. **10 December:** Evita and Perón get married at a religious ceremony in La Plata, Buenos Aires Province. **28 December:** Joins her husband on his national presidential campaign tour on the *Descamisado* Train.

1946 **8 February:** Attends a rally to support the Perón–Juan Hortensio Quijano ticket at the Luna Park Stadium in Buenos Aires. As Perón is not feeling well, Evita addresses his supporters on behalf of the leader. Starts delivering a speech but is unable to finish it as the audience demands Perón's presence. **18 February:** Visits Bahía Blanca, Buenos Aires Province. **27 February:** Gives first official political speech supporting women's civil rights. **20 March:** Evita's close friend Anita Jordán dies of cancer. **May:** Begins visiting factories with Isabel Ernst and Lillian Lagomarsino de Guardo. **5 May:** Makes a pilgrimage to Luján to thank Our Lady of Luján for Perón's victory at the ballot. **4 June:** Attends Perón's presidential inauguration ceremony at Congress. Later, Evita and Perón visit the Unzué Palace, the presidential residence. **July:** Starts working as a mediator between Perón and labor union representatives in an office located at the Central Post Office in Buenos Aires. She is also involved in events and activities to aid disadvantaged children. **25 July:** Gives a radio speech as part of the campaign supporting the reduction in the cost of living. The speech is broadcast by Radio del Estado and Red Argentina de Radiodifusión. **3 August:** The Asociación del Personal de Hospitales y Sanatorios Particulares, the private hospital workers' union, hosts an event in her honor and names her Argentina's "First Samaritan." As Evita feels too unwell to attend the event, she expresses her gratitude in a speech delivered from the presidential residence. **15 August:** Travels to Rosario to distribute clothes and food. **16 August:** Visits the Argentine Mint with Perón. **September:** Moves her office from the Central Post Office to the Secretariat of Labor and Social Welfare. **11 September:** Visits the Chamber of Deputies to show her interest in the female suffrage bill approved by the Senate on 21 August. **October:** Evita's activities as both first lady and Perón's collaborator increase considerably. **17 October:** First anniversary of the Peronist Loyalty Day. Attends the celebrations with Perón. **26 October:** Visits Alta Gracia, Córdoba Province, to inaugurate a polyclinic. **30 November:** Travels by plane to San Miguel de Tucumán in Tucumán Province as part of a provincial tour and makes a speech. **24 December:** Delivers a Christmas Eve message on Radio del Estado and Red Argentina de Radiodifusión.

1947 January: Buys *Democracia*, which becomes the first Peronist newspaper. Evita's speeches in favor of the right of women to vote in elections are published regularly in this paper. Considers herself the champion of women's suffrage and promotes the participation of women in politics. **11 January:** Visits Rosario together with Perón to lay the foundation stone for a power plant. **February:** The press announces Evita's official trip to Europe, the Rainbow Tour. The purpose of this diplomatic mission is to represent a "rainbow" rather than an axis between Argentina and Spain. **8 April:** Together with Perón, makes a stop in Junín on her way to Mendoza. **9 April:** Participates in the Grape Harvest Festival in Mendoza. **25 May:** Attends the celebrations of the May Revolution and meets Spanish ambassador José María de Areilza y Martínez de Rodas. **26 May:** Meeting with the Spanish ambassador to finalize the details of her welcome reception in Madrid. **2 June:** José María Freire organizes a farewell party in honor of Evita at the Secretariat of Labor and Social Welfare. **5 June:** A great farewell party is held for Evita at the Sociedad Rural Argentina in Buenos Aires. **6 June:** Embarks on Rainbow Tour. Departs from Morón Airport with her brother Juancito, Lagomarsino de Guardo, Francisco Muñoz Azpiri, Julio Alcaraz, Alberto Dodero, Emilio Abras, Francisco Aisina, Captain Adolfo Gutiérrez, her aide-de-camp Colonel Jorge Ballofet, and two dressmakers. She is also joined by the Count of Foxá III and Marquess of Armendáriz IV Agustín de Foxá y Torroba. Evita and her entourage make a brief stopover at Augusto Severo International Airport (formerly Parnamirim Airport) in Brazil, where Evita addresses Brazilian women. **7 June:** Evita's aircraft lands at the airport in Dakhla (then known as Villa Cisneros), Western Sahara. She is welcomed by Minister of Foreign Affairs Alberto Martín-Artajo Álvarez and his wife and Francisco Franco Bahamonde's secretary Francisco Franco Salgado-Araujo and his wife, among others. **8 June:** Evita's flight from Dakhla to Madrid makes a layover at Gando Airport in Las Palmas de Gran Canaria. Evita is greeted by the captain-general of the Canary Islands, Francisco García-Escámez Iniesta, among others. In Madrid, Evita is greeted by Franco; his wife María del Carmen Polo y Martínez-Valdés (hereafter Carmen Polo); and their daughter María del Carmen Franco y Polo, among others. Receives a spectacular welcome and is taken to the Royal Palace of El Pardo, where she stays for seven nights. Gives a radio speech on Radio Nacional de España. **9 June:** Franco decorates her with the Great Cross of Isabella the Catholic at the Royal Palace of Madrid. Delivers a public speech and visits some public hospitals and working-class districts. In the evening, attends a gala function at the Royal Palace of El Pardo and receives gifts. **10 June:** Together with Carmen Polo, the Argentine ambassador Pedro Radío, and his wife, visits the national craft market in Madrid in the morning. Later visits the Royal Site of San Lorenzo de El Escorial and the Santa María del Buen Aire National Camp. Upon her return to the Royal Palace of El Pardo, delivers a radio address to the Argentine people on Radio Nacional de España. Following an evening folk-dance show performed in her honor, representatives of each region of Spain present Evita with a complete outfit of a traditional costume. **11 June:** Evita and Carmen Polo visit Ávila in the morning and Medina del Campo in the afternoon via Arévalo. They arrive in Segovia in the evening and later travel to La Granja de San Ildefonso. Finally, they return to Madrid. **12 June:** In the morning, meets representatives of the Mercantile and Industrial Labor Union of Madrid and a group of publishers and booksellers at the Royal Palace of El Pardo. Arrives at the decorative arts exhibition at the Retiro Exhibition Palace in Madrid at 1:30 p.m. A bullfight is held in her honor at Las Ventas Bullring at 6 p.m. Attends a gala function at the Madrid City Hall at 10 p.m. Later enjoys Lope de Vega's *Fuenteovejuna* at the Español Theater. **13 June:** Arrives in Toledo at 2:30 p.m. After a dance and music show, has lunch at the city hall. In addition, visits the Primate Cathedral of St. Mary of Toledo and the Alcázar. Upon her return from Toledo, pays a visit to the residence hall Hogar Ciudad Universitaria de Auxilio Social in Madrid. At midnight, attends a celebration in the gardens of the Retiro Park. **14 June:** Visits the University City of Madrid around midday and the Prado Museum shortly after 1:30 p.m. Then, attends a reception in her honor hosted at the Argentine Embassy in Madrid. In the evening, continues touring the city. Visits Casa de las Flores, the Workers' Social Training School, the housing estate Our Lady of the Pillar, and the training center Our Lady of the Doves. Upon her return to the Royal Palace of El Pardo, attends Holy Mass and receives the imposition of the scapular of Our Lady of Mount Carmel. After the ceremony, gives a speech addressing Spanish women on Radio Nacional de España. The last event of the day is a gala function in honor of Franco and his family organized by Evita at the Ritz Hotel. **15 June:** The people of Madrid bid farewell to Evita, who departs from Adolfo Suárez Madrid–Barajas Airport toward the city of Granada. The plane carrying Evita arrives at Armilla Air Base near Granada at 7:14 p.m. After receiving a jovial welcome, makes her first stop at the Basilica of Our Lady of Sorrows. Then tours the streets of the city by car to finally reach the Alhambra Palace Hotel, where she stays for one night. Attends a gala function at the Granada City Hall at 11:45 p.m. and then visits the Alhambra. **16 June:** In the afternoon, visits the Generalife, the Granada Cathedral, and the Royal Chapel of Granada. After having lunch at the National Factory of Gunpowder and Explosives in El Fargue neighborhood, gives a speech addressing the factory workers. In the evening, leaves Granada by plane and arrives at Tablada Air Base in Seville. On her journey toward the city, Evita is hailed by the crowds. Arrives at the Alfonso XIII Hotel, where she spends three nights. Shortly after that, visits the Seville City Hall and receives a great number of gifts. Finally, attends a gala function at the Mudejar Pavilion. **17 June:** Leaves the Alfonso XIII Hotel to go to the Seville Cathedral at around 2:20 p.m. Arrives at St. Giles Church at around 3 p.m. After having lunch at the Alfonso XIII Hotel, visits the Royal Tobacco Factory and later the Torre Pavadel Estate, property of the National Institute of Rural

Development and Colonization. In the evening, attends a gala function at the Captaincy General Building. **18 June:** Takes a break from her busy schedule in the morning and leaves Seville toward the province of Huelva, where she visits the Monument to the Discovery Faith in the city of Huelva and the Friary of La Rábida in the town of Palos de la Frontera. Later visits the residence hall at the University of Santa María de la Rábida. Returns to Seville. **19 June:** In the morning, leaves Seville from Tablada Air Base and arrives in Santiago de Compostela. She is welcomed by local authorities at Santiago–Rosalía de Castro Airport (then known as Lavacolla Airport) at around 1 p.m. Attends a gala function at the Pazo de Raxoi. Greets the large crowd gathered at the Plaza de España. Takes part in the procession of the enthronement of Our Lady of Luján's image at the Santiago de Compostela Cathedral. At 3 p.m., has lunch at the Compostela Hotel, where she then rests for two hours. Before leaving for Pontevedra Province at 8 p.m., plants a tree known as La Perona in the Alameda Park. Arrives at the Monument to García Barbón in Vigo at 10:30 p.m. and is welcomed by the local authorities. Following a welcoming ceremony at the Plaza del Capitán Carrasco, attends a gala function at the city hall. Finally, leaves for the Castrelos Palace, where she spends two nights. **20 June:** In the morning, leaves for the Naval Military Academy located in the city of Marín. Arrives in Vigo at 6:10 p.m. Following a gala function at the Casino, enjoys a folklore party at the Royal Boat Club. **21 June:** Leaves Vigo at 12:45 p.m. After stopping at lunchtime at the Pazo de Lourizán, continues her journey toward Lavacolla Airport. She is bid farewell and departs for Zaragoza at 5:40 p.m. Arrives at Valenzuela Air Base, Zaragoza, at 7:50 p.m. Following a warm welcome, visits the Cathedral-Basilica of Our Lady of the Pillar. Travels to her temporal residence in Our Lady of Cogullada Monastery, located 4 kilometers (2.5 miles) from Zaragoza. Finally, attends a gala function at La Lonja Palace. **22 June:** Following Holy Mass at the church in the Cogullada residence at around 2 p.m., receives numerous gifts and has lunch. Leaves Zaragoza from Valenzuela Air Base shortly after 7 p.m. Arrives at El Prat Air Base at 8:05 p.m. Continues her journey to Barcelona via El Prat de Llobregat. Arrives at the Plaza de España at 8:45 p.m., where she receives a warm welcome. In an open-top car, travels to the Cathedral of the Holy Cross and St. Eulalia and eventually arrives at the Pedralbes Royal Palace, where she stays during her stay in Barcelona. Finally, attends a gala function at the Barcelona City Hall. **23 June:** Following the gala, enjoys the performance of William Shakespeare's *A Midsummer Night's Dream* by the Compañía de Teatro Español de Madrid at the Montjuic Gardens. Rests during the morning and leaves her residence at around 2 p.m. Has lunch on board of the *Hornero*, an Argentine cargo ship. Returns to the Pedralbes Royal Palace at 5 p.m. Takes part in a small event at the palace and receives several gifts. Later, visits the National Palace and the International Trade Fair. In the evening, enjoys the St. John's Eve festivities at the prestigious tennis club Real Club de Tenis de Barcelona. **24 June:** Leaves the Real Club de Tenis de Barcelona and arrives at the Pueblo Español Architectural Museum in the Montjuic Park at 2:35 a.m., where she is entertained by a music show that marks the end of the festivities. Has lunch at the Pedralbes Royal Palace and tours the city in the afternoon. Following a gala function at the Palace of the Generalitat of Catalonia in the evening, attends a festival organized in her honor at the St. James Square. **25 June:** Stays at the Pedralbes Royal Palace in the morning and later has lunch with Franco and his wife Carmen Polo. Visits the Santa María de Montserrat Abbey in the evening. **26 June:** Has lunch with Franco and his family. Evita's farewell speech is broadcast by Radio Nacional de España from the Pedralbes Royal Palace at 2:30 p.m. Following a festive farewell ceremony at Plaza de España, leaves Spain from El Prat Air Base at 3:50 p.m. Arrives at Rome–Ciampino International Airport, Italy, at 6:10 p.m. and is greeted by Foreign Minister Count Carlo Sforza, the wife of Prime Minister Alcide De Gasperi, and the Argentine ambassadors to Rome and the Vatican. Meanwhile, thousands of people are gathered outside the Argentine Embassy in Rome to welcome Evita. **27 June:**

Evita is granted a 20-minute audience with Pope Pius XII. **28 June:** In a ceremony at the Argentine Embassy, accepts on behalf of Perón the Cross of St. Gregory the Great, granted by the Pope. **29 June–5 July:** Spends time in both Rome and Milan. Attends several receptions and events. In Rome, tours the city and visits an orphanage and the Tomb of the Unknown Soldier. Enjoys a performance of Giuseppe Verdi's *Aida* at the Baths of Caracalla. Attends a reception organized by the Suffrage Association, where she expresses her support of women's suffrage. Travels to Milan to visit the Argentine stand at the Industrial Exhibition. Together with Sforza, tours the exhibition, attends a luncheon in her honor, and enjoys Claudio Monteverdi's *L'Orfeo* at La Scala Opera House. Back in Rome, meets President Enrico De Nicola and visits Villa Borghese Museum and the catacombs. **6 July:** Leaves Rome and takes a 10-day vacation in Rapallo. **14 July:** Appears on the cover of *Time*. **17 July:** Returns to Rome and travels to Lisbon. **18–20 July:** Has lunch with President António Óscar Fragoso Carmona, tours the city and nearby towns and visits working-class neighborhoods and soup kitchens. Unofficially meets the former Italian king Umberto II and the Spanish prince Juan de Borbón. **21 July–2 August:** Arrives at Orly Airport in France and is greeted by Minister of Foreign Affairs Georges Bidault, Argentine ambassador Julio Victorica Roca, and other Latin American ambassadors. During her stay, a commercial treaty is signed between Argentina and France by which France gets a loan to buy Argentine wheat and meat. To celebrate this treaty, a reception is organized at the French Ministry of Foreign Affairs. At the end of the ceremony, Evita is bestowed the Legion of Honor by Bidault. Evita's schedule includes lunch with President Vincent Auriol at the Castle of Rambouillet, a reception at the Maison de l'Amérique Latine, a gala function organized by Victorica Roca, a visit to Notre Dame, and a meeting with Msgr. Angelo Roncalli, who would become Pope John XXIII in 1958. In addition, visits Napoleon Bonaparte's tomb and Versailles. Travels to Monaco for a brief vacation and is bestowed the Gold Medal of the Principality of Monaco by the local authorities. **3–9 August:** Arrives in Geneva, Switzerland. Visits the UN headquarters. Tours the country. While in Bern, a tomato is thrown at Evita but does not hit her. Another incident takes place in Lucerne, where two stones are thrown at the vehicle transporting the first lady. Her visit to Switzerland marks the end of her European tour. **10 August:** Flies to Dakar via Lisbon. In Dakar, Evita has lunch and speaks to Perón on the phone for an hour. From Dakar, boards the *Buenos Aires* ship to Brazil. **15 August:** Arrives in Recife, Brazil, where she stays for two days. **17 August:** Flies to Rio de Janeiro to attend the Rio Conference. Stays at the Copacabana Palace and meets President Eurico Gaspar Dutra. Addresses the Brazilian people in a message broadcast by Rádio Nacional. Visits a charity and the Ministry of Labor, has lunch at the Tijuca National Park, attends several gala functions, and holds a press conference. She is awarded the distinction of Commander of the Order of the Southern Cross. **21–23 August:** Arrives in Montevideo and is welcomed by Chancellor Mateo Marques Castro, First Lady Matilde Ibáñez de Batlle Berres, the Uruguayan ambassador to Argentina Eugenio Martínez Thedy, and the Argentine ambassador to Uruguay Gregorio T. Martínez, among others. Meets President Luis Conrado Batlle Berres at the Government House. Attends a gala function at the Cabildo. Attends two receptions, the first organized by the Uruguayan Association for the Protection of Children and the second by the Argentine Embassy. **23 August:** Arrives in Buenos Aires by ship at around 3 p.m. Receives a warm welcome by Perón, members of the cabinet, labor union representatives, her mother and sisters, and thousands of Peronist supporters. **23 September:** Women's suffrage law is promulgated by Perón. To mark this event, a celebration is held in the Plaza de Mayo. Evita delivers a speech addressing Argentine women from the balcony of the Pink House.

1948 January–December: Has a packed work schedule during these months. Relentlessly deals with issues related to labor unions—meetings, organization of new labor unions, signing contracts, visits to factories, and attending ceremonies and events—while providing social assistance to people in need. Evita's hectic lifestyle remains the same for the next two years. **21 February:** Visits Río Cuarto, Córdoba Province, with Perón and delivers a speech. **24 February:** Visits San Francisco, Córdoba Province, together with Perón to inaugurate a drinking water plant. Gives a brief speech. **25 February:** Visits the military factory in San Francisco. **8 July:** The Fundación de Ayuda Social María Eva Duarte de Perón (María Eva Duarte de Perón Social Aid Foundation) is officially created. **21 July:** Her article "Por qué soy peronista" (Why I Am a Peronist) is published in *Democracia*. **30 September:** Attends a railroad workers' event held at the port in Rosario, where she delivers an impassionate speech. **25 November:** Visits the city of Bahía Blanca in Buenos Aires Province.

1949 May: Visits the national territory of Chaco to inaugurate the Evita neighborhood in Resistencia and starts planning the provincialization of Chaco. **25 July:** Attends opening ceremony of the first national assembly of Perón's party, the Partido Peronista (PP), at the Luna Park Stadium, Buenos Aires. **26 July:** First national assembly of Peronist women at the Cervantes Theater in Buenos Aires. **29 July:** Foundation of the PP women's branch, the Partido Peronista Femenino (PPF), led by Evita. **21 September:** Evita and Perón attend the opening of the new building that will house the University of Buenos Aires School of Law.

1950 9 January: Collapses at the opening of a new office of the taxi drivers' union. This is one of the first public episodes that suggests her health is deteriorating. **12 January:** Evita is hospitalized and operated on for appendicitis by Dr. Oscar Ivanissevich. **24 January:** Collects Perón from the Pink House after work. This is the first time Evita leaves the Unzué Palace after surgery. **27 January:** Resumes her work. **February–June:** Has an extremely busy work schedule during the first half of the year. Tours the country to attend several political events, including ceremonies commemorating the 100th anniversary of General José de San Martín's death. **3 February:** Sails with Perón on the *Tecuara* to San Lorenzo, Santa Fe Province. **5 February:** Opens the finals of the Evita Children's Soccer Championships. **17 February:** Presents keys of 427 homes built by the Fundación Eva Perón in the Saavedra neighborhood, Buenos Aires. **21 February:** Meets Assistant Secretary of State for Inter-American Affairs Edward Gr. Miller Jr. They visit several buildings built by the foundation, have a refreshment at the Hogar de la Empleada General San Martín (Home for the Employed Women General San Martín), and attend a gala function in honor of Miller. **22 February:** Meets delegates of the Texas Federation of Women's Clubs at the Pink House. **24 February:** Attends the opening of the Rights of the Elderly Park. **3 May:** Organizes a dinner at the Hogar de la Empleada General San Martín in honor of the new Labor Queen crowned during the 1 May celebrations. **4 May:** Has lunch with PPF delegates at the Olivos Presidential Residence. **25 May:** Attends a gala function at the Colón Theater as part of the May Revolution celebrations. **5 June:** Arrives in San Salvador de Jujuy in Jujuy Province to open a home-school and the Clínica de Recuperación Infantil de Termas de Reyes (Termas de Reyes Child Rehabilitation Clinic). **9 July:** Attends a gala function at the Colón Theater as part of the Independent Day celebrations. **16 August:** Visits Mendoza to celebrate the 100th anniversary of General José de San Martín's death. **19 August:** Organizes a reception for the wives of the Foreign Military Missions' chiefs at the Hogar de la Empleada General San Martín. **17 October:** The Confederación General del Trabajo (General Confederation of Labor) or CGT awards Evita the Distinction of Recognition necklace. **29 October:** Attends with Perón the closing session of the National Eucharistic Congress in Rosario.

1951 January: The activities of the Fundación Eva Perón are shown in the Eva Perón and Her Social Work exhibition, organized by the Secretariat of Information and Press. **February:** Launches Perón's presidential campaign by announcing the PPF's support for his reelection in November 1951. **24 February:** Opening of the Policlínico Presidente Perón (President Perón Polyclinic) in Avellaneda, Buenos Aires Province. **March:** Opening of the Escuela Superior Peronista (Peronist School). In addition, presides over the sessions at the Third Inter-American Conference on Social Security in Buenos Aires. **15 March:** Delivers her first lecture on the history of Peronism at the Escuela Superior Peronista. **29 March:** Delivers her second lecture on the history of Peronism at the Escuela Superior Peronista. **5 April:** Delivers her third lecture on the history of Peronism at the Escuela Superior Peronista. **9 April:** Meets Israeli labor minister Golda Meir. Welcomes the governor, ministers, and legislators of Buenos Aires Province at the Ministry of Labor and Social Welfare. **12 April:** Delivers her fourth lecture on the history of Peronism at the Escuela Superior Peronista. **19 April:** Delivers her fifth lecture on the history of Peronism at the Escuela Superior Peronista. **10 May:** Delivers her sixth lecture on the history of Peronism at the Escuela Superior Peronista. **19 June:** Addresses Congress and requests the provincialization of the national territories of La Pampa and Chaco. **5 July:** In honor of the presidential couple, La Pampa is renamed Eva Perón and Chaco, Presidente Perón. **2 August:** The Perón–Eva Perón ticket for the November 1951 presidential elections is proclaimed. **22 August:** The Cabildo Abierto is held on 9 de Julio Avenue in Buenos Aires. Crowds gather to support the Perón–Eva Perón ticket. Evita officially accepts the candidacy for vice president of the country. **23 August:** Collapses from pain and exhaustion at a public event. **31 August:** Broadcasts her renunciation of the candidacy. **September–October:** Remains bedridden in the presidential residence. **22 September:** Dr. Jorge Albertelli and Dr. Humberto Dionisi carry out a pelvic exam on Evita. **28 September:** Starts a radium treatment that lasts for five days. **29 September:** Reportedly purchases 5,000 automatic pistols, 1,500 machine guns, and a huge quantity of ammunition from Prince Bernhardt of the Netherlands for Perón's protection. **15 October:** Launch of Evita's book *La razón de mi vida* (*My Mission in Life*). **17 October:** Receives a first-class distinction by the unions in recognition of her renunciation and the Great Peronist Medal by Perón (extraordinary grade). **3 November:** Admitted to the Policlínico Presidente Perón in Avellaneda. **6 November:** Undergoes a hysterectomy at the Políclino Presidente Perón. **7 November:** A report from the Secretary of Information and Press informs that Evita has tolerated well the surgical procedure. **9 November:** Delivers a radio address to the nation. In the address, she says, "Not voting for Perón is treason for an Argentine." **11 November:** Evita is allowed to vote from her hospital bed. **7 December:** Broadcasts a message thanking the *descamisados* ("shirtless ones," referring to working-class people) for supporting Perón in the elections. **14 December:** Discharged from the Políclino Presidente Perón.

1952 **May:** Evita's abdominal pain returns. **1 May:** Gives last public speech from the balcony of the Pink House. **7 May:** Evita is awarded the Spiritual Leader of the Nation title. **4 June:** Attends Perón's second inauguration. **16 June:** Evita is awarded the Order of the Liberator General San Martín. **June–July:** Begins working on her second book *Mi mensaje* (*In My Own Words*). **26 July:** Dies at 8:23 p.m. (officially 8:25 p.m.), aged 33. Embalming process begins that very same night by Dr. Pedro Ara. **27 July:** Evita's funeral begins. Her body lies in state at the Ministry of Labor and Social Welfare for 13 days. **9 August:** Her coffin is taken to Congress. **10 August:** Her coffin is taken to the CGT headquarters and placed on the second floor of the building, where it remains until 1955. **17 October:** Perón reads out Evita's will to the crowds. Release of *Y la Argentina detuvo su corazón* (*And Argentina's Heart Stopped*), a documentary depicting Evita's impressive funeral made by Twentieth Century-Fox.

1953 **July:** Dr. Ara finishes Evita's mummifying procedure. Her body remains at the CGT headquarters.

1955 **16 September:** With the support of army battalions in several provinces, the

CHRONOLOGY

navy revolts against Perón's government and declares the Liberating Revolution from Córdoba Province. **20 September:** Perón flees the country. **23 September:** Lieutenant General Eduardo Ernesto Lonardi delivers his inaugural address as acting president of Argentina. The "de-Peronization" of the country begins. **November:** Evita's body is removed from the CGT headquarters and placed under the care of Colonel Carlos de Moori Koenig. **13 November:** General Pedro Eugenio Aramburu is appointed acting president of Argentina.

1957 **April:** President Aramburu orders the dispatch of Evita's body to Italy. Evita is buried under the name Maria Maggi de Magistris in the Maggiore Cemetery in Milan, where it remains until 1971.

1960s Emergence of the left-wing Peronist guerrilla group the Montoneros. Their goal is to overthrow the military government and restore Perón to power. They consider the late Evita a symbol of liberation and political change.

1970 **29 May:** Former president Aramburu is abducted from his residence in Buenos Aires and later assassinated by the Montoneros.

1971 **September:** Evita's body is removed from the Maggiore Cemetery and sent to Perón, who is residing in Madrid. Her corpse remains in Madrid until 1974, under the watch of Perón, his third wife, Isabel Martínez de Perón, and Dr. Ara.

1973 **20 June:** Perón returns to Argentina after 18 years. On the same day, there is a violent confrontation between Peronists who are gathered to welcome Perón at Ezeiza International Airport. Following this confrontation, Perón tilts toward the anticommunist, right-wing faction of the PP. In doing so, he paves the way for the persecution, torture, imprisonment, and killing of guerrilla and other left-wing Peronist groups' members, marking the beginning of what came to be known as the Dirty War in Argentina. **12 October:** Perón takes office as the newly elected president of Argentina.

1974 **1 July:** Perón dies of a heart attack. **October:** The Montoneros steal Aramburu's body from the Recoleta Cemetery in Buenos Aires and wish to exchange it for Evita's. **November:** Evita's body is brought back to Argentina and placed in the chapel of the Olivos Presidential Residence next to Perón's coffin.

1976 **October:** Evita's body is handed over to her family by the military junta that seized power in March of the same year. **22 October:** Her body is entombed in the Duarte family mausoleum in the Recoleta Cemetery. **19 November:** Tim Rice and Andrew Lloyd Webber release the rock opera concept album *Evita*.

1978 **21 June:** The musical *Evita* opens at the Prince Edward Theater in London.

1979 **8 May:** U.S. premiere of the musical *Evita* at the Dorothy Chandler Pavilion in Los Angeles.

1996 **14 December:** The movie *Evita*, directed by Alan Parker and starring Madonna, premieres in the United States.

2010 **8 March:** Argentine president Cristina Fernández de Kirchner names Evita Woman of the Bicentennial.

2011 **26 July:** Unveiling of south-facing mural of Evita on the Ministry of Social Development Building in Buenos Aires to commemorate the 59th anniversary of her death. **24 August:** Unveiling of north-facing mural of Evita on the Ministry of Social Development Building in Buenos Aires to celebrate the 60th anniversary of Evita's bid for vice president.

2012 **25 July:** Unveiling of the Argentine 100-peso banknote bearing the portrait of Evita. **31 July:** Launch of *Mi mensaje* to commemorate the 60th anniversary of Evita's death.

2019 **May:** Argentines honor Evita on what would have been her 100th birthday with different activities and events, including talks, exhibitions, and artistic performances.

Introduction

YOUNG EVITA

The youngest of five children, Evita was born Eva María Ibarguren in the impoverished rural town of Los Toldos, Buenos Aires Province, on 17 May 1919 to Juan Duarte and Juana Ibarguren. Like her siblings, Evita was born out of wedlock, given that her father was a married man who had a family in the nearby village of Chivilcoy. The stigma of illegitimacy, coupled with poverty, shaped Evita's entire life. Her father worked as an estate manager on Estancia La Unión, the ranch where she was presumably born. Following Evita's birth, the family moved to a house on the main street in Los Toldos, but they only lived there for a short period as Duarte moved back to his family in Chivilcoy, abandoning Doña Juana—as Evita's mother was known—and his children when Evita was less than a year old. A plausible reason for his action was that he may have fallen out of favor with the landowners and was thereby left out of work. Poverty-stricken Doña Juana and her children were forced to move to a tiny house by the railroad and live off Doña Juana's meager earnings as a seamstress. When Evita was six years old, her estranged father was killed in a car accident near Chivilcoy. Attending his funeral turned into a shameful occasion for Evita and her family because they were denied access to the wake on the grounds of not being Duarte's legitimate children. Only after the intervention of the mayor of Chivilcoy were they granted permission to attend.

As a child, Evita passed her days playing with her dog León and her sister Erminda on a piece of land beside the railroad, but she did not have many toys. Once, Evita asked for a doll for Christmas, but all her mother could afford was one with a broken leg. That did not matter to her as she loved her new toy all the same. Friends were few too. Like her siblings, Evita was ostracized by the other children in the village because her illegitimacy was considered scandalous. To overcome this stigma, Evita, like her siblings, used her father's surname, making herself known as Eva María Duarte.

Her formal education got off to a bumpy start. She attended school for the first time at the age of eight and then had to repeat second grade, probably due to her poor attendance. When her family moved out of Los Toldos, she was forced to leave primary school temporarily. Her sister Elisa had found work at the local post office in Junín—a more important city than Los Toldos—and Doña Juana saw an opportunity to give her family a better future. The Duartes, as they called themselves, moved to Junín at some point during the first half of 1930, and Evita was enrolled in third grade at Catalina Larralt de Estrugamou School in Junín the same year. She was not a particularly bright student but was fond of reciting poetry and would often entertain younger pupils with her recitations. Her childhood dream, however, was to become an actress. Her love for acting was strengthened in 1933, when she was invited to participate in a play titled *Arriba estudiantes* (Come on Students) at the National School of Junín. A year later, she made her radio debut. The precise circumstances of the debut are unclear. In

Mi hermana Evita (My Sister Evita), Erminda claims that Evita made her radio debut on 1 October 1934, when Radio Cultura in Buenos Aires broadcast a program dedicated to the town of San Carlos de Bolívar in the province of Buenos Aires. As part of the program, Evita recited the poem "¿Adónde van los muertos?" (Where Do the Dead Go?) by the Mexican poet Amado Nervo. Other sources suggest that Evita traveled to Buenos Aires to make her radio debut at Radio La Nación by filling in for someone called Miss Kelly. Either way, Evita's trip to Buenos Aires in 1934 certainly nurtured her dreams of becoming a famous actress.

ARTISTIC LIFE

Evita's drive to pursue an acting career might have motivated her to leave Junín at the age of 15. She returned to Argentina's capital city in 1935, this time to stay. Although this move has been attributed to an encounter she had with the Argentine tango singer Agustín Magaldi back in Junín, it is plausible that she traveled to Buenos Aires on her own. In any case, she was not completely alone in the big city since her brother Juancito, who was a conscript in Buenos Aires, almost certainly looked after his younger sister.

All beginnings are hard, and Evita's new life in Buenos Aires was by no means an exception to this rule. She did not despair, however. Her strong determination enabled her to secure an acting role a few months after her arrival. She made her stage debut on 28 March 1935 with the theater company Compañía Argentina de Comedias in the play *La señora de los Pérez* (Mrs. Pérez), in which she played the role of a maid. That play marked the beginning of an increasingly busy schedule, but while she would work for several theater companies, she remained a supporting actress. Although the stage did not afford her the opportunity to become the star she yearned to be, it was certainly a place that provided invaluable lessons and lifelong friends.

Despite lacking education and training as an actress, Evita eventually managed to work in film and radio during her short but relatively prosperous acting career. By 1943, she gradually shifted to working exclusively as a film and radio actress. As in the theater, Evita did not get major parts in films, except for her starring role in *La pródiga* (The Prodigal Woman). She launched her film career with a bit part in *¡Segundos afuera!* (Seconds Out!), a comedy produced by Argentina Sono Film in 1937. Three years later, she was cast as a supporting actress in *La carga de los valientes* (Only the Valiant). This was followed by another bit part in *El más infeliz del pueblo* (The Unhappiest Man in Town), while in *Una novia en apuros* (A Bride in Trouble) and *La cabalgata del circo* (Circus Cavalcade) she appeared once again in supporting roles. In 1945, Evita secured a three-film contract with the studio Estudios San Miguel. This, in turn, raised her salary considerably, allowing her better living standards. In the end, Estudios San Miguel would produce just one film with Evita in the lead, *La pródiga*. The shooting of *La pródiga* was completed by the end of 1945, but the studio faced considerable pressure to cancel its release due to Evita's imminent marriage to the presidential candidate Colonel Juan Domingo Perón. The film was eventually given as a wedding gift to the couple and never shown to the public until 1984. Evita's performance in film did not receive the praise she desired. She would, nevertheless, gain more acclaim and recognition in the radio industry.

Evita came to the attention of radio listeners in 1935 thanks to her performance in *radioteatros* or serial radio dramas at Radio París. Over the years, frequent radio appearances ensued. Her big break came when she was hired by Radio Belgrano in 1943 to star in a series of *radioteatros* titled *Heroínas de la historia* (Heroines in History). In the same year, she became the leader of the radio employees' union, the Asociación Radial Argentina (Argentine Radio Association). The following year, Evita's popularity skyrocketed, but during this time, her acting career became intertwined with politics. After meeting Perón, Evita was cast in the lead role in *Hacia un futuro mejor* (Toward a Better Future). This was a propaganda radio program supporting both Perón's political ideology and the Revolution of 1943 that toppled the corrupt government of President Ramón Antonio Castillo (1942–1943). Besides her budding political activity, she continued appearing in *radioteatros* and secured a major contract with Radio Belgrano that allowed her to achieve financial security. Becoming Radio Belgrano's leading actress made her one of the industry's best paid stars of the 1940s. As her popularity increased, so did her appearances in show-business magazines. She landed four covers in 1944 alone, the same year she met Perón.

EVITA AND PERÓN

In January 1944, an earthquake in the western Argentine province of San Juan left an estimated 10,000 people dead, more than 12,000 injured, and 90 percent of the buildings in the city of San Juan destroyed. If the San Juan earthquake shook the lives of thousands of Argentines, it also stirred Evita's, changing it forever. The Argentine newspapers covered the devastation through powerful images of orphaned children, collapsed houses, and homeless families. These photos arguably struck a chord with the Argentine people, who made donations and organized fund-raising campaigns to help the victims. Evita was among the many actors who took to the streets of Buenos Aires to collect money for the victims of the earthquake, and it was probably there that she and Perón met face-to-face. As secretary of labor and social welfare, Perón was in charge of launching the relief campaign with which Evita collaborated, but it was the fund-raising gala at the Luna Park Stadium in Buenos Aires that saw the beginning of their romantic relationship.

Organized by Perón, the well-attended fund-raising event held on 22 January 1944 was a turning point in Evita's life. She arrived at the Luna Park Stadium together with her friend Rita Molina and, during the event, Perón and Evita struck up a conversation. Despite their age difference—she was 25 and he was 48—they hit it off immediately and left the stadium together that night. Barely a few weeks later, Evita and Perón made their first public appearance together at Radio Belgrano. By September 1944, the couple had moved in together in two adjacent apartments on Posadas Street in the upmarket neighborhood of Barrio Norte, Buenos Aires.

Once she became Perón's mistress, her interest in politics was strengthened. At the time, it was unusual for women to partake in political discussions, but that did not stop her from being present at the political gatherings Perón held in their apartment. Although she refrained from intervening in the conversations, her mere presence exasperated many of Perón's peers, not to mention her presence at official ceremonies. Concurrently, she started to display her political engagement at work. On the set of *La cabalgata del circo*, she attempted to enlist her fellow actors to support Perón. In her propaganda radio program *Hacia un futuro mejor*, she did not miss out on any opportunity to extol Perón and his work. It was also evident that the program was addressed to those who would later become Perón's most fervent supporters, namely, the disenfranchised masses of Argentina. Whereas Perón was building his political career, Evita was evolving into his best ally.

More than anything else, the events of October 1945 were decisive for their relationship. Perón's rising influence on the government in tandem with his political ambition drew the ire of factions of the army that wished to get rid of him. As a result, he was taken prisoner to Martín García Island, from where he wrote two letters to Evita professing his love for her. In one of the letters, he promised her they would marry after his release, and that is exactly what happened. Perón was released from prison on 17 October thanks to the unconditional support of the working class. Perón and Evita secretly tied the knot in a civil ceremony on 22 October. To conceal her illegitimacy, Evita produced a false birth certificate stating that her name was María Eva Duarte. In other words, not only did she change her surname, she also changed her given names. In doing so, she was in fact emulating the common practice of the Argentine upper class by which a female given name was usually preceded by "María." Only two witnesses were present at the ceremony, Perón's closest collaborator, Domingo Alfredo

Mercante, and Evita's brother Juancito. On 10 December, they had an equally secret Catholic wedding at San Francisco de Asís Church in La Plata. This time the witnesses were Mercante and Doña Juana. Following the wedding, the couple spent their honeymoon at Perón's country house in San Vicente, Buenos Aires Province. By marrying Perón, Evita had taken the huge leap from mistress to legitimate wife. Moreover, her professional life changed dramatically, as she basically retired from show business in favor of first campaigning alongside her husband and then taking on the role of first lady of Argentina.

That the wife of a presidential candidate would campaign together with her husband was unprecedented in Argentina. In doing so, she definitely broke gender barriers, but that turned out to be merely the beginning of an impressive and prolific political career. Evita began to transform the conventional role of the first lady from social hostess to that of a more visible, active participant in her husband's administration. As first lady, she was a leader in her own right and definitely one of the most active first ladies in the history of Argentina. Among many other undertakings, she devoted a huge amount of time to meeting with underprivileged Argentines. She visited factories, orphanages, and hospitals; dealt with labor unions; represented Argentina abroad; set up a welfare organization; advocated women's political rights; and founded her own political party. Her political career spanned just six years, but her endeavors were plentiful. One of them was her tour of Europe in 1947.

RAINBOW TOUR

In the 1940s, the bond between Argentina and Spain manifested itself at both economic and ideological levels. During World War II, both countries adopted neutrality but for different reasons. Whereas Argentina's intention was to sign agreements with both the Axis powers and the United States and to maintain a significant level of commerce with Britain, Axis powers' sympathizer Spain remained neutral mainly because it needed the food supplies offered by democratic countries. After the war, while the rest of Europe was benefiting from the Marshall Plan, Spain found itself diplomatically and economically isolated due to its previous alliances with Germany and Italy. Ideologically, a significant element of the population in Argentina, like in Spain, sympathized with right-wing Catholic beliefs as well as anticommunism and took a dislike to U.S. imperialism. Honoring their cultural and ideological connection, Argentina signed a contract with Spain in 1946 by which the European country would get a loan to buy Argentine wheat and meat. Owing to the immediate Argentine response to Spain's request for financial help, the alliance and fraternity between the countries were reinforced. Thus, President Perón was invited to visit Spain by the Spanish leader Francisco Franco Bahamonde as a way of maintaining the excellent diplomatic relations established between the two nations. Nevertheless, while Perón was helping Franco's Spain, Argentina was finally improving its relations with the United States and taking its place within the United Nations. A visit by Perón himself to a fascist country would have been too diplomatically provocative if Argentina wanted to keep its improved position. Consequently, Evita traveled to Spain instead of Perón, and other countries were added to the tour as a way of making the visit to Spain appear less political.

As her husband's personal envoy, the first lady embarked on a tour of Europe on 6 June 1947. The trip came to be known as the Rainbow Tour because her mission was to stretch a "rainbow of beauty" and send a message of peace between the American and European continents to improve cultural and diplomatic relationships. Aside from her visit to Spain, the tour included Italy, Vatican City, Portugal, France, Monaco, and Switzerland. Evita's official visit to Spain, however, was by far the most memorable. She spent 18 days touring the country. Everywhere Evita went, she was hailed by crowds thronging the streets. She attended countless banquets, was honored at lavish public receptions, and was presented with countless gifts. For Spaniards, Evita was bringing not only the help they needed to survive but also a breath of fresh air to an impoverished country. She was held up as a role model for society because she was an exemplary Catholic wife working to improve the lives of women, children, workers, and people in need. Overall, she was perceived as an ambassador of peace and a gentle, glamorous, and beautiful woman. In addition, she made herself even more popular by distributing 100-peseta notes—a considerable amount at the time—to the crowds. Following Spain, Evita and her entourage carried on the trip around the rest of Europe and finally returned to Argentina on 23 August 1947.

Evita's Rainbow Tour was one of the most discussed topics in press agendas around the world in 1947. Influenced by the opinions of the dominant political ideologies of the time, the news media tended to present facts about the tour with some interpretation. While some news reports were inclined to describe the trip as a complete success, others sustained that the trip was in fact a smokescreen for secret political maneuvers such as the deposit of money in Swiss bank accounts and the preparation of the future arrival of Nazis in Argentina. Likewise, news about Evita was commonly reported in a dualistic positive-negative fashion. Such reporting played a significant role in the development of Evita's "white and black myths" or, in other words, her dichotomous mythological public persona. A case in point was the reporting of Evita's way of dressing. Indeed, Evita had an impressive wardrobe and expensive jewels, an undeniable fact since she showed them publicly, particularly during her European tour. In Spanish newspapers, Evita's sartorial elegance was presented as a symbol of her prestigious social status, honoring her role as the wife of the president of one of the richest countries in the world. In U.S. publications, on the contrary, Evita's physical appearance was portrayed as lavishness, which denoted her lack of sympathy toward Spain, self-interest, and materialism. The information given was true in that she dressed extravagantly, but what came to determine her image, however, was how that extravagance was presented in the print media. Undoubtedly, opposing press reports about Evita fed into the construction of her international image.

Not only did the Rainbow Tour make Evita (in)famous worldwide, it also paved the way for her transformation into the iconic Evita that we know today. Following the tour, she adopted a simpler style of clothing and would usually appear with her hair pulled back into a bun. Evita would only go back to her glamorous style when attending gala functions and official events. Henceforth, she would mostly channel her energy into dealing with domestic affairs, championing women's suffrage, creating the charitable foundation Fundación Eva Perón, and establishing her own political party, the Partido Peronista Femenino (PPF).

FUNDACIÓN EVA PERÓN

The Fundación Eva Perón, initially called the Fundación de Ayuda Social María Eva Duarte de Perón (María Eva Duarte de Perón Social Aid Foundation), was perhaps Evita's most outstanding achievement. The first lady's social assistance activities began in early 1946, when people started flocking to her office in the knowledge that she would support them in any way she could. Two years later, she set up the foundation, which, broadly speaking, aimed at ameliorating the standards of living of the underprivileged in Argentina. Among the foundation's most important goals were the provision of monetary and in-kind assistance and the building of houses, hospitals, and educational and welfare establishments. Despite its pivotal role, it was often seen as a corrupt organization that ultimately sought to popularize the government and finance the Peróns' lifestyle. Whether the generosity and love Evita demonstrated toward the poor were based on genuine feelings or her only objective was to increase Peronist popularity through very calculated actions is not clear. What is certain is that the foundation was one of the most effective forms of propaganda for Peronism, regardless of Evita's true intentions.

While Evita issued a personal check for 10,000 Argentine pesos as the initial capital for the foundation, all subsequent funding came from union and business contributions, taxes, and levies. The foundation's expenses were commonly supported by an exchange-of-favors system. If, for instance, Evita asked for a contribution from the workers' unions, she would give something in return. Since the foundation was exempt from taxes and controls, it did not need to justify its finances and thus did not need to keep financial records. Although there were undoubtedly cases of extortion and irregularities, there is no question about Evita's commitment to the foundation and the significant advances this organization brought to Argentine society as regards social assistance, education, and health care. However, the foundation was not Evita's only cause. She was also deeply involved in the enfranchisement of all Argentine women.

WOMEN'S SUFFRAGE AND THE PARTIDO PERONISTA FEMENINO

By entering the political arena, Evita pushed the boundaries of what it meant to be first lady, but more importantly, her incursion into politics shaped Argentine women's political future. While universal and compulsory male suffrage in the country was legally permitted with the 1912 Sáenz Peña Law, Argentine women had to wait until 23 September 1947 to be granted the right to vote nationwide and to be voted for. The women's suffrage movement in Argentina had emerged much earlier. Anarchist and socialist women, such as Julieta Lanteri, Alicia Moreau de Justo, Cecilia Grierson, and Alfonsina Storni, among others, had advocated female suffrage during the first part of the 20th century; the western province of San Juan had allowed women to vote in all provincial elections by 1927; and Perón himself had supported women's suffrage while he was secretary of labor and social welfare. Months after becoming Argentina's first lady, Evita began an active campaign advocating women's political rights. She delivered dramatic speeches in support of the women's suffrage bill, which was being discussed in Congress, and held rallies for women's rights. Her intervention in this matter resulted in the unprecedented participation of women in politics, as both voters and candidates in elections. Through her campaign for female suffrage, she contributed toward improving women's standing in society but also increasing the Peronist electoral body. Evita made female suffrage a Peronist cause. The passing of the legislation was celebrated in the emblematic Plaza de Mayo in Buenos Aires, where Perón handed Evita a copy of the law he had just signed. She in turn delivered a speech, encouraging women to belong to a party that would fight for social justice under the leadership of Perón. As such, success in gaining female suffrage led, almost two years later, to the foundation of her political party, the PPF.

Following the reform of the Argentine Constitution of 1949, the Partido Peronista (PP) embarked on a restructuring process to promote the affiliation of female members. After a series of meetings held for members of the party from 25 to 29 July 1949, the PPF was officially set up as a branch of the PP, and Evita was appointed the party leader. Although a separate party, the PPF was subordinate to the leadership of Perón, a fact that Evita made clear in her opening speech when she said, "Our movement is inspired theoretically and doctrinally by Perón's words. . . . For a woman to be a Peronist means loyalty and blind confidence in Perón." While he was the undisputed leader, Evita was his female counterpart, and he had entrusted her with the task of leading the PPF. Such a prestigious and powerful position constituted an official recognition of her political status in Argentina. To be the leader of the PPF was not merely an honorary position; it required stamina, leadership, and outstanding organizational skills. Evita had them all.

In addition to all her undertakings, such as running her foundation and dealing with the labor unions, Evita was devoted to the creation of the PPF. She personally selected the 23 party delegates, who relocated to the provinces and national territories of Argentina to organize the local branches of the PPF. She made sure that the women she entrusted with this task met certain criteria. Charisma, people skills, and the ability to deliver speeches to large audiences were essential requirements for delegates. Evita monitored their activities, demanded frequent reports, and insisted on having an intricate understanding of their work. The PPF was an enormous success. After only two years, it had recruited 500,000 members and opened more than 3,000 branches throughout the country. Moreover, on 11 November 1951, the women of Argentina were able to cast the ballot for the first time in a national election. Perón received 62.5 percent of the vote and 2,441,558 women of the 3,816,460 who voted did so for the Peronist ticket. Evita's hard work had paid off. However, she was forced to cast her own vote from a hospital bed after undergoing surgery to treat an illness that would be the ultimate cause of her death.

ILLNESS AND DEATH

Evita died of cervical cancer at the young age of 33, arguably as a result of never taking heed of her body's warning signs. She had always experienced health issues, and while she would take time away from her acting career to rest, her busy political schedule was prioritized above all else. The first indication that her health had begun to deteriorate was when she collapsed while on public duty on 9 January 1950. Shortly after this incident, she was admitted to hospital, where she underwent an appendectomy and was allegedly recommended a screening test—a recommendation she disregarded completely. Following the procedure, she was forced to take a few days off, but she had hardly recovered when she resumed work on 27 January.

After the appendectomy, her life became busier than ever. She consequently skipped meals, had a poor diet, slept too little, and had virtually no free time. Neglecting her health caught up with her, so much so that on 23 August 1951 she collapsed again, and on 24 September she could not get out of bed to go to work. At that time, she was experiencing severe abdominal pain, vaginal bleeding, and extreme weakness. It is highly likely that the symptoms and the pressure from her family and close collaborators made her give in and undergo a physical examination under general anesthesia. A biopsy confirmed that she was suffering from advanced cervical cancer. Ironically, Perón's first wife had died from the same disease. As weeks passed, Evita became drastically thin. Sick and bedridden, she made her last public appearance in June 1952, at Perón's second inauguration as president of Argentina. Too weak to stand and weighing less than 40 kilograms (88 pounds), Evita had to be propped up in a cagelike contraption to ride next to Perón in an open car through the Mayo Avenue in Buenos Aires.

Evita was oblivious to her disease as the diagnosis of cervical cancer was concealed from her, a normal practice at the time. She was told that she had a fibroma. She was treated with radium implants to stop the bleeding and then had a hysterectomy performed by the renowned American oncologist Dr. George Pack. However, the surgical procedure could not stave off the disease, and abdominal pain had returned by May 1952. A new examination revealed that the cancer had spread and that she had developed pulmonary metastases. At 8:23 p.m. on 26 July 1952, she passed away at the presidential residence in Buenos Aires, surrounded by Perón, her mother, her sisters, her brother Juancito, and her close collaborators, Oscar Lorenzo Nicolini, Atilio Renzi, Héctor José Cámpora, and Raúl Alejandro Apold.

FUNERAL AND BODY

The premature death of Evita ushered forth a wave of mourning that permeated the nation and spoke volumes about her significance in the Argentine consciousness. News of her death was broadcast throughout the country as soon as she passed away, and hundreds of thousands of people from all over Argentina made their way to the presidential residence to mourn Evita. The country came to a standstill. Stores closed; cinemas, bars, and restaurants emptied. A period of national mourning was decreed for one month. All members of the Confederación General del Trabajo (General Confederation of Labor) or CGT were asked to wear a black tie or ribbon as a sign of respect. Flags on public buildings were flown at half-mast, and lampposts in every city, town, and village in Argentina were draped in black. Tributes poured in from such world dignitaries as

INTRODUCTION

Britain's Queen Elizabeth and U.S. President Harry S. Truman.

As soon as Evita had taken her last breath, the distinguished Spanish physician Dr. Pedro Ara started the embalming process that would preserve Evita's corpse only long enough for public viewing. Dr. Ara worked against the clock, and the day after her death Evita's body was ready to lie in state at the Ministry of Labor and Social Welfare, where she previously had her office. The lines to see her body stretched in multiple directions around city blocks. For days, citizens filed through, touched, kissed, and even collapsed on her coffin. On 9 August, the government had to call the public viewing to an end for fear that the exposure would damage the corpse. On 11 August, Evita's corpse was taken through the streets of Buenos Aires. This was followed by an impressive funeral cortege that accompanied the casket to the headquarters of the CGT. Two million people lined the streets and threw flowers as the cortege passed. She was given a funeral fit for a head of state, showing how much public support she had from the Argentine people.

The odyssey of her corpse was as dramatic as her life, and many years had to pass before she was buried. Once the embalming process was over in July 1953, Evita's corpse remained in the CGT while the mausoleum where she would be laid to rest was being built, but the project was never completed. After Perón was ousted by the country's new military rulers in 1955, Evita's corpse was removed from the building of the CGT and hidden in the most unlikely places in an attempt to erase her from the national memory. But the military rulers' plan was unsuccessful, and wherever the corpse was hidden, lighted candles and flowers appeared. Thus, another plan was devised with the collusion of the high echelons of the Catholic Church. The body of Evita was smuggled out of Argentina in 1957 and buried in the Maggiore Cemetery in Milan under the false name Maria Maggi de Magistris. Her body would remain there until 1971.

By 1971, Argentina had seen a wave of military coups d'état that led to economic depression and social instability. The only plausible solution seemed to be the return of Perón from his exile in Madrid, Spain. Perón accepted the offer on condition that the body of Evita be returned to him. Her embalmed corpse was handed over to Perón in September 1971, but three more years passed before she would return to Argentina thanks to President Isabel Martínez de Perón. For a brief time, her body was displayed alongside the closed casket of Perón in the Olivos Presidential Residence. The military coup that seized power in Argentina in 1976 finally allowed her body to be buried. On 22 October of the same year, she was entombed inside the Duarte family mausoleum under three plates of steel in the glamorous Recoleta Cemetery in Buenos Aires and has remained there ever since. Today, Evita's resting place, which is always covered in fresh flowers, is one the most visited sites in Argentina—a living proof that she has never been forgotten.

Entries A–Z

ABRAS, EMILIO. One of the official photographers of the **Pink House**, Emilio Abras accompanied Evita on her 1947 **Rainbow Tour** and was responsible for organizing her contacts with the press while she was visiting Europe.

ACEVEDO PÉREZ, MARÍA GEORGINA CECILIA (1917–1994). María Georgina Cecilia Acevedo Pérez married **Héctor José Cámpora** in 1937, and they had two children, Héctor and Carlos. She became close to Evita in the late 1940s. Following Evita's **Rainbow Tour**, the two ladies would often be seen together at public events. Acevedo Pérez was part of Evita's loyal group of collaborators, which included **María Elena Caporale de Mercante**, **Teresa Adelina Fiora**, and **Emma Nicolini**. She remained by Evita's side until the first lady passed away in 1952.

ACOSTA, CLOTILDE. See GUEVARA, NACHA.

ACOSTA MACHADO, AMÉRICO (1922–1990). This Argentine radio and theater actor was at the peak of his career when he shared the stage with Evita in 1944. Acosta Machado had been hired by the **Compañía Candilejas** to replace the former leading actor **Pablo Racioppi** in the *radioteatro Una rosa en el río* (A Rose in the River) at **Radio Belgrano**. Acosta Machado and Evita also collaborated in the *radioteatro Llora una emperatriz* (An Empress Cries) when he was filling in for **Florindo Ferrario**. He performed in the 1946 Argentine film *Deshojando margaritas* (Depetaling Daisies). *See also* HEROÍNAS DE LA HISTORIA.

ADOLFO SUÁREZ MADRID–BARAJAS AIRPORT. Located 12 kilometers (7.45 miles) from **Madrid** city center, this airport opened in 1931 and is currently one of the largest and busiest airports in Europe. It was originally known as Madrid–Barajas Airport, but it changed its name to Adolfo Suárez Madrid–Barajas Airport in 2014 in honor of the first elected prime minister of democratic Spain. As part of Evita's **Rainbow Tour**, her joyful seven-day trip to the Spanish capital ended on 15 June 1947. On that day, hundreds of people filled the streets of Madrid as Evita rode toward Madrid–Barajas Airport together with **Francisco Franco Bahamonde**, his wife, and his daughter, among others. Visibly moved by the size of the crowd and its outpouring of affection and enthusiasm, Evita gave a wave from the steps of the plane that would take her to **Granada** and was seen looking out of its window before it took off.

ALBERTELLI, JORGE (1908–1996). This Argentine gynecologist, who was one of the **Fundación Eva Perón**'s medical advisers, became Evita's personal physician. On 21 September 1951, Minister of Technical Affairs **Raúl Mendé** summoned Dr. Albertelli to the **Pink House** to request his services because Evita had been diagnosed with advanced cervical cancer. Before committing to treating her, Dr. Albertelli consulted with Dr. **Humberto**

Dionisi about the diagnosis. Dionisi was the gynecologist who had carried out Evita's pelvic exam and cervical biopsy. The following day, the two physicians performed another pelvic exam on Evita and reportedly disclosed the sad news of Evita's terminal illness to **Juan Domingo Perón**. Dr. Albertelli was subsequently entrusted with the responsibility for treating Evita. He moved to the **Unzué Palace** to be close to his patient and started treating her with radium, then a standard treatment. Following the treatment, Evita was to undergo a hysterectomy, and Dr. Albertelli was convinced that he would be the one performing it. However, Mendé had other plans. After consulting with Dr. **Abel Canónico**, Mendé entrusted the renowned American oncologist Dr. **George Pack** with the procedure. As a result, Dr. Pack performed the hysterectomy and Dr. Albertelli collaborated with him. On 31 December 1951, Dr. Albertelli moved out of the Unzué Palace. In 1994, he published a book titled *Los "cien días" de Eva Perón* (The "Hundred Days" in Eva Perón's Life), in which he outlines details of Evita's illness.

ALCARAZ, JULIO (1902–1985). Julio Alcaraz was Evita's hairdresser and the creator of her famous chignon bun hairstyle. They met at the studio **Pampa Film**, where he worked as a hairstylist, while she was playing a supporting role in *La carga de los valientes* (Only the Valiant). Legend has it that Evita asked him to give her a hairstyle like that of Bette Davis—the American actress—but he refused to do so, arguing that he was a creator not an imitator. He styled and colored Evita's hair blonde for her performance in *La cabalgata del circo* (Circus Cavalcade) and continued doing so as long as she lived. After quitting show business, Evita attended his hair salon in Buenos Aires, but once she became Argentina's first lady, Alcaraz would go to the presidential residence to style her hair every morning. He also accompanied Evita on her **Rainbow Tour** to take care of her hair and her jewelry. During the embalming of her body in 1952, he was called on to color and style her hair for the last time. *See also* BODY OF EVITA; UNZUÉ PALACE.

ALCÁZAR OF TOLEDO. This stone fortress looms prominently over the city of **Toledo**, Spain. During the Spanish Civil War (1936–1939), Colonel José Moscardó Ituarte, a Nationalist, held the building against siege by the Republican forces between July and September 1936. The Republicans demanded the Nationalists' surrender in exchange for the life of Moscardó's son Luis, whom they held hostage. As Moscardó did not comply with the Republicans' request, his son was executed. The colonel's defense and eventual victory became one of the most heroic episodes during the war. While visiting Toledo on 13 June 1947, Evita, **María del Carmen Polo y Martínez-Valdés**, and their entourage were welcomed by Moscardó and the fortress's former defenders at the Alcázar. Evita visited the museum, the chapel, the infirmary, and the basement where women and children took refuge during the siege. Deeply moved after hearing Luis's story, Evita said to Moscardó, "Today's world already knows his glory, but history will immortalize it." Nowadays, the Alcázar houses the Army Museum and a library. *See also* RAINBOW TOUR.

ALEA BUILDING. This building, located in the block bounded by Bouchard, Viamonte, and Leandro N. Alem Streets in Buenos Aires, was the headquarters of **Alea S.A.** between 1951 and 1955. The city block, which had historically belonged to the Catalinas Warehouses and Mole Company Limited, had been sold to Yatahi, a company owned by the businessman **Alberto Nicolás Dodero**, in 1945. Four years later, the southern part of the block was sold to the Agrupación de Trabajadores Latinoamericanos Sindicalizados (a Latin American labor union confederation) whose leader, Carlos Vicente Aloé, became the president of Alea S.A. Two buildings were erected in the newly acquired land lot, the Alea and the Atlas. The former had an underground refuge built for **Juan Domingo Perón** and Evita. Although not solidly built, the bunker was approximately eight meters (26 feet) deep and had an independent power generator, air-conditioning, and a safe where administrative files belonging to the government were kept. Apparently, neither Perón nor Evita ever set their foot in the shelter. In 1955, Alea S.A. was dismantled and the underground bunker opened to the public—some of Evita's clothes and jewelry were among the objects displayed. However, by 1956, the conditions of the Alea Building and its bunker were deteriorating rapidly. The building fell into decay until 1996, when President **Carlos Saúl Menem** decided that it would house the General Archive of the Nation, but the project was never completed. In 1998, the building was bought and remodeled by the multinational corporation Cargill, and Perón's bunker was transformed into an underground garage. The former Alea Building is currently known as the Samsung Building. *See also* LIBERATING REVOLUTION.

ALEA S.A. Between the late 1940s and early 1950s, the Peronist government pursued a campaign to bring the owners of newspapers, magazines, and radio stations into line with the Peronist ideology. In some cases, the government forced them to sell their business to the state. Those who got rid of their business without causing trouble could aspire to hold a managerial position in their former companies. Such was the case of **Jaime Yankelevich**, a renowned businessman who sold his radio station to the state but continued managing it. By 1947, the government was in control of numerous media companies, so President **Juan Domingo Perón** saw the need to set up a conglomerate from which all the state-owned media businesses could be run. This resulted in the emergence of the media group Alea S.A., placed under the management of Perón's administrative secretary, Carlos Vicente Aloé, who was reportedly appointed to this position by Evita. From 1951 to 1955, the headquarters of Alea S.A. was located at the **Alea Building** in Buenos Aires. The media group continued operating until the **Liberating Revolution** dismantled it in 1955. *See also* ANTI-ARGENTINE ACTIVITIES CONGRESSIONAL COMMITTEE; *CRÍTICA*; *DEMOCRACIA*; DEMOCRACIA S.A.; *EL MUNDO*; *LA ÉPOCA*; PERONISM.

ALHAMBRA. This UNESCO World Heritage Site is located in **Granada**, Spain. As part of her **Rainbow Tour**, Evita paid a visit to this magnificent Moorish fortress and palace complex. Following a gala function at the **Granada City Hall** on 15 June 1947, Evita together with the rest of the guests continued the celebrations at the Alhambra, which was beautifully illuminated. The first lady of Argentina was given a tour of the Moorish palace and fortress and later enjoyed music and dance shows at the Garden of the Partal.

ALHAMBRA PALACE HOTEL. Located a short walk from the **Alhambra** in **Granada**, Spain, this luxury hotel was opened by King Alfonso XIII in 1910. Evita spent a night at the Alhambra Palace Hotel on 15 June 1947 while touring the country as part of her **Rainbow Tour**. Upon her arrival after 8 p.m., she was given a 21-gun salute by an artillery battery and was presented with flowers. The artillery soldiers were charged with guarding the hotel during Evita's stay in Granada. The first lady and her entourage were assigned to exquisite rooms on the first floor. Later in the evening, the guests left the hotel to attend a gala function at the **Granada City Hall**.

ALOÉ, CARLOS VICENTE (1900–1978). *See* ALEA BUILDING; ALEA S.A.

ÁLVAREZ, MARÍA EUGENIA (1927–). María Eugenia Álvarez became a nurse at the age of 17 after completing a two-year nursing program run by the **Society of Beneficence of Buenos Aires**. She met Evita in 1949, when the first lady paid a visit to the hospital where Álvarez was working. She was part of a group of nurses that the **Fundación Eva Perón** sent to Peru to provide aid to the victims of an earthquake. Álvarez was the director of the **Escuela de Enfermeras Eva Perón** from 1951 to 1955. Following Evita's appendectomy in 1951, she became Evita's personal nurse and took care of Evita until the moment the first lady passed away in 1952. In 2010, Álvarez published a book titled *La enfermera de Evita* (Evita's Nurse). In 2020, a newly built hospital to deal with the COVID-19 pandemic in Argentina was named after her.

AMANDA ALLEN CHILDREN'S CITY. *See* CIUDAD INFANTIL AMANDA ALLEN.

ANTENA. Launched in 1930 by **Jaime Yankelevich**, this show-business magazine was a weekly supplement that publicized **Radio Belgrano** and eventually **Radio Belgrano y la Primera Cadena Argentina de Broadcasting.** *Antena* centered on articles about artists, theater, music, and cinema. In 1937, the magazine was acquired by Yankelevich's friend and businessman Julio Korn. On 22 April 1939, *Antena* published Evita's portrait with an article announcing *Los jazmines del 80* (The Jasmines of 1880), an upcoming *radioteatro* starring the young actress. On 20 May of the same year, Evita landed her first magazine cover. She graced the cover of *Antena* with a portrait by **Sivul Wilenski** that shows Evita wearing a black hat with a veil. At the peak of her career, Evita was featured on the front cover of *Antena* three more times—on 1 June and 21 September 1944 as well as on 15 February 1945. *See also* HEINRICH, ANNEMARIE.

ANTI-ARGENTINE ACTIVITIES CONGRESSIONAL COMMITTEE. The relationship between **Peronism** and the mass media in Argentina was marked by violence, detention of journalists, censorship, expropriations of newspapers, control over radio stations, manipulation of advertising, and deliberate restrictions on paper distribution. Aiming to monopolize the Argentine press and broadcasting industry, the Peronist government gradually began intimidating media businesses' owners into being more in line with the Peronist ideology and, in some cases, into selling their companies to the state. Once in power, President **Juan Domingo Perón** declared publicly that he would eradicate the "anti-Argentine" behavior transmitted by certain media. Under the guise of fighting anti-Argentine attitudes and activities, Perón was trying to oppress all those who did not agree with his government's policy. Therefore, he set out to police the political orientation of the mass media through two main agencies: the **Secretariat of Information and Press**, headed by **Raúl Alejandro Apold**, and the Anti-Argentine Activities Congressional Committee, also known as the Visca–Decker Commission—named after its main leaders, the national legislators José Visca and Rodolfo Decker. Although this committee was originally formed to investigate police tortures, Perón soon found out that he could control the media through allegations of anti-Argentine activities. The committee's inspections in search of anti-Argentine activities led to hundreds of newspapers being shut down. The criteria to consider an activity anti-Argentine was, however, highly questionable. For example, to commemorate the centennial of General **José de San Martín**'s death, all publications were forced to mention this event in their headlines. As many publications disregarded the decree, the government took advantage of this and closed several newspapers. Other businesses' closures could be based on trivial offences or justified by alleging that they had poor facilities or inadequate sanitary conditions. When Perón was ousted in 1955, all Peronist organizations, including the Visca–Decker Commission, ceased to function. *See also* ALEA S.A.; LIBERATING REVOLUTION.

ANTIPUEBLO. In Peronist discourse, this term refers to those individuals or groups who oppose the *pueblo. Antipueblo*—literally meaning "against the people"—is a synonym for *oligarca, vendepatria,* and *cipayo.*

APOLD, RAÚL ALEJANDRO (1898–1980). This Argentine journalist and politician had two passions: journalism and aviation. At the age of 19, he became the secretary of General Pablo Riccheri and later worked for several papers, including *La Época* and *El Mundo.* For the latter, he used to cover aviation issues, which led him to pay frequent visits to different government offices. Throughout the years, he got to know the right people in politics, who helped him to advance his career. Aside from working as a journalist, he held other positions: he was a film and theater producer, an artist representative, and a press officer and lobbyist for the studio **Argentina Sono Film**. One of his most important achievements was to be able to get raw stock for the national film industry during World War II. The neutral position adopted by Argentina had resulted in many economic restrictions; one of them was the import ban on raw stock from the United

States. Apold's key intervention to prevent a halt in the production of film enhanced his position in the local cinema industry.

Although there are many versions of how he became acquainted with Colonel **Juan Domingo Perón**, the most trustworthy is that he met the colonel before the **Revolution of 1943** through General Ángel María Zuluaga, a pioneer in Argentine aviation. Apold allegedly assisted Perón during the 1945–1946 presidential campaign and influenced the leader to value the importance of exerting control over the mass media to gain political power. By January 1947, Apold was overseeing the Directorate General for Information Distribution, an agency under the **Secretariat of Information and Press**. Concurrently, Evita named him editor-in-chief of *Democracia*, the first newspaper bought by her and the first one to belong to the media group **Alea S.A.** Apold made the secretariat the Peronist propaganda agency par excellence. He oversaw the publication of thousands of brochures, newspapers, and magazines that exalted the Peronist government. In addition, all Peronist imagery—photographs and footage—was exclusively produced and distributed by the secretariat. It is believed that Apold orchestrated the events that set the foundation for the Peronist social imaginary, such as the **Peronist Loyalty Day**, Evita's **candidacy for vice president**, and her eventual renunciation. The "creator" of **Peronism**, as the Argentine journalist Silvia Mercado calls him, was also responsible for such popular slogans as "Perón cumple, Evita dignifica" (Perón fullfils, Evita dignifies) and the countless complimentary titles that described Evita, including *La abanderada de los humildes* (The Standard-Bearer of the Poor). Evita's death was one of his great productions: he published many reports about her supposed improvement and then modified the time of her death by two minutes to achieve a more memorable number. He also prompted the filming of Evita's funeral, which was released as a documentary titled *Y la Argentina detuvo su corazón* (And Argentina's Heart Stopped). Apold's influence was crucial for the Peronist government to succeed in controlling the mass media and the arts. Near the end of Perón's second term (1952–1955), Apold's successful career came to an end. *See also* ANTI-ARGENTINE ACTIVITIES CONGRESSIONAL COMMITTEE; STATE FUNERAL OF EVITA; TIME OF EVITA'S DEATH.

ARA, PEDRO (1891–1973). This Spanish physician became Evita's embalmer. He had studied in Vienna, worked in **Madrid**, and embalmed, among others, the body of the famous Spanish composer Manuel de Falla. As soon as Evita's death appeared imminent, **Juan Domingo Perón** hired Dr. Ara to preserve the **body of Evita**. He commenced his work shortly after her death on 26 July 1952 to prepare the body for an encounter with the public. Evita was exposed to public visitation for 13 days. As Dr. Ara had not prepared the corpse for so sustained an exhibition, he had to bore some holes in the coffin to equalize the temperature inside and clear the mist developed inside the glass plate. After the 13-day public display, Evita was first taken to the Argentine Congress to be given the honors of a head of state and then to the headquarters of the **Confederación General del Trabajo (CGT)**, where Dr. Ara could continue his work. Once in the CGT, Dr. Ara placed her body in baths of acetate and potassium nitrate and pumped it with chemicals again and again. Finally, he coated her skin with flexible plastic so that it could be touched and exhibited. The entire process of embalming the corpse took him a year. In his final report to the government, Dr. Ara wrote that Evita's corpse contained all its internal organs and could cope with indefinite contact with the air. He also proposed that he should keep the key to the coffin in which Evita was lying. In 1971, Evita's body was disinterred from the Maggiore Cemetery in Milan and delivered to Perón, who was living in exile in Madrid. As her body had suffered some minor damages, Dr. Ara's skills came into play once again. *See also* STATE FUNERAL OF EVITA.

ARAMBURU, PEDRO EUGENIO (1903–1970). This Argentine de facto president, who governed the country between 1955 and 1958, took part in the 1955 military coup d'état that toppled President **Juan Domingo Perón**.

Unlike his predecessor General **Eduardo Ernesto Lonardi**, President Aramburu showed that he was a hard-line general. During his mandate, he banned the use of Peronist symbols, ordered the arrest of many political and union leaders, barred the **Partido Peronista** from participating in future elections, declared illegal the mentioning of Perón and Evita, and decreed the execution of a group of Peronists who had attempted to overthrow his government. His aim was clear, namely, to eradicate **Peronism** from Argentine society at any price. During Aramburu's presidency, the **body of Evita** was sent to Europe and buried in a secret location, unknown even to him. On receiving the information about the burial of the body in a sealed letter, Aramburu instructed his lawyer to pass it on to the incumbent president of Argentina upon his death. Despite being a de facto president, Aramburu had stated that his intention was to call for general elections "neither a minute too soon nor a minute too late." Indeed, elections were held on 23 February 1958 and **Arturo Frondizi** was elected president of Argentina. Aramburu, for his part, continued to be politically active and founded his own political party. On 29 May 1970, he was abducted from his apartment by the **Montoneros** guerrilla group. After being interrogated as to the whereabouts of Evita's body, he was assassinated. The Montoneros requested Evita's body in exchange for Aramburu's. Like Evita, Aramburu is buried in the Recoleta Cemetery in Buenos Aires. *See also* CABANILLAS, HÉCTOR EDUARDO; LIBERATING REVOLUTION.

AREILZA Y MARTÍNEZ DE RODAS, JOSÉ MARÍA DE (1909–1998). This Spanish politician and diplomat served as Spanish ambassador to Argentina between 1947 and 1950. In this capacity, his main mission was to achieve a new trade agreement between Spain and Argentina to increase the supply of wheat and meat, and thereby alleviate the serious needs of the Spanish population. However, the tense relationship between Evita and Areilza almost jeopardized his mission. Six days after Areilza presented his credentials to President **Juan Domingo Perón**, Evita summoned him to her office at the **Secretariat of Labor and Social Welfare** to finalize the details of her official visit to Spain, which was part of her **Rainbow Tour**. In his memoirs, Areilza states that Evita accused him of ruining her visit to Spain. Apparently, Areilza was to award Evita the Great Cross of Isabella the Catholic in Argentina on behalf of the Spanish government, but that did not suit her. Evita's wish was to be decorated with the order during her visit to Spain and in the presence of a large audience. Although that was exactly what happened, the relationship between Areilza and Evita never got back on track. Reportedly, their bickering led Areilza to quit his position as Spanish ambassador to Argentina in 1950.

ARGENTINA DE HOY. *Argentina de hoy* (The Argentina of Today) is a 1949 propaganda documentary produced by the Argentine **Secretariat of Information and Press**. It showcases the **New Argentina**, highlighting the achievements of both President **Juan Domingo Perón** and Evita. The documentary opens with an overview of Argentine geography followed by a sequence of shots depicting a series of thriving industries from across Argentina as well as infrastructure improvements. The film also features the work of the **Fundación Eva Perón**, including the **Escuela de Enfermeras Eva Perón**, the **Ciudad Infantil Amanda Allen**, the *proveedurías*, and the **senior residences**. In an attempt to capture other aspects of the New Argentina, the documentary focuses on the importance of education and culture, the development of tourism, and the prominent role of sports. The images are accompanied by voice-over narration to inform the audience that the New Argentina is the result of the work of the Perón administration. By centering only on the prosperity of the country, this documentary is a biased portrayal of Argentina.

ARGENTINA SONO FILM. Screenwriter and director Luis Moglia Barth and cinema entrepreneur Ángel Mentasti produced their first film, *¡Tango!*, in Buenos Aires in 1933. Their collaboration resulted in the creation of the film production company Argentina Sono Film. *¡Segundos afuera!* (Seconds Out!), which was produced and released by this company in 1937, was Evita's debut film.

ARGENTINE ANTI-COMMUNIST ALLIANCE. *See* TRIPLE A.

ARGENTINE CONSTITUTION OF 1949. Under the banner of social justice, the first Peronist government introduced new political, social, and economic policies. Some of these included the proclamation of the **Bill of Rights of the Workers** and the **Decalogue of the Rights of Seniors**, the declaration of economic independence at the Historical House of Tucumán, and the passing of the law granting women the right to vote. The Peronist government then saw the need to amend and update the Argentine Constitution of 1853 to consolidate and promote the above reforms. Hence, this major constitutional revision—which took place between January and March 1949—incorporated new social, political, and economic rights and policies, including the unlimited reelection of the president, the national ownership of energy sources, and equal rights for men and women in marriage. In addition, several secretariats were given the rank of ministries. In 1956, during the **Liberating Revolution** government, President **Pedro Eugenio Aramburu** repealed the amended document and reinstalled the former 1853 constitution. *See also* PERONISM.

ARGENTINE INSTITUTE FOR THE PROMOTION OF TRADE. Before taking office, **Juan Domingo Perón** adopted a number of measures that were to serve as a basis for his government project. As a result of these measures, the Central Bank of Argentina was nationalized and the Argentine Institute for the Promotion of Trade was created. The latter was set up in 1946 to expand the Argentine economy and conquer new international markets. The economist and businessman **Miguel Miranda** had a key role in both institutions. He was named head of the institute and president of the bank. The institute was closed in 1958 during the government of the **Liberating Revolution**.

ARMILLA AIR BASE. Located six kilometers (3.72 miles) from **Granada**, this is one of the oldest aerodromes still in operation in Spain. Evita and her entourage arrived at Armilla Air Base on 15 June 1947 at 7:15 p.m. After being welcomed by the local authorities, Evita traveled to Granada, where she stayed for two days as part of her **Rainbow Tour**.

ASOCIACIÓN ARGENTINA DE ACTORES (AAA)/ARGENTINE ACTORS' ASSOCIATION. This artists' labor union was founded on 18 March 1919. Evita became a member of the Asociación Argentina de Actores in January 1939.

ASOCIACIÓN RADIAL ARGENTINA (ARA)/ARGENTINE RADIO ASSOCIATION. By 1943, Evita was a relatively well-established actress and began to get involved in labor union activities. On 3 August of the same year, Evita figured as one of the founders of the Asociación Radial Argentina (ARA) and eventually became its president. This was the first organization created to defend the rights of workers in the radio industry. The **Secretariat of Labor and Social Welfare** gave official recognition to the ARA in May 1944.

ATENEO CULTURAL EVA PERÓN. Created by Evita, this institution was officially opened on 5 October 1950. The opening speech was delivered by its president, the Argentine actress **Fanny Navarro**. Evita herself had appointed Navarro to preside over the institution in August of the same year. Located at 570 Diagonal Roque Saenz Peña Street in Buenos Aires, the Ateneo Cultural Eva Perón offered a space where actresses could meet, chat, rehearse, read, and purchase clothes and makeup at affordable prices. However, the idea of setting up the Ateneo also furthered a political agenda, namely to attract a new pool of voters and disseminate the ideology of **Peronism**. The combination of the two would in turn benefit the reelection of **Juan Domingo Perón** as president of Argentina. From its inception, the Ateneo arguably functioned as an extension of the **Partido Peronista Femenino**. In 1951, Navarro managed to collect the signatures of approximately 3,000 actresses to support the reelection of Perón. In addition, those actresses affiliated to the Ateneo actively supported Evita's **candidacy for vice president** at the **Cabildo Abierto**. With the death of Evita in 1952, the institution was dissolved and transformed into the **Unidad Básica Cultural Eva Perón**, headed by **Delia Parodi**.

AUGUSTO SEVERO INTERNATIONAL AIRPORT. Named after the Brazilian politician and aviator Augusto Severo de Albuquerque Maranhão, this airport served the city of Natal, Brazil, until 2014, the year it was closed to civil aviation. On 7 June 1947, the plane carrying Evita and her entourage to Africa made a brief stopover at this airport. Following a warm welcome, Evita held a press conference addressing Brazilian women. On the same day, Evita continued her journey toward **Dakhla** as part of her **Rainbow Tour**.

ÁVILA. Located in the province of Ávila in the autonomous community of Castile and León, Spain, this city is particularly known for its medieval walls dating back to the 11th century. Evita visited Ávila while touring Spain in 1947. She arrived in the city on 11 June at 11:23 a.m. together with **María del Carmen Polo y Martínez-Valdés**. Both ladies were welcomed by the local authorities at the Gate of St. Vincent, one of the nine gates in the city walls. After visiting the Royal Monastery of St. Thomas and the Convent of St. Teresa of Jesus, they left the city at 2:45 p.m. *See also* MEDINA DEL CAMPO; RAINBOW TOUR.

AYRINHAC, NUMA (1881–1951). Born in Aveyron, France, Numa Ayrinhac emigrated to Argentina with his parents at the age of five, settling in the agricultural colony of Pigüé, Buenos Aires Province. His interest in painting led him to study with the Argentine painter Ernesto de la Cárcova. During the government of **Juan Domingo Perón**, Evita commissioned Ayrinhac to paint portraits of her mother and her brother Juancito. His most famous work, however, is the full-body portrait of Perón and Evita in gala attire. The painting features the happy and radiant couple standing on a red carpet and turning slightly toward the right as if they are amused by something the artist did not capture on the canvas. This is the only painting that survived the destruction of Peronist iconography propelled by the **Liberating Revolution**. In 1950, Ayrinhac painted the official portrait of Evita that appeared on the cover of *La razón de mi vida* (*My Mission in Life*). This portrait was destroyed by the Liberating Revolution government.

Banner featuring iconic portrait of Evita painted by the French Argentine artist Numa Ayrinhac.

B

BARCELONA. The capital city of the autonomous community of Catalonia in Spain, Barcelona was the last stop on Evita's official visit to that country in 1947. She arrived in the city of Barcelona on 22 June 1947 and remained there until 26 June. As in everywhere else in Spain, she was warmly welcomed by the authorities and the citizens alike. Shortly after her arrival, Evita visited the Cathedral of the Holy Cross and St. Eulalia, which shone in its fullest splendor and where a Te Deum was sung in her honor. Hundreds of civilian, ecclesiastic, and military authorities filled the cathedral to welcome Evita. When she stepped out of the church, the crowd cheered and waved Argentine and Spanish flags. Hundreds of thousands of people flooded the streets of Barcelona to catch a glimpse of her. During her stay, she had a tight schedule that included gala events, official luncheons, homages to Catalan workers, meetings with labor unions, and festivals, among other activities. General **Francisco Franco Bahamonde**; his wife, **María del Carmen Polo y Martínez-Valdés**; and their daughter had arrived from **Madrid** to welcome Evita and accompany her during her last days in Spain. *See also* RAINBOW TOUR.

BASILICA OF OUR LADY OF SORROWS. One of the most impressive baroque churches in Spain, this is a must-see attraction in **Granada**. It was built in the 17th century and houses the image of the patron saint of the city, Our Lady of Sorrows. Upon her arrival in Granada on 15 June 1947, Evita visited this basilica, where she was welcomed by the archbishop, the parish priest, and the Our Lady of Sorrows Fraternity, among others. She prayed before the image of Our Lady of Sorrows, visited the museum of the basilica, and received gifts from the fraternity. In addition, Evita was offered a replica of the image of Our Lady of Sorrows for the eponymous fraternity in Argentina. In turn, Evita gave a generous donation to the parish priest. *See also* RAINBOW TOUR.

BENÍTEZ, HERNÁN (1907–1996). This Argentine Jesuit priest was very close to the Peróns. How he became acquainted with **Juan Domingo Perón** is not clear. Some sources state that he administered last rites to Perón's first wife, **Aurelia Gabriela Tizón**, in 1939. Other sources claim that the two men met at El Salvador Church, where Perón would attend services just to listen to Benítez's homilies. He was so well known for his eloquence in public speaking that his services where broadcast on the radio. In 1943, collaboration between Benítez and Perón started to emerge due to their common concern, social justice. He supported the **Revolution of 1943** and reportedly penned some of the documents of the **Grupo de Oficiales Unidos**. On Good Friday 1944, he crossed paths with Evita at **Radio Belgrano**, where he preached to the radio audience. After the broadcast of his Good Friday preaching, she approached him and arranged to meet him a few days later at the Jesuit school of El Salvador, but he never turned up. A year later, when Perón introduced him to his wife, Evita reminded Benítez that he had stood her up. Despite the incident, he became Evita's confessor and one of her chief advisers. It has been stated that he also officiated at Perón and Evita's religious wedding ceremony, but this has never been confirmed. In 1947, Perón commissioned him to organize Evita's **Rainbow Tour**, a request he willingly accepted. He traveled to Spain and **Rome** and arranged Evita's meeting with **Pope Pius XII**. His involvement with the Peróns, in tandem with his active participation in the organization of the tour, was not looked favorably upon by the Jesuit authorities in Argentina. As a result, Benítez was not allowed to return to his country of birth. Instead, he was asked to seclude himself in a monastery in Salamanca, Spain. He complied with the request but became very ill. To be able to leave Europe, Benítez asked to become a secular priest, and the **Vatican** granted him permission to do so. On his return to Argentina in the late 1940s, Evita named him spiritual leader of the **Fundación Eva Perón**. This led him to work closely with her. He was by Evita's side when she died and gave her last rites. *See also* CANONIZATION OF EVITA; WEDDING OF EVITA.

BID FOR VICE PRESIDENT. *See* CANDIDACY FOR VICE PRESIDENT.

BILL OF RIGHTS OF THE WORKERS. The first significant labor legislation was introduced in Argentina by decree-laws between 1943 and 1945 by Secretary of Labor and Social Welfare **Juan Domingo Perón**. He continued working relentlessly toward the improvement of working conditions in Argentina. On 24 February 1947, once he had become president of Argentina, Perón proclaimed the Bill of Rights of the Workers at a solemn ceremony organized by the **Confederación General del Trabajo** at the Colón Theater in Buenos Aires. The bill included the description of 10 basic rights: the right to work, the right to fair remuneration, the right to training, the right to decent working and living conditions, the right to health, the right to well-being, the right to social security, the right to the protection of the family, the right to economic improvement, and the right to the defense of professional interests. These rights were eventually regularized and included in the **Argentine Constitution of 1949**. *See also* SECRETARIAT OF LABOR AND SOCIAL WELFARE.

BIRTH CERTIFICATE OF EVITA. Officially, Evita and **Juan Domingo Perón** were married in a civil ceremony on 22 October 1945. Early in 1945, Evita's sister **Elisa Duarte** reportedly arrived at the registry office in **Los Toldos** to request changes of details on Evita's birth certificate. The officer in charge, however, refused to comply and advised her to submit her case in writing. Perón's wife-to-be was determined to change a few details on her birth certificate and thereby bury the stigma of being an illegitimate child. Following the refusal at the registry office, Evita's birth certificate was mysteriously destroyed and a new one appeared just before her wedding to Perón. This new file showed that she was born María Eva Duarte to **Juan Duarte** and **Juana Ibarguren** in Junín on 7 May 1922. She was in fact born Eva María Ibarguren in Los Toldos on 7 May 1919. The original birth certificate was never recovered. *See also* FREUDE, RODOLFO "RUDI" LUDOVICO; WEDDING OF EVITA.

BLOMBERG, HÉCTOR (1889–1955). Son of the naval architect Pedro Blomberg and the Paraguayan writer Ercilia López, Blomberg was a renowned Argentine poet, librettist, dramatist, songwriter, translator, and journalist. Influenced by his father, Blomberg developed a taste for traveling and sailing that was regularly mirrored in his writings. He published his first book of poems in 1912 and started writing *radioteatros* in the 1920s. His *radioteatros* combined fact and fiction, were generally connected to 19th-century (political) events, and frequently included songs. In 1939, he wrote a series of *radioteatros* which were performed by the **Compañía de Teatro del Aire**, headed by Evita and **Pascual Pellicciotta**. Over the years, Blomberg collaborated with several popular newspapers and magazines, such as *La Razón* and *Caras y Caretas*.

BODY OF EVITA. Shortly after Evita's death on 26 July 1952, the Spanish pathologist and embalmer Dr. **Pedro Ara** began the embalming of Evita's corpse. Although it was not yet prepared for permanent preservation, her body lay in state at the Ministry of Labor and Social Welfare, where it remained for 13 days. Once the funeral was over, Evita's remains were taken to the **Confederación General del Trabajo (CGT)**, where Dr. Ara continued the mummifying process. Within a year, the body's preservation process was complete. As the vast monument where it was to be placed was yet to be built, President **Juan Domingo Perón** decided to keep the corpse in the CGT headquarters. In 1955, a military coup d'état ousted Perón, and the new rulers started the "de-Peronization" of the country, a hostile campaign to erase **Peronism** from Argentina. The new anti-Peronist government feared that Evita's body could be used as a symbol to join forces against them. Therefore, military troops led by Colonel **Carlos Eugenio de Moori Koenig** removed the body from the CGT headquarters and hid it in the most unlikely places, but wherever the corpse was hidden, lighted candles and flowers appeared. In 1957, the corpse was smuggled out of Argentina and buried in the Maggiore Cemetery in Milan, Italy, under the name Maria Maggi de Magistris. This information, however, remained highly confidential. President **Pedro Eugenio Aramburu** received an envelope with details about the location of the corpse, but he directed his lawyer to pass the information on to the incumbent Argentine president once Aramburu himself had died. In 1970, Aramburu was kidnapped, interrogated, and killed by the Peronist guerrilla group **Montoneros**. Aramburu's death was intended not only as retribution for the killing of fellow guerrilla comrades in 1956 but also as part of a demand for the repatriation of Evita's remains. It was President **Alejandro Agustín Lanusse** who eventually negotiated with the Montoneros for the return of Evita's corpse. Once the place of Evita's grave was disclosed, the remains were exhumed and transported to **Madrid**, where Perón had been residing since 1960. However, when Perón returned to Argentina in 1973 and became president for the third time, he left Evita behind. Upon Perón's death in 1974, his wife and successor, **Isabel Martínez de Perón**, was faced with the Montoneros' demand for the return of Evita's body once again. After stealing Aramburu's corpse from his resting place in the Recoleta Cemetery in Buenos Aires, the Montoneros demanded the exchange of it for Evita's. As a result, President Martínez de Perón organized the repatriation of Evita's remains, which arrived in Buenos Aires in November 1974. The casket with Evita's remains was placed next to Perón's in the crypt of the **Olivos Presidential Residence**. However, her body lay there only until 1976, when a military coup d'état ousted President Martínez de Perón. The new military government under the leadership of General **Jorge Rafael Videla** removed Evita's corpse from the presidential residence, handed it over to her family, and agreed to have it entombed in the **Duarte family tomb** in the Recoleta Cemetery, where it lies to this day under three plates of steel. *See also* CABANILLAS, HÉCTOR EDUARDO; LIBERATING REVOLUTION; NATIONAL COMMISSION FOR THE EVA PERÓN MONUMENT; SECRETARIAT OF LABOR AND SOCIAL WELFARE; STATE FUNERAL OF EVITA.

BORLENGHI, ÁNGEL GABRIEL (1904–1962). This leading union representative participated in the protests that led to the release of **Juan Domingo Perón** from prison in 1945. Borlenghi was convinced that Perón's work as secretary of labor and social welfare would improve the conditions of the working class in Argentina. Together with other like-minded labor leaders, he participated in the creation of the **Partido Laborista** to back Perón in the 1946 presidential election and later supported the dissolution of this political party to rechart it as the Partido Único de la Revolución. Following Perón's victory, Borlenghi was appointed minister of interior and became a key cabinet member. He contributed to Perón's control of the **Confederación General del Trabajo**, and after the failed 1951 military coup d'état, his ministry wielded power over the provincial and national police forces. Unlike other ministers, Borlenghi remained in his ministerial job until three months before the military coup d'état of 1955 ousted Perón. One of the reasons for this longevity was probably the good rapport he had with Evita. Not only was he part of the Argentine delegation that traveled to **Rio de Janeiro** to meet Evita after her **Rainbow Tour**, he also credited Evita with gaining the right to vote for Argentine women in a speech he made on the day **female suffrage** was granted in Argentina. Airbrushing Argentine feminists from that historical moment, he claimed that "after so many years in need of someone capable of leading her to victory, the Argentine woman has found in María Eva Duarte de Perón the true leader of her demands." *See also* LIBERATING REVOLUTION; PARTIDO PERONISTA; SECRETARIAT OF LABOR AND SOCIAL WELFARE.

BRAMUGLIA, JUAN ATILIO (1903–1962). This Argentine labor lawyer was minister of foreign affairs from 1946 until 1949. As head of the Foreign Ministry, Bramuglia was in charge of navigating Argentina's foreign relations in a "third way," which meant cultivating positive relations with the United States and the Soviet Union. In 1948, Bramuglia was appointed head of the UN Security Council for Argentina. In that capacity, he was successful in having the countries involved in the Berlin Blockade form a committee to solve this major international crisis. Despite his successful undertakings, Bramuglia presented his resignation as cabinet member to President **Juan Domingo Perón** several times. Although his reasons could not be pinned down to one single episode, his differences with Evita played a role in his decision to step down. Aside from opposing Evita's **Rainbow Tour**, he initially refused to submit her proposal for the United Nations' adoption of the **Decalogue of the Rights of Seniors**, but he eventually gave in. Evita, for her part, instructed radio stations to refrain from mentioning him or his accomplishments. She directed *Democracia* to have his image removed from the newspaper and to airbrush him from group photographs. *See also* ALEA S.A.

BRIDE IN TROUBLE, A. *See UNA NOVIA EN APUROS.*

BUNKER OF JUAN DOMINGO PERÓN. *See* ALEA BUILDING.

CABANILLAS, HÉCTOR EDUARDO (1914–1998). A virulent anti-**Peronist**, Colonel Héctor Eduardo Cabanillas played an instrumental role in the collapse of the second government of **Juan Domingo Perón** in September 1955. In 1956 and during the **Liberating Revolution** regime, Cabanillas was appointed head of the Argentine military intelligence, thus replacing Colonel **Carlos Eugenio de Moori Koenig**, who had kept Evita's embalmed body concealed in his office. Since he had not received instructions as to what to do with the **body of Evita**, Cabanillas decided to leave it where it had been lying. However, news on the location of the body ostensibly leaked out. Consequently, Cabanillas was instructed by President **Pedro Eugenio Aramburu** to secretly bury Evita. He devised a plan with the collusion of the Catholic priest Francisco Rotger to bury Evita's remains in the Maggiore Cemetery in Milan, Italy. He procured counterfeit passports for Evita and himself, took all the necessary measures to conceal his clandestine undertaking, and escorted the coffin from Argentina to Italy. After burying Evita, Cabanillas returned to Argentina. In 1958, he was appointed military attaché to the Argentine Embassy in **Paris**, retiring the following year. Summoned by President **Alejandro Agustín Lanusse** in 1971, Cabanillas was instructed to exhume Evita's remains and return them to Perón, who was then residing in **Madrid**. In September 1971, Cabanillas handed Evita's corpse over to Perón. Cabanillas was one of the main sources for **Tomás Eloy Martínez**'s novel *Santa Evita*. One of Cabanillas's last public appearances was in the 1997 documentary *Evita: la tumba sin paz* (Evita: The Peaceless Tomb), directed by Tristán Bauer. In the film, he gives his testimony on the death of Evita and the tribulations of her corpse.

CABILDO ABIERTO. Held on 22 August 1951, the Cabildo Abierto was a massive public assembly convened by the **Confederación General del Trabajo (CGT)** to propose the **Juan Domingo Perón**–Eva Perón ticket for the 1952 presidential election. At 5:20 p.m., Perón, several of his cabinet members, and officials of the CGT appeared on the makeshift stage on 9 de Julio Avenue, Buenos Aires. Evita, however, was not among them. While the leader of the CGT, **José Espejo**, was delivering his opening speech, the crowds frequently interrupted him, demanding Evita's presence. Espejo excused Evita's absence by claiming that her modesty had stopped her from attending the Cabildo Abierto. As the clamor of the crowd persisted, Espejo exited the stage and, a few minutes later, he returned with Evita. The crowd cheered euphorically when she appeared on the stage. During her speech, which became a dialogue between the crowd and Evita, she never made clear whether she accepted the **candidacy for vice president** or not. The Cabildo Abierto testified to Evita's significance for the Argentine people and the synergy between them.

CABRERA DE FERRARI, IRMA. Evita's personal live-in maid from 1946 to 1952, Irma Cabrera de Ferrari remained by her side until the day Evita died. In an interview in 1969, she mentioned that Evita was always kind to her except for once, when she gave Evita a bottle of alcohol to disinfect her hands and face after she had kissed a leper. Evita was so angry with her that she threw the bottle against the wall.

CÁMPORA, HÉCTOR JOSÉ (1909–1980). This dentist served as president of Argentina from 25 May until 13 July 1973. Cámpora showed his budding interest in politics already in high school, where he was chosen president of the students' union. He studied dentistry at the National University of **Córdoba** and moved to the town of San Andrés de Giles in Buenos Aires Province to work as a dentist. He married **María Georgina Cecilia Acevedo Pérez** in 1937 and became the mayor of San Andrés de Giles in 1944. He presided over the Chamber of Deputies from 1948 to 1952. In 1951, together with the leaders of the **Confederación General del Trabajo**, he spearheaded the popular movement that propelled Evita's **candidacy for vice president**. Cámpora won the 1973 presidential election, but once he took office it was immediately clear that he was merely preparing the way for the return of **Juan Domingo Perón** to Argentina. After 49 days, he resigned to call for new elections, thus allowing Perón to become president of Argentina for the third time. Cámpora died in exile at the age of 71. The modern left-wing Peronist political youth organization La Cámpora is named after him. *See also* MONTONEROS.

CANDIDACY FOR VICE PRESIDENT. With the 1952 presidential election fast approaching, more than 1,000,000 Peronist supporters gathered on 9 de Julio Avenue—one of the major thoroughfares in Buenos Aires—on 22 August 1951 to ask Evita to be the Peronist vice presidential candidate. This entailed running for office alongside **Juan Domingo Perón**. After making an emotional speech, she seemed to consent to do so. On 31 August of the same year, however, she announced in a radio broadcast her immutable decision not to run for vice president, declaring that her renunciation reflected her true intentions. She added that she had never wanted to gain any political glory but the love of Perón and her *descamisados*. She also stated that she only wished to be remembered as Evita, the humblest Peronist collaborator to serve the people of Argentina. *See also* CABILDO ABIERTO.

CANÓNICO, ABEL (1910–2000). This Argentine oncologist was a friend of the leading American oncologist Dr. **George Pack**. Once Evita's inner circle of collaborators knew that a surgery was needed to save her life, Minister of Technical Affairs **Raúl Mendé** approached Dr. Canónico to consult with him as to who would be the best surgeon to perform a hysterectomy. He recommended Dr. Pack. Shortly after that, he was dispatched to the United States for the purpose of persuading the American oncologist to perform Evita's hysterectomy. Being successful in his mission, he escorted Dr. Pack to Argentina, stayed with him at the **Olivos Presidential Residence** during the American's visit, and was even present at Evita's big surgery. When Evita's death was imminent, Dr. Canónico was consulted once again as to who would be the best embalmer. On that occasion, he recommended Dr. **Pedro Ara**. *See also* BODY OF EVITA.

CANONIZATION OF EVITA. Evita's charismatic personality permitted her to forge a bond with Argentina's disadvantaged in an unprecedented way. She began her passionate and dramatic speeches by addressing these neglected Argentines as "my dear *descamisados*." She embraced them, provided assistance for them, comforted the sick, and let them kiss her. To them, she was a saint, and the devotion people felt for her was manifested everywhere. While she was recruiting female delegates for the **Partido Peronista Femenino**, a woman who called into her office told her, "It isn't servility and it isn't just adulation, but I have never touched a saint of flesh and blood. Let me kneel before you and kiss you." Her ties with the underprivileged, coupled with her extreme fanaticism toward **Juan Domingo Perón**, her youth, her rags-to-riches story, her tragic end, and, last but not least, Peronist propaganda furnished her with such quasi-religious titles as "Lady of Hope,"

"Mother of the Innocents," "Queen of Labor," "Standard-Bearer of the Descamisados," and "Bridge of Love."

If **Peronism** is conceived as a secular religion, Evita was the Virgin Mary of the movement. Indeed, the Peronist movement insisted on her association with the Virgin, which in turn resulted in that devotion to Evita seemingly superseding that to the Virgin. The newspaper *Democracia*, purchased by Evita in 1947, was one of her best allies in promoting her sainthood, as she was often referred to as a saint in its pages. But the pinnacle of her secular "canonization" was reached in October 1951, when it was publicly announced that she was ill with anemia. Evita was in fact suffering from cervical cancer, but this was not publicly disclosed. Perón hailed his wife by declaring 18 October 1951 St. Evita's Day. In May 1952, when her demise was imminent, the Argentine Congress officially named Evita the Spiritual Leader of the Nation. Before she died, the Catholic priest **Hernán Benítez** led the nation in prayers for her recovery, declaring her a martyr sent by God as a model of self-sacrifice and faith. As a result, altars with Evita's likeness surrounded by flowers and lighted candles appeared around the country. Upon her death on 26 July 1952, her body was prepared as if it were a holy relic and the **Vatican** received thousands of letters urging that she be canonized. Three years later, when Perón was overthrown, the military government organized an anti-Peronist campaign to erase Peronism from Argentina. Far from making Evita vanish from the shared public memory, the anti-Peronist campaign and the subsequent disappearance of her body accentuated her iconic quasi-religious status. In 2019, the **Confederación General del Trabajo** launched a campaign to push for Evita's canonization by the Roman Catholic Church. *See also* BODY OF EVITA; FUNDACIÓN EVA PERÓN; ICON; LIBERATING REVOLUTION; ST. PERÓN'S DAY; STATE FUNERAL OF EVITA.

CAPORALE DE MERCANTE, MARÍA ELENA (1901–1982).

Daughter of Italian immigrants, Caporale was brought up in a middle-class Buenos Aires family. After marrying **Domingo Alfredo Mercante** at the age of 21, she moved in with her in-laws and lived with them until they passed away. The mother of two, she lived a life dedicated to her family, but Mercante's election to governor of Buenos Aires Province in 1946 was a turning point in her sheltered existence. She made friends with Evita and escorted her to different public events. In her capacity as the governor's wife, she received petitions from individual members of the public and provided direct social aid to them. Like Evita's social assistance, Caporale's was channeled through an organization called the Obra de Ayuda Social de la Gobernación de Buenos Aires (Government of Buenos Aires Social Aid Foundation). Her active role in social assistance made her honorary president and vice president of several institutions in the province of Buenos Aires. During the first assembly of the **Partido Peronista Femenino (PPF)**, Caporale was named Evita's secretary and was one of the three signatories of the assembly's minutes. She oversaw the organization of the *unidades básicas* for the PPF in Buenos Aires Province and opened the main local branch on 5 November 1949. Caporale would become Evita's political arm in the province of Buenos Aires. Her speeches, coupled with her social and political activities, made her so well known that she appeared in the newspapers *Democracia*, *El Argentino*, and *El Día*. As her power and popularity grew, however, her relationship with Evita started to deteriorate.

CARRILLO, RAMÓN (1906–1956).

Known as the architect of the modern Argentine health system, this neurosurgeon, physician, academic, and public health advocate served first as secretary of health and then as minister of health during the administration of **Juan Domingo Perón**. Being an advocate for social medicine, he believed that access to universal free health care was a **human right**, a belief that led him to launch a national scheme to implement universal health care in Argentina. The scheme improved the health of the Argentine population by introducing preventive medicine and by bringing health-care access to rural areas in the form of new hospitals, clinics, sanitation, and vaccine programs. During his tenure, the number of hospital beds doubled and the number of health-care workers on government payrolls tripled. He set up national health-care programs that contributed to decreasing the tuberculosis mortality rate, ending typhus and brucellosis, and lowering infant mortality. To accomplish his plan, he worked closely with the **Fundación Eva Perón**. In July 1954, he resigned as a cabinet member on account of his poor health as well as the rivalries that emerged within **Peronism**. In memory of his legacy, the current Argentine 5,000-peso banknote features the portrait of Dr. Carrillo together with another Argentine physician, Dr. Cecilia Grierson. *See also* PUBLIC HEALTH CARE.

CARTA A EVA. Directed by Agustí Villaronga, *Carta a Eva* (Letter to Eva) is a two-episode Spanish miniseries that was broadcast on Spanish television in 2013. It garnered several accolades and many positive reviews. With a focus on Evita's interaction with the then Spanish first lady, **María del Carmen Polo y Martínez-Valdés**, the miniseries follows Evita's official visit to Spain in 1947. The series shows Evita, during her visit, successfully interceding for Juana Doña, a communist militant who is awaiting execution. A letter written by Doña's son reaches Evita, revealing that Doña has been condemned to death by the regime of **Francisco Franco Bahamonde** for a bomb attack on the Argentine Embassy in **Madrid**. *See also* RAINBOW TOUR.

CASTILLO, RAMÓN ANTONIO (1873–1944). This Argentine lawyer governed the country from 1940 to 1943. From September 1940 to June 1942, he was the acting president because the incumbent president, Roberto Ortíz—who had won the elections by vote rigging—was seriously ill. After Ortíz passed away, Castillo became president and remained in power until he was overthrown by the **Revolution of 1943**. His was the last presidential mandate during the period known as the **Infamous Decade**.

CASTIÑEIRA DE DIOS, JOSÉ MARÍA (1920–2015). This celebrated Argentine poet was a devout Catholic and a Peronist supporter. Castiñeira de Dios was one of **Juan Domingo Perón**'s close collaborators. He presided over Perón's pro-candidacy board in 1945, served as secretary of culture during Perón's first presidential term (1946–1952), and was named director of the **José de San Martín** National Institute. Castiñeira de Dios worked closely with Evita too. Together they reportedly founded the **Peña Eva Perón**. The phrase *volveré y seré millones* (I will be back and will be millions), commonly associated with Evita, was first popularized by Castiñeira de Dios. He included it in his 1962 poem "Eva Perón." Together with other authors, he attended the book launch of Evita's autobiography *La razón de mi vida* (*My Mission in Life*) in 1951. Following the **Liberating Revolution**, he was part of the Peronist resistance that opposed **Pedro Eugenio Aramburu**'s government. Over the years, Castiñeira de Dios held different positions in the administrations of Perón and **Carlos Saúl Menem**, published a myriad of works, and was the recipient of many awards and distinctions. Concurrently, he built a career in advertising. He oversaw the advertising campaigns for Knorr Suiza and Cross & Blackwell. He also held managerial positions at Fiat, Nestlé, and McCann Ericson. *See also* CHÁVEZ, BENITO ENRIQUE "FERMÍN."

CATALINA LARRALT DE ESTRUGAMOU SCHOOL. Evita attended this primary school, located in the heart of **Junín**, Buenos Aires Province, once she and her family moved to this city in 1930. According to her educational records, Evita completed her primary education at this school when she was 14. The detail of her age is noticeable given that the normal school-leaving age at the time was 11. Due to economic difficulties, she started attending the only primary school in **Los Toldos** at the age of eight and resumed her education in the third grade at Catalina Larralt de Estrugamou School when she was 11. With only six years of formal education, Evita left for Buenos Aires in 1935 to pursue an acting career. *See also* FORMAL EDUCATION OF EVITA.

CATHOLIC SACRAMENTS OF EVITA. Evita was raised Catholic. Although no document exists of her baptism, it is believed that she, her sister Erminda, and her brother Juancito were baptized at the same time at Our Lady of the Pillar Church in Los Toldos, Buenos Aires Province, on 21 November 1919. Her baptismal name was Eva María Ibarguren but, like her siblings, she always used her father's surname, Duarte. The priest who baptized the siblings was Carmelo Vicone, and their godparents were Antonio Ochotorena and Paz Michotorena, two acquaintances of Evita's mother, **Juana Ibarguren**. Evita reportedly received First Communion in 1926 together with Erminda and Juancito. *See also* BIRTH CERTIFICATE OF EVITA; DUARTE, ERMINDA; DUARTE, JUAN "JUANCITO" RAMÓN; WEDDING OF EVITA.

CAUDILLISMO. The Spanish word *caudillo* (leader) comes from the Latin *capitellum*, which means "little head." In Argentina, as in the rest of Latin America, caudillismo refers to a system of political power based on the leadership of and allegiance to a strongman who shows autocratic tendencies. Although caudillismo flourished in the mid-19th century, some historians also regard 20th-century Latin American leaders—such as **Juan Domingo Perón**—as caudillos. *See also* PERONISM.

CAUDILLO. *See* CAUDILLISMO.

CENTROS INDEPENDIENTES/INDEPENDENT CENTERS. This was a loose political coalition of conservative leaders that emerged spontaneously after 17 October 1945. It went into coalition with the **Partido Laborista** and the **Unión Cívica Radical**–Junta Renovadora to back **Juan Domingo Perón**'s presidential candidacy. Members of the Centros Independientes were appointed to important positions during Perón's first and second mandates (1946–1955). *See also* PERONIST LOYALTY DAY.

CEREIJO, RAMÓN ANTONIO (1913–2003). This Argentine economist, who served as minister of finance from 1946 to 1952, had close ties with Evita. As her financial adviser, he was present whenever Evita received monetary donations from the delegations of labor union representatives and workers who went to see her. He eventually proposed the opening of a bank account to deposit that money. Cereijo was also the administrator and managing general agent of the **Fundación Eva Perón** and presided over the commission that organized the Evita Children **Tournaments**.

CHÁVEZ, BENITO ENRIQUE "FERMÍN" (1924–2006). Commonly known as Fermín Chávez, this Argentine journalist, historian, poet, and Peronist militant had a long and prolific career. Mostly remembered as a revisionist, Chávez authored more than 40 books questioning official Argentine history. He studied humanities and philosophy in Argentina, and Ancient Hebrew, theology, canon law, and archeology in Cuzco, Peru. During the first Peronist government, he launched his career in journalism by collaborating with a great number of newspapers and magazines as well as the **Confederación General del Trabajo** press office. By 1950, he was working at the Secretariat of National Public Health. In the same year, he joined the **Peña Eva Perón**. After **Juan Domingo Perón** was ousted in 1955, Chávez was part of the Peronist resistance that opposed **Pedro Eugenio Aramburu**'s government. While in exile, Perón sent Chávez personal letters and invited the writer to accompany him on his flight back to Argentina in 1973. *See also* CASTIÑEIRA DE DIOS, JOSÉ MARÍA; LIBERATING REVOLUTION; VENTURINI, AURORA.

CHILDREN'S REPUBLIC, THE. *See* REPÚBLICA DE LOS NIÑOS.

CICCONE, MADONNA LOUISE (1958–). The American singer, songwriter, and actress known as Madonna played the role of Evita in the eponymous musical film directed by Alan Parker. As an actress, she had played in, among others, *Desperately Seeking Susan*, *Dick Tracy*, and *A League of Their Own* before landing the leading role in *Evita*. While Madonna had been criticized as an actress, her performance as Evita gave credibility to her acting career. The challenge of interpreting a character with such historical importance, strong personality, and cultural characteristics let Madonna show the world that she could increase the scope of her artistic skills. Madonna's rendition of **"Don't Cry for Me Argentina"** was praised highly. The casting of Madonna, in turn, resulted in an avalanche of publicity for the film and Evita's story, resulting in what Marta E. Savigliano calls the "Madonnification of Evita." Peronist supporters, however, took the choice of the steamy singer playing Evita as a further attack on Argentine history and dignity. *See also EVITA CONCEPT ALBUM; EVITA MUSICAL: AMERICAN STAGE PRODUCTION; EVITA MUSICAL: BRITISH STAGE PRODUCTION.*

CINE ARGENTINO. Founded in 1938, *Cine Argentino* was one of the few Latin American magazines exclusively devoted to film. Evita landed the cover of *Cine Argentino* on 27 March 1941. The photograph was part of a series of covers portraying young actresses with popular soccer players. The image features Evita and Argentine soccer player Bernardo Gandulla, both wearing Boca Juniors outfits and kicking a soccer ball.

CIPAYO. The term *cipayo* acquired a new meaning under the work of historical revisionists in Argentina. The Argentine writer **Arturo Martín Jauretche** popularized the use of *cipayo* to describe a person supporting foreign interests and imperialism. **Juan Domingo Perón** borrowed this term and employed it in his discourse. For Perón, a *cipayo* was any professional backing imperialism and pursuing an economic benefit. In Peronist ideology, *cipayo* is a synonym for *vendepatria*, *oligarca*, and *antipueblo*. *See also PUEBLO.*

CIRCUS CAVALCADE. *See LA CABALGATA DEL CIRCO.*

CIUDAD ESTUDIANTIL PRESIDENTE JUAN DOMINGO PERÓN. The **Fundación Eva Perón** inaugurated this building complex on 27 October 1951. It was built next to the **Ciudad Infantil Amanda Allen** in Belgrano, Buenos Aires, which had opened its doors in 1949. The Ciudad Estudiantil Presidente **Juan Domingo Perón** served mainly as a boarding school for socially disadvantaged students who arrived in Buenos Aires from the **interior of Argentina** without their families to complete their secondary education. The complex included dormitories, dining rooms, recreational rooms, theater workshops, a library, a printing studio, hair salons, and medical centers. Furthermore, students had access to a variety of sport activities, such as soccer, basketball, fencing, riding, swimming, and sprinting. The teaching approach consisted of integrating theory and practice, with an emphasis on topics related to the social sciences and technology. The mission of the school was to develop the country's future leaders. Following the **Liberating Revolution**, it became a detention center for Peronist union leaders and politicians. Like the Ciudad Infantil Amanda Allen, it served as a medical center over the years.

CIUDAD INFANTIL AMANDA ALLEN. Also known as Ciudad Infantil Evita, this miniature city was opened by the **Fundación Eva Perón** in Belgrano, Buenos Aires, on 14 July 1949. The city was named in honor of one of the foundation's nurses, Amanda Allen, who passed away after being gravely injured in a plane crash on returning to Argentina from an aid mission to Ecuador. The children's city assisted socially disadvantaged children between the ages of two and six. Serving as a **home-school**, the building complex included dormitories, dining areas, parks, a swimming pool, a movie theater, as well as medical and dental centers, among other facilities. Evita herself looked after the interior decoration of the different buildings. The city had approximately 700 children in-house daily, with half of them living on the premises. The morning hours were devoted to educational activities that followed the Montessori and Froebel methods. In addition, the children could take part in gardening, dance, and music classes. After lunch, they usually spent time in the parks and enjoying the rest of the facilities. During the **Liberating Revolution**, the city was seriously damaged and ceased functioning. Over the years, the premises served as a psychophysics rehabilitation hospital. The Ciudad Infantil Amanda Allen was declared a national historical monument in 2013.

CIUDAD UNIVERSITARIA ESTUDIANTIL PRESIDENTE PERÓN. Since 1957, this university campus has been part of the National University of **Córdoba**, Argentina. In 1949, the government of Córdoba Province began negotiations with the **Fundación Eva Perón** to start a new project on the land once occupied by the National School of Agriculture. Three years later, the province transferred to the foundation two-thirds of the land. The foundation then committed itself to building a **senior residence**, a **home-school**, and the Ciudad Universitaria Estudiantil Presidente Perón there. The university campus was initially conceived of as a series of residence halls, a main building, parks, and sports facilities. Designed by the Argentine architect Jorge Sabaté, the university campus included both new buildings and restored premises belonging to the former National School of Agriculture. Most of the buildings on the modern university campus were named after such countries as Spain, Mexico, Chile, Peru, and France. Following the 1955 military coup d'état, the Ciudad Unversitaria Estudiantil Presidente Perón was handed over to the National University of Córdoba. See also LIBERATING REVOLUTION.

COMPAÑÍA ARGENTINA DE COMEDIAS. Evita made her stage debut with this theater company in Buenos Aires in 1935. The Compañía Argentina de Comedias was managed by actor **José Franco** and director Joaquín de Vedia. The company's leading actress was Franco's daughter **Eva Franco**. The 15-year-old Evita was hired by the company to play the role of a maid in *La señora de los Pérez* (Mrs. Pérez), which premiered at the Comedia Theater in Buenos Aires on 28 March 1935. Even though Evita had only one line, "Dinner is served," she was mentioned in a review in *Crítica*. Evita worked with this company until January 1936. Other plays in which she had small roles were *Cada casa es un mundo* (Every Home Is a Different World), *Madame Sans-Gêne*, and *La dama, el caballero y el ladrón* (The Lady, the Gentleman, and the Thief). See also PELLICCIOTTA, PASCUAL.

COMPAÑÍA ARGENTINA DE ESPECTÁCULOS CÓMICOS. This theater company was first known as Compañía de Teatro **Pierina Dealessi**. Eventually, it became the Compañía Argentina de Espectáculos Cómicos, with Dealessi as the leading actress and Rafael Firtuoso as the director. Evita was hired by the company in March 1938 to play a bit part in *La gruta de la fortuna* (The Grotto of Fortune). The play opened at the Liceo Theater in Buenos Aires on 17 March. Evita worked for this company for the rest of the year. Other plays in which she performed were *¡Si los viejos levantaran la cabeza!* (If the Old Could See This!), *El cura de Santa Clara* (Santa Clara's Priest), and *Una noche en Viena* (A Night in Vienna). See also PELLICCIOTTA, PASCUAL.

COMPAÑÍA CANDILEJAS. This theater company was directed by the popular librettist Félix Martinelli Massa. In May 1942, Evita and her **Compañía Juvenil de Radioteatro** joined the Compañía Candilejas at **Radio El Mundo**. The leading artists were Evita and **Pablo Racioppi**. Sponsored by Radical Soap, the company performed romantic **radioteatros** on weekdays, including *Una promesa de amor* (A Promise of Love), *Infortunio* (Misfortune), *El rostro y el aullido del lobo* (The Face and the Howl of the Wolf), *Mi amor nace en ti* (My Love Is Born in You), and *La otra cara de la máscara* (The Other Side of the Mask). See also VALLE, PABLO OSVALDO.

COMPAÑÍA CÓMICA SIMARI-SIMARI. In 1940, Evita joined the theater company Compañía Cómica Simari-Simari, managed by brothers Leopoldo and **Tomás Simari**. She appeared in bit parts in three plays performed by the company at the Smart Theater in Buenos Aires: Ivo Pelay's *¡Llegaron parientes de España!* (Our Family from Spain Is Here!), Ricardo Hicken's *Corazón de manteca* (Heart of Butter), and Antonio Botta's *¡La plata hay que repartirla!* (Money Should Be Spread Around!). The plays, which opened on 20 July, 1 August, and 16 August, respectively, were not successful and ran for less than two weeks.

COMPAÑÍA DE ARMANDO DISCÉPOLO. In March 1937, the respected author and theater director **Armando Discépolo** announced that he would direct a new theater company in Buenos Aires and that their debut play would be *La nueva colonia* (The New Colony) by the Italian dramatist Luigi Pirandello. Before the announcement, the company was already rehearsing the play, translated by Discépolo himself. Evita was cast in the role of Nella, a woman from the countryside, and had a few lines in the third act. The play premiered at the Politeama Theater in Buenos Aires on 5 March. Despite Discépolo's and the main cast's excellent reputation, the play received mixed reviews from critics and ran for less than a week. The entire experience was, nevertheless, quite positive for Evita. Apart from gaining experience under the direction of Discépolo, she was mentioned in *Crítica*. The review on 6 March stated that "Juana Sujo, Eva Duarte, **Anita Jordán**, and Jordana Fain acted gracefully in well-directed group scenes."

COMPAÑÍA DE CAMILA QUIROGA. Evita joined the distinguished actress **Camila Quiroga**'s theater company in Lucienne Favre's *Mercado de amor en Argelia* (Market of Love in Algeria), which opened at the Astral Theater in Buenos Aires on 5 January 1939. The play was adapted by Gaston Baty and translated by the Argentine director **Edmundo Guibourg**. Evita was cast as the psychic odalisque Baya. Reportedly, Evita got the part thanks to her friendship with Guibourg and Quiroga's daughter Nélida.

COMPAÑÍA DE COMEDIAS MUÑOZ-FRANCO-ÁLVAREZ. In May 1936, Evita joined the comedy theater company of Pepita Muñoz, **José Franco**, and Eloy Álvarez on a tour of the Argentine cities of **Rosario, Mendoza**, and **Córdoba**. Their debut play, *Miente y serás feliz* (Lie and You Will Be Happy), opened at the Odeón Theater in Rosario on 22 May. Among the plays performed by the company, *El beso mortal* (The Mortal Kiss) was the most successful. Reportedly, Evita did not finish the tour as she left the company after Franco's wife learnt about the alleged affair between Evita and Franco.

COMPAÑÍA DE COMEDIAS Y SAINETES RINALDI-CHARMIELLO. This small theater company was directed by the renowned comedians Leonor Rinaldi and Francisco Charmiello. Evita had a brief appearance in *No hay suegra como la mía* (There Is No Mother-in-Law Like Mine), performed by this company at the Liceo Theater in Buenos Aires between 5 November 1937 and 6 March 1938. The play was such a big hit that Radio Splendid began broadcasting the company's evening performance.

COMPAÑÍA DE PABLO SUERO SIERO. Evita joined the theater company of **Pablo Suero Siero** in December 1936. Suero translated *The Children's Hour* by Lillian Hellman into Spanish and called the play *Las inocentes*, which premiered at the Corrientes Theater in Buenos Aires at the beginning of December. Evita played the role of a student named Catalina, but she was not mentioned in the newspaper reviews. The company also performed *Las inocentes* at the 18 July Theater in Montevideo, Uruguay, between 14 and 20 January 1937.

COMPAÑÍA DE TEATRO DEL AIRE. Between May and September 1939, Evita became the leading actress of this theater company. She performed in a series of *radioteatros* written by the poet and writer **Héctor Blomberg**. Broadcast by **Radio Mitre** and **Radio Prieto**, the series began on 1 May with *Los jazmines del 80* (The Jasmines of 1880), and it was the first time Evita had a starring role. Broadcast every day except Sundays, *Los jazmines del 80* was a hit. As a result, Evita gained popularity and was featured in such magazines as *Antena* and *Sintonía*. Other *radioteatros* performed by the company were *Las rosas de Caseros* (Caseros's Roses) and *La estrella del pirata* (The Pirate's Star). *See also* PELLICCIOTTA, PASCUAL.

COMPAÑÍA DEL PRADO-DE PAULA. The leading artists of this theater company were

Blanca del Prado and Francisco de Paula. Sponsored by Lever Bros., their *radioteatros* were broadcast daily on **Radio Belgrano**. Between March and April 1943, Evita reportedly signed a six-month contract with **Linter Publicidad**, an advertising agency that sponsored her. Thanks to this contract, she performed with the Compañía del Prado-de Paula in several *radioteatros*, including Boris Zipman's *El amor de una esposa* (A Wife's Love), Rafael García Ibañez's *Los desesperados* (The Desperate), and Claudio Rivera's *Así era mi casa* (My House Was Like This).

COMPAÑÍA JUVENIL DE RADIOTEATRO. In December 1941, Evita secured a contract with **Radio Argentina** to be the leading actress of this theater company. Sponsored by Radical Soap, the Compañía Juvenil de Radioteatro went on the air every morning between January and February 1942. The leading actor and director of the company was **César Mariño**, who was also the director of *radioteatro* shows at Radio Argentina. The company performed two *radioteatros*. The first one was a romantic comedy entitled *Amanecer* (Dawn), written by the artistic director of Radio Argentina, **Roberto Gil**. The second one was Manuel Barberá's *Cara sucia* (Dirty Face), which was broadcast in February. The Compañía Juvenil de Radioteatro moved to **Radio El Mundo** and joined the **Compañía Candilejas** in May 1942.

COMPAÑÍA REMEMBRANZAS. Evita was hired by this theater company to perform several *radioteatros* at **Radio Belgrano** between August and September 1937. The first one was Manuel Ferradás Campos's *Oro blanco* (White Gold), based on a poem by Luis Solá. This *radioteatro* was sponsored by **Antena** magazine.

COMPAÑÍA ROMANCES DEL PUEBLO. Directed by writer Atilano Ortega Sanz, this theater company took part in the show *La fiesta de Juan Manuel* (Juan Manuel's Party), which was broadcast on **Radio Mitre** daily. Allegedly, Evita joined Ortega Sanz's company in July 1942. She was the leading actress in the *radioteatro La calandria ciega* (The Blind Calandra Lark). Between September and December, the company toured the country performing different plays, including *La calandria ciega*. Ortega Sanz was a pioneer in offering theater performances in the **interior of Argentina**.

CONFEDERACIÓN GENERAL DEL TRABAJO (CGT)/GENERAL CONFEDERATION OF LABOR. Founded on 27 September 1930, the Confederación General del Trabajo (CGT) is the major labor union federation in Argentina. After 1943, the CGT welcomed the pro-labor landmark social reforms promoted by Colonel **Juan Domingo Perón** and eventually became the mainstay of **Peronism**. CGT members played a key role in the 17 October 1945 demonstration to release Perón from prison and in Perón's victory in the 1946 presidential election. Perón was not alone in building a strong relationship with the CGT labor unions. Through her work as a mediator between the unions and Perón, Evita earned the CGT's respect and support. When Evita died in 1952, her coffin was taken to the CGT headquarters on 10 August and remained there until 1955. The CGT headquarters building, located at 802 Azopardo Street, San Telmo, Buenos Aires, was donated by Evita through her foundation and opened by Perón on 18 October 1950. *See also* BODY OF EVITA; CABILDO ABIERTO; FUNDACIÓN EVA PERÓN; PARTIDO PERONISTA (PP)/PERONIST PARTY; PERONIST LOYALTY DAY; STATE FUNERAL OF EVITA.

CONQUISTA. The only newspaper of the **Partido Peronista Femenino (PPF)**, *Conquista* was published twice a month. Its first issue came out on 7 May 1955. The date of publication was not chosen randomly. It coincided with the day and month Evita was born. Aside from praising Evita's work and legacy, the newspaper featured the activities and achievements of the local branches of the PPF. *Conquista* ceased to be published in September 1955, when **Juan Domingo Perón** was toppled. *See also* LIBERATING REVOLUTION; *UNIDADES BÁSICAS*.

COPI. *See EVA PERÓN* PLAY.

CÓRDOBA. Located 700 kilometers (435 miles) northwest of Buenos Aires, Córdoba is the capital city of the eponymous province and the second most populous city in Argentina. In 1936, Evita was on a tour of **Rosario**, Córdoba, and **Mendoza** with the **Compañía de Comedias Muñoz-Franco-Álvarez**. After a successful season in Mendoza, the company went to Córdoba, and Evita made her debut in this city on 3 September. Evita returned to Córdoba during the presidential campaign of 1945–1946, accompanying her husband and presidential candidate **Juan Domingo Perón** on board the *Descamisado* **Train**. As first lady, she visited the province of Córdoba on different occasions.

CÓRDOBA, IRMA (1913–2008). This Argentine theater, radio, and television actress had a prolific career. She was born in Corrientes Province and moved to Buenos Aires at the age of nine. Córdoba met Evita in 1935, when they both were with the **Compañía Argentina de Comedias**. Whereas Córdoba was already an accomplished actress, Evita was in the early stages of her acting career. In an interview with *Radiolandia 2000* on 4 April 1980, Córdoba mentioned that Evita felt a little inhibited, most likely because she was surrounded by renowned actors such as **Eva Franco**, Felisa Mary, and Enrique Serrano. In another interview with the writer Noemí Castiñeiras, Córdoba stated that Evita was keen on reciting poetry and that she did it as a pastime in the dressing rooms. Córdoba also told Castiñeiras that one day Evita went to her house to ask her if she had any dresses for sale. Back then, actresses had to pay for their own stage clothes. This proved to be difficult for Evita, who had very little money. As Córdoba sympathized with Evita's situation, she allowed her to pay for the clothes in installments.

CRÍTICA. This evening newspaper was founded in 1913 by the Uruguayan journalist Natalio Botana in Buenos Aires. The paper gradually adopted a colloquial, modern, controversial, and sensationalist approach, focusing on sports and crime reports. On 29 March 1935, *Crítica* mentioned Evita in a review of *La señora de los Pérez* (Mrs. Pérez), a play in which Evita had a small role. This was Evita's debut play, and the review noted that "Eva Duarte was very correct in her brief intervention." When Botana died in a car accident in 1941, *Crítica* passed to his wife, Salvadora Medina Onrubia de Botana. Together with *La Razón*, *Noticias Gráficas*, *La Vanguardia*, *La Prensa*, *El Mundo*, and *La Nación*, *Crítica* was one of the papers that strongly opposed the presidential candidacy of **Juan Domingo Perón** during the 1945–1946 general election campaign. In 1951, amid financial difficulties, the Botana family was forced to sell the paper, which became part of the Peronist media conglomerate **Alea S.A.** Although in circulation until 1962, *Crítica* was never returned to the Botana family. *See also* ANTI-ARGENTINE ACTIVITIES CONGRESSIONAL COMMITTEE.

CULTURAL ATHENAEUM EVA PERÓN. *See* ATENEO CULTURAL EVA PERÓN.

D

DAKHLA. Known in Spanish as Villa Cisneros, Dakhla is a city located in Western Sahara. It was occupied by Spain between 1884 and 1975. This disputed territory is currently the capital of the Moroccan administrative region of Dakhla-Oued Ed-Dahab. Evita arrived in Dakhla on 7 June 1947 as part of her **Rainbow Tour**. She was welcomed by Minister of Foreign Affairs **Alberto Martín-Artajo Álvarez**, **Francisco Franco Bahamonde**'s secretary **Francisco Franco Salgado-Araujo**, and their respective wives, among others. Evita attended her first official gala function in Spain at the military casino in Dakhla. The gala function was followed by a brief press conference. After spending the night at the governor's house, Evita and her entourage traveled to **Madrid** via **Las Palmas de Gran Canaria**. *See also* GANDO AIRPORT.

DAMAS Y DAMITAS. This weekly women's magazine was founded by Emilio Ramírez in 1939. Although *Damas y Damitas* encompassed some show-business information, it featured mainly articles about fashion, beauty, home, cookery, and maternity, among other topics. Thanks to a subscription and mail-order system, the magazine had a wide circulation, especially among urban and rural middle-class women. Evita graced the cover of this magazine on 13 December 1939. The photo by **Sivul Wilenski** shows Evita wearing a daring outfit by the standard of those days—a light coat, a pair of mini shorts, and just a shawl serving as a top. According to the then editorial manager of *Damas y Damitas*, **Vera Pichel**, Evita needed to appear on the front cover of a magazine that was not devoted to show business to boost her acting career.

DAMONTE BOTANA, RAÚL (1939–1987). *See EVA PERÓN* PLAY.

DEALESSI, PIERINA (1894–1983). This Italian Argentine theater and film actress worked together with Evita throughout 1938 for the **Compañía Argentina de Espectáculos Cómicos**, in which Dealessi was the leading actress. As rehearsals finished late in the evening, Dealessi worried about Evita's safety while heading back home. Hence, she offered that Evita could stay over at her place. The young actress slept on a couch in Dealessi's sitting room and usually left early in the morning. Eventually, Dealessi and Evita became very close friends. In 1950, when Evita set up the **Ateneo Cultural Eva Perón**, she asked Dealessi to be a member of its board of directors.

DECALOGUE OF THE RIGHTS OF SENIORS. One of the main goals of the **Fundación Eva Perón** was to improve the living conditions of the elderly in Argentina. Hence, on 28 August 1948, Evita introduced the Decalogue of the Rights of Seniors in a solemn ceremony at the **Secretariat of Labor and Social Welfare**. This document introduced fundamental social rights that were to be guaranteed to the elderly. The rights were primarily concerned with the provision of housing, food, clothing, health care, and recreation, and were eventually included in the amended **Argentine Constitu-**

tion of 1949. As part of this undertaking, the foundation inaugurated the Hogar para Ancianos Coronel Perón (Senior Residence Colonel Perón), on 17 October 1948 in Burzaco, Buenos Aires Province. Argentina became a pioneer as regards the recognition of the rights of the elderly when it submitted a document on old age rights, based on the decalogue, to the UN General Assembly on 4 December 1948. The preamble of the document read, "That old age rights, having the same origin and purpose as other universal social safeguards, are essential for the improvement of living conditions of the worker and for his welfare when his physical strength is at an end and he is exposed to poverty and neglect." Although the resolution languished in the UN, more than 50 countries acknowledged the importance of Evita's document and decided to implement similar rights too. See also SENIOR RESIDENCES.

DEMOCRACIA. Focused on agricultural and labor-related news, this tabloid paper was founded by Antonio Molinari, Fernando Estrada, and Mauricio Birabent in Buenos Aires in 1945. Initially, it was an evening paper, but after a few months in circulation it became a morning publication issued from Monday to Saturday. Together with *La Época*, *El Laborista*, and *El Pueblo*, *Democracia* supported **Juan Domingo Perón**'s presidential candidacy during the 1945–1946 general election campaign. Under the auspices of Carlos Vicente Aloé, *Democracia* was acquired by the state in November 1946 and **Raúl Alejandro Apold** was named the daily's editor-in-chief. The purchase was carried out thanks to a loan received from the Central Bank of Argentina, whose president was **Miguel Miranda**. In January 1947, the paper changed its profile, becoming Evita's mouthpiece and the first paper to be part of the media conglomerate **Alea S.A.** See also DEMOCRACIA S.A.

DEMOCRACIA S.A. In November 1946, Antonio Molinari, Fernando Estrada, and Mauricio Birabent sold the Peronist government their publishing company Democracia S.A., which published the papers *Democracia* and *Rosario*. Under the management of Carlos Vicente Aloé, Democracia S.A. became part of the media conglomerate **Alea S.A.** in 1947. See also ANTI-ARGENTINE ACTIVITIES CONGRESSIONAL COMMITTEE.

DE-PERONIZATION OF ARGENTINA. See ARAMBURU, PEDRO EUGENIO; LIBERATING REVOLUTION.

***DESCAMISADO* TRAIN.** Named after the *descamisados* or working-class people, *El Descamisado* was a train in which the presidential candidate **Juan Domingo Perón** toured the **interior of Argentina** during the 1945–1946 presidential campaign. Evita joined Perón on board the train on 28 December 1945 to partake in the campaign. It was the first time in the history of Argentina that a candidate's wife campaigned side by side with her husband. During the tour, large numbers of people gathered at train stations to be able to see and touch her.

DESCAMISADOS. This term was first employed by **Juan Domingo Perón** on 17 October 1945. On that day, people had gathered in the central **Plaza de Mayo**, Buenos Aires, to demand Perón's release from prison. When he finally appeared on the balcony of the **Pink House**, he gave a speech and addressed the crowd as *descamisados* or "shirtless ones," referring to the fact that many of them were not wearing shirts. It was a hot day, and most people had taken off their shirts. Some had even bathed in the fountains in the Plaza de Mayo while waiting for Perón's release. After that day, the use of this term would emphasize and celebrate the courage and loyalty shown by working-class people toward Perón and **Peronism**. See also PERONIST LOYALTY DAY.

DÍAZ, JULIETA (1977–). This famous Argentine actress, known for her work in film, television, and theater, interpreted Evita in the 2011 film *Juan y Eva*, directed by Paula de Luque.

DIONISI, HUMBERTO (1901–1988). Head of the Cancer Institute of **Córdoba** and professor at the National University of Córdoba, Dr. Humberto Dionisi was a renowned Argentine gynecologist who diagnosed Evita's cervical cancer. In August 1951, he was summoned by Minister of Technical Affairs **Raúl Mendé** to perform a gynecological examination on Evita. As he agreed to the request, the government organized a military flight that brought him from Córdoba to Buenos Aires in secret. He carried out the examination and removed a sample of tissue for testing. A few days later, the results showed that she was suffering from advanced cervical cancer. However, Dr. Dionisi made it clear to the government that he was not able to treat the patient due to his many commitments back in Córdoba. Yet he stayed on in Buenos Aires until the treatment was entrusted to Dr. **Jorge Albertelli**. Both Dr. Dionisi and Dr. Albertelli performed a second pelvic exam on Evita together before the former's return to Córdoba.

DIRTY WAR. Also known as the Process of National Reorganization, the Dirty War—in Spanish, *guerra sucia*—is a period in Argentine history spanning from 1976 to 1983, during which the military junta that ruled the country kidnapped, tortured, and murdered between 10,000 and 30,000 civilians without any regard for the law. The term *Dirty War* was employed by the military to claim that they were waging a war to maintain social order and eradicate left-wing political opponents, a practice that had been carried out by the **Triple A** or the Argentine Anti-Communist Alliance, since **Juan Domingo Perón**'s third term in office (1973–1974). As many of those abducted were never heard from again, and evidence of their arrests was never recorded nor proofs of their deaths found, they came to be known as the *desaparecidos*, or the disappeared. Initially, the target group was young and politically mobilized supporters of left-wing **Peronism**. However, the threats and abductions were eventually extended to anyone suspected of being aligned with leftist or socialist ideas, including labor union members, freethinkers, academics, artists, teachers, and journalists. The abductees were taken to clandestine detention camps, where the majority of them were tortured, raped, and even killed. The growing evidence of **human right** violations in Argentina led to the emergence of the Mothers of the Plaza de Mayo in 1977. Constituted by the mothers of those who went missing, the movement openly challenged the military regime by starting to march in protest in the emblematic **Plaza de Mayo** in Buenos Aires. *See also* MONTONEROS.

DISCÉPOLO, ARMANDO (1887–1971). This Argentine theater director and playwright is considered the creator of the *grotesco criollo*—the Argentine version of the grotesque genre. He was the first of five children of the Italian musician Santos Discépolo and Luisa de Lucchi and brother of the famous poet and tango composer Enrique Santos Discépolo. He was initially an actor but soon discovered that acting was not his vocation. Following his father's death, Discépolo began writing short plays. Over the years, he became an established playwright. Evita performed under the direction of Discépolo in *La nueva colonia* (The New Colony) at the Politeama Theater in Buenos Aires in March 1937. *See also* COMPAÑÍA DE ARMANDO DISCÉPOLO.

DODERO, ALBERTO (1887–1951). Born and raised in Montevideo, Uruguay, Dodero moved to Buenos Aires after World War I. He became one of the major shipping tycoons in South America in the mid-20th century. His shipping fleet allegedly transported thousands of Nazi criminals and collaborators from Europe to South America. As he was close to the Peróns, he financed Evita's trip to Europe and presented the couple with a high-rise building in Buenos Aires. His wife, Betty Sundmark, an American ex–chorus girl from Chicago, befriended Evita for a time. *See also* RAINBOW TOUR.

DODERO, ALBERTO NICOLÁS (1915–1997). Nephew of **Alberto Dodero**, Alberto Nicolás Dodero was a lawyer and the head of the Argentine Shipping Company Dodero, which had an active participation in the implementation of the national shipping policy. He sold the land where the **Alea Building** was later erected to the Agrupación de Trabajadores Latinoamericanos Sindicalizados (a Latin American labor union confederation) in 1949.

"DON'T CRY FOR ME ARGENTINA." This song was composed by Andrew Lloyd Webber and Tim Rice for the *Evita* concept album. Released in 1976, the original version was recorded by the English singer and actress Julie Covington. This catchy tune, which was at the top of the British hit parade in 1976, portrays not only Evita's public persona but also her private side. *See also* EVITA MUSICAL: AMERICAN STAGE PRODUCTION; *EVITA* MUSICAL: BRITISH STAGE PRODUCTION.

DUARTE, BLANCA (1908–2005). The first of five children of **Juana Ibarguren** and **Juan Duarte** and older sister of Evita. After completing her primary education in **Los Toldos**, she moved to Bragado, Buenos Aires Province, to continue studying. She then moved to **Junín** to join her family and to complete her teacher training. Upon finishing her studies, she was offered a position as a primary school teacher at a local school in Junín. Thanks to her job, she was able to contribute to the family economy. In 1940, she married Justo Álvarez Rodríguez, a lawyer whom she had met at her mother's pension in Junín.

DUARTE, ELISA (1909–1967). The second of five children of **Juana Ibarguren** and **Juan Duarte** and older sister of Evita. As she secured a job at the post office in **Junín**, the rest of the family followed suit and left **Los Toldos** in 1930. In 1936, she married Major Alfredo Arrieta, who had frequented her mother's pension in Junín. She died of peritonitis at the age of 52.

DUARTE, ERMINDA (1916–2012). The fourth of five children of **Juana Ibarguren** and **Juan Duarte** and older sister of Evita. She was Evita's playfellow during the siblings' childhood in **Los Toldos**. Upon moving to **Junín** in 1930, she started her postprimary education at the town's National School, where she became involved in the school's drama club. Knowing Evita's passion for acting, Erminda would invite her to take part in the school plays organized by the club. In 1936, she caught pleurisy, and Evita, who was on a tour, paid her a visit at the family's home in Junín. She was with Evita while her sister was bedridden and at the moment she passed away on 26 July 1952. In 1971, she traveled to **Madrid** with her sister **Blanca Duarte** to take part in the process of repatriating Evita's remains and, one year later, she published *Mi hermana Evita* (My Sister Evita), a book that pays tribute to the memory of Evita and vindicates the figure of their mother. *See also* BODY OF EVITA.

DUARTE, JUAN (1872–1926). Father of Evita, husband of Estela Grisolía, and partner of **Juana Ibarguren**, known as Doña Juana. Duarte came from a wealthy family from Chivilcoy, Buenos Aires Province. In 1901, he left his wife and children in Chivilcoy and moved to **Los Toldos**, a small town in the province of Buenos Aires, to work as a property manager for the Malcom family, who owned **Estancia La Unión**, a ranch situated 20 kilometers (12.4 miles) from Los Toldos. Duarte received a portion of whatever profits he made working the land and eventually became the owner of his own farm. In 1908, he was made a judge of peace in recognition of the local influence he had then acquired. By that time, he was already involved in a relationship with Doña Juana, and the couple lived together as a family. They had four daughters—Blanca, Elisa, Erminda, and Evita—and one son—Juan. Nonetheless, his wife and children from Chivilcoy would come and visit him from time to time. In the early months of 1920, when Evita was about to turn one, Duarte left his farm, Doña Juana, and their children and returned to his family in Chivilcoy. On 8 January 1926, he died in a car accident. On hearing the news of his death, Doña Juana decided to attend the funeral. She dressed the children in black mourning clothes and the whole family traveled to Chivilcoy. It was the first time Evita had ever left her hometown. Although the family was initially refused entry at the funeral, Evita and her siblings managed to have a brief, last look at their father thanks to the intervention of the mayor of Chivilcoy, who was none other than Grisolía's brother.

DUARTE, JUAN "JUANCITO" RAMÓN (1914–1953). The third of five children of

Juana Ibarguren and **Juan Duarte** and older brother of Evita. Born in **Los Toldos**, Buenos Aires Province, Juancito moved to the provincial town of **Junín** together with his mother and sisters at the age of 16. Once there, he found a job as a delivery man for a pharmacy and began contributing to the family income. After completing military service in Buenos Aires, Juancito remained in the city, where he shared an apartment with Evita. The siblings were very close and looked after each other in good and bad times. In 1939, he was accused of embezzling money from the savings bank where he had found work after conscription. Evita sold her belongings to pay off Juancito's debt, thus preventing him from going to jail. Juancito found a new job as a salesman for **Juan Guereño Rodríguez**'s soap company. When Evita met **Juan Domingo Perón** in 1944, Juancito's life was forever changed. Through her influence, he was first appointed inspector of the Casino of Mar del Plata in the province of Buenos Aires, and when Perón took office in 1946, Juancito became his private secretary, having an influential role in the government. Juancito accompanied Evita on her **Rainbow Tour**. He never married but had several mistresses. He amassed a fortune by doubtful means. Accused of corruption, he died under mysterious circumstances. *See also* NAVARRO, FANNY.

DUARTE FAMILY TOMB. This tomb in the Recoleta Cemetery in Buenos Aires contains Evita's remains, which are reportedly buried five meters (16.4 feet) deep under three plates of steel. Although Evita passed away in 1952, her body was placed in the Duarte family tomb first in 1976. Her entombment took place after the military government that had seized power in Argentina that same year handed the corpse over to her family. Nowadays, the tomb is one of the most popular sites of pilgrimage and tourism in Argentina. Its iron grillwork door is always covered in fresh flowers and notes left by Evita's admirers and, on every 26 July—the anniversary of her death—the crowds grow into the thousands. Ironically, the tomb is marked with the Duarte family name even though Evita's father, **Juan Duarte**, never recognized her as his daughter. Apart from Evita, in the tomb lie her brother Juancito, her sister Elisa, her sister's husband Alfredo Arrieta, and her mother, **Juana Ibarguren**. *See also* BODY OF EVITA.

DUHALDE, EDUARDO ALBERTO (1941–). This Argentine lawyer, who joined the **Partido Peronista** during his youth, was appointed mayor of Lomas de Zamora County, Buenos Aires Province, in 1973 but was forced out of office in 1976 by the country's new military rulers. With the return to democratic rule in Argentina in 1983, he returned to politics and was elected national deputy in 1987. He was **Carlos Saúl Menem**'s running mate in 1989 but stepped down as vice president of Argentina in 1991 to run for governor of Buenos Aires Province, an election he won. He was reelected in 1995, but when he left office in 1999 his image was tarnished by accusations of corruption, and the province was virtually bankrupt. He unsuccessfully ran for president in 1999. However, in the midst of the political, social, and economic unrest that shook Argentina in 2001, Duhalde became interim president on 2 January 2002 and served until 25 May 2003. During his presidency, he proposed to move the **body of Evita** from the Recoleta Cemetery in Buenos Aires to the mausoleum at the **San Vicente country house**. However, this was never carried out.

EL AMIGO DEL PUEBLO. Playing a key social role, this newspaper was issued between 14 October 1933 and 6 January 1940 in **Junín**, Buenos Aires Province. Managed by María Peralta Thorp de Leonard, *El Amigo del Pueblo* stood out in a time when women were not supposed to be in managerial positions or interested in what was covered by the broadsheets. In addition, the paper's editor-in-chief published interviews discussing **female suffrage**. From its inception, it covered education, politics, sports, show business, as well as social issues such as unemployment, poverty, and thefts. Evita was mentioned in this daily on 28 April 1934. The very short text devoted to her explained that Evita had traveled to Buenos Aires to perform at **Radio La Nación**. Throughout the years, *El Amigo del Pueblo* would continue publishing information on the young actress's career, including Evita's theater debut in 1935. *See also* COMPAÑÍA ARGENTINA DE COMEDIAS.

EL LABORISTA. This tabloid morning newspaper was founded by the **Partido Laborista (PL)** in January 1946 in Buenos Aires. Under the management of **Ángel Gabriel Borlenghi**, *El Laborista* adhered to a simple writing style addressed to the general public. The PL and thus *El Laborista* supported the **Juan Domingo Perón–Juan Hortensio Quijano** ticket during the 1945–1946 presidential campaign. After the disbanding of the PL in June 1946, *El Laborista* was transferred to state ownership, becoming part of **Alea S.A.** in 1947. Following Perón's overthrow in 1955, *El Laborista* was returned to the former PL's leader, **Cipriano Reyes**. *See also* DEMOCRACIA; *EL PUEBLO*; *LA ÉPOCA*; LIBERATING REVOLUTION; *TRIBUNA*.

EL MÁS INFELIZ DEL PUEBLO. Directed by Luis Bayón Herrera and produced by **Establecimientos Filmadores Argentinos**, *El más infeliz del pueblo* (The Unhappiest Man in Town) was released in March 1941. It tells the story of an office clerk who marries his boss's goddaughter in exchange for a promotion to chief of staff at the city council. The unfortunate consequences of his marriage and promotion come to light as soon as he ties the knot. Evita's participation in this film was minimal, playing the role of one of the guests at the wedding reception.

EL MUNDO. This morning tabloid newspaper was founded in Buenos Aires in 1928 by the Englishman Albert Haynes, owner of **Haynes Publishing**. The paper was an immediate success due to its cheap price, simple and short reports, abundance of pictures, and clear thematic sections. Before becoming part of the Peronist propaganda apparatus in 1947, *El Mundo* had followed an independent line, albeit subtly defending the interests of the British in Argentina. The paper had also been among the publications supporting **Juan Domingo Perón**'s opposition during the 1945–1946 presidential campaign. It went into bankruptcy in 1967. *See also* ALEA S.A; ANTI-ARGENTINE ACTIVITIES CONGRESSIONAL COMMITTEE.

EL PUEBLO. This was the major Argentine Catholic newspaper in the first half of the 20th century. It was founded in 1900 and was initially solely sold by subscription but eventually became a daily newspaper. Like most Argentine papers, *El Pueblo* was revamped during the 1920s with the purpose of becoming a more popular, mass-appealing, Catholic daily. *El Pueblo* offered the same sections as other papers such as ***La Prensa***, ***La Razón*** and ***Crítica*** but employed a simple conservative language. Ideologically, its editorial was antiliberal, antisocialist, and anticommunist, traits that it shared with the fundamentalist Catholicism typical of the time. *El Pueblo*, as well as ***Democracia*** and ***El Laborista***, supported **Peronism**, in particular during **Juan Domingo Perón**'s first term as president between 1946 and 1952. The daily mirrored Perón's pro-Catholic policy and his close collaboration with the Catholic Church. Nevertheless, the editorial and graphic design of the paper declined in quality during the Peronist years. Even though there was an attempt to improve the paper between 1953 and 1954, the crIsIs that emerged between the Catholic Church and Perón at the end of 1954 led to its closure. Following the **Liberating Revolution**, the paper reappeared but finally ceased publication in 1960.

EMBALMING OF EVITA. *See* ARA, PEDRO; BODY OF EVITA.

ERNST, ISABEL (1924–2000). Born in Cologne, Germany, Ernst migrated with her parents to Uruguay and later to Argentina, where the family settled. She worked as a teacher in the Buenos Aires Jansen primary school until 1943—the year she met Colonel **Domingo Alfredo Mercante**. Although Mercante was a married man, he and Ernst started a romantic relationship that would last until Mercante's demise. Persuaded by Mercante, she changed jobs in January 1944 and started to work as the secretary of Mercante's cousin, Hugo Mercante, at the **Secretariat of Labor and Social Welfare**. Ernst's role was to meet with union delegations and prepare reports on their demands before they were received by **Juan Domingo Perón**. As such, Ernst developed excellent contacts with union representatives. When Evita became involved in politics, Ernst became her private secretary. She was present at each of Evita's meetings with union leaders. She would stand behind Evita taking notes and making suggestions. In 1949, she stopped her collaboration with Evita because she got pregnant out of wedlock with Mercante's child. Mercante was at that time the governor of Buenos Aires, and Ernst's pregnancy was frowned upon.

ESCRIBE EVA PERÓN. The book *Escribe Eva Perón* (*The Writings of Eva Perón*) is a collection of 15 articles written by Evita and published in the newspaper ***Democracia*** in the second half of 1948. Addressing political and social issues, the articles helped to showcase and reinforce Evita's political position. More specifically, the articles dealt with the work of the government, **Peronism**, the **Fundación Eva Perón**, the reform of the Constitution, the *descamisados*, and the rights of the elderly, among other themes. The best known of these essays was probably "Por qué soy peronista" (Why I Am a **Peronist**), in which Evita claimed that being a Peronist was the duty of every Argentine citizen. The articles appeared every Wednesday under the heading "Escribe Eva Perón" and were accompanied by the official portrait of Evita. By mid-November, she stopped writing them, and although the reason is not known, it is believed that it was due to her tight schedule. The articles were compiled and published for the first time as a book-length publication in 1950. The volume has also been published under the title *Por qué soy peronista por Eva Perón* (Why I Am a Peronist by Eva Perón). *See also* ARGENTINE CONSTITUTION OF 1949; DECALOGUE OF THE RIGHTS OF SENIORS.

ESCUELA DE ENFERMERAS EVA PERÓN. This avant-garde nursing school was created in 1948 as part of the Public Health Analytical Scheme promoted by the Peronist government. The scheme had been proposed by the neurosurgeon Dr. **Ramón Carrillo**. He highlighted the need for further substantive improvements in the Argentine health system. His strategy involved the following three basic steps: first, to cure the sick; second, to prevent illnesses; and third, to address the sociocultural factors that prompted illnesses, such as the lack of basic hygiene and proper nutrition. In order to successfully carry out the project, manpower in the health sector needed to be increased, especially nurses. As a result, Dr. Carrillo asked the secretary of the Nursing School at the Peralta Ramos Hospital of Buenos Aires, **Teresa Adelina Fiora**, to reorganize the nursing schools in the country and to update their curricula. In less than a year, the Escuela de Enfermeras Eva Perón opened its two-year reorganized course in nursing for women between 18 and 34 years old. Those students who could not afford the course fees were subsidized by the **Fundación Eva Perón**. Nurses were trained in subjects such as general pathology and therapeutics semiology, anatomy and physiology, hygiene and epidemiology, national defense and public disasters, first aid, medical and surgical infirmary, social medicine, pediatrics, dietetics, gynecology, and obstetrics.

ESCUELA SUPERIOR PERONISTA. **Juan Domingo Perón** created this school on 4 December 1950 for the dissemination of his doctrine and the training of political cadres. The Escuela Superior Peronista was officially opened in Buenos Aires on 1 March 1951 and its head was Minister of Technical Affairs **Raúl Mendé**. It was divided into five departments: management, administration, dissemination, doctrine, and teaching. The administrative department oversaw the economic and financial organization of the school and the magazine *Mundo Peronista*. The dissemination department was responsible for the writing of *Mundo Peronista* and the editing of all doctrinal publications. The doctrine department preserved, studied, and classified Perón's and Evita's speeches. The teaching department supervised all matters related to courses, lectures, conferences, and students. The classes consisted of male and female students in equal numbers. Only students who had been members of the **Partido Peronista** for a year were able to enroll. In addition, each candidate had to provide three referees who were involved in either labor union, political, or governmental activities. The students could avail of three courses—basic, superior, and advanced—which lasted between three and six months each. The modules of the basic course were basic principles of **Peronism**, organization of Peronism, and achievements of Peronism. The superior course offered modules such as *justicialismo*, Peronist social policy, Peronist economic policy, ethics of *justicialismo*, and the constitution of *justicialismo*. The advanced course consisted of two modules, history of Peronism and political leadership, delivered by Evita and Perón, respectively. The nine lectures given by Evita were both tape-recorded and published in book format in 1952. At the end of the course, students had to sit for a problem-solving exam. In other words, they had to provide solutions to a problem that required a plan of action. Evita's lessons could go on posthumously thanks to the recordings of her lectures. The lesson was then divided into two sections: the first was listening to the recordings and the second was an open discussion based on the recorded topic. The school ceased functioning after the 1955 military coup d'état. *See also* LIBERATING REVOLUTION.

ESPEJO, JOSÉ (1911–1980). This labor union leader served as the head of the **Confederación General del Trabajo (CGT)** from December 1947 to December 1952. A staunch **Peronist**, Espejo was loyal to Evita and had been handpicked by her for the prominent role of secretary general of the CGT. On behalf of the CGT, Espejo awarded Evita a Distinction of Recognition on 17 October 1950 for her support of the Argentine labor movement. In his capacity as the leader of the CGT, he promoted and officially announced the **Juan Domingo Perón–Eva Perón** ticket at the **Cabildo Abierto** rally held on 9 de Julio Avenue in Buenos Aires on 22 August 1951. Aside from his work at the CGT, he was appointed vice president of the convention that drafted the **Argentine Constitution of 1949**. He also collaborated with the

Fundación Eva Perón and held various positions in government agencies. With the death of Evita, Espejo was removed as head of the CGT and succeeded by Eduardo Vuletich. Following the ousting of Perón in 1955, Espejo was incarcerated in Río Gallegos, Santa Cruz Province, but managed to escape from prison, fleeing to Chile in 1957. He returned to Argentina during the presidential mandate of **Arturo Frondizi**. *See also* GAY, LUIS.

ESTABLECIMIENTOS FILMADORES ARGENTINOS. Businessmen Julio Joly, Alfredo Wilson, and Clemente Lococo founded this film production company in Buenos Aires in 1937. Evita had a bit part in the film *El más infeliz del pueblo* (The Unhappiest Man in Town), which was released by this company in 1941. Establecimientos Filmadores Argentinos ceased production in 1955.

ESTANCIA LA UNIÓN. In the first decade of the 20th century, the Argentine government appropriated the lands belonging to the Mapuche community in **Los Toldos**, Buenos Aires Province, and distributed them among new owners. Evita's father, **Juan Duarte**, was named property manager of part of these lands, the Estancia La Unión, owned by the Malcom family. Doña Juana, Evita's mother, worked as a maid on the ranch. Located 20 kilometers (12.4 miles) from Los Toldos, the ranch was apparently Evita's birthplace. Juana Rawson de Guayaquil, a Mapuche woman who had previously assisted Doña Juana during labor, arrived at La Unión on 7 May 1919 to deliver Evita. Seemingly, the building where the birth took place was torn down to prevent it becoming a Peronist shrine. However, according to the records at the civil registry in **Junín**, Buenos Aires Province, Evita's birthplace was not Los Toldos. The document, which was allegedly forged, attests that she was born in Junín on 7 May 1922. *See also* BIRTH CERTIFICATE OF EVITA; IBARGUREN, JUANA; WEDDING OF EVITA.

ESTUDIOS BAIRES. This film production company was founded by *Crítica*'s owner Natalio Botana in partnership with *Crítica*'s deputy editor Eduardo Bedoya in the 1930s. The studios were located in the town of Don Torcuato, Buenos Aires Province, and ceased production after Botana's death in 1943. Although short-lived, this company released several films, including *Una novia en apuros* (A Bride in Trouble), in which Evita had a small role.

ESTUDIOS SAN MIGUEL. This film production company was founded and owned by the renowned Spanish businessman Miguel Machinandiarena and his brother Narciso. Built between 1937 and 1940, the facilities included offices, a power plant, as well as a carpentry, a plaster, and a costume workshop. Furthermore, an area of 22,400 square meters (241,111 square feet) provided both outdoor filming facilities and provisional accommodation for artists and technicians. By then, the cinema industry in Argentina followed the Hollywood star system; that is, each studio hired well-established radio and theater artists and turned them into movie stars. Among Estudios San Miguel's main stars were **Libertad Lamarque Bouza** and Hugo del Carril. Evita signed her first contract with the studio to appear in a supporting role in *La cabalgata del circo* (Circus Cavalcade) along with Lamarque and del Carril. In October 1944, she secured a second contract to make three films with them. The first film was going to be *Amanece sobre las ruinas* (Dawn over the Ruins), a movie about the **San Juan earthquake**, but later it was announced that instead Evita would be starring in *La pródiga* (The Prodigal Woman). The latter was the last film in which Evita took part before becoming **Juan Domingo Perón**'s wife. Due to financial difficulties, the studio ceased production by 1952.

EUROPEAN TOUR. *See* RAINBOW TOUR.

EVA, EL GRAN MUSICAL ARGENTINO. This Argentine musical, which had been seven years in gestation, premiered at the Maipo Theater in Buenos Aires in May 1986. *Eva, el gran musical argentino* (Eva, the Great Argentine Musical) was produced as a response to Tim Rice and Andrew Lloyd Webber's musical *Evita*.

The Argentine musical starred the renowned Argentine performer **Nacha Guevara**, who also directed and coauthored the libretto with the Argentine writer Pedro Orgambide. The music was composed by the Argentine musician Alberto Favero, who also acted as the musical director. Divided into two acts and not claiming absolute historical veracity, the musical tells the story of Evita from the moment she arrives in Buenos Aires as a 15-year-old until her death. In an attempt to depict an independent Evita, **Juan Domingo Perón** barely appears in the musical, and emphasis is put on Evita's acting career and her incursion into politics before becoming Argentina's first lady. *Eva, el gran musical argentino* struck a chord with the Argentine audience and was praised highly thanks to Guevara's brilliant performance. The musical was restaged at the Argentino Theater in **La Plata**, Buenos Aires Province, on 17 September 2008. This revival was arguably linked to Guevara's foray into politics. The opening night was attended by President **Cristina Fernández de Kirchner** and Daniel Scioli, the governor of the province of Buenos Aires. On 21 October 2008, the musical was transferred to the Lola Membrives Theater in Buenos Aires, where it ran until 19 April 2009.

EVA DE LA ARGENTINA. Directed by María Seoane and released in 2011, the movie *Eva de la Argentina* (Eva from Argentina) follows the interweaving stories of Evita and the Argentine writer Rodolfo Walsh, who comments on the actions and characters of the story in voice-over narration. Blending flashbacks and flash-forwards, this animated film, which also incorporates archival footage, photographs, and audio materials, adds to the various films that portray Evita. Through the workings of crime fiction and melodrama, the story is constructed around the question posed by Walsh on the whereabouts of Evita's corpse, unravelling the events that have led to its disappearance. Searching for the truth about her body, Walsh unveils the life and death of Evita from the moment her father passes away in 1926 until October 1976, when her remains are finally placed in her family's mausoleum in the Recoleta Cemetery in Buenos Aires. Concurrently, the viewer follows the plight of Walsh as he lives in secrecy during the rule of the last military junta in Argentina until his own disappearance in 1977. *See also* BODY OF EVITA.

EVA DOESN'T SLEEP. *See EVA NO DUERME.*

EVA FROM ARGENTINA. *See EVA DE LA ARGENTINA.*

EVA NO DUERME. Directed by Pablo Agüero, the film *Eva no duerme* (Eva Doesn't Sleep) was released in 2015. Divided into three main segments and interspersed with newsreel footage, the story follows the eerie journey of Evita's corpse from her death on 26 July 1952 to its return to Argentina in 1974. The three segments that make up the film are pitted against a country ridden with military regimes. The entire story is bookended by a night when Admiral **Emilio Eduardo Massera** abducts Evita's embalmed body from the **Olivos Presidential Residence** and buries it in the Recoleta Cemetery in Buenos Aires in 1976. In voice-over narration, Massera expresses his resentment toward both Evita and the *descamisados*. This elliptical narrative unfolds in flashback describing Dr. **Pedro Ara**'s work, the abduction of the **body of Evita** from the headquarters of the **Confederación General del Trabajo** in 1955, and the kidnapping and execution of former president **Pedro Eugenio Aramburu**.

EVA PERÓN: LA VERDADERA HISTORIA. Directed by Carlos Desanzo and released in 1996, the film *Eva Perón: la verdadera historia* (Eva Perón: The True Story) follows the last year of Evita's life. It opens with Evita's bid for the vice presidency in 1951; narrates the failed 1951 military coup d'état, her illness, and her unsuccessful surgeries; and closes with her death on 26 July 1952. The story is interspersed with flashbacks of Evita's childhood, her acting career, and her encounter with **Juan Domingo Perón**. The Argentine actress Esther Goris stars as Evita. Goris's skinny body and shrill voice bear a resemblance to Evita's during the final stages of her life. *Eva Perón: la verdadera historia* was spawned by another movie, namely, Alan Parker's *Evita*, and came to be known as the Argentine counterpart of Parker's film. Contrary to *Evita*, *Eva Perón: la verdadera historia* is a low-budget film but more historically accurate.

EVA PERÓN: THE TRUE STORY. See EVA PERÓN: LA VERDADERA HISTORIA.

EVA PERÓN FOUNDATION. See FUNDACIÓN EVA PERÓN.

EVA PERÓN HOME/MUSEUM. The reopening of this museum on 6 May 2019 was one among many events that celebrated the 100th anniversary of Evita's birth. The museum—Evita's childhood home—is located in the town of **Los Toldos**, Buenos Aires Province. Named a provincial historical monument and national historical monument, the museum opened its doors for the first time in 2004. Since being remodeled, the museum currently boasts a cultural complex that surrounds it.

EVA PERÓN NURSING SCHOOL. See ESCUELA DE ENFERMERAS EVA PERÓN.

EVA PERÓN **PLAY.** This theater play was written in French in 1969 by the Argentine playwright Raúl Damonte Botana, known as Copi. The play—a queer interpretation of Evita—is a grotesque farce about the last days of Evita's life. It was premiered in 1970 in the L'Épée de Bois Theater in **Paris**. News had spread that the play insulted the memory of Evita, and a group of **Peronists** arrived to stop the performance. They hurled stink bombs, tore down the set, bullied the cast, and threatened to burn down the playhouse before the intervention of the police. Copi's play was staged in England in 1974—two years before the release of the rock opera *Evita* by Tim Rice and Andrew Lloyd Webber. It is therefore possible that the play inspired Rice and Lloyd Webber to create the famous rock opera. Despite its performance in English and the existence of translations of it into other languages since the 1970s, the *Eva Perón* play only became well known outside of France after Copi's death in 1987. See also EVITA CONCEPT ALBUM; *EVITA* MUSICAL: AMERICAN STAGE PRODUCTION; *EVITA* MUSICAL: BRITISH STAGE PRODUCTION.

EVA PERÓN ROOM. See KIRCHNER CULTURAL CENTER.

EVITA: SU LEGADO DE PUÑO Y LETRA. *Evita: su legado de puño y letra* (Evita: Her Legacy) is a book that includes two of Evita's works, **La palabra, el pensamiento y la acción** (The Word, the Thought, and the Action) and **Escribe Eva Perón** (*The Writings of Eva Perón*). First published in 2009, the volume features an introduction by the Argentine political scientist Pablo Adrián Vázquez.

"EVITA CAPITANA." "Evita capitana" (Evita, the Captain), which is the feminine version of the **"Marcha peronista"** (Peronist March), was the anthem of the **Partido Peronista Femenino (PPF)**. It was used by the PPF during their gatherings and activities. The song borrows the melody from the "Marcha peronista" but changes the lyrics, praising Evita's leadership and Peronist women's loyalty to Evita. The lyrics were probably written by the Argentine composer Rodolfo Sciammarella. The last time the crowds sang "Evita capitana" for Evita was on 1 May 1952, when she made her last public appearance on the balcony of the **Pink House**.

EVITA CHILDREN TOURNAMENTS. See TOURNAMENTS.

EVITA CITY. Founded in 1947 by the Peronist government, Evita City is located in La Matanza County, Buenos Aires Province. It was originally designed as a garden city; that is, a self-contained community surrounded by greenbelts. This garden city has residential areas and such facilities as schools, libraries, sports clubs, and churches. Named after Evita, the city features a street layout built in the shape of her profile.

***EVITA* CONCEPT ALBUM.** As with their previous collaboration, *Jesus Christ Superstar* (1971), Andrew Lloyd Webber and Tim Rice first released the rock opera *Evita* in record form (a double album), and it was only then that the stage performance followed. Written in English with sections in Spanish and Latin, *Evita* the double album chronicles the life of Evita, with the character of the Argentine revolutionary Che Guevara as the main narrator of the story. The recording consists of 23 songs, opening with the announcement of Evita's death on 26 July 1952 and followed by her funeral. Then, the narrative is taken back in time to the moment the 15-year-old Evita leaves her hometown of **Junín**, up until her death. The release of the recording in November 1976 proved to be a fruitful way of introducing a musical work intended for the theater in order to test the reaction to the music alone. The two-record album became a best-seller in the UK and the rest of Europe, with **"Don't Cry for Me Argentina"** at the top of the British hit parade—almost 1,000,000 copies were sold in the UK in 1976.

Evita does not have a unique original source, but it emerged from the revision of several sources that included a radio broadcast, a documentary, a biography, and a historical text. The return to Argentina of **Juan Domingo Perón** in 1973 to assume office for the third time and of Evita's embalmed body on 17 November 1974 (19 years after its disappearance) were given blanket coverage by the media in Argentina and abroad. Rice got the idea of creating *Evita* one evening late in 1973, while hearing the last 10 minutes of a BBC radio broadcast. Those 10 minutes encouraged him to listen to a repeat of the entire program a few days later. Rice knew nothing about Evita, except that she had appeared on Argentine stamps while he was at school, that she was good-looking, and that she was dead. Rice and Lloyd Webber had been searching for their next project together after *Jesus Christ Superstar*, and when Rice suggested his idea to Lloyd Webber, they both agreed that the story of Evita could be the one strong enough to follow *Superstar*. Rice and Lloyd Webber did not consider Evita a role model, but they agreed to compose and write music having Evita in mind owing to the fact that they believed that her Cinderella story, her death at such a young age, and the devotion she inspired among the Argentine people would captivate audiences worldwide. She interested them as a subject due to the dramatic possibilities of her life. They saw the potential in her short life story to develop a successful album and, in all likelihood, the economic benefits this could bring. *See also EVITA* FILM; *EVITA* MUSICAL: AMERICAN STAGE PRODUCTION; *EVITA* MUSICAL: BRITISH STAGE PRODUCTION.

***EVITA* FILM.** This 1996 musical film directed by Alan Parker was produced by Robert Stigwood, Alan Parker, and Andrew G. Vajna. The screenplay was written by Alan Parker and Oliver Stone, and the music was composed by Andrew Lloyd Webber. Exactly 20 years after the release of the *Evita* concept album, the image of Evita was once more reconstructed through the film adaptation of both the concept album and the musical stage productions. The film was partly shot in Argentina, where President **Carlos Saúl Menem** granted the crew permission to film at the **Pink House**. *Evita* premiered in New York and Los Angeles on 25 December 1996 and in the rest of the United States on 10 January 1997. Parker revamped Evita's image by intensifying her melodramatic appeal, but more importantly, he made her story contemporary and commercial by casting Madonna as Evita. The success of the concept album and the musical coupled with the casting of one of the most famous singers in the world made the film an immediate box-office hit and Evita's image a global **icon**. *See also* CICCONE, MADONNA LOUISE; *EVITA* MUSICAL: AMERICAN STAGE PRODUCTION; *EVITA* MUSICAL: BRITISH STAGE PRODUCTION; TRANSNATIONAL ICONIC IMAGE OF EVITA.

EVITA MUSEUM. This museum, which opened its doors on 26 July 2002, is located at 2988 Lafinur Street in the Palermo neighborhood of Buenos Aires. It is housed in a mansion designed by architect Estanislao Pirovano and built for the Carabassa family in 1923. In 1948, the mansion was purchased by the **Fundación Eva Perón** and transformed into a shelter for women and children with no resources. The museum features videos, historical photos,

Evita's bust in the Evita Museum at 2988 Lafinur Street, Buenos Aires.

books, posters, and Evita's memorable wardrobe. It also houses a library and the **Instituto Nacional de Investigaciones Históricas Eva Perón**. *See also* TEMPORARY HOMES.

EVITA MUSICAL: AMERICAN STAGE PRODUCTION. The U.S. premiere of *Evita* took place on 8 May 1979 at the Dorothy Chandler Pavilion in Los Angeles. After a nine-week run, *Evita* played seven weeks at the San Francisco Orpheum Theater and finally moved to Broadway, where it opened on 25 September 1979. In order to enter the U.S. market, Tim Rice and Andrew Lloyd Webber had to overcome several difficulties. First, *Evita* the album had never caught on in the United States, which meant that they would have to start all over again with the marketing of the show. Second, Rice, Lloyd Webber, and director Harold Prince were informed by the U.S. Actors Equity that the British cast would not be allowed to play in the United States. Finally, they had to adjust *Evita* in order to comply with the antagonistic political view of Evita and **Peronism** that had been constructed mainly by the U.S. media. The changes did not affect Evita's lyrics or performance directly, but such changes assured audiences would have no doubt that she was putting up a show as part of a fascist government through the character of Che. Though the unsavory side of Peronism was certainly highlighted in the U.S. stage production, this was achieved through the narration of Che, not through Evita, who remained depoliticized. The result was that her story remained astonishing and moralistic rather than repulsive. Despite getting mixed reviews, once again *Evita* was a hit, settling down for a four-year run on Broadway and winning seven Tony Awards and six Drama Desk Awards for its 1979–1980 season. *See also* EVITA CONCEPT ALBUM; *EVITA* FILM; *EVITA* MUSICAL: BRITISH STAGE PRODUCTION.

EVITA MUSICAL: BRITISH STAGE PRODUCTION. The success of the ***Evita* concept album** led to preparations for the British stage production, which was premiered at the Prince Edward Theater in London. The British stage performance of *Evita* was reviewed in positive and negative terms by the press from both political and musical perspectives. While the theater adaptation of the recording was generally well received, some critics continued to reinterpret *Evita* in accordance with ideological questions that reinforced the negative image Evita and **Peronism** acquired in the English-speaking world in the late 1940s and early 1950s. The international success of this musical has allowed it to remain present in the entertainment industry for more than 40 years. Since its premiere in London in 1978, *Evita* has been performed in more than 50 countries, including the United States, Australia, Spain, Mexico, South Africa, New Zealand, Hungary, Brazil, and Japan. The latest revival of *Evita* took place in 2019 at the Regent's Park Open Air Theater in London. *See also* *EVITA* FILM; *EVITA* MUSICAL: AMERICAN STAGE PRODUCTION.

EVITA PERÓN MINISERIES. Starring Faye Dunaway as Evita and James Farentino as **Juan Domingo Perón**, this miniseries was produced and directed by Marvin J. Chomsky and aired on NBC in 1981. As it was shot in Mexico, the landscape does not do justice to the flat Argentine Pampas, where Evita was raised. Not historically accurate either, the miniseries follows Evita from the moment her father passes away in 1926 until her own death. Evita is portrayed as a promiscuous and vindictive woman whose ruthlessness and ambition eventually destroy her.

EVITAPERON.ORG. This website, at https://www.evitaperon.org/index.htm, provides information about Evita's life and legacy as well as the work of the **Fundación Eva Perón**. The site, which offers its contents in English, Spanish, and French, is developed and maintained by Evita's family. It includes articles, photographs, and video footage.

EZEIZA MASSACRE. After an 18-year exile, **Juan Domingo Perón** officially returned to Argentina on 20 June 1973. Thousands of people gathered to welcome him near Ezeiza International Airport in Buenos Aires, including right- and left-wing **Peronists**. Perón was traveling by plane along with left-wing Peronist **Héctor José Cámpora**, who had been elected president in 1973. To prevent Perón from becoming a candidate for these elections, President **Alejandro Agustín Lanusse** had announced that eligible candidates had to be residents in Argentina by August 1972. Since Perón did not fulfill this requisite, his candidacy was barred, and in turn, he chose Cámpora to "represent" him in the elections. Since Perón's departure in 1955, ideological polarities between right- and left-wing Peronists had triggered hostilities that usually unleashed violent confrontations such as the one that took place at Ezeiza. While waiting for the return of their leader, the more orthodox, right-wing Peronists opened fire on the revolutionary, left-wing Peronists, targeting the **Montoneros** and the **Juventud Peronista** in particular. At least 13 people died and hundreds were wounded. Shortly after the massacre, Cámpora resigned, new elections were called in September 1973, and Perón became president of Argentina for the third time. Before passing away on 1 July 1974, President Perón had tilted toward the anticommunist, right-wing faction of the **Partido Peronista**. In doing so, he paved the way for the persecution, torture, imprisonment, and killing of guerrilla and other left-wing members of Peronist groups, marking the beginning of what became known as the **Dirty War** in Argentina. *See also* HUMAN RIGHTS IN ARGENTINA.

FACULTY OF ENGINEERING BUILDING. Located at 850 Paseo Colón Avenue in Buenos Aires, this neoclassical building that is home to the Faculty of Engineering at the University of Buenos Aires was originally conceived to provide a suitable space for the **Fundación Eva Perón**. Evita's wish was to have an entire building to house her foundation. The building was designed in 1950 by the Directorate General for Architecture, an agency under the Ministry of Public Works, and construction began in 1951. However, Evita died before the building was completed. Following President **Juan Domingo Perón**'s overthrow in 1955, the building was attacked by anti-Peronist militants, who destroyed, beheaded, and threw the 10 statues that decorated it into the Río de la Matanza. In 1956, the building was handed over to the University of Buenos Aires. *See also* LIBERATING REVOLUTION; TOMASSI, LEONE.

Faculty of Engineering Building at the University of Buenos Aires, originally conceived to provide a suitable space for the Fundación Eva Perón.

FARRELL, EDELMIRO JULIÁN (1887–1980). This general preceded **Juan Domingo Perón** as president of Argentina. After graduating as second lieutenant, he began his military career in **Mendoza** Province, where he specialized in mountaineering fighting. He was sent to Italy to train with the Alpine regiments of the Italian army in 1924. In 1941, he rose to the rank of general and was appointed head of the Inspectorate of Mountain Troops in Buenos Aires. He supported the 1943 military coup d'état that toppled President **Ramón Antonio Castillo**. During the government of General **Pedro Pablo Ramírez**, Farrell served as minister of war and then as vice president. Following Ramírez's overthrow, Farrell became president of Argentina on 24 February 1944. Under pressure from the United States, Farrell declared war on Germany and Japan in 1945. He remained in power until 4 June 1946, the day Perón was sworn into office. *See also* GRUPO DE OFICIALES UNIDOS (GOU)/UNITED OFFICERS GROUP; REVOLUTION OF 1943.

FASCISM. *See* GRUPO DE OFICIALES UNIDOS (GOU)/UNITED OFFICERS GROUP.

FEMALE SUFFRAGE. As secretary of labor and social welfare, **Juan Domingo Perón** decided to develop a policy to address the importance of the role of women in society. To that end, the Directorate General for Labor and Women's Assistance was created on 3 October 1944. In 1945, a commission pro women's suffrage, supported by Perón, raised a petition to the government requesting compliance with the Act of Chapultepec, by which signatory countries were committed to granting the vote to women. However, this petition failed to garner enough support. It was not until 23 September 1947—once Perón had become president of Argentina—that women in that country were granted suffrage rights. Evita was instrumental in the success of the campaign for voting rights to female citizens. Whereas female suffrage had been pursued from a socialist and pacifist political point of view during the 1920s and 1930s, Evita began to advocate it from a nationalist Catholic angle, which was consistent with the ideology of the **Partido Peronista (PP)**. At the beginning of 1947, Evita began an active campaign advocating women's political rights. She delivered dramatic speeches in support of the women suffrage bill, which was being discussed in Congress, and held rallies for women's rights. Evita's campaign for female suffrage was the way she found of improving women's social conditions and of increasing the Peronist electoral body. On the day the law was passed, Evita gave a speech from the balcony of the **Pink House** stating that she welcomed the passing of the legislation but, at the same time, encouraged women to belong to a party that would fight for peace under the leadership of Perón and with faith in God. Her active involvement in women's rights resulted in the unprecedented participation of women in politics, both as voters and as candidates at elections. Success in obtaining female suffrage led to the foundation of the **Partido Peronista Femenino** on 29 July 1949. This party was set up as a branch of the PP. Its leader was Evita, and its motto was unconditional loyalty to Perón. *See also* PERONISM; SECRETARIAT OF LABOR AND SOCIAL WELFARE.

FERNÁNDEZ, ALBERTO ÁNGEL (1959–). This Argentine lawyer, professor, and politician became president of Argentina on 10 December 2019. Fernández studied law at the University of Buenos Aires, graduating in 1983. Although he became affiliated with the **Unión Cívica Radical** during his student days, he later switched to the **Partido Justicialista**. He was appointed chief of staff by President **Néstor Kirchner** in 2003 and retained the same post during the administration of **Cristina Fernández de Kirchner**. A conflict between the agricultural sector and the government ensued in 2008. Fernández was the chief negotiator, but the negotiations failed and he resigned. As a private citizen, he became a severe critic of President Fernández de Kirchner. In 2017, there were signs of rapprochement between the two, and she became his running mate for the 2019 presidential election. He managed to integrate different factions of **Peronism** into a coalition dubbed **Frente de Todos**.

FERNÁNDEZ, MARÍA ASUNCIÓN "ASUNTA."

She was one of Evita's fashion assistants between 1946 and 1952. National fashion houses assigned an employee to accompany the first lady all day long as fashion assistants. Asunta, as she was known, worked for the fashion house Henriette and oversaw the wardrobe for Evita's **Rainbow Tour**. Upon Evita's return from Europe, Asunta used to go to the presidential residence daily. Her task was to select the most appropriate outfits according to Evita's activities for the day. In addition, Asunta traveled twice a year to **Paris** to buy gowns and *tailleurs* for Evita. The garments came back by plane or ship, where they hung to avoid wrinkling. Asunta was by Evita's side until her death. She transformed an unworn white dress into Evita's shroud. *See also* JAMANDREU, FRANCISCO "PACO" VICENTE; PALMOU, JUANA.

FERNÁNDEZ DE KIRCHNER, CRISTINA (1953–).

Born in the suburb of Tolosa, **La Plata**, Buenos Aires Province, this politician is the incumbent vice president of Argentina. She studied law at the National University of La Plata, where she met her soon-to-be husband, **Néstor Kirchner**, who introduced her to **Peronism**. After she married Kirchner in 1975, the couple moved to his hometown of Río Gallegos, Santa Cruz Province. There she became active in local politics and was elected deputy to the provincial legislature of Santa Cruz in 1989. During the 1990s and 2000s, she was involved in national politics. She represented Santa Cruz in the Senate and also served in the Chamber of Deputies. During her time in Congress, she was among President **Carlos Saúl Menem**'s most fervent critics, voting against his legislative policies. By the time her husband was elected president of Argentina in 2003, Fernández de Kirchner had already cemented her political influence to such an extent that she succeeded him in 2007, thus becoming the first female elected president in Argentina.

During her mandates—she was reelected in 2011—she deliberately appeared in front of images of Evita, whom she called her spiritual mentor. In fact, the evocation of Evita's political actions and ideals by Fernández de Kirchner has been one of the strongest factors in keeping the fascination with Evita alive in Argentina. Férnandez de Kirchner, who ruled the country until 2015, grabbed every opportunity to eulogize Evita as the paradigm of the ideal **Peronist**. Her two terms coincided with the 60th anniversary of Evita's death and Argentina's celebrations of the bicentennial of the 1810 May Revolution. In relation to the former, Fernández de Kirchner organized a week of celebrations that included several events and concerts. One of the highlights of the week was the lighting of the two **murals of Evita** hanging from the Ministry of Social Development Building on 9 de Julio Avenue in Buenos Aires. The creation of the murals had been commissioned to celebrate the 59th anniversary of Evita's death in 2011. Regarding the commemorations of the 1810 May Revolution, Fernández de Kirchner named Evita the Woman of the Bicentennial, highlighting that "all Argentine women identify with her. No one can deny the historical role she has fulfilled in this country and in the world."

FERRARIO, FLORINDO (1897–1960).

This Argentine theater, radio, and film actor began his acting career in the early 1920s. He worked for **Camila Quiroga**'s and José Podestá's theater companies, among others. His radio career started in 1938 in the *Noticioso Mobiloil* at **Radio El Mundo**. Ferrario and Evita starred in the radio series *Heroínas de la historia* (Heroines in History) at **Radio Belgrano** in 1943. At that time, Ferrario was in the prime of his career after the success of the film *Stella*, in which he had a starring role. Ferrario had a prolific film career, taking part in approximately 30 films between 1930 and the late 1950s.

FINOCHIETTO, RICARDO (1888–1962).

Dr. Ricardo Finochietto was a distinguished Argentine surgeon who founded the surgical school for postgraduates at the Rawson Hospital of Buenos Aires in 1938. Among his students was Dr. **Oscar Ivanissevich**, who would later become Evita's personal physician. Dr. Finochietto was also one of the **Fundación Eva Perón**'s medical advisers and the director of one of the foundation's hospitals, the **Policlínico Presidente Perón** in Avellaneda County, Buenos Aires Province. Following the skirmishes between Dr. Ivanissevich and Evita, Dr. Finochietto reportedly became Evita's personal physician. However, a gynecologist was needed to treat Evita's cervical cancer. Given that gynecology was not Finochietto's specialty, Dr. **Humberto Dionisi** and later Dr. **Jorge Albertelli** were summoned to treat the patient. After Dr. Dionisi and Dr. Albertelli examined Evita, she was informed that a surgical procedure was necessary and that Dr. Finochietto would oversee it. Although he officially appeared as the person who performed the surgery, it was a trick to mislead Evita and hide from her the fact that the operation would be carried out by an American, Dr. **George Pack**.

FIORA, TERESA ADELINA. Teresa Adelina Fiora was an Argentine nurse who became Evita's right hand at the **Fundación Eva Perón**. Up to 1946, she had been the secretary of the Nursing School at the Peralta Ramos Hospital of Buenos Aires. In 1946, Dr. **Armando Méndez de San Martín**—head of the Directorate General for Social Assistance—entrusted her with the task of reorganizing the nursing program of the school. In collaboration with a group of physicians led by Dr. **Jorge Albertelli**, Fiora updated the curricula. The nursing school was eventually named **Escuela de Enfermeras Eva Perón**, and Fiora was appointed director of the school. In 1949, she became actively engaged with the **Partido Peronista Femenino (PPF)**. Given that she was a dynamic, lively, and efficient woman, Evita named her delegate of the PPF to the city of Buenos Aires. Fiora opened a local branch of the PPF in the working-class neighborhood of Presidente Perón on 27 January 1950. The opening speech she delivered on that occasion praised Evita's work and leadership to the skies. *See also* UNIDADES BÁSICAS.

FLORES, MARÍA. *See* MAIN, MARY.

FORMAL EDUCATION OF EVITA. In 1927, when Evita was eight years old, she started her elementary education at School Number 1 in **Los Toldos**, Buenos Aires Province. She was enrolled as Eva María Duarte and not Eva María Ibarguren, which was her birth name. According to her school records, her attendance was poor, and this may have been the reason she repeated second grade. In 1930, when she was in third grade, she moved with her family to **Junín**, Buenos Aires Province, continuing her elementary education there. *See also* BIRTH CERTIFICATE OF EVITA; CATALINA LARRALT DE ESTRUGAMOU SCHOOL; REPETTI, PALMIRA.

FOXÁ Y TORROBA, AGUSTÍN DE (1906–1959). Born Count of Foxá III and Marquess of Armendáriz IV, this nobleman was a renowned Spanish diplomat, journalist, writer, and poet. He earned a degree in law and began his diplomatic career in 1930. De Foxá y Torroba became friends with the Spanish politician José Antonio Primo de Rivera, and they both were regulars at the Lion café in **Madrid**, where the fascist political organization Falange Española used to get together. On behalf of the Spanish government, de Foxá y Torroba joined Evita on her journey from Argentina to Spain in June 1947. *See also* RAINBOW TOUR.

FRANCO, EVA (1906–1999). The first of three children of Ernesta Morandi and the actor **José Franco**, Eva Petrona Talía Franco—better known as Eva Franco—was an Argentine theater and film actress. Coming from a family of actors, Franco made her stage debut at the age of five. She gained popularity in her teenage years when she worked in her father's theater company. During her lifetime, Franco performed in approximately 14 films and 200 plays under the direction of renowned film directors, writers, and playwrights such as Federico García Lorca. In 1935, Evita secured her first theater role with the **Compañía Argentina de Comedias**, in which Franco was the leading actress. In an interview with *Radiolandia 2000* on 4 April 1980, Franco described Evita as a girl with beautiful skin and, like most novice actors, full of hope and enthusiasm. Franco was one of the most celebrated artists of her generation. Due to a long, thriving career, she was the recipient of several awards and was declared Honorary Citizen of Mar del Plata, Buenos Aires Province, where she passed away at the age of 92.

FRANCO, JOSÉ (1886–1966). Argentine theater and film actor, husband of Ernesta Morandi and father of Herminia, Nélida, and **Eva Franco**. He was also one of the founders of the **Asociación Argentina de Actores**. During his lifetime, he managed several theater companies and employed Evita on two occasions. She was hired by the **Compañía Argentina de Comedias** in 1935 and, the following year, by the **Compañía de Comedias Muñoz-Franco-Álvarez**. While touring Argentina with the latter, Evita reportedly had an affair with him. After hearing the rumors, José Franco's wife paid a visit to the company and asked her husband to dismiss Evita.

FRANCO BAHAMONDE, FRANCISCO (1892–1975). This Spanish general, who ruled Spain from 1939 to 1975, was a fascist dictator who came to power after overthrowing the leftist Republican government in the Spanish Civil War (1936–1939). With the fall of fascism in Europe in 1945, Spain was ostracized by the United Nations and excluded from the U.S. financial support to reconstruct Europe. As Argentina was the only country that still had excellent diplomatic relations with Spain, Franco invited President **Juan Domingo Perón** to visit Spain in 1947. Perón turned down the invitation due to political reasons, but Evita traveled to Spain instead of him. Franco, who was accompanied by his wife and daughter, welcomed Evita in **Madrid** on 7 June 1947. The next day, Franco bestowed upon her the Grand Cross of Isabella the Catholic, Spain's highest honor. On that occasion, Franco delivered a speech praising the ideals of **Peronism** and gave schoolchildren and workers in Madrid the day off to celebrate Evita's visit. He and Evita addressed the crowds from the balcony of the **Royal Palace of Madrid**. After Perón was toppled in 1955, Franco invited him to settle in Spain. *See also* LIBERATING REVOLUTION; RAINBOW TOUR.

FRANCO SALGADO-ARAUJO, FRANCISCO (1890–1975). This Spanish military officer was a cousin and close collaborator of **Francisco Franco Bahamonde**. Franco Salgado-Araujo started his military career in **Toledo**, Spain, in 1908. He took part in several battles and received decorations for meritorious service. In 1928, he became Franco's aide-de-camp, a position he held until 1975. Franco Salgado-Araujo was among those who welcomed Evita in **Dakhla** on 7 June 1947 while she was touring Spain. *See also* MARTÍN-ARTAJO ÁLVAREZ, ALBERTO; RAINBOW TOUR.

FRANCO Y POLO, MARÍA DEL CARMEN "NENUCA" (1926–2017). Spanish aristocrat and only daughter of **Francisco Franco Bahamonde** and **María del Carmen Polo y Martínez-Valdés**. She married Cristóbal Martínez-Bordiú y Ortega. The couple had seven children, all born at the **Royal Palace of El Pardo**. Nenuca—also known as Carmelilla, Carmencita, Cotota, and Morita—was among those who welcomed and bid farewell to Evita during her visit to Spain in June 1947. *See also* RAINBOW TOUR.

FREIRE, JOSÉ MARÍA (1901–1962). This Argentine politician served as minister of labor and social welfare between 1949 and 1953. Freire came from a disadvantaged family from the Barracas neighborhood in Buenos Aires. He started working in the glass industry at an early age and continued to do so for 40 years. Eventually, he became the secretary of press and propaganda of the glass industry labor union, which had traditionally been disorganized and fragmented. Secretary of Labor and Social Welfare **Juan Domingo Perón** unified and organized this labor union in 1944, and Freire became one of the union's front men. After being named secretary of labor and social welfare in 1946, Freire worked closely with Evita. They both had their offices at the

Secretariat of Labor and Social Welfare. Initially, Evita dealt with labor unions' issues herself and Freire assisted the first lady. She gradually detached herself from that role to focus more on the activities of the **Fundación Eva Perón**. It was then that Freire could fulfil his role as secretary and, following the amendment of the **Argentine Constitution in 1949**, as a cabinet minister.

FRENTE DE TODOS/FRONT FOR ALL. This electoral alliance led by **Alberto Ángel Fernández** and **Cristina Fernández de Kirchner** was created on 12 June 2019. Encompassing different movements and ideologies, such as **Peronism**, **Kirchnerism**, feminism, socialism, and communism, Frente de Todos is a center-left coalition supported by the **Confederación General del Trabajo**. In 2019, Fernández and his running mate Fernández de Kirchner were elected president and vice president of Argentina, respectively, on the Frente de Todos ticket.

FRENTE JUSTICIALISTA DE LIBERACIÓN (FREJULI)/JUSTICIALIST LIBERATION FRONT. Created on 6 December 1972, this electoral alliance was formed by the **Partido Justicialista**, the Movimiento de Integración y Desarrollo (Integration and Development Movement) led by former president **Arturo Frondizi**, and other minor parties. The FREJULI won control of Argentina's legislature on 25 May 1973 with the victory of the Peronist **Héctor José Cámpora**, who resigned shortly thereafter to make way for the reelection of **Juan Domingo Perón**. The alliance was dissolved on 24 March 1976, when the military junta led by **Jorge Rafael Videla** outlawed all political parties in Argentina.

FRENTE JUSTICIALISTA DE UNIDAD POPULAR (FREJUPO)/JUSTICIALIST FRONT OF POPULAR UNITY. This electoral coalition integrated by the **Partido Justicialista** and other smaller political parties was created in 1989 to back the presidential candidacy of **Carlos Saúl Menem**. It was dissolved in 1995.

FRENTE PARA LA VICTORIA (FPV)/FRONT FOR VICTORY. This center-left Peronist electoral alliance was integrated by a faction of the **Partido Justicialista** and other political parties. It was founded on 1 March 2003 by the then presidential candidate **Néstor Kirchner**, who led it until his death in 2010. Ideologically, it identified with **Kirchnerism**. It was dissolved on 12 June 2019.

FREUDE, LUDWIG (1890–1956). A very influential businessman and the director of the Transatlantic German Bank in Buenos Aires, Ludwig Freude was a German citizen and a Nazi sympathizer who settled in Argentina in the 1930s. He met **Juan Domingo Perón** in **Mendoza**, where Perón was the commanding officer of a detachment of mountain troops and Freude's construction company was building the road between the cities of San Juan and Mendoza. The two men became lifelong friends. Freude owned a cabin called Ostende, which was located on Tres Bocas Island in the Tigre Delta—30 kilometers (18 miles) from Buenos Aires. When Perón was forced to resign as a cabinet member in October 1945, Freude offered him and Evita his cabin to reflect on their future. Freude became a supporter of Perón and donated a significant amount of money to Perón's political campaign. To celebrate Evita's birthday in May 1946, Freude threw a magnificent party in Ostende and presented her with an apartment in the Buenos Aires neighborhood of Belgrano. When Germany launched a bid to have him extradited, Perón speeded Freude's naturalization process to become an Argentine citizen and thereby avert extradition.

FREUDE, RODOLFO "RUDI" LUDOVICO (1922–2003). A member of **Juan Domingo Perón**'s private secretariat and, for a period of time, a close friend to Evita, Rudi Freude was the son of **Ludwig Freude**. When Perón was forced to resign as a cabinet member in October 1945, Rudi suggested that Perón and Evita should leave their apartment on Posadas Street and spend some time on the island of Tres Bocas in the Tigre Delta—30 kilometers (18 miles) from Buenos Aires—where Rudi's father owned a cabin. The couple accepted his offer. Years later Perón would remember the two days he spent with Evita on Tres Bocas as the best days of his life. Once Perón became president of Argentina in 1946, he named Rudi his chief of intelligence. His agents apparently discovered that Evita was an illegitimate child born in 1919 and not in 1922, as attested on the birth certificate she produced at her wedding. This probably happened just before Evita's **Rainbow Tour** because on the plane to **Dakhla** she wrote a farewell letter to Perón advising him against putting his trust in Rudi. In the letter, she wrote: "Beware of Rudi, he likes money. . . . I left **Junín** when I was thirteen years old. . . . I didn't tell you when I left because I was sad enough as it was and didn't want to add to all of that." Rudi reportedly used his position as chief of intelligence to organize a covert network that facilitated the entry of suspected Croatian, Belgian, French, and German war criminals into Argentina. See also BIRTH CERTIFICATE OF EVITA; PERONIST LOYALTY DAY; WEDDING OF EVITA.

FRONDIZI, ARTURO (1908–1995). This Argentine lawyer, who became president of Argentina in 1958, showed his interest in politics when he was a law student at the University of Buenos Aires. He joined the **Unión Cívica Radical** in 1930 and was their vice presidential candidate in the 1951 presidential election, which was overwhelmingly won by **Juan Domingo Perón**. Although Frondizi was a member of the opposition during Perón's first two mandates, he supported Perón's social and economic program. Frondizi won the 1958 presidential election with the support of proscribed **Peronists**. During his presidency, Frondizi put a series of austerity measures in place that burdened the poor and middle classes, resulting in strikes, demonstrations, and confrontations with the police. Although his economic policies were harsh, they would eventually lead to rapid industrialization and economic resurgence. However, lifting the ban on the **Partido Peronista** in the midterm elections of 1962 resulted in a military coup d'état that removed Frondizi from government in March of that year. Like Perón, Frondizi, was sent to **Martín García Island**, where he remained for a year and a half. Frondizi supported the Peronist candidate **Héctor José Cámpora** in the 1973 presidential election.

FUNDACIÓN EVA PERÓN. This foundation emerged as a result of Evita's involvement in social assistance and the need to centralize that assistance. In her role as the first lady of Argentina, Evita showed, from the beginning, that she was different from her predecessors: she would attend every official event with President **Juan Domingo Perón**, speak on his behalf, and visit factories, workshops, and hospitals on her own. By July 1946—a few months into Perón's first term—she was working three days a week in an office located at the Central Post Office, where she received workers and labor union leaders who wanted a meeting with Perón as well as ordinary citizens who needed a favor or financial assistance. Evita listened to all of them and acted promptly. On 23 September 1946, she moved her office to the **Secretariat of Labor and Social Welfare**, and in doing so, her role as Perón's representative was made official, but her activities went beyond her office work.

In December 1946 and with Christmas fast approaching, Evita, aided by the steward of the presidential residence, **Atilio Renzi**, distributed cider and panettone bread (two iconic items that Argentines enjoy at Christmas) to the less privileged. News about Evita's social assistance and promptness spread like wildfire. By 1948, she was receiving 12,000 letters daily requesting help. She had the means to help people, but her work was disorganized and needed a solid structure. As a result, the Fundación de Ayuda Social María Eva Duarte de Perón (María Eva Duarte de Perón Social Aid Foundation) was created on 8 July 1948. Its objectives were to provide monetary assistance or in-kind relief to the disadvantaged; to build houses for families in need; to build, among others, educational establishments, hospitals, and homes; and to contribute to the creation of jobs for the less privileged. At its height, the foundation employed 14,000 workers on a permanent basis, including 6,000 construction workers, and 26 priests. It awarded scholarships, organized youth soccer **tournaments**, and built homes, hospitals, other welfare establishments, and modern schools in the poorest areas of Argentina. The organization changed its name to the Fundación Eva Perón on 25 September 1950. The foundation was funded through a percentage of workers' salaries as well as private funds. It also accepted in-kind donations, which were mostly given with political motives. Compared with other state agencies, the foundation received more funds despite dealing in the same area. *See also* CIUDAD ESTUDIANTIL PRESIDENTE JUAN PERÓN; CIUDAD INFANTIL AMANDA ALLEN; CIUDAD UNIVERSITARIA ESTUDIANTIL PRESIDENTE PERÓN; ESCUELA DE ENFERMERAS EVA PERÓN; HOGAR DE LA EMPLEADA GENERAL SAN MARTÍN; HOME-SCHOOLS; LAS DELICIAS; *PROVEEDURÍAS*; SENIOR RESIDENCES; TEMPORARY HOMES; THOUSAND SCHOOLS SCHEME; *TURISMO SOCIAL*.

GANDO AIRPORT. This airport is located 19 kilometers (12 miles) to the south of **Las Palmas de Gran Canaria**, on eastern Gran Canaria. Evita arrived at Gando Airport on 8 June 1947. She was greeted by the captain-general of the Canary Islands, **Francisco García-Escámez Iniesta**, and other authorities. Upon her arrival, **Radio Nacional de España** broadcast a brief message by Evita addressed to Spanish women. *See also* RAINBOW TOUR.

GARCÍA-ESCÁMEZ INIESTA, FRANCISCO (1893–1951). This Spanish military officer started his military career at the age of 16 in **Toledo**, Spain. Thereafter, he developed a successful career. He took part in two armed conflicts, the Rif War (1920–1927) and the Spanish Civil War (1936–1939), fighting on the Nationalist side. Upon the Nationalists' victory, he served as military governor of **Barcelona**. In 1942, he became the military governor of **Seville**, and the following year, he was named captain-general of the Canary Islands. García-Escámez Iniesta was among those who welcomed Evita at **Gando Airport** on 8 June 1947 while she was touring Spain. *See also* RAINBOW TOUR.

GAY, LUIS (1903–1988). This telephone workers' union leader participated in the massive labor demonstration in support of **Juan Domingo Perón**'s liberation on 17 October 1945. Following the release of Perón, Gay together with other union leaders founded the **Partido Laborista**, one of the political parties that supported Perón's presidential candidacy. Gay had joined the **Confederación General del Trabajo (CGT)** in 1944 and was made head of this labor organization in late 1946 against Perón's candidate, **Ángel Gabriel Borlenghi**. His victory over Borlenghi did not suit Perón, whose aim was to consolidate his power by wielding influence in the Argentine labor movement. Perón tried to influence Gay but was not successful. Consequently, he had him expelled from the CGT three months after his appointment on false grounds of treason. A delegation of American labor organizers and members of the International Labor Organization had arrived in Buenos Aires in January 1947 at the invitation of the CGT. Perón seized this opportunity to accuse Gay of selling the CGT to the United States. As a result, Gay was forced to leave Buenos Aires after a series of threats against his life. He was succeeded by Aurelio Hernández, who led the CGT for a few months, until **José Espejo**—Evita's handpicked candidate—was appointed leader of the Argentine labor organization. *See also* PERONIST LOYALTY DAY; REYES, CIPRIANO.

GENERALIFE. Built in the 13th century in **Granada**, Spain, the Generalife was the summer palace of the Nasrid dynasty. The building was part of Evita's itinerary during her visit to Granada in 1947. She arrived at the ancient palace on 16 June shortly after 1:30 p.m. While appreciating a beautiful panoramic view of the city, Evita was given a detailed explanation of how historical buildings like the Generalife were preserved. *See also* RAINBOW TOUR.

GIL, ROBERTO "ERREGÉ" (1908–1981). This Argentine journalist, writer, songwriter, librettist, and radio host developed his career in the radio, film, and theater industries. Erregé, as he was known, wrote a myriad of *radioteatros* and worked for Radio del Pueblo, Radio Splendid, **Radio Argentina**, **Radio Prieto**, and **Radio El Mundo**. In 1936, he was named artistic director of Radio Prieto and Radio Argentina. Evita and Erregé worked together at Radio Argentina at the end of 1941, when Erregé paired Evita with **César Mariño** to lead the **Compañía Juvenil de Radioteatro**. In all probability, however, Evita might have met Erregé before 1941. *Sintonía* magazine published an article on 10 July 1940 describing a celebration in honor of Erregé in which Evita was a guest.

GRANADA. Granada is the capital city of the eponymous province in the autonomous community of Andalusia, southern Spain. The city, which is famous for its Moorish heritage dating back to the Moorish occupation of the Iberian Peninsula (711–1492), is home to one of the most visited monuments in Spain, the **Alhambra**—a fortified Moorish palace. As part of her official visit to Spain, Evita was in Granada on 15 and 16 June 1947. Accompanied by her entourage and the Argentine ambassador to Spain, **Pedro Radío**, among others, Evita arrived in the city to a grand welcome. Granada was decorated with Argentine and Spanish flags, and people lined the streets to catch a glimpse of her. She made her first stop at the **Basilica of Our Lady of Sorrows** to pray. Following a brief rest at the **Alhambra Palace Hotel**, she attended a gala function at the **Granada City Hall** and visited the Alhambra by night. The following day, she visited other attractions and delivered a speech to the workers of the National Factory of Gunpowder and Explosives in the neighborhood of El Fargue. *See also* RAINBOW TOUR.

GRANADA CITY HALL. Marked by Moorish architecture, this imposing building fronts the Plaza del Carmen in **Granada**, Spain. During her stay in this city, Evita attended a gala function in her honor at the Granada City Hall.

On 15 June 1947, the first lady of Argentina arrived at the city hall at approximately 11:45 p.m. While dinner was being served, the guests could enjoy a repertoire of songs played by a band. Following dinner, Evita was presented with a painting by the mayor of Granada. *See also* RAINBOW TOUR.

GRASA. The use of the expression *grasa* (grease) in Argentina denotes a certain attitude on the part of the speaker. A word utilized pejoratively by the Argentine upper class to refer to poor people, *grasa* means to be a person with vulgar habits and preferences. However, Evita used this term (and its diminutive *grasita*) affectionately to address her followers or ***descamisados***. By employing *grasa* or *grasita* lovingly, she contradicted the standard usage of the words, possibly to emphasize that being a *grasa* or *grasita* was not something of which to be ashamed. Furthermore, the affective use of this pejorative term reinforced Evita's image as a person who sympathized with the Argentine working class. In doing so, she shared their poverty as well as their rejection of the oligarchy. *See also* OLIGARQUÍA.

GREAT CROSS OF ISABELLA THE CATHOLIC. *See* AREILZA Y MARTÍNEZ DE RODAS, JOSÉ MARÍA DE; FRANCO BAHAMONDE, FRANCISCO; ROYAL PALACE OF MADRID.

GRUPO DE OFICIALES UNIDOS (GOU)/UNITED OFFICERS GROUP. This secret *loggia* was formed by a group of junior officers within the Argentine army in the early 1940s. Its initials in Spanish, GOU, stand for Grupo de Oficiales Unidos (United Officers Group), but other alleged names are ¡Gobierno! ¡Orden! ¡Unidad! (Government! Order! Unity!) or Grupo de Obra Unificación (Unification Work Group). Although information about this group is limited, it is known that its members shared nationalist and anticommunist ideologies. Historians have identified Colonel **Juan Domingo Perón** as one of its leading creators. In 1937, Perón traveled to Europe on a study tour. He learned about fascism in Italy and was deeply shocked by the aftermath of the Spanish Civil War (1936–1939). When he returned to Argentina in 1941, he saw the need to make a radical change in the Argentine government and society. His ideology was far from being a copy of fascism, except for the fascist principles in relation to labor legislation—to eliminate class struggle by organizing labor unions controlled by the state—which most certainly influenced his policy in later years. However, while fascism tried to crush the working class, Perón made labor legislation the basis for his success. His pro-labor policy managed not only to organize the workers' unions but also to keep them under control and to guarantee their support. Apart from this, Perón was interested in implementing a nationalist-industrial plan, unlike fascism and Nazism, which were mainly attracted by large (foreign) capital. Soon, Perón shared his views with other army officers and decided to take action. On 4 June 1943, the military overthrew President **Ramón Antonio Castillo**, putting an end to the **Infamous Decade**. The GOU supposedly orchestrated this coup d'état, which in fact had neither a leader nor a tangible plan. This event, which is also known as the **Revolution of 1943**, led to a series of military governments until 1946, the year Perón won the presidential election in Argentina.

GUARDO, RICARDO CÉSAR (1908–1984). Ricardo César Guardo was a successful dentist who had his own practice in the elegant neighborhood of Barrio Norte in Buenos Aires. He was married to **Lillian Lagomarsino**, with whom he had four children. He met **Juan Domingo Perón** before 1946 and was so moved by his ideas that he went into politics. Guardo would often meet Perón to discuss politics. During one of those meetings, Evita asked Guardo to accompany her to buy a gown for the pre-inaugural dinner to be held on 4 June 1946 at the **Pink House**. He managed to arrange a private fitting for Evita in the fashionable Buenos Aires store Bernarda and assisted her in purchasing a gown of her liking. Guardo also introduced his wife to the Peróns, and the two couples befriended each other for a while. He was president of the Chamber of Deputies from 1946 to 1948, but the relationship between him and Perón eventually deteriorated and he was replaced by another dentist, **Héctor José Cámpora**. Once Perón was ousted, Guardo and his family went into exile.

GUEREÑO RODRÍGUEZ, JUAN (1888–1961). Born in Crémenes, Spain, Juan Guereño Rodríguez arrived in Argentina in 1907. Once he settled in Buenos Aires, he started working in the soap industry. His great initiative and hard work made him a very successful businessman. By 1961, his company, Establecimientos Fabriles Guereño S.A., had more than 1,000 employees in Argentina. Over the years, Guereño Rodríguez's soap company became a regular sponsor of *radioteatros*. In the late 1930s, Evita's brother **Juan Ramón Duarte**, who worked for Guereño Rodríguez, reportedly got Evita a two-month contract to star in the commercials for Radical soap, one of Guereño Rodríguez's brands. This was a career breakthrough for her. Due to this contract, she succeeded in finding work at different radio stations. During 1941, she secured a five-year contract with Guereño. Allegedly, Evita's first sponsored radio program by Radical soap was *La hora de las sorpresas* (The Hour of Surprises) at **Radio Argentina**.

GUEVARA, NACHA (1940–). Born Clotilde Acosta, Nacha Guevara is a prolific Argentine singer-songwriter, dancer, and actress. She rose to fame in the late 1960s owing to her one-woman shows in which she criticized the status quo severely. By the mid-1970s, she had become an artist of great renown but nonetheless controversial. After receiving death threats from the far-right secret organization **Triple A**, Guevara fled Argentina with her family. She attempted to return to the Argentine stage in 1975, but the theater in which she was set to perform was bombed and two people were killed. Following the attack, she went into exile first to Peru and then to Mexico, where she pursued a successful career. Between 1978 and 1982, she lived and worked in **Madrid**. With the advent of democracy in Argentina in 1983, Guevara returned to her country of birth. In 1986, she played Evita in the musical *Eva, el gran musical argentino*, which premiered at the Maipo Theater in Buenos Aires.

Being coauthored by Guevara and composed mostly abroad, *Eva, el gran musical argentino* was the Argentine counterpart of Tim Rice and Andrew Lloyd Webber's **Evita**. In 2008, Guevara revisited *Eva, el gran musical argentino*, and the musical was restaged at the Argentino Theater in **La Plata**, Buenos Aires Province. The premiere was attended by President **Cristina Fernández de Kirchner** and Daniel Scioli, the governor of the province of Buenos Aires. The revival of the musical and the presence of these high-ranking politicians on opening night marked Guevara's incursion into politics. Her political career, however, was short-lived. After securing a seat in the Argentine Chamber of Deputies, she resigned.

GUIBOURG, EDMUNDO "PUCHO" (1893–1986). Husband of Anita Levín, this writer, dramatist, librettist, film director, translator, journalist, and theater critic was known by his artistic name Pucho. In the early stages of his career, he worked as a cartoonist for the daily *Última Hora*. His first theater review was published in *Tribuna* magazine in 1912. He started working for the daily **La Vanguardia** In 1913 and was eventually named editorial secretary. Between 1927 and 1932, he was *Crítica*'s news correspondent in **Paris**. Upon his return to Buenos Aires, Pucho started writing theater reviews for the same newspaper. He also collaborated with other important newspapers, such as **La Prensa** and **La Nación**. It was Pucho who gave Evita her first mention in a Buenos Aires paper. While reviewing *La señora de los Pérez* (Mrs. Pérez) for *Crítica* on 29 March 1935, Pucho stated that Evita was very correct in her brief performance. Indeed, Pucho supported Evita's career by mentioning her in his reviews despite her minor roles. In 1939, Evita was cast in a supporting role in *Mercado de amor en Argelia* (Market of Love in Algeria), and the director of the play was Pucho. In his memoirs, Pucho narrates how Evita befriended his wife, Anita. At a point, Evita used to visit them almost every afternoon and was very close to the couple. As their protégé, Evita was reportedly helped by Pucho in getting a speaking role in *Mercado de amor en Argelia*. *See also* COMPAÑÍA DE CAMILA QUIROGA.

GUIÓN. Evita graced the cover of this weekly film magazine on 24 January 1940. Perhaps one of the most daring of the young actress's photographs, the cover of *Guión* features a smiling Evita wearing a polka dot swimsuit. The photograph had been taken by **Annemarie Heinrich** in 1939.

H

HACIA UN FUTURO MEJOR. *Hacia un futuro mejor* (Toward a Better Future) was a propaganda radio series that commemorated the **Revolution of 1943** and promoted **Juan Domingo Orlando Perón**'s political ideology. Evita performed the role of an ordinary woman who urged the Argentine people to support the revolution. To that end, she used simple, straightforward, and passionate language, and her speech was interspersed with fragments from Perón's speeches. Audiences could listen to the program twice a week for more than a year. The first episode was broadcast on **Radio Belgrano** on 17 June 1944, and the librettists were **Francisco Muñoz Azpiri** and later Antonio Giménez. From August, it was broadcast on **Radio del Estado**. This program represented a landmark in Evita's career because she was able to develop not only her acting but also her political skill set and knowledge. Her participation in this program marked the beginning of her political career.

HAYNES PUBLISHING. This media company was founded in 1904 by the Englishman Albert Haynes, who had arrived in Argentina in 1887 to work for the Buenos Aires Western Railway. Following his decision to settle in Argentina, he entered the publishing industry and launched his first magazine, *El Hogar*, which became a great success. Other publications would follow, including *Mundo Infantil*, *Mundo Atómico*, *Mundo Argentino*, *Mundo Deportivo*, *Mundo Agrario*, *Mundo Radial*, *Caras y Caretas*, *PBT*, *Selecta*, **Sintonía**, and **El Mundo**. Haynes's widely read publications included magazines that were targeted at specific social groups. In addition, Haynes also owned the **Red Azul y Blanca de Emisoras Argentinas**. In its heyday, Haynes employed nearly 3,000 people. When **Juan Domingo Perón** took office, Haynes was one of the major publishing companies in the country. In November 1948, the former president of the Central Bank of Argentina **Domingo Maroglio** acquired 51 percent of the company's shares, but the Haynes family continued to be financially connected to their business. Nonetheless, the new leaders of the company were Peronists **Miguel Miranda** and Carlos Vicente Aloé, who were named director and deputy director, respectively. Following Miranda's death in 1954, Aloé became the director. Under the control of the Peronist government, Haynes Publishing took a different direction and focused on promoting **Peronism** and its leaders. A new addition to the existing publications was *Mundo Peronista*. The government of the **Liberating Revolution** oversaw the company for a couple of years until it was bought by a group of businessmen who also owned Radio Rivadavia, the Bank of Buenos Aires, and the mining company Aluminé. Haynes Publishing went into bankruptcy in 1967. *See also* ALEA S.A.; ANTI-ARGENTINE ACTIVITIES CONGRESSIONAL COMMITTEE; SECRETARIAT OF INFORMATION AND PRESS.

HEINRICH, ANNEMARIE (1912–2005). This German-born, naturalized Argentine photographer arrived in Argentina in 1926. Her father decided to migrate to Argentina after having been injured during World War I. The family first settled in Larroque, Entre Ríos Province, where Heinrich's uncle Karel introduced Heinrich to photography. Once settled in Villa Ballester, Buenos Aires Province, Heinrich improved her photography skills with the Austrian photographer Melita Lang and at **Sivul Wilenski**'s studio, where she worked as his assistant. In addition, Heinrich had a photo studio at her home where she could further develop her skills and interest in photography. She opened her own professional studio and officially became a photographer in 1930. Specializing in portraits and nudity, she photographed the biggest stars of Argentine theater, cinema, and radio, aside from collaborating with numerous magazines such as **Antena**, **Radiolandia**, and **Guión**. Furthermore, she was an expert in the use of lightning and the retouching of prints. In 1939, she took photographs of Evita, who was at the time a 20-year-old actress. Recalling that session in an interview, Heinrich said that the first time she portrayed Evita was for **Sintonía** magazine. Heinrich was asked to take good and sexy photographs if possible, but she could not do so because Evita, according to the photographer, was not sexy but only a very modest and simple girl.

HEROÍNAS DE LA HISTORIA. In September 1943, **Antena** announced that Evita and **Florindo Ferrario** would star in a radio series entitled *Heroínas de la historia* (Heroines in History) at **Radio Belgrano**. This was a life-changing event for Evita as the job was well paid, she gained national recognition, and she was able to move to an affluent neighborhood in Buenos Aires. Sponsored by Radical soap, each program of the series was broadcast daily and lasted approximately a month. The librettists **Francisco Muñoz Azpiri** and Alberto Insúa provided the scripts, biographies about significant women in world history. The first biography, *Madame Lynch, la amazona del destino* (Madame Lynch, Destiny's Warrior), described the tragic love story between Elisa Lynch and the Paraguayan president Francisco Solano López. The series continued with *La mujer que nos dieron* (The Woman We Were Given) and *Llora una emperatriz* (An Empress Cries), the story of Charlotte of Belgium and later Charlotte of Mexico. Other **radioteatros** in this series included *Mi reino por el amor* (My Kingdom for Love), the story of Queen Elizabeth I; *Un ángel pisa la escena* (An Angel Enters the Scene), the story of the French actress Sarah Bernhardt; *Nieva sobre mi ensueño* (Snow in My Reverie), the story of Russia's last empress, Alexandra Feodorovna; *¡Éxtasis!* (Ecstasy!), the story of Madame George Sand; *Sumisión* (Submission), the story of Margarita Weil de Paz; and *Alucinación* (Hallucination), the story of Rosario López Zelada. Evita also impersonated Lola Montes in *Reina de reyes* (Queen of Kings), Madame Chiang Kai Shek in *Una mujer en la barricada* (A Woman at the Barricade), Eleonora Duse in *Fuego en la ciudad muerta* (Fire in the Dead City), Lady Hamilton in *La paloma del águila* (The Dove of the Eagle), Empress Joséphine in *La doncella de Martinica* (The Maiden of Martinique), Eugénie de Montijo in *La sangre de la reina huele a claveles* (The Queen's Blood Smells of Carnations), Isadora Duncan in *La danzarina del paraíso* (Paradise's Dancer), Catherine the Great in *Una lágrima al viento* (A Tear in the Wind), and Anne of Austria in *El ajedrez de la gloria* (The Chess of Glory), among others. The series spanned two years, from October 1943 to October 1945, and was brought to a halt due to the events that led to 17 October 1945. *See also* GUEREÑO RODRÍGUEZ, JUAN; PERONIST LOYALTY DAY.

HISTORIA DEL PERONISMO. In 1951, Evita delivered nine lectures on Peronist history and its ideals at the newly founded **Escuela Superior Peronista**. These lectures were published in 1952 under the title *Historia del peronismo* (History of Peronism). The first lecture set the tone by eulogizing **Juan Domingo Perón**, calling him a genius and comparing him with Napoleon. The purpose of the lectures, as Evita admits in the book, was to learn to admire Perón and not to teach history. The hyperbolic language she used in her lectures transformed Perón into a quasi-deity and the Argentine people into a privileged group because they had a unique leader in Perón. Sprinkled with references to the Bible, classical antiquity, the French and the Russian Revolutions, and her **Rainbow Tour**, her lectures had a clear message. She claimed that Perón was greater than the greatest men in history because everything he did, he did it for his people. Moreover, according to Evita, Perón was not a politician but an artist—the creator of the **New Argentina**.

HISTORICAL MUSEUM 17 OCTOBER. This museum is located at **Juan Domingo Perón**'s **San Vicente country house** in the town of San Vicente, Buenos Aires Province. Perón and Evita used to spend their weekends at this house to escape the rigors of daily life. The museum's collection, offers a wide variety of objects and documents that belonged to Perón and Evita. The theme of the museum's collection is based on the three main pillars of **Peronism**: social justice, economic independence, and political sovereignty. One of the highlights of the museum is a car given to Perón as a present by the chairman of Fiat. Visitors also have access to Perón's mausoleum and to a replica of the train he used during his 1951 presidential campaign.

HISTORY OF PERONISM. See HISTORIA DEL PERONISMO.

HOGAR DE LA EMPLEADA GENERAL SAN MARTÍN. Inaugurated on 30 December 1949 by the **Fundación Eva Perón**, this residence for working women was located on the central Mayo Avenue in Buenos Aires. Its main purpose was to assist two different groups of women: those women who could not afford accommodation and those who needed a place where they could have a daily meal. Whereas the former group of women was provided a room at an affordable price, the latter group was granted access to this facility as long as they did not have relatives in Buenos Aires. Residents had to follow simple rules. They were asked to return to the premises before 10 p.m. and say goodbye to boyfriends at least 300 meters (330 yards) away from the residence. Visitors were not allowed. The building could accommodate 500 women. Apart from dormitories, it included two restaurants, one for the residence beneficiaries and the other for both the beneficiaries and the general public. The foundation spared no expense in the construction of this building. The home included such amenities as a small library, a sewing workshop, and a music room on each floor. The housekeeping was carried out by uniformed personnel. Regarding their health, women had access to a practitioner, a dentist, and a nutritionist. Moreover, residents who got sick were usually treated and cared for in-house. Like the rest of the institutions run by the foundation, the home was closed after the 1955 military coup d'état. *See also* LIBERATING REVOLUTION; TEMPORARY HOMES.

HOME FOR THE EMPLOYED WOMEN GENERAL SAN MARTÍN. *See* HOGAR DE LA EMPLEADA GENERAL SAN MARTÍN.

HOME-SCHOOLS. With the idea of creating a safe space for disadvantaged children, the **Fundación Eva Perón** opened 20 home-schools across Argentina between the late 1940s and early 1950s. In the past, the home-schools run by the **Society of Beneficence of Buenos Aires** required children to wear uniforms, be identified with a number, and work. Evita created home-schools that were quite the opposite. Children neither worked nor wore uniforms but chose their own clothing. Moreover, whenever possible, children spent weekends and public holidays with their families. If they could not visit their families, they were assigned a tutor. Parents who wanted to send their children to the home-schools had to write a letter to Evita explaining their social and personal situation. Then, the foundation's social workers visited each candidate's home to corroborate the information provided in the letters. Evita's home-schools accepted children between four and 10 years old. Some children were residents, whereas others just spent the day at the home-schools. All of these children attended public schools; received school supplies, clothes, and shoes; and had regular health screenings done. The home-schools were lively spaces—with flowers, books, and toys—where children could avail themselves of meals, extracurricular activities, and tutoring. Like the rest of the Peronist institutions, the home-schools ceased to function after the military coup d'état of 1955. *See also* CIUDAD INFANTIL AMANDA ALLEN; LIBERATING REVOLUTION.

HOSPITAL TRAIN. This train was part of the ambitious **public health care** program launched by the Ministry of Health in conjunction with the **Fundación Eva Perón**. It provided health care for people in remote areas of Argentina. It was equipped with laboratories, a generator, a pharmacy, X-ray rooms, a waiting room, an operating theater, and a delivery room. The train, which toured Argentina from 1 August to 14 November 1951, offered free medical and dental check-ups, X-rays, vaccinations, and medicine.

HUMAN RIGHTS IN ARGENTINA. A blend of popular support and authoritarian rule characterized **Juan Domingo Perón**'s first two mandates (1946–1955). While his government championed the rights of the destitute, the elderly, and the working class, it also engaged in a number of authoritarian practices. Perón's political opponents were arrested, the media was censored, and students' textbooks were rewritten. As the Argentine economy declined during his second mandate, Perón became increasingly authoritarian. The last straw was when he attempted to separate church and state. This enraged the leaders of the Catholic Church. After excommunicating Perón, the upper echelons of the church encouraged a clique of military officers to plot a coup d'état against the president. The period between Perón's overthrow in 1955 and **Héctor José Cámpora**'s presidency in 1973 saw restrictions of personal and political freedom, social unrest, terrorism, and a rise in violence. In an attempt to put an end to the chaotic situation, Perón returned to Argentina in 1973 to run for office for the third time. His return, however, was not auspicious as a violent confrontation between right-wing and left-wing **Peronists** ensued the day he landed. That event—known as the **Ezeiza massacre**—ignited an even more chaotic period during which killings and kidnappings became the order of the day. Upon Perón's death in 1974, his third wife, **Isabel Martínez de Perón**, took over the presidency but was unable to stop the wave of violence that raged across the country. As a result, she was deposed in 1976 by a military coup d'état. The new leaders of the nation ruled with an iron fist. Known as the **Dirty War**, the period between 1976 and 1983 was marked by the escalation of human right abuses. Thousands of people went missing and were never seen again. Political dissidents and anyone suspected of being aligned with leftist, socialist, or social justice causes were abducted, tortured, and murdered. The 1976–1983 military regime was the most violent and cruel in the history of Argentina. Human rights groups have estimated that more than 30,000 people were "disappeared" at the hands of the military dictatorship. In 1977, the mothers and grandmothers of the disappeared began gathering in the **Plaza de Mayo**, demanding the whereabouts of their children. The protests of this group, coupled with rampant unemployment, inflation, a debilitated economy, and a lost war against the United Kingdom, led to the fall of the military regime in 1983. Democratically elected, Raúl Alfonsín was inaugurated president of Argentina on 10 December 1983. The first item on his agenda was to create a truth commission that would investigate the fates of the disappeared. This led to the creation of the Comisión Nacional sobre la Desaparición de Personas (National Commission of the Disappearance of Persons) or CONADEP, which published *Nunca más* (Never Again), a report of the atrocities committed by the military juntas. During the Alfonsín administration, the perpetrators of human rights violations were prosecuted, but a faltering economy forced Alfonsín to resign. He was succeeded by **Carlos Saúl Menem**, who took office in 1989. As the Menem administration maintained that the support of the military forces would benefit the country, the president pardoned all members of the military regime either already convicted or still indicted. With the rise to power of the Peronist **Néstor Kirchner** in 2003, the pardons were revoked. The government of Kirchner garnered local and international support by revoking amnesty laws for the members of the last military regime. Former president **Cristina Fernández de Kirchner**, who succeeded Kirchner, continued her husband's human rights policies. In 2015, Argentine politics shifted to the right, and the center-right leader Mauricio Macri became president of Argentina. Human rights were not a priority for the government of Macri. During his mandate (2015–2019), perpetrators of crimes against humanity were granted shorter prison terms by double-counting days served in pretrial detention, a ruling that has of course perpetuated impunity in the country. *See also* ANTI-ARGENTINE ACTIVITIES CONGRESSIONAL COMMITTEE; LIBERATING REVOLUTION; LÓPEZ REGA, JOSÉ; MASSERA, EMILIO EDUARDO; MONTONEROS; TRIPLE A; VIDELA, JORGE RAFAEL.

I

IBÁÑEZ MENTA, NARCISO (1912–2004). This Spanish radio and television librettist, actor, and theater director came from a family of performers and musicians—his parents were lyrical singers. His first appearance on a stage was at a very early age. After touring Spain and South America, his parents decided to settle in Buenos Aires. Eventually, Ibáñez Menta married the Argentine actress Pepita Salvador. He reached the zenith of his career as a horror theater actor in the 1930s. Ibáñez Menta would become a legend in the horror genre, performing not only in theater but also in film and television. He collaborated several times with his son Narciso Ibáñez Salvador, who also developed a career as an actor, librettist, and film and television director. Evita and Ibáñez Menta worked together on a Christmas Eve special show at **Radio Belgrano** in 1944.

IBARGUREN, EVA MARÍA (1919–1952). Evita, as she is referred to throughout this book, was born out of wedlock in **Los Toldos**, Buenos Aires Province, Argentina. She was the fifth of five children of Judge of Peace **Juan Duarte** and his partner **Juana Ibarguren**. See other entries dealing with her family, her acting career, her relationship with **Juan Domingo Perón**, her European tour, her foundation, her political career, her political party, her illness, her funeral, and her corpse.

IBARGUREN, JUANA (1894–1971). Mother of Evita and daughter of Petronia Núñez and Joaquín Ibarguren, Juana Ibarguren, best known as Doña Juana, was a woman of humble origins. Apparently, Núñez had arrived in **Los Toldos**, Buenos Aires Province, along with the soldiers who were waging a military campaign against the indigenous populations in the area. She lived with Ibarguren, a Basque carter, for some time and had two daughters, Liberata and Juana. Doña Juana met **Juan Duarte** when she was 15 or 16 years old and became his mistress. They had five children, Blanca, Elisa, Juan, Erminda, and Evita. Although Doña Juana and Duarte were not married, the couple lived as a family, and she adopted the name Duarte and so did her children. She and her children lived in a house on the main street of Los Toldos for a brief period of time. In 1920, Duarte abandoned her and their children and returned to his family in Chivilcoy, Buenos Aires Province. Impoverished, Doña Juana and her children moved to a two-room house by the railroad. Although she worked as a seamstress to support her family, her reputation as a kept woman always preceded her. On 8 January 1926, she and her children traveled to Chivilcoy to attend Duarte's funeral, but Estela Grisolía, Duarte's wife, refused to let them in. Only after pleading to Grisolía's brother were they allowed to attend the funeral. This was probably the first time Evita witnessed injustice in her life. In 1930, Doña Juana and her children moved to the town of **Junín**, Buenos Aires Province. As the elder children started working, the family was better off than in Los Toldos, but Doña Juana continued sewing and offered meals to single gentlemen in her house. Some sources suggest that Doña Juana accompanied Evita to

Buenos Aires to take part in an audition for a small radio contract in 1935.

ICON. The etymological idea underlying the definition of the term *icon* is that of similarity. In the 19th century, icon denoted a representation of some sacred personage, in painting, bas-relief, or mosaic. This representation was regarded as sacred and honored with worship or adoration in the Eastern Orthodox Church. One of the main functions of religious icons was to set out roles for the population to adopt in order to conform to church- and state-sponsored norms of behavior. When applied to people, the term *icon* denotes a person worthy of veneration or someone regarded as a representative symbol. Although referring to nonreligious people, this definition of the term suggests a connection with the concept of religious icon. The scholar Sarah Misemer employs the concept of secular icon to identify icons that are neither purely religious nor completely disconnected from the sacred. She argues that in the process of becoming a public figure, there is a moment when people collectively agree to consider a person as an example of how to conduct oneself in society. That person becomes the carrier of a set of values in a particular society and in a particular context. Among the myriad of images that Evita acquired between the late 1940s and early 1950s, the image of the Peronist Evita gave her iconic status. The reason lies in that the majority of people in Argentina saw her as the keeper of the values and ideology that marked their society. *See also* TRANSNATIONAL ICONIC IMAGE OF EVITA.

ICONIC IMAGE OF EVITA. *See* ICON; TRANSNATIONAL ICONIC IMAGE OF EVITA.

IDEOLOGY OF PERONISM. *See* JUSTICIALISMO.

IMBERT, ANÍBAL FRANCISCO (1897–1954). This Argentine army officer and radio engineer was the head of the Secretariat of Communications during the military government of President **Pedro Pablo Ramírez**. Under his government, radio actors were required to obtain permits to be able to work, and Imbert was in charge of granting them. As Evita was among those who obtained the permits, rumor broke out that Imbert was Evita's lover, but this has never been confirmed. He did not belong to the **Grupo de Oficiales Unidos**, but he was close to **Juan Domingo Perón**.

IN MY OWN WORDS. See MI MENSAJE.

INFAMOUS DECADE. This term, coined by the Argentine journalist José Luis Torres, refers to the political period that began in 1930 with the ousting of President Hipólito Yrigoyen and ended with the 1943 military coup d'état that would eventually propel the election of **Juan Domingo Perón** as president of Argentina. The period owes its name to the fact that a conservative coalition of parties, known as the Concordancia, stayed in power by rigging elections and repressing political opposition. Yet the Infamous Decade saw the expansion of the industrial sector in Argentina through an economic policy that replaced foreign imports with domestic production. This import-substitution industrialization in tandem with the crisis affecting rural Argentina resulted in the migration of thousands of people to the city of Buenos Aires in search of work. Evita was among those who left their small communities in the **interior of Argentina** and moved to the capital. *See also* CASTILLO, RAMÓN ANTONIO; GRUPO DE OFICIALES UNIDOS (GOU)/UNITED OFFICERS GROUP; REVOLUTION OF 1943.

INSTITUTO NACIONAL DE INVESTIGACIONES HISTÓRICAS EVA PERÓN (INIHEP)/EVA PERÓN NATIONAL INSTITUTE OF HISTORICAL RESEARCH. Sponsored by the Argentine Ministry of Culture, the Instituto Nacional de Investigaciones Históricas Eva Perón (INIHEP) was created on 23 September 1998. In short, the INIHEP aims to promote Evita's life, work, and principles. Not only does it function as a research and publication center, it also houses a bibliographic and documentary archive. The INIHEP is located in the same building as the **Evita Museum** at 2988 Lafinur Street in Buenos Aires. This

Former temporary residence at 2988 Lafinur Street, Buenos Aires. This historical building currently houses the Instituto Nacional de Investigaciones Históricas Eva Perón and the Evita Museum.

museum was created in 2002 as part of the INIHEP, and it also operates under the auspices of the Ministry of Culture. *See also* TEMPORARY HOMES.

INTERIOR OF ARGENTINA. Argentina is divided into 23 provinces and one autonomous city, Buenos Aires. The city of Buenos Aires is surrounded by Greater Buenos Aires, which comprises 24 counties in Buenos Aires Province. The interior of Argentina is that part of the country that lies beyond Buenos Aires City and Greater Buenos Aires. Evita herself hailed from the interior of Argentina. She toured the interior first as an actress, then as the presidential candidate's wife, and finally as the first lady of Argentina.

IVANISSEVICH, OSCAR (1895–1976). This renowned Argentine surgeon worked very closely with **Juan Domingo Perón** very early on. When Perón took office in 1946, Dr. Ivanissevich was named administrator of the University of Buenos Aires. In the following year, he was appointed ambassador to the United States with the aim of learning from the American education system in order to use it as a possible model for a reform of the Argentine system. While abroad, Dr. Ivanissevich did not miss out on any opportunity to praise Perón. He would drop into classrooms and deliver speeches about the greatness of Perón to American pupils. From 1948 to 1950, he joined Perón's cabinet as secretary of education, but with the reform prompted by the **Argentine Constitution of 1949**, he became minister of education. His influence on **Peronism** was remarkable: he reportedly authored the lyrics of the "**Marcha peronista**"—the official song of the **Partido Peronista**; linked Peronism to nationalism and religion; and made discipline, piety, and nationalism the main values to be instilled in Argentine primary education. Aside from this, Dr. Ivanissevich was the surgeon who performed an appendectomy on Evita on 12 January 1950. At least two versions exist as to what happened when the surgery was carried out. One claims that Dr. Ivanissevich noted that there was an abnormality in Evita's uterus, yet he did not do a pelvic exam and only commented on it with his surgical team. The other states that he asked Evita to have a gynecological examination done, but she refused and was furious with him. This episode allegedly cost him his ministerial position. He was again appointed minister of education from 1974 to 1975 during the presidency of **Isabel Martínez de Perón**.

JAMANDREU, FRANCISCO "PACO" VICENTE (1925–1995). This Argentine actor, fashion designer, and costume designer, known as Paco Jamandreu, designed part of Evita's wardrobe and became one of her closest friends. Evita hired him to design her clothes after she moved in with **Juan Domingo Perón**. Jamandreu was gay, a homosexual, to use the terminology of the day, and as the Peronist regime considered homosexuals deviant, he ended up in prison several times. On those occasions, Evita interceded to get him out. When Evita was terminally ill and therefore bedridden, Perón contacted Jamandreu and asked him to design an entire new wardrobe to cheer her up, which he did. While he fell from grace after Perón was overthrown in 1955, he reemerged as one of Argentina's most celebrated fashion designers thanks to the costumes he created for the films of the Argentine director Armando Bó. In 1981, Jamandreu published his memoirs in *Evita fuera del balcón* (Evita Outside the Balcony), a book that describes his friendly relationship with Evita. He died of a heart attack while he was designing the costumes for a film.

JAURETCHE, ARTURO MARTÍN (1901–1974). This Argentine writer, revisionist, philosopher, and politician was initially a member of the **Unión Cívica Radical (UCR)**. Due to ideological differences, some members of the UCR began questioning the leadership of the party from 1935. It was then that Jauretche and others founded the Fuerza de Orientación Radical de la Joven Argentina (FORJA), a group of dissident members of the UCR. Toward 1943, Jauretche was FORJA's sole leader. With the advent of World War II, FORJA fully supported the idea of Argentina adopting a neutral position. Thus, after President **Pedro Pablo Ramírez** severed relations with the Axis powers, FORJA welcomed his ousting by the **Grupo de Oficiales Unidos**. Henceforth, FORJA allied with **Juan Domingo Perón** and Jauretche eventually became a Peronist supporter. Over the years, Perón and Evita would constantly employ terminology popularized by Jauretche in their discourse such as *pueblo*, *oligarquía*, *oligarca*, *vendepatria*, and *cipayo*.

JORDÁN, ANITA (1917–1946). This Argentine theater, radio, and film actress was one of Evita's close friends. In the early stages of her acting career, Evita found in Jordán the support she needed to face hardship in Buenos Aires. The two young aspiring actresses shared boarding house rooms, clothes, and dressing rooms. They also shared the stage in **Armando Discépolo**'s play *La nueva colonia* (The New Colony), which opened at the Politeama Theater in Buenos Aires on 5 March 1937. They worked together in *La carga de los valientes* (Only the Valiant) in 1940. Jordán became a relatively successful film actress. Between 1934 and 1944, she was cast in 10 films. However, her career was cut short when she was diagnosed with metastatic cervical cancer in the early 1940s. After a long, painful battle with the disease, she finally passed away at the Cancer Institute of Buenos Aires. Evita was among those who attended Jordán's funeral.

JUAN AND EVA. *See JUAN Y EVA.*

JUAN Y EVA. Directed by Paula de Luque and released in 2011, the movie *Juan y Eva* (Juan and Eva) is based on the eponymous novel by the Argentine writer Jorge Coscia. It tells the romantic story between **Juan Domingo Perón** and Evita from the moment they meet in 1944 until Perón's release from prison in 1945. Their romantic relationship is pitted against the political scenario of the time. As such, the film portrays not only their mutual attraction but also the different factions within the military, the imprisonment of Perón on **Martín García Island**, and the role of the labor unions in his liberation. Evita's character in the film underscores her strong personality and her unconditional support to Perón. The Argentine actress **Julieta Díaz** delivers a compelling performance in her role as Evita.

JUNÍN. Located 260 kilometers (161 miles) west of Buenos Aires, Junín is known as the hometown of Evita although she only lived there for five years. Junín was originally a fort that suffered frequent attacks by indigenous people. Despite this, its population continued to grow, owing to its strategic location in the Argentine Pampas as well as the arrival of the Central Argentine Railway in 1880 and the Buenos Aires and Pacific Railway in 1884. As a result, migrants arrived in Junín looking for jobs in the railroad workshops. Due to this rapid growth, Junín was declared a city by 1906. Evita and her family moved to Junín in 1930 because **Elisa Duarte**, Evita's eldest sister, found a job in the city's post office. Apparently, Junín meant very little to Evita, and she left it in 1935 to pursue an artistic career in Buenos Aires. *See also* LOS TOLDOS, GENERAL VIAMONTE.

JUSTICIALISMO. Deriving from the concept of social justice, *justicialismo* was the official ideology of the political movement known as Peronism. The leader of the movement, **Juan Domingo Perón**, first introduced *justicialismo* at a philosophy conference at the University of Cuyo in **Mendoza** in 1949. Devised by Perón, the doctrine of *justicialismo* systemized his ideas into a political and social theory. Perón's *justicialismo* put forward the idea that within a society there were four necessary but competing forces: idealism, materialism, individualism, and collectivism. He believed that *justicialismo* under his tutelage could balance these competing forces in Argentine society through the notion of a "third position," which was neither Marxist nor liberal. In terms of foreign policy, Perón's third position entailed that Argentina would become a flagship country leading a bloc of nations autonomous from Washington and Moscow. His position was in fact an attempt to achieve a truly national sovereignty. As domestic policy goes, the third position meant that Perón attempted to create a new society relying on hierarchical principles and eschewing class conflict. His idea of community was one of direct state intervention in order to ensure harmony between laborers and employers. One of the main underpinnings of *justicialismo* was Catholicism. Perón would often say that his doctrine was the true embodiment of Catholic social teaching. This in turn caused him trouble with the church as he became an object of deification by his followers. Evita, his most fervent follower, once said, "[My] only religion was Peronism and [my] only tenet was faith in Perón." On 17 October 1950, Perón announced the **Twenty Peronist Tenets**, also known as the Twenty Truths of *Justicialismo*, in commemoration of the fifth anniversary of the Peronist movement. These tenets represented the essence of his political philosophy. *See also* CANONIZATION OF EVITA.

JUVENTUD PERONISTA (JP)/PERONIST YOUTH. Emerging as the Movimiento de la Juventud Peronista (Peronist Youth Movement) in 1951, this Peronist youth group ceased to exist after the overthrow of President **Juan Domingo Perón** in 1955. Two years later, it was refounded as Juventud Peronista (JP) by factory worker Gustavo Rearte despite the proscription of **Peronism** at the time. Influenced by the Cuban Revolution and other guerrilla movements, the JP evolved into a resistance movement, carrying out its first act of armed resistance under the name Ejército Peronista de Liberación Nacional. From its ranks emerged some of the clandestine armed organizations that would confront the military regimes of the 1960s and 1970s. At the first national congress of the JP, held in October 1963, the JP issued a declaration demanding the restitution of the remains of Evita to Argentina, among other things. *See also* BODY OF EVITA; MONTONEROS.

K

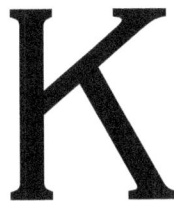

KARTULOVICH "KARTULO," EMILIO (1895–1961). Born in Croatia, this naturalized Chilean and Argentine citizen was a journalist, editor-in-chief, film director, librettist, and racing car driver. Kartulo, as he was known, came from an affluent family. His father was a well-known politician who had to flee his native Croatia after the Austrio-Hungarian government put a price on his head. Hence, he arrived in Chile with his family in 1900. As a young man, Kartulovich was interested in aviation and car racing. He competed in numerous races and won several titles. In addition, he became a successful show-business entrepreneur in Argentina. He was the owner of Radio La Voz del Aire, founder of the film production company Rayton Cinematográfica Argentina, and editor-in-chief of *Sintonía* magazine. Kartulovich and Evita met in the late 1930s. Reportedly, they had a love affair that prompted Evita's regular appearances in *Sintonía*.

KIRCHNER, NÉSTOR (1950–2010). Born in the small coastal city of Río Gallegos in Santa Cruz Province, Néstor Kirchner joined the **Juventud Peronista** while he was a law student at the National University of **La Plata**. In 1975, he married **Cristina Fernández**, a fellow law student and political activist, and the couple moved to Río Gallegos, where they set up a law firm. Briefly imprisoned due to his political beliefs during Argentina's last military dictatorship (1976–1983), Kirchner was elected mayor of Río Gallegos in 1987 and governor of Santa Cruz in 1991. Endorsed by the outgoing president **Eduardo Alberto Duhalde**, Kirchner ran for president on the **Frente para la Victoria** ticket. On 25 May 2003, he was sworn in as president of Argentina. Despite finding a country in tatters when he took office, he managed to bring economic growth through his policies. One of his greatest achievements was the reopening of trials against **human rights** abuses that had been committed by the military dictatorship. In 2007, he could have run for reelection and won, but he stood aside and let his wife compete for the presidency. She then became Argentina's first elected female president. The Kirchners constituted the most important political marriage in Argentina since that of Evita and **Juan Domingo Perón**. *See also* DIRTY WAR.

KIRCHNER CULTURAL CENTER. Named after former Argentine president **Néstor Kirchner**, this cultural center located in the former Buenos Aires Central Post Office opened its doors on 21 May 2015. This nine-floor Beaux-Arts-style building houses, among other attractions, a concert hall; five auditoriums; 18 halls for poetry reading, performance art, and other events; and the Eva Perón Room. This room re-creates the headquarters of the **Fundación Eva Perón**, featuring the large desk used by Evita and mail bags containing letters addressed to her. It also exhibits toys, bicycles, and boxes of cider bottles, all of which were distributed by Evita and her foundation among the disadvantaged in Argentina.

KIRCHNERISM. Under the banner of populism, this center-left political movement emerged as a result of **Néstor Kirchner's** victory in the 2003 presidential election. It was based on the structure of the **Partido Justicialista**, different types of social movements, and the **Confederación General del Trabajo**. Resistance to neoliberal policies, economic nationalism, and cultivating the support of the middle class were central to Kirchnerism. During the governments of Kirchner (2003–2007) and **Cristina Fernández de Kirchner** (2007–2015), images of **Juan Domingo Perón** and Evita were used to link the Kirchners to the Peróns.

L

LA CABALGATA DEL CIRCO. Directed by Mario Soffici and Eduardo Boneo, *La cabalgata del circo* (Circus Cavalcade) is a 1945 Argentine film that gave rise to a myth surrounding the confrontation between **Libertad Lamarque Bouza**—the leading actress who played Nita in the film—and Evita—who had a supporting role as Chila. The film follows the lives of two siblings, Nita and Roberto Arletty, from 1880 to 1945. Born into a family of circus artists, Nita and Roberto travel the Argentine Pampas, bringing their shows to rural villages. They are accompanied by their parents and other siblings as well as a cohort of associates, among whom is Chila. Roberto and Chila fall in love and they tie the knot, but their marriage is short lived. Chila leaves Roberto because she resents Nita's

Still from the 1945 movie *La cabalgata del circo* (Circus Cavalcade). From left to right, Ana Nieves, Evita, Elvira Quintana, and José Olarra.

lead in the circus company. As a result, Chila disappears from the plot. On the same day of Chila's departure, the circus company is hired to perform at a Buenos Aires theater and their nomadic life is forever changed. Nita eventually marries and starts a family while Roberto becomes an internationally renowned artist. The film closes with an image of the aging siblings watching *La cabalgata del circo* in a theater. The on-screen rivalry between Nita and Chila was also enacted outside the cinematic narrative. During the shooting of the movie, problems arose between Lamarque and Evita due to their different political views and the fact that Evita would arrive late on the film set or interrupt the shooting of the movie to attend to matters related to **Juan Domingo Perón**. Evita would excuse herself by saying that she was Perón's personal assistant and that there were more important things than shooting a film. This enraged Lamarque, who did not hide her resentment toward Evita. Legend has it that Lamarque actually slapped Evita in the face, but Lamarque herself always denied it.

LA CAPITAL. Founded by journalists Ovidio Lagos and Eudoro Carrasco in November 1867, *La Capital* is the oldest Argentine tabloid daily still in circulation. It started as an evening publication in **Rosario**, Santa Fe Province, but became a morning paper in August 1868. Lagos was an active advocate for Rosario to be the new capital city of the country, and thus he named the paper *La Capital* as part of his lobbying campaign. Evita's first solo picture was published by *La Capital* on 26 July 1936. The young actress was part of a touring company. Their debut play opened at the Odeón Theater in Rosario on 22 May. At the end of the season, *La Capital* published an article with information about the company together with a photograph of Evita. The caption read, "Eva Duarte, young actress who has managed to stand out during the season that ends today at the Odeón." *See also* COMPAÑÍA DE COMEDIAS MUÑOZ-FRANCO-ÁLVAREZ.

LA CARGA DE LOS VALIENTES. Directed by Adelqui Millar and produced by **Pampa Film**, this movie was released on 12 June 1940. Set in 1827, *La carga de los valientes* (Only the Valiant) is a historical drama that depicts a fictionalized version of the battle of Carmen de Patagones. This was an armed conflict between Argentina and Brazil that took place in the surroundings of Carmen de Patagones, nowadays a town in Buenos Aires Province. The focus of the film is on the rivalry between a lieutenant and a gaucho—the Argentine equivalent to the cowboy—over a young lady. The denouement of the story comes when the two men become comrades in arms to repel the invading Brazilian forces, and the gaucho perishes in the battle. Evita's participation in the film is minimal, appearing in the opening scenes as Aurora, an attractive young woman who lives with her wealthy parents in Buenos Aires. The lieutenant is infatuated with her, but he is soon dispatched to Carmen de Patagones by his superior, and Aurora disappears from the plot.

LA ÉPOCA. *La Época*, which was the mouthpiece of the **Unión Cívica Radical (UCR)** until the early 1940s, was an evening newspaper founded by the Radical politician José Cantilo in Buenos Aires in 1916. In the 1930s, the paper was bought by another member of the UCR, Eduardo Colom, who was a supporter of **Juan Domingo Perón**'s policy. Under Colom's management, *La Época* backed the Peronist government unfailingly. In 1949, Colom sold *La Época* to the state but kept his position as editor-in-chief until 1951, when the paper was incorporated into **Alea S.A.** Due to his unconditional support of **Peronism**, Colom was entitled to a seat in the Chamber of Deputies. Following the **Liberating Revolution**, *La Época* continued to be issued only for a few months. A reissue of the Peronist *La Época* in September 1983 was short-lived, and the paper ceased publication in the same year.

LA GRANJA DE SAN ILDEFONSO. This royal site is located 10 kilometers (6.2 miles) from **Segovia** in the autonomous community of Castile and León, Spain. Boasting a royal palace, a glass factory, and Versailles-like gardens, it is a token of the glory of the 18th-century Spanish monarchy. Evita, together with **María**

del Carmen Polo y Martínez-Valdés and their entourage, was in La Granja de San Ildefonso on 11 June 1947 as part of her **Rainbow Tour**. The visitors arrived at 8:25 p.m.; toured the palace, where some refreshments were served; and enjoyed the fountain water shows in the impressive gardens.

LA MUJER DEL LÁTIGO: EVA PERÓN. See MAIN, MARY; *WOMAN WITH THE WHIP: EVA PERÓN, THE.*

LA NACIÓN. This historic liberal-conservative newspaper was founded by the former president of Argentina Bartolomé Mitre in Buenos Aires in 1870. *La Nación*—known as the newspaper of the bourgeoisie—did not endorse **Juan Domingo Perón** but the candidates of the Unión Democrática (Democratic Union) during the 1945–1946 presidential campaign. Between 1946 and 1955, *La Nación* managed to avoid governmental intervention by taking a guarded viewpoint on **Peronism**, unlike other papers that also opposed Perón, such as *La Prensa* and *Crítica*. After years of living in fear of being expropriated, the paper's owners finally decided to take a different approach and focused on establishing friendlier terms with the Peronist government. The Mitre family is still the proprietor of the newspaper. *See also* ANTI-ARGENTINE ACTIVITIES CONGRESSIONAL COMMITTEE; SECRETARIAT OF INFORMATION AND PRESS.

LA PALABRA, EL PENSAMIENTO Y LA ACCIÓN. The book *La palabra, el pensamiento y la acción* (The Word, the Thought, and the Action) is a collection of quotes that stem from Evita's speeches. The quotes, which outline Evita's ideas, beliefs, and intentions, make up brief paragraphs grouped into chapters. Each of the chapters addresses such themes as social aid, work, childhood, social justice, education, religion, women, politics, and culture. This publication has also appeared under the title *Su palabra, su pensamiento y su acción* (Her Word, Her Thought, and Her Action).

LA PAMPA. Sparsely populated, La Pampa is a landlocked province located in the middle of the country. It was a national territory until 1952, the year it attained provincial status, allegedly owing to a proposal by Evita. The new province was renamed Eva Perón but reverted to its original name in 1955.

LA PERONA. While visiting the city of **Santiago de Compostela**, Spain, Evita planted a tree belonging to the fir species in the Alameda Park on 19 June 1947. Known as La Perona, the tree, which now stands 22 meters (72 feet) high, can be found at the Ferradura walk in the park and is currently one of the city's favorite attractions. *See also* RAINBOW TOUR.

LA PLATA. Founded in 1882, La Plata is the capital of Buenos Aires Province. Evita reportedly lived in this city for a few months in 1943 while she was performing in a *radioteatro* at a local radio station. She returned to La Plata in 1945 to marry **Juan Domingo Perón** at San Francisco de Asís Church. Following Evita's death in 1952, the city changed its name to Ciudad Eva Perón. The change of name was proposed by the local **Partido Peronista**, and the bill approving it was passed by the legislature of the Buenos Aires Province. Once Perón was ousted, the military government restored its original name. *See also* WEDDING OF EVITA.

LA PRENSA. One of the most powerful and influential morning papers in Argentina, *La Prensa* was founded in 1869 by the Argentine statesman José C. Paz. Between 1898 and 1943, its editor-in-chief was Paz's son, Ezequiel Paz, who was succeeded by his nephew, Alberto Gainza Paz. Soon after its foundation, this liberal, conservative paper gained reputation as a trusted source of information. *La Prensa* and other independent media businesses faced government harassment between the late 1940s and early 1950s. During the 1945–1946 presidential campaign, major papers such as *La Prensa* had given their unconditional support to **Juan Domingo Perón**'s opposition, the Unión Democrática (Democratic Union). After becoming president, Perón initiated an intimidation campaign against his opponents in the media industry,

La Prensa being one particular target. He tried to boycott the paper in 1947 by describing it as anti-Argentine. However, the Peronist government's efforts were not successful until 1951, when the news vendors' union organized a strike against *La Prensa*. The protest turned violent—one news vendor died and several were wounded. Evita had met the news vendors and allegedly encouraged them to mount the strike against the paper to demand better salaries. It was no secret that she abhorred *La Prensa*. Furthermore, the fact that the instigators who started the shooting were purportedly not news vendors supports the idea of the Peronist government trying to gain control over the paper through a fabricated conflict. Indeed, *La Prensa* was expropriated and became the mouthpiece of the **Confederación General del Trabajo**, which openly supported Perón. *La Prensa* was returned to the Gainza Paz family on 3 February 1956, but due to financial problems, the paper was sold in 1993. Currently, the paper is part of the media group La Capital, owned by the businessman Florencio Aldrey. *See also* ANTI-ARGENTINE ACTIVITIES CONGRESSIONAL COMMITTEE; LIBERATING REVOLUTION.

LA PRÓDIGA. Directed by Mario Soffici and produced by **Estudios San Miguel**, *La pródiga* (The Prodigal Woman) is the only movie in which Evita played the lead. Having had smaller roles in other films, she probably used her relationship with **Juan Domingo Perón** to get the starring role in this one. Although the main role had been offered to the actress Mecha Ortíz—the Argentine Greta Garbo—she was eventually replaced by Evita. The reason for this change was that the Argentine film industry was under a U.S. embargo on raw film stock, yet Evita managed to access the coveted celluloid through Perón. *La pródiga* was completed in September 1945. While the film was ready to be released in December of the same year, the events of October and Evita's marriage to Perón put an enormous pressure

Still from *La pródiga* (The Prodigal Woman), in which Evita played the role of Julia, a wealthy widow. Julia is surrounded by poor villagers.

Still from *La pródiga* (The Prodigal Woman), the only movie in which Evita played the lead. Julia burns a love letter.

on the studios not to release it. Instead, the film was given to the newlyweds as a wedding gift and was not released until 16 August 1984.

Regarding the plot, the film tells the story of Julia, an extremely wealthy widow—played by Evita—who lives on a sumptuous estate located in Valle de Piedras Albas, a valley inhabited by poor villagers. The arrival of an engineer in the valley is the turning point in Julia's life as he falls in love and moves in with her. The villagers, for their part, frown upon their relationship because the couple is not married. The plot bears striking similarities with Evita's role as Argentina's first lady. Like Evita, Julia refuses to openly disclose her past life; she is referred to as "la Señora" and "mother of the destitute"; she helps the poor villagers; and she dies childless and young. Additionally, Julia's sleek hair and elegant attire bear more than a passing resemblance to Evita, who was always impeccably groomed. Evita was so keen on the film that she watched it while she was recovering from her appendicitis surgery in 1950. *See also* PERONIST LOYALTY DAY; WEDDING OF EVITA.

LA RAZÓN. This evening newspaper was founded in 1905 in Buenos Aires by the Argentine journalist Emilio Morales. In 1911, it was bought by the journalist José Cortejarena, who modernized the paper. When Cortejarena died in 1921, *La Razón* had several editors-in-chief. In 1937, Ricardo Peralta Ramos, the husband of one of Cortejarena's daughters, became the majority shareholder and the new editor-in-chief. Together with *Crítica*, ***Noticias Gráficas***, *La Vanguardia*, *La Prensa*, *El Mundo*, and ***La Nación***, *La Razón* was part of the press that supported **Juan Domingo Perón**'s opposition during the 1945–1946 general election campaign. In 1951, *La Razón* was bought by the state. Despite having sold all his shares to the Peronist government, Peralta Ramos continued as the leading figure of both *La Razón* and **La Razón S.A.** During the government of the **Liberating Revolution**, Peralta Ramos and his lawyer and business partner Marcos Satanowsky once again found themselves in conflict with the authorities over the management and ownership of *La Razón*. The de facto government did not recognize Peralta Ramos or Satanowsky but Perón as the legitimate owner of the paper. Over the years, *La Razón* had different owners and went through financial difficulties. Its last edition was in December 2017. *See also* ALEA S.A.; ANTI-ARGENTINE ACTIVITIES CONGRESSIONAL COMMITTEE.

LA RAZÓN DE MI VIDA. This book, attributed to Evita, was published in Argentina in 1951 with an initial print-run of 300,000 copies. Largely a summary of Evita's history and relationship with **Peronism**, the volume is written in the present tense, consists of 59 chapters, and is divided into three parts: the motivation behind her work, the connection between her work and the Argentine working class, and the link between her work and women in Argentina. As the first-person narrator, Evita focuses on what she regards as the brilliance of the Peronist doctrine and its values, namely, class equality, universal love, and self-sacrifice. More importantly, *La razón de mi vida* (*My Mission in Life*) foregrounds her views of **Juan Domingo Perón** as the leader and father of the nation. The use of short sentences and paragraphs, coupled with the reiteration of terms connected to emotions, conveys an overall conversational and sentimental tone throughout the book.

Despite the broad consensus by its contemporary (Peronist) Argentine readers that the book was a manifestation of Evita's honest work and feelings toward the Argentine people, scholars agree that its main purpose was to function as a propaganda piece. The book was initially ghostwritten by the Spanish journalist **Manuel Penella de Silva**, who opted for a narrative in the first person based on conversations with Evita. When the book was ready, Perón asked **Raúl Mendé**, a member of his cabinet, to edit *La razón de mi vida*. Mendé allegedly corrected the book by suppressing its original feminist approach and by transforming it into praise of Perón and Peronism. In any case, the content of the volume was carefully planned and revised, which discredits the notion that the text comprises Evita's genuine and unfiltered thoughts. A second reason that supports the idea that *La razón de mi vida* is a political tract is its controversial categorization as an autobiography. The book does not claim to be an account of real-life events, and it does not provide essential biographical details of, for instance, Evita's childhood or youth, but only a recounting of her feelings and political life from the moment she met Perón. All in all, the choice to advertise it as an autobiography cannot be interpreted merely as a mistake or lack of knowledge of narrative genres. It seems more likely that selling it as an autobiography was a strategy to emphasize Evita as the author of the book and provide an account narrated directly by its protagonist. As such, it increased its appeal for its intended readership. Peronism made *La razón de mi vida*—and thus Evita—gain prestige and reputation by decreeing that the book was to be employed as reading material in Argentine schools. The volume was the first of Evita's publications to be officially launched, a fact that signaled the importance given to both book and author. Unlike any other of Evita's publications, *La razón de mi vida* became a best seller in Argentina after her death in 1952. It has been translated into Arabic (1951), French (1952), German (1952), English (1953), and Italian (1953), among other languages. *See also* AYRINHAC, NUMA.

LA RAZÓN S.A. Ricardo Peralta Ramos was the majority shareholder and manager of this media company, which owned **La Razón** and the **Red Argentina de Emisoras Splendid**. Peralta Ramos sold La Razón S.A. to the president of the National Economic Council, **Miguel Miranda**, in 1951 but continued to hold his managerial position.

LA VANGUARDIA. This respected socialist morning newspaper was founded in Buenos Aires in 1894 by the leader of the Partido Socialista (Socialist Party) or PS, Juan B. Justo, among others. In 1896, it became the official paper of the PS, and its founder described it as the voice of the working class. Its pages served as a vehicle for spreading news about the PS, encouraging internal discussions, making the PS position known, and reporting on various events relevant to the socialists, such as strikes, celebrations, and commemorations. In the early 1940s, *La Vanguardia* was closed several times due to its criticism of the military government, which was characterized by the paper as pro-Nazi and fascist. Hence, *La Vanguardia* was opposed to the 1945 presidential candidacy of **Juan Domingo Perón**. After countless inspections by the Peronist government, the paper was finally closed in 1947, using a noise ordinance as an excuse for the closure. Nonetheless, *La Vanguardia* appeared a week later as a clandestine publication, and it would continue to be published weekly. Meanwhile, the editor-in-chief of *La Vanguardia*, Américo Ghioldi, and the rest of the staff were intimidated, persecuted, or imprisoned, and eventually some of them went into exile in Uruguay. Following the 1955 military coup d'état, *La Vanguardia* reopened its doors and has been in operation since then. *See also* ANTI-ARGENTINE ACTIVITIES CONGRESSIONAL COMMITTEE; LIBERATING REVOLUTION; SECRETARIAT OF INFORMATION AND PRESS.

LAGOMARSINO DE GUARDO, LILLIAN (1911–2012). Wife of **Ricardo César Guardo**, mother of four, and Evita's companion, she met Evita at the Peróns' country house in **San Vicente**, Buenos Aires Province, in 1946. Some months after that first encounter, Evita called Lillian and asked her to come to her office. From that moment on, the two women would speak on the phone practically every morning, and their relationship evolved as Evita started to send her car to pick up Lillian. Evita required Lillian to sit quietly in her office while she met with different people. Lillian soon became a key person in Evita's life, to such an extent that she accompanied Evita to diplomatic functions, galas at the Colón Theater, and opening ceremonies. Coming from a wealthy background, Lillian advised Evita what was appropriate to wear and inspected the costly gifts Evita received since she could distinguish between a fake and a real gemstone. Such was their closeness that Lillian accompanied Evita on her **Rainbow Tour**. During the trip, she did not leave Evita's side and she even slept the first nights in **Madrid** on a couch in Evita's bedroom. However, the relationship between the two women cooled down once Guardo was replaced by **Héctor José Cámpora** as the president of the Chamber of Deputies on 1 May 1948.

LAMARQUE BOUZA, LIBERTAD (1908–2000). This famous actress and singer, who developed her artistic career between Argentina and Mexico, shared the stage with Evita. Lamarque was born in **Rosario**, Argentina, to a militant anarchist. Together with six siblings, she started her acting career in plays inspired by anarchist ideas. She had her first professional appearance as an actress at the age of 12. In 1926, and after moving to Buenos Aires with her family, she began singing tangos at the theaters on Corrientes Avenue. Six years later, she won a national tango contest and became universally known as the "queen of tango." Lamarque was also involved in acting and, by the time she died, she had appeared in more than 60 films. The release of *Madreselva* (Honeysuckle) on 5 October 1938 was a landmark in her career. From then on, the singer and actress was the most popular artist in Argentine cinema. She and Evita appeared in ***La cabalgata del circo*** (Circus Cavalcade). Popular legend has it that during the filming a furious row ensued between the two actresses. The row ended with Lamarque supposedly slapping Evita in the face, but she herself denied that she had slapped Evita. Lamarque made one more film in Argentina, *Romance musical* (Musical Romance), after which she learned that she had been blacklisted and departed for Mexico. During the golden age of Mexican cinema, her career blossomed, and she continued to work in Mexico until her death in 2000.

LANUSSE, ALEJANDRO AGUSTÍN (1918–1996). This Argentine military officer participated in a coup d'état that failed to oust President **Juan Domingo Perón** in 1951. Due to his participation, he was punished with a life term in jail. However, once Perón was toppled in 1955, Lanusse was released from jail and promoted to the rank of lieutenant colonel. He was named commander-in-chief of the army in 1968 and, three years later, led a coup d'état that would bring him to power. He assumed the post of president of Argentina on 22 March 1971. During his mandate, he began the process of returning Argentina to democratic rule by legalizing all non-Marxist political parties, including the **Partido Justicialista**. As social unrest escalated in the country, Lanusse concluded that the only way to stop it was to bring Perón back from exile. He began secret negotiations with him in **Madrid** and returned the **body of Evita** to Perón in September 1971 as a sign of good faith. In 1973, presidential elections were held, and **Héctor José Cámpora** won them. Lanusse stepped down as president on 24 May 1973.

LARRAURI, JUANITA (1910–1990). Juana Larrauri de Abramí was an Argentine tango singer and politician better known as Juanita Larrauri. Aside from a few tours in the **interior of Argentina** and neighboring countries, Larrauri built her singing career in radio. She started out as a tango singer at Radio Nacional (later **Radio Belgrano**) in 1931 but would continue to perform at, among others, Radio Rivadavia, **Radio Prieto**, and Radio del Pueblo. With the rise of **Juan Domingo Perón** to power, she became a staunch supporter of **Peronism**. She was among the women who backed Evita in her campaign for **female suffrage**. While her active participation in politics put an end to her singing career, it led her to become a member of the National Committee of the **Partido Peronista Femenino (PPF)**. She was appointed delegate of the PPF to the province of Entre Ríos and was elected national senator for the same province in 1951. In the same year, she recorded the anthem of the PPF, "**Evita capitana**" (Evita, the Captain). Following Evita's death, she presided over the National Commission for the Eva Perón Monument. *See also* PINK ROOM.

LAS DELICIAS. This was the first warehouse of what would be the **Fundación Eva Perón**. Soon after **Juan Domingo Perón** became president of Argentina in 1946, Evita began to assist the disadvantaged classes of Argentina. She would drive with the steward of the **Unzué Palace** and her right-hand man, **Atilio Renzi**, to the poor neighborhoods in Buenos Aires to give away food and clothes. Initially, Evita received people at the palace to listen to their needs, and people would also write letters to her asking for help. Evita's social work was rapidly supported by labor unions across the country. Delegations of workers visiting her would bring donations, usually of what they produced and manufactured. These were stored in a garage of the palace. According to Renzi, the palace staff named the store Las Delicias after Perón stated that all the goods were "una delicia para los necesitados" (a delight for those in need). With the help of Renzi, **Irma Cabrera de Ferrari**, the chef Bartolo, and the rest of the personnel at the palace, Evita would sort, pack, and label the goods for distribution.

LAS PALMAS DE GRAN CANARIA. Founded in 1478, this city is the capital of three jurisdictions, the Gran Canaria Island, the province of Las Palmas, and the autonomous community of the Canary Islands. Evita arrived at **Gando Airport** in Las Palmas de Gran Canaria on 8 June 1947 as part of her **Rainbow Tour**. From the airport, Evita was driven to Las Palmas followed by a caravan of cars. In the city, hundreds of people lined the streets to welcome her. Evita phoned **Juan Domingo Perón** from the local government office and attended Holy Mass at Las Palmas Cathedral. She returned to the airport to have lunch and left Las Palmas at 2 p.m. for **Madrid**.

LAS VENTAS BULLRING. Located in the district of Salamanca, **Madrid**, this is the largest bullring in Spain and the third largest in the world. Evita attended a bullfight at Las Ventas Bullring on 12 June 1947 during her official visit to Spain. She arrived at 5:50 p.m. and was welcomed by an imposing bullring, with thousands of people cheering for Spain and Argentina. Evita sat in the presidential box—the best seat in the bullring—together with **Francisco Franco Bahamonde**, his wife, his daughter, and **Lillian Lagomarsino de Guardo**, among others. *See also* FRANCO Y POLO, MARÍA DEL CARMEN "NENUCA"; POLO Y MARTÍNEZ-VALDÉS, MARÍA DEL CARMEN; RAINBOW TOUR.

LASCANO GONZÁLEZ, JULIO (1905–1986). Head of the anatomic pathology services at the Italiano Hospital of Buenos Aires, this Argentine physician diagnosed Evita's cervical cancer. He processed her tissue sample, which was obtained from the biopsy performed by Dr. **Humberto Dionisi**, and wrote the pathology report.

LETTER TO EVA. *See CARTA A EVA.*

LIBERATING REVOLUTION. This term refers to the civic-military coup d'état that ousted President **Juan Domingo Perón** in September 1955 and the subsequent de facto regime that ruled Argentina between 1955 and 1958, known as the government of the Liberating Revolution. Perón's second administration had been marked by such issues as economic instability, (political) censorship, conflicts with the Catholic Church, long-continued hostilities with the navy and armed forces, and escalation of violence between the government and anti-Peronist civic and military groups. These were some of the factors that led the navy—with the support of army battalions in several provinces—to revolt against Perón's government on 16 September 1955 and declare from **Córdoba** Province the Liberating Revolution. The leaders of the military uprising were General **Eduardo Ernesto Lonardi**, General **Pedro Eugenio Aramburu**, and Admiral **Isaac Francisco del Ángel Rojas**. Once Perón was ousted, Lonardi became the de facto president and Rojas the vice president. Meanwhile, Perón sought refuge in the Paraguayan Embassy. Eventually, he settled in Spain, where he remained until 1973. Despite working together to depose Perón, the three leaders of the coup d'état would soon be in strong disagreement over their political beliefs. While Lonardi stood for a nationalist-Catholic faction of military men with a more conciliatory approach, Aramburu and Rojas represented a more liberal military group with a fervent anti-Peronist ideology. As a result, Lonardi was ousted on 13 November 1955, Aramburu assumed the presidency, and Rojas remained as vice president. The government of the Liberating Revolution made significant political and ideological changes, including the implementation of a hostile anti-Peronist policy. The "de-Peronization" of Argentina aimed to eradicate **Peronism** at any cost. As such, Peronist supporters were persecuted, imprisoned, and, in several cases, executed. Peronist institutions were closed, and the use of Peronist terminology was banned. The **body of Evita** was removed from the headquarters of the **Confederación General del Trabajo** to an unknown location. Finally, the **Partido Peronista** was not allowed to run in the presidential election held in February 1958, which was won by the candidate of the **Unión Cívica Radical** Intransigente, **Arturo Frondizi**.

LINTER PUBLICIDAD. In 1938, Evita worked as a model for this advertising company. She participated in the short advertising film *La luna de miel de Inés* (Inés's Honeymoon) with Claudio Martino.

LISBON. Evita paid a visit to the Portuguese capital from 17 to 21 July 1947 as part of her **Rainbow Tour**. She was welcomed by Prime Minister Antonio Oliveira Salazar, attended a luncheon hosted by President Óscar Fragoso Carmona, traveled to different seaside villages, visited workers' houses and community dining halls, and met unofficially with the former Italian king Umberto II and the Spanish prince Juan de Borbón. She was advised that her meeting with the Spanish prince might seem discourteous to **Francisco Franco Bahamonde**, whom she had met in **Madrid**, but she is reported to have said, "I'll go where I want and if fatty doesn't like it, that's too bad."

LLAMBÍ, BENITO PEDRO (1907–1997). A member of the **Partido Peronista**, this Argentine military officer, politician, and diplomat had a long diplomatic career, serving as Argentina's ambassador to **Switzerland**, Sweden, Iran, and Thailand during **Juan Domingo Perón**'s first two mandates (1946–1955). Llambí was a personal friend of Perón and a member of the **Grupo de Oficiales Unidos**. When Perón was appointed secretary of labor and social welfare, Llambí became one of his close collaborators. He was also in charge of organizing Perón's inaugural ceremony in 1946. While Evita was touring Europe in 1947, Llambí, who was the Argentine ambassador to Switzerland, organized and hosted Evita's visit to this country. In the same year, Llambí persuaded **Manuel Penella de Silva** to travel to Argentina and write a biography of Evita. However, Llambí seems to have used his official position for dubious activities. From the Argentine Embassy in Switzerland, he reportedly arranged for Nazi criminals and collaborators to reach Argentina. *See also* RAINBOW TOUR.

LOBOTOMY OF EVITA. In a 2011 journal article, the Yale professor Dr. Daniel Nijensohn reported that Evita underwent a prefrontal lobotomy—a procedure used for treating intractable pain from cancer and other diseases. Allegedly, the surgery took place without her consent and in a makeshift operating theater in a back room of the **Unzué Palace** sometime between May and June 1952. It was probably performed in the highest confidentiality and in the middle of the night. The neurosurgeon in charge was apparently Dr. James Poppen, an international expert on the use of lobotomy and a sympathizer of **Peronism**. Following the operation, Dr. Poppen was reportedly taken aback by Evita's rapid decline and early death. Seemingly, Evita stopped eating after the lobotomy. In another study from 2016, Dr. Nijensohn and his team put forward another argument accounting for Evita's lobotomy. They concluded that the procedure was in fact performed with the intention of modifying her belligerent behavior and impulsive personality. In the 1950s, lobotomy was in fact used to treat uncontrollable aggression and impulsive violence. However, Dr. Nijensohn himself has noted that absolute confirmation of the procedure has not been possible yet as the exhumation of her corpse is not an option. *See also* BODY OF EVITA; DUARTE FAMILY TOMB.

LONARDI, EDUARDO ERNESTO (1896–1956). Army officer Eduardo Ernesto Lonardi held a personal grudge against **Juan Domingo Perón**, whom he replaced as military attaché to Chile in 1937. Apparently, Perón intended to transfer materials in violation of Chilean espionage laws but left it to Lonardi to collect the data without briefing him. Lonardi was caught red-handed and arrested by Chilean agents. Although he was later released thanks to the intervention of the Argentine Embassy, Perón blamed him for the scandal, which fueled Lonardi's resentment against him. After criticizing Evita's **candidacy for vice president** and plotting against Perón in a conspiracy that failed, he was forced to retire. In 1955, he was one of the leaders of the **Liberating Revolution**, a coup d'état that not only toppled Perón but also installed Lonardi as president of Argentina. On 22 September 1955, Lonardi swore himself in as provisional president of Argentina. His slogan, "neither victors nor vanquished," showed that he was devoted to national unity and reconciliation, but his policy did not please everybody. He lost the confidence of the military and the civilians who had supported the Liberating Revolution. On 13 November 1955, he was replaced by General **Pedro Eugenio Aramburu**.

LÓPEZ REGA, JOSÉ (1916–1989). This Argentine police officer gained **Juan Domingo Perón**'s trust, becoming his private secretary during the Peronist leader's exile in Spain. Due to his knowledge and practice of black magic and occultism—an interest he shared with **Isabel Martínez de Perón**—he was called El Brujo (The Wizard). He was one of the two men in charge of opening Evita's coffin once it was exhumed and delivered to Perón at his residence in Spain. Evita's remains were placed in an upstairs guest room of the residence. López Rega, who claimed that Evita felt bored and lonely, reportedly placed a little doll inside the coffin. Furthermore, he would allegedly ask Martínez de Perón to lie on top of Evita's coffin while he burned candles and performed different rituals. Upon his return to Argentina, he served as minister of social welfare during Perón's third presidency and continued in this position during Martínez de Perón's mandate. One of his most notorious activities as a cabinet member was the creation of the **Triple A** or Argentine Anti-Communist Alliance. *See also* BODY OF EVITA.

LOS TOLDOS, GENERAL VIAMONTE. Located approximately 310 kilometers (180 miles) from Buenos Aires, Los Toldos is the capital town of General Viamonte County in Buenos Aires Province. It was founded on 2 November 1892 by Electo Urquizo, who had donated the land where the Los Toldos train station was built. Before its foundation, Los Toldos had been the settlement of an indigenous tribe originally from Chile. **Estancia La Unión** on the outskirts of Los Toldos is renowned for being Evita's birthplace. When Evita's father abandoned the family, Evita and her family were forced to move to a modest house by the railroad. They lived there until 1930, the year they moved to **Junín**. Nowadays, Evita's former house is a museum, which was opened on 4 June 2004. *See also* DUARTE, JUAN; EVA PERÓN HOME/MUSEUM; IBARGUREN, JUANA.

LUJÁN. Located 68 kilometers (42 miles) north west of Buenos Aires, the city of Luján is well known for its Neo-Gothic Basilica of Our Lady of Luján. Every year millions of people make pilgrimages to Luján. Evita visited the basilica on different occasions. On 20 January 1940, her sister Blanca married the Argentine lawyer Justo Álvarez Rodríguez first at a civil ceremony in **Junín** and later the same day at a religious ceremony at the Basilica of Our Lady of Luján. Evita was among the guests at both ceremonies. On 5 May 1946, she went on a pilgrimage to the basilica along with her husband, **Juan Domingo Perón**, to thank Our Lady of Luján for his victory at the ballot. A year later, Evita accompanied Perón on an official visit to the city. The presidential couple attended the National Marian Congress held in Luján. *See also* DUARTE, BLANCA.

LUNA PARK STADIUM. This multipurpose arena located at the corner of Corrientes and Bouchard Avenues in the heart of Buenos Aires is the Argentine equivalent of Madison Square Garden. It opened as a boxing venue in 1932, but it was also used for Nazi and fascist events during World War II. In 1944, the stadium provided the setting for the meeting between Evita and **Juan Domingo Perón**. Throughout her life, Evita attended several events held at this venue. In 1945, she led a rally to support Perón's presidential campaign at the Luna Park Stadium. *See also* SAN JUAN EARTHQUAKE.

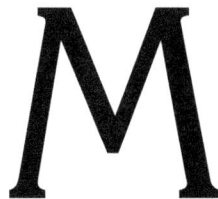

MACRI, ANA CARMEN (1916–). This Argentine feminist worked as a secretary in the Department of Radiology at the Rivadavia Hospital of Buenos Aires. With the rise of **Juan Domingo Perón** to power, she became a staunch **Peronist**. In 1948 and at the recommendation of Dr. **Armando Méndez de San Martín**—head of the Directorate General for Social Assistance—Macri was appointed head of the **temporary home** situated at 2899 Lafinur Street in Buenos Aires. There she met Evita, who named her secretary and delegate to the ninth Inter-American Conference of Women, held in Bogotá, Colombia. In 1949, she became politically engaged through her active participation in the **Partido Peronista Femenino (PPF)**. Evita appointed her delegate of the PPF to the province of Tucumán and later to the province of Santa Fe. Macri carried out a Herculean task opening 658 local branches of the PPF in the course of two years. In 1952, she was elected to Congress. *See also* UNIDADES BÁSICAS.

MADONNA. *See* CICCONE, MADONNA LOUISE.

MADRID. The capital city of Spain, Madrid lies on the Río Manzanares in the center of the country. As part of her **Rainbow Tour**, Evita and her entourage arrived in Madrid on 8 June 1947 and stayed at the **Royal Palace of El Pardo** until 15 June. Evita was welcomed by **Francisco Franco Bahamonde**; his wife, **María del Carmen Polo y Martínez-Valdés**; and their daughter, among others. During her stay in Madrid, Evita explored the city's must-see historical and cultural attractions. She also visited factories, neighborhoods, educational institutions, and charitable organizations. Furthermore, she attended a constant series of gala events and received countless gifts. Always accompanied by Franco's wife, Evita also traveled to the nearby cities of **Ávila**, **Medina del Campo**, **Segovia**, and **La Granja de San Ildefonso**. *See also* LAS VENTAS BULLRING; MADRID CITY HALL; PRADO MUSEUM; ROYAL PALACE OF MADRID; ROYAL SITE OF SAN LORENZO DE EL ESCORIAL; SANTA MARÍA DEL BUEN AIRE NATIONAL CAMP; UNIVERSITY CITY OF MADRID.

MADRID CITY HALL. The **Madrid** City Hall was originally located at the Casa de la Villa in the Plaza de la Villa, Madrid. On 12 June 1947, a gala function was held at the city hall in honor of Evita, who was visiting Madrid as part of her **Rainbow Tour**. She arrived with **Francisco Franco Bahamonde** and his wife, **María del Carmen Polo y Martínez-Valdés**, at 10 p.m. The three guests were welcomed by the local authorities. Following the gala event, Evita enjoyed a tour of the Casa de la Villa and admired the valuable works of art exhibited in its rooms, including a unique collection of tapestries.

MAGALDI, AGUSTÍN (1898–1938). Most accounts of Evita's life maintain that this famous Argentine tango singer met Evita in **Junín** when she was 15. She supposedly fell in love with him and asked him to take her with him to Buenos Aires. There is, however, no evidence to support this claim. The Junín newspapers of the time did not report any of his shows in the city in either 1934 or 1935. It is highly probable that their paths crossed, but that might have happened once Evita was living in Buenos Aires. They probably met at **Radio París**, where they both worked in 1935.

MAGGI DE MAGISTRIS, MARIA. *See* BODY OF EVITA; CABANILLAS, HÉCTOR EDUARDO.

MAIN, MARY (1903–1998). This novelist wrote the controversial biography of Evita *The Woman with the Whip: Eva Perón*. Born to British parents in Buenos Aires, Main grew up in the privileged Anglo-Argentine society and married the British engineer James Main in 1927. Fourteen years later, the couple moved to the United States, where Mrs. Main started writing short stories for the *Saturday Evening Post, Collier's*, and other magazines. In 1950, the publishing company Doubleday commissioned her to write a biography of Evita. As the biography was highly critical of Evita, **Juan Domingo Perón**, and the Peronist government, at first Main appeared under the pseudonym of María Flores as a precaution for fear of Peronist reprisals. She died aged 95 at her home in the United States.

"MARCHA PERONISTA." Officially known as "Los muchachos peronistas" (Peronist Boys), the "Marcha peronista" (Peronist March) is still one of the most powerful symbols of allegiance to **Peronism**. This political anthem extols the figure of **Juan Domingo Perón** by calling him the first worker and praising his greatness. Its origins are uncertain. While some sources claim that the tunes stem from carnival music, others suggest that the melody was the work of the Argentine composer Rodolfo Sciammarella. In relation to the lyrics, there appears to be strong consensus that they were written by Secretary of Education Dr. **Oscar Ivanissevich** on a flight from **Córdoba** to Tucumán in 1948. His motivation arose from the news of an attack on the lives of Perón and Evita, allegedly perpetrated by the labor union leader **Cipriano Reyes**. Dr. Ivanissevich's original song was performed for the first time at the Coventry Hotel in Tucumán. The Argentine actor, director, and tango singer Hugo del Carril recorded it on 17 October 1949. Played countless times during Perón's first two mandates, it was banned by decree following his overthrow in 1955. The "Marcha peronista" has been re-recorded in different versions, among which there is one devoted to Evita, **"Evita capitana"** (Evita, the Captain).

MARIÑO, CÉSAR. Eduardo Malcolm César Salvador Mariño, better known as César Mariño, was an Argentine actor who had a prolific film career between the 1930s and 1950s. He also worked in radio and theater. In 1942, Mariño was the director of *radioteatros* at **Radio Argentina**. Early that same year, his boss and Radio Argentina's artistic director, **Roberto Gil**, called him into his office and introduced him to Evita. Gil announced that Evita was going to be the new leading actress. According to Mariño, Gil was more interested in Evita's sponsor, Radical soap, than in Evita herself. He had to perform and direct Evita, two challenging tasks since she was not a particularly good actress. However, Mariño recalls that Evita's docile, modest, and serious personality compensated her poor acting skills. *See also* COMPAÑÍA JUVENIL DE RADIOTEATRO; GUEREÑO RODRÍGUEZ, JUAN.

MARMO, ALEJANDRO (1971–). Alejandro Marmo is a self-taught Argentine sculptor who makes art from recycled materials. He supports the promotion of social inclusion through art and has therefore spearheaded art projects in poor districts in Argentina. In the mid-1990s, Marmo started a new project, dubbed "Art in the Factory," which repurposes abandoned factories, recycles the materials found in those places, and involves former factory workers in making artwork. The two **murals of Evita** that now hang from the Ministry of Social Development Building on 9 de Julio Avenue in Buenos Aires constituted the pinnacle of Marmo's project. They were crafted in an industrial area of Avellaneda County, Buenos Aires Province, by factory workers. *See also* SANTORO, DANIEL.

MAROGLIO, DOMINGO ORLANDO (1902–?). This businessman was the president of the Central Bank of Argentina between 17 July 1947 and 19 January 1949. During the presidency of **Juan Domingo Perón**, Maroglio bought 51 percent of **Haynes Publishing**'s shares in November 1948. Once in the hands of the Peronist government, Haynes's numerous publications constantly featured Evita and Perón.

MARTÍN GARCÍA ISLAND. This island of approximately two square kilometers (0.7 square miles) is located in the Río de la Plata between Uruguay and Argentina. For most of the 20th century, the island served as a prison for several ousted presidents of Argentina, such as Hipólito Yrigoyen in 1930 and **Arturo Frondizi** in 1962. From 11 to 17 October 1945, the future president of Argentina **Juan Domingo Perón** was also held prisoner on Martín García. As the island is a strategic point of great importance, Argentina and Uruguay disputed its jurisdiction for years. On 19 November 1973, the dispute was settled when the two countries reached an agreement establishing Argentine jurisdiction over it. Martín García Island is currently a natural and historical reserve. *See also* PERONIST LOYALTY DAY.

MARTÍN-ARTAJO ÁLVAREZ, ALBERTO (1905–1979). This Spanish politician served as minister of foreign affairs between 1945 and 1957 during **Francisco Franco Bahamonde**'s regime. Martín-Artajo Álvarez was among those who welcomed Evita in **Dakhla** on 7 June 1947. Between 10 and 18 October 1948, he was on a diplomatic visit to Argentina to repay Evita's. The minister's agenda in Argentina included luncheons, speeches, and public gatherings. During his visit, he was accompanied by both **Juan Domingo Perón** and Evita. *See also* FRANCO SALGADO-ARAUJO, FRANCISCO; GARCÍA-ESCÁMEZ INIESTA, FRANCISCO; RAINBOW TOUR.

MARTÍNEZ, TOMÁS ELOY (1934–2010). This Argentine journalist and writer was forced to leave his country by President **Isabel Martínez de Perón**'s government and lived in exile in Venezuela for eight years before migrating to the United States in 1983. Martínez authored several nonfiction books on Argentine history and **Peronism** and published seven novels, among which are *La novela de Perón* (*The Perón Novel*) and *Santa Evita*. According to Martínez, both *La novela de Perón* and *Santa Evita* resulted from years of research and interviews. During his lifetime, he argued that the stories he had gathered could only be told through fiction.

MARTÍNEZ DE PERÓN, ISABEL "ISABELITA" (1931–). Isabel Martínez de Perón (née María Estela Martínez Cartas) was Latin America's first woman president. Born in La Rioja, the capital of the eponymous northwestern Argentine province, she moved to Buenos Aires with her family after her father passed away. She changed her name to Isabel on the day of her confirmation in the Catholic Church. After dropping out of school, she became a night club dancer and met **Juan Domingo Perón** in Panama while she was on a Latin America tour with a dance troupe. As a result of the encounter, she gave up dancing and became Perón's personal assistant. She moved with him to **Madrid**, where he was going to live in exile, and married him on 15 November 1961. During the 1960s and 1970s, she traveled back and forth between Spain and Argentina to build political support for her husband. On one of those trips, she apparently met **José López Rega** and pressed Perón to name him his private secretary. When Perón finally returned to Argentina in 1973 and ran for president, she was his vice presidential running mate. On 23 September 1973, the couple won a landslide victory. With the death of Perón on 1 July 1974, she became Argentina's president. She inherited a country on the verge of anarchy: a deeply divided Peronist movement, political and social turmoil, labor unrest, a high unemployment rate, and soaring inflation. Although she attempted to implement different measures, she did not manage to bring order into the chaotic situation. Under her mandate, the sociopolitical situation worsened: the economy collapsed, inflation soared, and guerrilla activity increased. López Rega, who was then minister of social welfare and her private secretary, had founded the **Triple A**, a right-wing secret organization that unleashed a wave of killings, thus fueling even more violence. She was urged to resign on several occasions, but she refused to do so. On 24 March 1976, she was deposed by a military coup d'état and held under house arrest for five years. In 1981, she went into exile in Spain, where she has lived until now. *See also* DIRTY WAR; HUMAN RIGHTS IN ARGENTINA; PERONISM.

MASSERA, EMILIO EDUARDO (1925–2010). The Argentine navy military officer Emilio Eduardo Massera was a member of the junta that overthrew President **Isabel Martínez de Perón** in March 1976 and enforced one of the most brutal military regimes in Argentina. He was responsible for turning the Navy Mechanics School in Buenos Aires into a clandestine detention camp. After the fall of the military regime in 1983, Massera was convicted of having committed crimes against humanity. He served five years of a life sentence before President **Carlos Saúl Menem** granted him amnesty. *See also* DIRTY WAR; HUMAN RIGHTS IN ARGENTINA.

MAZZA, MIGUEL ÁNGEL (1909–1955). This Argentine army doctor was **Juan Domingo Perón**'s personal physician and a friend of Evita and Perón. On 14 October 1945, while Perón was held prisoner on **Martín García Island**, Mazza paid him a visit under the pretext of examining the prisoner. During the visit, Perón entrusted Mazza with the task of delivering a letter to Evita. In the letter, he promised that they would marry as soon as he retired from the army. The letter also mentioned the visit of Mazza and the fact that Perón would try to return to Buenos Aires by any means necessary. The visit gave Mazza and Perón the opportunity to devise a plan that would lead to Perón's release. As part of the maneuver, Mazza reported that the prisoner's health was compromised due to the unfavorable climate on the island. This resulted in the transfer of Perón to the Military Hospital in the Palermo neighborhood of Buenos Aires on the morning of 17 October 1945. Later that day Perón was released. Evita, who was anxious, had received the letter, and Mazza arranged for her to see Perón while he was in hospital. Mazza remained loyal to Perón and played an important role in the development of the Argentine Red Cross. *See also* PERONIST LOYALTY DAY; WEDDING OF EVITA.

MEDINA DEL CAMPO. Located in the autonomous community of Castile and León, Spain, this town welcomed Evita on 11 June 1947. The first lady of Argentina together with **María del Carmen Polo y Martínez-Valdés** and their entourage arrived in Medina del Campo at 3:45 p.m. Their first stop was at the Castle of La Mota, where they were welcomed by Pilar Primo de Rivera and other local authorities. The distinguished guests were given a tour of the castle, had lunch, and later continued touring the premises until 5:55 p.m. *See also* RAINBOW TOUR; SEGOVIA.

MEIR, GOLDA (1898–1978). Born Goldie Mabovitch in Kiev, Ukraine, Golda Meir was a renowned Israeli politician. Due to the Kiev pogroms, Meir and her family fled Ukraine in 1906 and immigrated to Milwaukee, Wisconsin. There she attended the Milwaukee Normal School and later became a leader in the Milwaukee Labor Zionist Party. In 1921, she and her husband, Morris Myerson, emigrated to Palestine. From the 1940s through the 1960s, Meir held various positions in the Israeli government, serving as prime minister of the country between 1969 and 1974. She visited Argentina in April 1951 in her capacity as labor minister. The reason for her visit was to thank Evita personally for the help the **Fundación Eva Perón** had given to the newly formed State of Israel. During the 1948 Arab–Israeli War, the foundation had sent humanitarian aid to Israel. Later in her life, Meir would remember the foundation's furniture, agricultural tools, sheets, and blankets that were still being used in Israeli kibbutzim.

MENDÉ, RAÚL (1918–1963). Born Raúl Mende, this Argentine cardiologist studied medicine at the National University of **Córdoba**, completing his studies in 1942. His interest in writing led him to publish his first book of poems in 1944. A supporter of **Peronism**, he became mayor of the city of Esperanza, Santa Fe Province, in 1946 and was later appointed provincial secretary of social welfare. He traveled to Buenos Aires to participate in the reform of the **Argentine Constitution of 1949** and remained there on account of his appointment as secretary of culture of Buenos Aires. By that time, Mendé had authored at least three books on Peronism. In November of the same year, President **Juan Domingo Perón** appointed him minister of technical affairs. In that capacity, he was in charge of overseeing, among other government agencies, the Argentine Atomic Energy Commission, the Argentine Council of Scientific Research, and the Argentine Antarctic Institute. He also led the **Escuela Superior Peronista** and contributed to writing some of Perón's speeches. He became very close to Perón and Evita and was held in high regard by them. Mendé, in return, did not miss out on any opportunity to praise them to the skies. Legend has it that Evita started calling him Mendé instead of Mende, his real surname, so as not to confuse him with another cabinet member by the name of **Armando Méndez de San Martín**. Seemingly, his influential position in the government and in the Peróns' private life led to the summoning of the renowned American oncologist Dr. **George Pack** to operate on Evita. Likewise, Mendé was part of the commission that approved the work of Dr. **Pedro Ara** on Evita's corpse. His good writing skills served him well when it came to rewriting *La razón de mi vida* (*My Mission in Life*). *See also* ALBERTELLI, JORGE.

MÉNDEZ DE SAN MARTÍN, ARMANDO (1902–1958). Armando Méndez de San Martín was an Argentine physician and a staunch **Peronist**. His close ties to Evita seemingly furthered his political career. He was first appointed administrator of the **Society of Beneficence of Buenos Aires** and then head of the Directorate General for Social Assistance. In 1950, he was named minister of education following Dr. **Oscar Ivanissevich**'s resignation.

Two significant undertakings marked Méndez de San Martín's tenure: the "Peronization" of school textbooks and the centralization of education. The former saw the transformation of the public school system into a site of Peronist indoctrination. Following Evita's death, for instance, homage to her memory was compulsory, and her ghostwritten autobiography *La razón de mi vida* (*My Mission in Life*) became mandatory reading in schools. The centralization of education was facilitated through an educational reform that granted the state the right to regulate both the internal administration of the universities and the content of the courses offered. Students had to be versed in the Peronist doctrine and the fundamentals of the **Argentine Constitution of 1949**. This of course enraged the university student body. Dr. Méndez de San Martín was the founder of the **Unión de Estudiantes Secundarios**. During his tenure, the Universidad Nacional Obrera opened its doors. *See also* UNIVERSIDAD TECONOLÓGICA NACIONAL.

MENDOZA. Located 1,037 kilometers (644 miles) west of Buenos Aires, Mendoza is the capital of its eponymous Argentine province. Mendoza is linked to the independence movement in Spanish America as General **José de San Martín**, who was the governor of modern-day Mendoza, San Juan, and San Luis Provinces, organized the Army of the Andes in this city to cross the Andes Mountains and liberate Chile from Spanish rule in 1817. The province of Mendoza is worldwide known for its wine, and the city holds an annual wine festival to celebrate the grape harvest. The massive event, which has been celebrated since 1936, features music, parades, and shows that last for a week. Evita visited Mendoza for the first time in 1936, while she was touring the **interior of Argentina** with the Compañía de Comedias Muñoz-Franco-Álvarez. She made her Mendoza debut with the play *Baturros y más baturros* (Nothing but Stubborn People) at the Municipal Theater on 30 July. Nine years later, in 1945, she returned to Mendoza, but this time as the wife of the presidential candidate **Juan Domingo Perón** and on board the *Descamisado* Train. Once she became the first lady of Argentina, she visited the city and the province of Mendoza on several occasions. She was on an official visit to the province together with Perón from 8 to 11 April 1947 to take part in the wine festival. On 16 August 1950, Evita visited Mendoza to celebrate the 100th anniversary of the death of General José de San Martín.

MENEM, CARLOS SAÚL (1930–2021). Born in the northwestern province of La Rioja, Argentina, Menem obtained his law degree from the National University of **Córdoba** in 1955. While he was a law student, he met Evita and **Juan Domingo Perón** in Buenos Aires. His interest in **Peronism** led him to become an active member of the **Juventud Peronista**. In 1973, he was elected governor of La Rioja but was deposed in 1976 by the military coup d'état that toppled the government of President **Isabel Martínez de Perón**. In 1989, Menem was elected president of Argentina. During his mandate, he opted for moving away from the traditional policies of Peronism; instead, he embraced neoliberalism as a way to recover from stagnation and hyperinflation. State companies were privatized, subsidies removed, the Argentine peso dollarized, public employment cut, and union power reduced. With these measures, he managed to reduce the inflation rate and provide political stability. However, the unemployment rate was still high and low-income earners were deeply affected by these neoliberal policies. Despite this, he was reelected in 1995 and governed the country until 1999.

MERCANTE, DOMINGO ALFREDO (1898–1976). This Argentine military officer and politician became one of the closest allies of **Juan Domingo Perón**. Encouraged by his mother, Mercante studied hard to pass the entrance examination for the Argentine Military Academy, where he was admitted in 1915. Four years later, he graduated with a commission as a second lieutenant in the artillery and served in the Argentine provinces of **Córdoba**, Corrientes, Buenos Aires, and Neuquén. While he was serving in the Neuquén Convuco Center, Mercante met General **Edelmiro Julián Farrell**, who later recruited him to the Inspectorate of Mountain Troops in Buenos Aires. Mercante struck up a friendship with Perón, who had also been appointed to the inspectorate. The two men found out that they had similar political ideas, namely, improving the lives of workers and their families. Mercante's allegiance to Perón was sealed when he became part of the **Grupo de Oficiales Unidos**. Apparently, the two men laid the foundations of what became known as **Peronism**. Mercante played a pivotal role in the liberation of Perón on 17 October 1945 as he planned and led successful mobilizations for Perón's release. Promoted to full colonel in December 1945, Mercante accepted Perón's offer of the nomination as his running mate for the presidential election. In January 1946, however, Mercante asked to be dropped from the ticket; instead, he ran for governor of Buenos Aires Province. In 1946, while Perón was elected president, Mercante became governor. During his administration, land reform was accelerated, 1,600 schools were built, and 146 housing developments were completed. Mercante's work improved the lives of the citizens of the province, and as his popularity grew, he started to be considered Perón's "natural" successor, which in turn became his liability. He fell from grace and was expelled from the **Partido Peronista** in 1953. As for his private life, in 1922 Mercante married **María Elena Caporale**, with whom he had two children, but Mercante also had numerous extramarital affairs, including his relationship with Evita's private secretary, **Isabel Ernst**. *See also* PERONIST LOYALTY DAY.

MI MENSAJE. *Mi mensaje* (*In My Own Words*) is a book attributed to Evita. It was written between 1951 and 1952 while she was confined to bed due to her illness, but the manuscript seemed to have disappeared until the Argentine newspaper *La Nación* announced its auction on 20 September 1987. The volume consists of 30 brief chapters in which Evita denounces the enemies of **Peronism** and addresses such topics as her political interests, her ambitions, and the role of the church in society. The first edition of the book was published in 1987 and the second in 1994. The latter was edited by the Peronist militant

Alberto Schprejer. Following the publication of the book, Evita's sisters, Blanca and Erminda, initiated legal proceedings against Schprejer since they believed Evita was not its author. In 2006, the jury confirmed that Evita was indeed the author of *Mi mensaje*. The definitive version of *Mi mensaje* was launched by the Argentine government on 31 July 2012 in a ceremony commemorating the 60th anniversary of Evita's death. *See also* DUARTE, BLANCA; DUARTE, ERMINDA.

MIRANDA, MIGUEL (1891–1953). The Argentine businessman and economist Miguel Miranda was the director of the **Argentine Institute for the Promotion of Trade** between 1946 and 1949 and the president of the Central Bank of Argentina between 1946 and 1947. Allegedly, it was thanks to Miranda that Evita got a loan from the Central Bank to buy *Democracia*, the first newspaper to be part of the state media conglomerate **Alea S.A.** In 1947, Perón named Miranda chair of the National Economic Council. In that capacity, Miranda promoted the nationalization of companies and public services, hitherto held by foreign capital, and accelerated the industrialization of the country. By 1949, Argentina's economy was under pressure, and thus Perón saw the need to make some changes in his economic policy. As a result, Miranda eventually resigned and was replaced by Roberto Ares and Alfredo Gómez Morales. Miranda retired to Montevideo in Uruguay and spent his last years there.

MONACO. The second smallest sovereign state in Europe and one the most luxurious places on the French Riviera, the Principality of Monaco was Evita's vacation spot during her **Rainbow Tour**. After her visit to Paris, she took a break and traveled with **Alberto Dodero** to Monaco, where she stayed at the Monte-Carlo Beach Hotel. Although Evita was on vacation in Monaco, her presence did not go unnoticed by the members of the Government Council, who awarded her the Gold Medal of the Principality of Monaco. Years after Evita's death, the Greek shipping magnate Aristotle Onassis bragged that he had slept with Evita in Monaco and that afterward he had rewarded her by donating money to one of her favorite charities. It is likely that Evita and Onassis met since he had lived in Argentina in his youth and was a friend of Dodero, but the meeting was not necessarily a sexual encounter.

MONTONEROS. In the years following the 1955 coup d'état, Argentina was affected by civil violence unleashed by the confrontation between the military and their opponents. The 1960s and 1970s saw the emergence of a left-wing Peronist guerrilla group dubbed the Montoneros. The name of the group referred to the *montoneras*—the paramilitary groups formed during the wars of independence from Spain that took place in Argentina and other Latin American countries in the 19th century. Most of the Montoneros had not been part of the original Peronist movement. Indeed, the majority were not working- but middle- and upper-middle class students and professionals. Their goal was to overthrow the military government and to restore **Juan Domingo Perón** to power. They were originally permeated with nationalist, Catholic, and socialist ideologies. However, as time passed on, the movement tilted more to socialist ideals and embraced the Peronist beliefs in social justice, economic development free of foreign influence, and political independence; in other words, they saw **Peronism** as a movement of national liberation. Moreover, they formed alliances with other leftist guerrilla groups, such as the Fuerzas Armadas Revolucionarias (Armed Revolutionary Forces) and the Ejército Revolucionario del Pueblo (People's Revolutionary Army). The Montoneros venerated not only Perón but also Evita. If the image of Evita represented the people's struggle against the oligarchy in the late 1940s and early 1950s, the late Evita became a symbol of liberation and political change for the Montoneros. She represented their anger, hatred, and unity against the military repression.

Their modus operandi usually consisted of kidnappings, killings, and robberies that particularly targeted the military. The group was notorious for kidnapping, interrogating, and killing former president **Pedro Eugenio**

Aramburu in 1970. The Montoneros considered Aramburu responsible for the 1956 León Suárez massacre—the unlawful shooting of a group of Peronist militants—and for the theft and disappearance of Evita's body in 1955. Furthermore, in 1974, they kidnapped Aramburu's corpse to demand the repatriation of Evita's body, which had been outside of Argentina for 19 years. When Perón returned to Argentina to run for president for the third time in 1973, there was a massive gathering near Ezeiza International Airport in Buenos Aires to welcome him back from an 18-year exile in Spain. The Montoneros were among the crowd. Undercover right-wing Peronist snipers opened fire on the crowd, targeting the Montoneros. This event, known as the **Ezeiza massacre**, marked a definitive rupture between left- and right-wing Peronist supporters. The confrontation between the two sides continued in the form of more killings and also kidnappings. By 1974, Perón tilted more toward the Peronist right, expelling the Montoneros from the **Partido Justicialista**, an action that increased the power of the extreme Peronist right. The latter was represented by the Argentine Anti-Communist Alliance or **Triple A**, set up by **José López Rega**. The Montoneros continued to be active until 1977. During the military dictatorship that ruled Argentina between 1976 and 1983, they launched major operations against the armed forces, but they were actively persecuted and eventually dismantled. *See also* BODY OF EVITA; DIRTY WAR; HUMAN RIGHTS IN ARGENTINA; LIBERATING REVOLUTION.

MONUMENT OF THE *DESCAMISADO*. To commemorate Evita's passing in 1952, a colossal monument was to be built in a park on Figeroa Alcorta Avenue in Buenos Aires. Under the supervision of Evita, the project was originally intended to honor **Peronist Loyalty Day** and the *descamisados*. The monument would comprise a mausoleum beneath the giant statue of a worker or *descamisado*—approximately 138 meters (450 feet) tall. The Italian painter and sculptor **Leone Tomassi** was the artist behind the construction of the monument. When Evita passed away, the government decided to modify the project. The monument was to be named after Evita, and her embalmed body was to be displayed in the mausoleum instead of the body of a worker, as was first proposed. However, all plans came to an end with the emergence of the **Liberating Revolution** in 1955. *See also* NATIONAL COMMISSION FOR THE EVA PERÓN MONUMENT.

MOORI KOENIG, CARLOS EUGENIO DE. A virulent anti-**Peronist**, Colonel Carlos Eugenio de Moori Koenig was the head of Argentine military intelligence when he abducted the body of Evita from the headquarters of the **Confederación General del Trabajo** on 24 November 1955. His duty was to bury Evita's corpse in the Chacarita Cemetery in Buenos Aires, but instead he kept it in his private office and showed it to visitors as a personal trophy. Rumors had it that Moori Koenig had been infatuated with Evita when she was alive and that he had developed a sick obsession with her corpse. Upon finding out what was happening, President **Pedro Eugenio Aramburu** instructed that the **body of Evita** should be removed from Moori Koenig's care. The colonel was allegedly sent to a prison in the town of Comodoro Rivadavia in the Argentine Patagonia. *See also* CABANILLAS, HÉCTOR EDUARDO.

MORÓN AIRPORT. This Argentine airport is located in the county of Morón, Buenos Aires Province. Evita departed from this airport toward Europe in June 1947. *See also* RAINBOW TOUR.

MOVIMIENTO NACIONAL JUSTICIALISTA. *See* PARTIDO JUSTICIALISTA (PJ)/JUSTICIALIST PARTY.

***MUNDO ARGENTINO*.** Evita graced the front cover of *Mundo Argentino* on 3 April 1940. The photograph depicts a portrait of a serious Evita. **Haynes Publishing** began issuing this women's magazine in the 1920s. Its content included general information, short stories, comics, as well as fashion and home sections.

MUÑOZ AZPIRI, FRANCISCO (1915–1968). This Argentine writer, librettist, and journalist wrote many of Evita's scripts during her career as a radio actress. He met Evita at **Radio Belgrano** in 1943 after she secured the Secretariat of Communications' approval to perform her radio series *Heroínas de la historia* (Heroines in History). He, together with Alberto Insúa, wrote most of the scripts of the aforementioned radio series. In 1944, Evita introduced him to **Juan Domingo Perón**, who appointed him head of the propaganda department at the **Secretariat of Information and Press** in June that year. From June 1944 until October 1945, Muñoz Azpiri would collaborate with Evita on the radio series *Hacia un futuro mejor* (Toward a Better Future), a propaganda program that furthered **Peronism** and extoled the figure of Perón. During Perón's presidential campaign, Muñoz Azpiri crafted some of the slogans of Peronism and wrote some of the leader's speeches. As Evita became more involved in politics, he was in charge of writing all her speeches. He also accompanied her on her 1947 European tour in his capacity as speechwriter. *See also* RAINBOW TOUR.

MURALS OF EVITA. In 2011, President **Cristina Fernández de Kirchner** inaugurated two metal cutout murals of Evita hanging from the Ministry of Social Development Building on 9 de Julio Avenue in Buenos Aires. Inspired by **Numa Ayrinhac**'s official portrait of Evita, the south-facing mural was unveiled at 8:25 p.m. —the official **time of Evita's death**—on 26 July to commemorate the 59th anniversary of her death. The north-facing portrait, which features a militant Evita, was unveiled on 24 August of the same year to celebrate the 60th anniversary of Evita's agreement to be **Juan Domingo Perón**'s running mate for the 1952 presidential election. A famous photograph of Evita taken at the 1951 August rally known as the **Cabildo Abierto** served as a model for the north-facing mural. The murals were designed by the sculptor **Alejandro Marmo**, who worked closely with the artist **Daniel Santoro**, while Fernández de Kirchner oversaw and backed the project. Weighing 15 tons each, the murals are 31 meters (101 feet) high and 24 meters (78 feet) wide.

South-facing metal cutout mural of Evita hanging from the Ministry of Social Development Building on 9 de Julio Avenue in Buenos Aires. Inspired by Numa Ayrinhac's official portrait of Evita, the mural was unveiled on 26 July 2011 to commemorate the 59th anniversary of her death.

North-facing metal cutout mural of a militant Evita hanging from the Ministry of Social Development Building on 9 de Julio Avenue in Buenos Aires. This mural was unveiled on 24 August 2011 to celebrate the 60th anniversary of Evita's agreement to be Juan Domingo Perón's running mate for the 1952 presidential election.

MY MISSION IN LIFE. Translated by Ethel Cherry from the original ***La razón de mi vida***, *My Mission in Life* was published in 1953 by Vantage Press in New York. If at first U.S. publishers were eager to publish the translation of Evita's book, the negotiations for publications rights were dropped when they realized that the actual topic of the book was **Peronism**. This was taken as an offense by the Argentine government, and gatherings were organized across the country as a way of protesting against the U.S. publishers. Despite the controversies surrounding it, the book was published but received hardly any reviews in the U.S. press due to the political, diplomatic, and ideological tension between the United States and Argentina that dated back to World War II. The few newspaper articles that reviewed the book classified it as a eulogy of Peronism, tapping into negative aspects of the Argentine government. For example, the *San Antonio Express*'s review was contained in an article that discussed press censorship in Argentina, linking the book with a government that controlled press freedom. Associations of this type inevitably conditioned the reception and review of Evita's book in the United States.

In relation to the translation itself, the rewriting of *La razón de mi vida* was produced under the influence of the image of Evita constructed in previous years in the United States. Although *My Mission in Life* does not portray Evita antagonistically, she remains foreign, distant, and a representative of a political ideology that was not accepted in the United States. This characterization was achieved through the use of translation strategies, namely, cultural borrowing and exoticism, supported by footnotes that tended to favor the specificities of the source text and its cultural context rather than conforming to values dominating U.S. culture. The footnotes and translation strategies used in *My Mission in Life* tend to evoke a sense of the foreign rather than to combat the alienating effect of the foreign text. The result was that the interlingual translation kept the target reader at a distance instead of evoking an emotional response and sympathies for Evita as the original did in Argentina and in Spain.

MYTH OF EVITA. *See* PERONIST AND ANTI-PERONIST MYTHS; POLITICAL MYTH; WHITE AND BLACK MYTHS.

N

NATIONAL COMMISSION FOR THE EVA PERÓN MONUMENT. Chaired by the Argentine senator **Juanita Larrauri**, the National Commission for the Eva Perón Monument was set up in July 1952 following the enactment of Law 14,124. The law provided for both the building of a monument in honor of Evita in Buenos Aires and the placement of the monument replicas in each province of Argentina. The monument in Buenos Aires was going to be Evita's final resting place. The mock-up, drawings, and final plans of the monument were exhibited to the public at the Ministry of Labor and Social Welfare on 26 July 1953. A statue of Evita, the statues of two *descamisados*, a secular basilica, and elaborate doors would be part of this impressive monument, which would be erected in the neighborhood of Recoleta, Buenos Aires. The project was funded through donations. The company Wayss y Fritag was in charge of it, and construction work started in January 1955. However, it was never completed due to the ousting of President **Juan Domingo Perón**. *See also* HISTORICAL MUSEUM 17 OCTOBER; LIBERATING REVOLUTION; MONUMENT OF THE *DESCAMISADO*; TOMASSI, LEONE.

NATIONAL TECHNOLOGICAL UNIVERSITY. *See* UNIVERSIDAD TECNOLÓGICA NACIONAL.

NAVARRO, FANNY (1920–1971). The Argentine actress Fanny Navarro started her artistic career as a tango singer. She made her film debut in 1937 with Luis José Moglia Barth's movie *Melodías porteñas* (Buenos Aires Melodies). Two years later, she was the leading character in Adelqui Migliar's film *Ambición* (Ambition). However, by 1949, the year she met Evita's brother Juancito, Navarro had not been able to secure a contract for three years. Her romantic relationship with Juancito would soon boost her career, however. In the same year, she was cast as a supporting actress in two films, *Mujeres que bailan* (Women Who Dance) and *Morir en su ley* (To Die in His Law). Her acquaintance with Juancito led her to become a staunch supporter of **Peronism** and a member of the **Partido Peronista Femenino**. Although committed to Peronism, she continued working in the Argentine film industry. Seeing Navarro's political potential, Evita appointed her president of the **Ateneo Cultural Eva Perón** and instructed her on politics. Navarro studied Evita's speeches, accompanied Evita in the daily activities of the **Fundación Eva Perón**, and stood by Evita at several events. The death of Juancito in 1953 was a setback for her artistic career since it became impossible for her to find work. Following the ousting of **Juan Domingo Perón** in 1955, Navarro was interrogated by Próspero Fernández Alvariño, who had exhumed Juancito's remains and cut his head off. During the interrogation, Fernández Alvariño showed her Juancito's head. The event had such an impact on her that she never fully recovered from the shock. *See also* DUARTE, JUAN "JUANCITO" RAMÓN.

NEW ARGENTINA. Introduced by the Peronist propaganda machine, the *New Argentina* referred to the period that began with the election of **Juan Domingo Perón** to the presidency in 1946. As Perón and Evita did not shy away from promoting their achievements, the concept was frequently included in their public speeches. In practice, the New Argentina was an umbrella term that included the political, economic, and social reforms that the Peronist government implemented to improve the living conditions of the working class. A propaganda documentary, which was titled *Argentina de hoy* (The Argentina of Today) and depicted the New Argentina through the achievements of Perón and Evita, was screened across the country in 1949.

NICOLINI, EMMA (1933–). Daughter of Oscar Lorenzo Nicolini, Emma Nicolini replaced **Isabel Ernst** as Evita's private secretary in 1949. Evita enjoyed the company of young Emma, who escorted her on official visits throughout Argentina.

NICOLINI, OSCAR LORENZO (1889–1956). This medical doctor, politician, and president of the Argentine Football Association between 1948 and 1949 was one of Evita's closest friends. Despite graduating from the University of Buenos Aires as a medical doctor, Nicolini started working at the Argentine postal service in the city of **Junín** in 1921. Seemingly, it was through his good offices that **Elisa Duarte**, Evita's eldest sister, secured a job in the Junín post office. After the military seized power in Argentina in 1943, Colonel **Aníbal Francisco Imbert** became secretary of communications and Nicolini his assistant. One of the regulations introduced by the military government was that actors should obtain a permit from the Secretariat of Communications to be able to work. As it was difficult to meet Colonel Imbert, actors approached Nicolini. Like her peers, Evita went to Nicolini to submit a radio broadcast project. With the project approved, she secured a five-year contract with **Radio Belgrano**. As a result, Evita and Nicolini forged a close friendship that would last until her demise. When **Juan Domingo Perón** became president of Argentina, Nicolini was appointed to the strategic post of secretary of communications, which eventually led to his position as minister of communications in 1949. As such, he held responsibility for improving telecommunications in Argentina, and one of his biggest achievements was facilitating the introduction of television broadcasting in the country. When Evita became bedridden due to her terminal illness, Nicolini would visit her daily until she passed away on 26 July 1952. *See also* REVOLUTION OF 1943.

NOTICIAS GRÁFICAS. Following the military coup d'état in September 1930, the evening paper *Crítica* was suspended. The then owner of *La Nación*, Jorge Mitre, saw the opportunity to fill the gap in the market left by *Crítica* and thus launched *Noticias Gráficas* in Buenos Aires on 10 June 1931. While this popular daily tabloid benefited from the absence of *Crítica*, once the latter returned to the market in 1932, *Noticias Gráficas* suffered serious financial difficulties. In 1938, the paper was bought by José Agusti, who remained its owner and editor-in-chief until 1947. Together with *Crítica*, ***La Razón***, ***La Vanguardia***, ***La Prensa***, ***El Mundo***, and *La Nación*, *Noticias Gráficas* supported **Juan Domingo Perón**'s opposition during the 1945–1946 presidential campaign. Under pressure from the Peronist government, Agusti decided to negotiate the transfer of his paper to the state in 1947. Not only did he get a large sum of money, he was also appointed ambassador to the 1948 UN General Assembly in **Paris**. In the meantime, *Noticias Gráficas* became part of **Democracia S.A.** *See also* ALEA S.A.; ANTI-ARGENTINE ACTIVITIES CONGRESSIONAL COMMITTEE.

OLIGARCA. See OLIGARQUÍA.

OLIGARCH. See OLIGARQUÍA.

OLIGARCHY. See OLIGARQUÍA.

OLIGARQUÍA. Argentine historical revisionists employed the term *oligarquía* (oligarchy) to refer to elite groups linked to the export of raw materials. According to historical revisionism, the mentality of the *oligarquía* was marked by liberal ideology to the detriment of national traditions. Historical revisionists also considered that because history was written by the *oligarquía*, it was inaccurate. As a result, they believed that official history had left out the participation of the people or *pueblo* in the development of the nation. Widely used in Peronist discourse, the terms *oligarquía*, *oligarca* (oligarch), and *pueblo*, together with ***vendepatria*** and ***cipayo***, were popularized by the Argentine revisionist **Arturo Martín Jauretche**. **Juan Domingo Perón** used this word to refer to those people and institutions that responded to the dictates of certain countries and defended the oligarchic economic model. In other words, he understood oligarchic governments as those that exploited their own people and acted as envoys of imperialist countries. Hence, in Peronist ideology, *oligarca* is a synonym for traitor, *vendepatria*, *cipayo*, and ***antipueblo***. The terms *oligarquía* and *pueblo* were discussed by Evita in the lectures she gave at the **Escuela Superior Peronista** in 1951. Referring to the Argentine *oligarquía* in **La razón de mi vida** (***My Mission in Life***), Evita states, "Our people have lived for more than a century under the rule of oligarchic governments whose main task was not to serve the people but rather to serve the interests of a privileged minority, perhaps refined and cultured, but sordidly selfish."

OLIVOS PRESIDENTIAL RESIDENCE. This residence currently serves as the Argentine president's official living quarters. Located in Vicente López County, to the north of Buenos Aires, the Olivos Presidential Residence is an estate of 32 hectares (79 acres) that comprises a manor-type house and elegantly manicured parkland. The design of the house was commissioned to Prilidiano Pueyrredón in 1851 and the building was completed in 1854. In 1913, the then owner of the estate, Carlos Villate Olaguer, bequeathed it to the government of Argentina on condition that it would be used as the president's official summer residence. During the presidency of **Juan Domingo Perón**, a screening room, an amphitheater, tennis courts, a reflecting pool, and a greenhouse were added to the amenities of the residence. After Evita's death, Perón opened the facilities to the girls' branch of the **Unión de Estudiantes Secundarios**. Allegedly, Perón had an affair with a 14-year-old girl who often trained at the residence. On 1 July 1974, Perón passed away at the Olivos Presidential Residence. Following her husband's death, President **Isabel Martínez de Perón** organized the return of Evita's embalmed body from **Madrid** and put it on public display next to the closed casket of Perón in the crypt of the Olivos Residence. Their bodies remained there until March 1976, when President **Jorge Rafael Videla**, who was unwilling to occupy the residence while the caskets were still there, decided to remove them. *See also* BODY OF EVITA; DUARTE FAMILY TOMB; RIVAS, NÉLIDA "NELLY" HAYDEÉ.

ONDANÍA. Evita featured on the cover of this magazine on 7 July 1944. The cover image is a portrait of Evita showing a timid smile. She is wearing her hair up and the tailor-made suit that would characterize her in later years.

ONE-HUNDRED-PESO BANKNOTE. On 25 July 2012, President **Cristina Fernández de Kirchner** unveiled a new 100-peso banknote bearing the portrait of Evita to commemorate the 60th anniversary of her death. The banknote is noteworthy due to two reasons. First, it was the first time a woman graced an Argentine bill. Secondly, the note had its origin in the design of a five-peso bill that the mint had planned to make after Evita's death on 26 July 1952 but which was never issued.

ONLY THE VALIANT. *See LA CARGA DE LOS VALIENTES.*

PACK, GEORGE (1898–1969). This American oncologist received his medical degree from Yale University in 1922. He joined the Memorial Cancer Center of New York—currently known as the Memorial Sloan Kettering Cancer Center—*as* an intern in 1926. After training at the Curie Foundation Institute of Radium in **Paris**, he returned to the cancer center as a resident surgeon in 1928. He was appointed chief of the Gastritis Service at the same center, developing it into a true oncologic service. Dr. Pack was highly regarded, and physicians from all over the world went to the Memorial Cancer Center to watch him operate and to study his methods of treating cancer. He was invited as a keynote speaker at a cancer conference in Buenos Aires organized by the Argentine oncologist **Abel Canónico** in 1951. When the news that Evita had cervical cancer reached **Juan Domingo Perón**, he wanted the best oncologist to operate on his wife. Dr. Canónico was consulted as to who would be the best surgeon to perform a hysterectomy on Evita and he recommended Dr. Pack, who was summoned to Buenos Aries in the strictest confidence. After examining Evita, he agreed to carry out the procedure. The hysterectomy was due on 6 November 1951 at one of the hospitals of the **Fundación Eva Perón**, the **Policlínico Presidente Perón** in Avellaneda, Buenos Aires Province. He performed extensive surgery because the cancer had spread to adjacent pelvic organs. Because his undertaking was a state secret and unknown even to Evita, Dr. Pack only entered the operating theater once Evita was anesthetized and left before she woke up. He remained in Argentina until Evita was stable. Dr. Pack never revealed his involvement in the operation while he was alive, and Evita died without knowing that he had performed surgery on her. *See also* ALBERTELLI, JORGE.

PALLAROLS CUNI, CARLOS. Carlos Pallarols Cuni was a famous Catalan silversmith who had migrated to Argentina with his family at an early age. Following Evita's death in 1952, he was commissioned to make a thin silver cover in the shape of a sleeping Evita to be placed on top of the casket that would contain her embalmed body. Pallarols never finished the project because President **Juan Domingo Perón** was toppled while he was working on it and the new authorities forced him to destroy his work. Pallarols melted the silver but managed to hide the molds. Pallarols's son, Juan Carlos Pallarols, recovered the molds and made a death mask of Evita in silver, which is now part of the exhibition of the Pallarols Museum in San Telmo, Buenos Aires. *See also* ARA, PEDRO; BODY OF EVITA; LIBERATING REVOLUTION.

PALMOU, JUANA. One of Evita's fashion assistants, Juana Palmou worked for the fashion house Paula Naletoff. Palmou's work was to have Evita's clothes ready and to advise her on each outfit for every hour and occasion. *See also* FERNÁNDEZ, MARÍA ASUNCIÓN "ASUNTA"; JAMANDREU, FRANCISCO "PACO" VICENTE; *TAILLEUR.*

PAMPA FILM. The former wool industry businessman Olegario Ferrando founded this film production company in partnership with Warner Bros. in Buenos Aires in 1936. Pampa Film was active for nine years and produced 27 films. Like most film studios in Argentina, Pampa Film followed the Hollywood star system. The studio hired well-established radio and theater artists and turned them into movie stars. Among their main stars were the actors Luis Sandrini and Mirtha Legrand. Evita worked for Pampa Film as a supporting actress and had a small role in *La carga de los valientes* (Only the Valiant), which was released on 12 June 1940.

PARIS. As part of her official visit to France, Evita visited the French capital from 21 July to 2 August 1947. On her arrival, she was welcomed by the French foreign minister, Georges Bidault; the Argentine ambassador to France, Julio Victorica Roca; and several Latin American ambassadors. She stayed at the famous Ritz Hotel, and to show the importance of her visit the Parisian authorities made Charles de Gaulle's car available to her during her stay. The day after her arrival, she attended a luncheon hosted by the French president, Vincent Auriol, at the Castle of Rambouillet, an event that propelled a series of protests by the Communist Party, labor unions, and the Spanish Maquis exiled in France. Evita's busy schedule included a gala event at the Maison de l'Amérique Latine, a banquet hosted by Bidault, a tour of Notre Dame, presiding over the signing of the French–Argentine Treaty of Commerce that granted France a loan for the purchase of wheat and meat, as well as visits to social welfare institutions, the Palace of Versailles, and Napoleon's tomb. Apparently, Evita skipped a visit to the Louvre because she was exhausted, but despite her fatigue she did pay a visit to the House of Christian Dior and left her measurements with him. Evita became one of Dior's most loyal and important customers, having pieces from his collections flown from Paris to Buenos Aires. Because Evita could not speak French, she did not feel as comfortable in Paris as she had felt in Spain or Italy and depended on **Lillian Lagomarsino de Guardo**'s interpretation skills. *See also* RAINBOW TOUR.

PARODI, DELIA (1912–1991). Delia Parodi (née Delia Delfina Degliuomini) married Juan Carlos Parodi in 1942. The couple came into contact with **Juan Domingo Perón**, and they actively collaborated with the relief campaign to aid the victims of the **San Juan earthquake**. Delia eventually got an administrative job at the **Secretariat of Labor and Social Welfare** where she would meet Evita in 1946. Her incursion into politics took place in 1950, when Evita named her subdelegate of the **Partido Peronista Femenino (PPF)** to the Belgrano neighborhood in Buenos Aires. There she helped to open a local branch of the PPF and recruit women party members. Her second political undertaking was as a delegate of the PPF to San Luis Province, where her work resulted in the opening of 350 PPF local branches. In July 1951, she traveled to Buenos Aires together with her subdelegates to attend a special gathering the Peróns were holding for the provincial female party members. The year 1951 was also when she became a member of the PPF National Committee and was elected to Congress. After Evita's demise in 1952, Perón took over as head of the PPF, but after realizing that he could not lead the party as Evita had done, he named Delia the new leader of the PPF in 1953. With Perón's overthrow in 1955, the PPF was dissolved and Delia imprisoned. Pardoned by President **Arturo Frondizi**, she went into exile in Uruguay. *See also UNIDADES BÁSICAS.*

PARTIDO JUSTICIALISTA (PJ)/JUSTICIALIST PARTY. After the dissolution of the **Partido Peronista** in 1955, **Peronists** sought to reorganize their participation in Argentina's political life. This process resulted in the creation of the Partido Justicialista (PJ), which was outlawed by de facto president Juan Carlos Onganía in 1966. On account of the proscription of political parties during Onganía's government, **Juan Domingo Perón**, who was living in exile, proposed that **Peronism** should be organized in terms of an inclusive movement instead of a party. The movement came to be known as

Movimiento Nacional Justicialista (National Justicialist Movement) or MNJ, and its aims were to support Perón's return to Argentina, to unite the internal factions of Peronism, and to plan a Peronist electoral victory. By 1970, Perón started negotiations with the de facto government, but this was not looked upon favorably by all the factions of the MNJ. Amid internal clashes in the MNJ, 1972 saw the official resurgence of the PJ. In 1973, a coalition dubbed **Frente Justicialista de Liberación**, which included the PJ and other minor parties, supported **Héctor José Cámpora**'s presidential candidacy. Since then, the PJ has integrated with different electoral alliances that have led to the victory of several Peronist candidates, including **Carlos Saúl Menem, Néstor Kirchner, Cristina Fernández de Kirchner**, and **Alberto Ángel Fernández**. *See also* EZEIZA MASSACRE; FRENTE DE TODOS; FRENTE JUSTICIALISTA DE UNIDAD POPULAR (FREJUPO)/JUSTICIALIST FRONT OF POPULAR UNITY; FRENTE PARA LA VICTORIA (FPV)/FRONT FOR VICTORY.

PARTIDO LABORISTA (PL)/LABOR PARTY. Modeled after the British Labor Party, this party was created by the labor union leaders **Cipriano Reyes** and **Luis Gay**, among others, in October 1945 to back **Juan Domingo Perón**'s presidential bid. The platform of the party called for land reform, the nationalization of public services, women's suffrage, and social welfare. The PL was one of the three parties that supported Perón's candidacy. The others were the **Unión Cívica Radical**–Junta Renovadora and **Centros Independientes**. The PL, however, supplied the majority of the votes for Perón in the February 1946 presidential election. Seeing it as a potential threat to his leadership, Perón dissolved it on 23 May 1946 and founded his own party, the Partido Único de la Revolución. *See also* PARTIDO PERONISTA (PP)/PERONIST PARTY.

PARTIDO PERONISTA (PP)/PERONIST PARTY. Juan Domingo Perón won the 1946 presidential election thanks to the backing of three political parties—the **Partido Laborista**, the **Unión Cívica Radical**–Junta Renovadora, and **Centros Independientes**—which he dissolved by alleging that there were internal conflicts. On 13 June 1946, he founded his own political party, the Partido Único de la Revolución, which came to be known as Partido Peronista (PP) in July 1947. The reason for this change was that his advisers believed that "Único" lent a totalitarian tinge to the party name. From the outset, the PP was controlled strictly by its leader and was divided into union and political branches. Perón used the political branch as a counterweight to the union branch in order to retain the total control of the party. A separate women's branch called **Partido Peronista Femenino (PPF)** was created under Evita's leadership in July 1949. Empowered by the constitution of the party, Perón resolved party disputes, supervised the choice of party leaders, set the agenda for meetings at all levels, and selected candidates for electoral offices. Perón, however, neglected the organization-building aspect of the PP as he did not believe in the usefulness of having a party. This eventually backfired on the PP when Perón was ousted in 1955 and President **Pedro Eugenio Aramburu** dissolved the Peronist parties with ease. In 1958, a political party under the name **Partido Justicialista**, led by Perón from the exile, emerged. *See also* JUVENTUD PERONISTA (JP)/PERONIST YOUTH; PERONISM.

PARTIDO PERONISTA FEMENINO (PPF)/PERONIST WOMEN'S PARTY. Success in obtaining **female suffrage** led to the foundation of the Partido Peronista Femenino (PPF) on 29 July 1949. It was set up as the women's branch of the **Partido Peronista (PP)**. The party was under the leadership of Evita, and its motto was unconditional devotion and loyalty to **Juan Domingo Perón**. At first, the newly formed party was called Movimiento Peronista Femenino (Peronist Women's Movement), and the change of name to Partido Peronista Femenino took place around May 1950. One of the PPF's aims was to promote female education and culture in the belief that women were de facto educators of their children. Evita's stance was that women should contribute actively to national life but without altering the traditional gender roles in society. In other words, Evita's intention was not to destabilize patriarchy. Her unorthodox feminist approach toward women's participation in politics did not undermine the impact of her actions on Argentine women. Her intervention in this matter resulted in the unprecedented participation of women in politics, both as voters and candidates in elections.

The first national assembly of the PPF took place on 26 July 1949 at the Cervantes Theater in Buenos Aires. During the assembly, it was agreed that the PPF would be one of the fundamental pillars of Peronism—together with the PP and the **Confederación General del Trabajo**—but with a degree of independence from its masculine counterpart. Unlike the PP, the organization of the PPF relied strongly on the *unidades básicas*, local party branches established nationwide. One of Evita's first undertakings was to carry out a national census of Peronist women. The census was overseen by appointed female Peronist delegates to all provinces and territories in the country. The aim of the census was not only to recruit female Peronist sympathizers but also to assist them in processing their voting papers and to address any personal, work, or health-related issues. By 1952, the PPF had registered approximately 500,000 members. In the 1951 Argentine general election, 109 candidates of the PPF were elected to offices, including 23 national deputies and six national senators. After Evita's death in 1952, the PPF continued to operate until Perón's overthrow in 1955. *See also* LIBERATING REVOLUTION; PINK ROOM.

PARTIDO ÚNICO DE LA REVOLUCIÓN/ONLY PARTY OF THE REVOLUTION. *See* PARTIDO PERONISTA (PP)/PERONIST PARTY.

PELLICCIOTTA, PASCUAL (1905–1985). Pascual Pellicciotta was a well-known Argentine theater, radio, film, and television actor. He had a long, prolific career that started in the 1920s. Pellicciotta worked with Evita several times. He first met the young actress when they were both hired by the **Compañía Argentina de Comedias** in 1935. They met again in 1938 while performing with the **Compañía Argentina de Espectáculos Cómicos**. Eventually, Pellicciotta and Evita became the leading artists in the **Compañía de Teatro del Aire** in 1939. During his acting career, Pellicciotta was cast in numerous films. His last appearance was in Eduardo Mignogna's docufilm *Evita, quien quiera oír que oiga* (Evita, They Who Want to Listen, Let Them Listen), in which he shares his memories of Evita. *See also* BLOMBERG, HÉCTOR.

PENELLA DE SILVA, MANUEL (1906–1969). This Spanish journalist, writer, and diplomat had strong links with the Francoist dictatorship. While working as a foreign correspondent in Berlin, Zurich, and Buenos Aires, he reportedly served as an agent for the Francoist secret service. Apparently, he arrived in Argentina with the help of the Argentine ambassador to **Switzerland, Benito Pedro Llambí**. At least two accounts explain the purpose of his travel to Buenos Aires. One states that Penella was to write about the positive effects of **Peronism** on Argentine society and thereby improve the international image of the South American country. The other claims that he approached Llambí with the idea of writing about the participation of women in politics, and the phenomenon of Evita was obviously worthy of being reported. He arrived in Argentina in May 1947 and after several attempts eventually managed to talk to Evita. In their first meeting, he persuaded her to publish her memoirs. The plan was that he would ghostwrite them. Evita seemed enthusiastic about the idea, but she had to consult with **Juan Domingo Perón** before embarking on the project. After securing Perón's approval, Pennella met daily with Evita and followed her to the many events where her presence was required. Afterward, they would sit and discuss what he would write. When the manuscript was ready, Evita handed a copy over to Perón, who in turn consulted with Minster of Technical Affairs **Raúl Mendé** and Minister of Education **Armando Méndez de San Martín**. As a result, Penella's original manuscript was rewritten and parts of it discarded. He was disappointed with Evita. The final version, which was published in October 1951 under the title *La razón de mi vida* (*My Mission in Life*) by Peuser, bore little resemblance to the original text written by Penella. In 2019, Penella's son, Manuel Penella Heller, published a book titled *Evita y yo: la verdadera historia del libro de Eva Perón* (Evita and I: The True Story of Eva Perón's Book), in which he included the original manuscript.

PEÑA EVA PERÓN. The Peña Eva Perón was the name of a group of poets, writers, and labor union members who met with Evita at the **Hogar de la Empleada General San Martín** in Buenos Aires. The story goes that Evita thought that the devout Catholic and Peronist supporter **José María Castiñeira de Dios** was "a bit **oligarch**." Therefore, she asked him to spend some time with her to see how she worked. One day, a woman with sores in her body approached him. Castiñeira de Dios asked the doctor on duty what the cause of the sores could be. The doctor responded that the sores could be anything, even a sign of syphilis. Hence, Castiñeira de Dios attempted to stop Evita from kissing the woman. Furious, Evita scolded him and kissed the woman's sores. When he got home that night, Castiñeira de Dios could not sleep, questioning his Christianity. He was so impressed by Evita that he dedicated a poem to her titled "Alabanza" (Praise). Evita then suggested that they should get together with other poets and writers so that Castiñeira de Dios could read his poem to them. That marked the beginning of the Peña Eva Perón. The *peña* was a gathering in which they could recite poems, laugh, relax, joke, gossip, and discuss politics and social welfare in a relaxed atmosphere. *See also* CHÁVEZ, BENITO ENRIQUE "FERMÍN."

PEREYRA IRAOLA PARK. This urban park stretching out over 10,246 hectares (25,318 acres) was declared a biosphere reserve by UNESCO in 2008. It is spread over the districts of Berazategui, Ensenada, Florencio Varela, and **La Plata** in Buenos Aires Province. On 7 January 1948, President **Juan Domingo Perón** announced that the San Juan and Santa Rosa Ranches—that is, the lands owned by the Pereyra Iraola family and others—were to be expropriated to build a public park. As a result, on 24 February 1950, the Perón administration renamed these lands Rights of the Elderly Park in honor of the **Decalogue of the Rights of Seniors** announced by Evita. Perón, Evita, and the governor of Buenos Aires, **Domingo Alfredo Mercante**, were present at the opening ceremony in Berazategui. After Perón was ousted, the military government restored the park's original name. Since then, there have been several unsuccessful attempts to rename it once more Rights of the Elderly Park.

PERÓN, JUAN DOMINGO (1895–1974). Argentine army general, politician, and husband of Evita, Juan Domingo Perón was born in Lobos, Buenos Aires Province. He was the younger of two sons of Juana Sosa Toledo and Mario Tomás Perón. Leaving his family behind, his father moved from Lobos to the Patagonia region in 1901 to pursue his dream of owning land and becoming a rancher. The family rejoined in Patagonia a year later. In 1904, Perón and his brother were sent away to a boarding school in Buenos Aires, where they received a strict Catholic education. At the age of 16, Perón entered military school, where he trained as an officer, excelling in sports, including fencing, skiing, and boxing. Once he graduated in 1913, he was posted to different military garrisons around Argentina. The early 1920s were years of labor conflicts in the South American country, and the army, in the absence of a sufficient police force, was frequently called in to maintain the peace. As an army officer, Perón successfully mediated a prolonged labor conflict in 1920 at the British-owned Forestal Land, Timber and Railways Company in Santa Fe Province. In 1926, he was promoted to captain and returned to Buenos Aires. On 5 January 1929, he married **Aurelia Gabriela Tizón**. She accompanied Perón to Chile when he was assigned military attaché to that country in 1936. Following their return from Chile, she died of cervical cancer. In 1939, Perón was sent to Europe as a military observer to see the development of fascism and Nazism. He returned to Argentina in 1941 and joined a secret group of military officers called **Grupo de Oficiales Unidos (GOU)**. The GOU plotted the 1943 coup d'état that overthrew the ineffective and corrupt civilian government of President **Ramón Antonio Castillo**. The military regimes of the following three years came increasingly under the influence of Perón, who had shrewdly requested for himself only the minor post of secretary of labor and social welfare. In 1944, as a protégé of President **Edelmiro Julián Farrell**, Perón rose to the rank of minister of war and then vice president. Supported by the *descamisados* and some sectors of the army, Perón's influence increased. A 1945 effort from within the military to quash his influence proved unsuccessful. Associates in the labor unions rallied the workers of Greater Buenos Aires, and Perón was released from custody on 17 October 1945. That night, he addressed 300,000 people gathered in the **Plaza de Mayo** from the balcony of the **Pink House**. His speech was broadcast on the radio to the country. On 22 October 1945, Perón married Evita, whom he had met during the relief work triggered by the **San Juan earthquake** in 1944. The next year, Perón was elected president of Argentina and Evita became his most fervent supporter. Preaching industrialization and government intervention, Perón promoted a "third position" that was neither capitalism nor communism. He brought needed benefits to industrial workers in the form of wage increases and fringe benefits, nationalized the railroads and other utilities, and financed public works on a large scale. In 1951, he was reelected president and began his second term in June 1952. Like Perón's first wife, Evita died of cervical cancer on 26 July 1952. Evita's death, in tandem with the economic stagnation in the country, was a setback for Perón. He was overthrown and fled to Paraguay on 19 September 1955. He then moved to Venezuela, where he lived in exile until 1958. He met his third wife, **Isabel Martínez**, in a nightclub in Panama, married her in 1961, and settled in Spain until 1974. Although any support of Perón was proscribed in Argentina, he had great leverage over Argentine politics, and candidates he supported frequently won elections. Perón eventually managed to convince both liberals and conservatives that he was their best choice, and by 1973, millions of Argentines were clamoring for him to return. In 1973, **Héctor José Cámpora**, a stand-in for Perón, was elected president of Argentina, thus paving the way for Perón's comeback. When Perón flew in from Spain on 20 June, more than 3,000,000 people thronged the airport to welcome him back. His arrival turned to tragedy when right-wing **Peronists** opened fire on left-wing Peronists known as **Montoneros**, killing at least 13. Perón was elected president of Argentina for the third time and took office on 12 October 1973. However, his third term was plagued by chaos as right- and left-wing Peronist organizations fought openly for power. He succeeded in controlling violence for a time, but he died of a heart attack on 1 July 1974. *See also* EZEIZA MASSACRE; PARTIDO PERONISTA (PP)/PERONIST PARTY; PERONISM; PERONIST LOYALTY DAY; SECRETARIAT OF LABOR AND SOCIAL WELFARE.

PERONISM. This unique Argentine political and social movement was founded by **Juan Domingo Perón**. Peronism emerged during the period 1943–1945, when Perón was secretary of labor and social welfare. In that capacity, Perón rallied the urban working classes against the landowning class and foreign businesses, introduced a broad range of social welfare benefits in order to improve the working conditions of unionized workers, and settled industrial disputes in favor of the unions as long as they pledged political allegiance to him. With Perón as president of Argentina, Peronism became a form of **caudillismo** of industrial society through which a patron–client relationship was forged. While Perón was the indisputable leader of the movement, Evita was the spiritual mentor of Peronism, and they both exploited their charisma at mass rallies outside the **Pink House** in the **Plaza de Mayo**. The Peronist movement relied on the **Partido Peronista**, the **Partido Peronista Femenino**, and the **Confederación General del Trabajo**. Its ideology was known by the name *justicialismo*. Notwithstanding the fact that the three tenets of *justicialismo* were national sovereignty, economic independence, and social justice, the movement split Argentina up into two irreconcilable camps. For the vast majority of the working class, Peronism meant the betterment of their living and working conditions through a notable distribution of income and their integration into the ideological state apparatus and the political system. However, for the political opposition, non-Peronist intellectuals, and artists, Peronism was a traumatic experience as anyone who stood against Perón or Evita was considered a traitor. Peronism did not disappear with the ousting of Perón in 1955. In 1973 and under the name of the **Partido Justicialista**, Peronism swept back into power. The turmoil caused by left- and right-wing **Peronists** after Perón's demise in 1974 shook the basis of Peronism to such an extent that the Peronist government of **Isabel Martínez de Perón** was overthrown by a military coup d'état in 1976. Peronism made a comeback on the political scene when the Peronist candidate **Carlos Saúl Menem** won the 1989 presidential election. By embracing free-market-oriented policies, he managed to open Peronism up for the upper classes. Peronism has evolved and adopted different labels throughout time. Candidates with Peronist leanings who have become presidents of Argentina are **Eduardo Alberto Duhalde**, **Néstor Kirchner**, **Cristina Fernández de Kirchner**, and **Alberto Ángel Fernández**. *See also* HUMAN RIGHTS IN ARGENTINA; MONTONEROS.

PERONIST. A Peronist is either a supporter of **Juan Domingo Perón**, a member of the **Partido Justicialista**, or an adherent of Perón's policies. *See also* JUSTICIALISMO; PARTIDO PERONISTA (PP)/PERONIST PARTY; PERONISM.

PERONIST AND ANTI-PERONIST MYTHS. The mythmaking surrounding Evita, which was elaborated by herself and others, has redefined the historical figure behind the myth. While the Peronist and anti-Peronist myths began to develop in the late 1940s and early 1950s, both myths claim to be a historical account of Evita's life. On the one hand, the Peronist myth focuses on the political image of Evita, defining her actions as exemplary. Additionally, this myth depicts Evita as the ideal woman because she complies with the traditional submissive and motherly roles, and her actions foreground the Virgin Mary's purity and moral strength. The anti-Peronist myth, on the other hand, hinges on the negative aspects of Evita's political career and centers its discussion on controversial aspects of her personal life. Scholars of **Peronism** tend to use the terms *Peronist* or *anti-Peronist mythology* or *narrative* to refer to Evita's myths, but there are also researchers who use the Spanish terms *mito blanco* and *mito negro* (**white and black myths**) to express the same idea.

PERONIST LOYALTY DAY. Celebrated on 17 October, Peronist Loyalty Day is a landmark in Argentine history. After the June 1943 military coup d'état that overthrew President **Ramón Antonio Castillo**, General **Pedro Pablo Ramírez** became president of Argentina, General **Edelmiro Julián Farrell** was named vice president, and Colonel **Juan Domingo Perón** was appointed secretary of labor and social welfare. In that capacity, Perón diligently promoted labor legislation and organized workers' unionization nationwide. While workers in Argentina received for the first time paid vacation days and pay raises, one of the most important changes brought by Perón was the rural workers' statute, which introduced minimum food and housing conditions, minimum wages, maximum hours, sick pay, and Sundays off. Through his work, Perón cultivated the labor unions and gained their support and respect. Perón's rising popularity and power, however, were not positively seen by business leaders, the middle and upper classes, the landed aristocracy, and some sectors of the armed forces. In February 1944, Ramírez resigned, Farrell became president, and Perón became secretary of war and vice president. Subsequently, the state of siege was lifted, and presidential elections were called for February 1946. On 19 September 1945, when Perón made a formal bid for the presidency, the government's opposition and Perón's own rivals marched through the streets of Buenos Aires, demanding that the Supreme Court take over the government and hold an election. The opposition was supported by the United States, which considered Perón a half-fascist, half-democratic candidate and thus a potential threat to democracy. Soon, the U.S. ambassador to Argentina, Spruille Braden, would join Perón's political opponents and denounce the fascist behavior of the colonel. Due to the political turmoil in the country, Farrell reimposed the state of siege. The anti-Peronist military then requested Perón's resignation and imprisonment. On 12 October 1945, Perón was taken to **Martín García**, a remote prison island. Under the pretense of being sick, however, Perón was transferred to a military hospital in Buenos Aires a few days later. In the meantime, Peronist supporters had organized a protest requesting Perón's release. On 17 October 1945, thousands of supporters (mostly working-class people) gathered peacefully in the **Plaza de Mayo** to demand his return. Not until Perón made a speech from the balcony of the **Pink House** did the crowds begin to disperse. This unprecedented peaceful gathering prompted Perón's discharge and brought him back to power. Even though Evita mentions her assiduous search for help while Perón was in prison in her book *La razón de mi vida* (*My Mission in Life*), historians tend to agree that she did not play a key role in the resolution of the crisis. It is generally accepted that union members such as **Cipriano Reyes** and Colonel **Domingo Alfredo Mercante** were the most important figures in launching the campaign to release Perón. *See also* GRUPO DE OFICIALES UNIDOS (GOU)/UNITED OFFICERS GROUP; MAZZA, MIGUEL ÁNGEL; REVOLUTION OF 1943; ST. PERÓN'S DAY.

PERONIST SCHOOL. *See* ESCUELA SUPERIOR PERONISTA.

PERONIST SONGS. During the first two mandates of **Juan Domingo Perón**, songs praising **Peronism**, Perón, and Evita were common. Songs celebrating Evita and her work emerged in tandem with the rise of her political figure. The best known of these songs is currently "**Evita capitana**" (Evita, the Captain), the feminine counterpart of the "**Marcha peronista**" (Peronist March). In honor of the 1948 children's soccer championship, a march titled "Marcha del primer campeonato de fútbol infantil Evita" (March of the First Children's Soccer Championship Evita) was played. The song was composed by Rodolfo Sciammarella and Carlos Artagnan Petit and interpreted by a boys' choir. To encourage Argentine women to vote for Perón in the 1952 presidential election, Antonio Helú and Enrique Maroni composed "La descamisada" (The Shirtless Woman), which was recorded by the Argentine tango singer Nelly Omar in 1951. "Madrecita de los pobres" (Little Mother of the Poor) by Félix Scolatti Almeyda and Alfonso Tagle Lara was recorded on 1 August 1951. "Versos de un payador a la señora Eva Perón" (A Folksinger's Verses to Mrs. Eva Perón) by the tango lyricist Homero Manzi and the tango singer Hugo del Carril eulogizes Evita and Perón. After Evita passed away, the tango lyricist Cátulo Castillo composed a cantata called "Serenata de la muerte de Eva" (Serenade to Eva's Death).

PICHEL, VERA. Born in **Junín**, Buenos Aires Province, this journalist and biographer worked for women's magazines from a very early age. Pichel was the editorial manager of ***Damas y Damitas*** when she met Evita in 1939. She eventually became very close to Evita. In 1993, Pichel published *Evita íntima* (Evita: A Personal Account), a biography about Evita's personal life.

PIETRANTONIO, ANGÉLICA CLARA (1919–). Angélica Clara Pietrantonio worked as a corset maker, dressmaker, and embroiderer until she was 88 years old. She grew up in the Florida neighborhood in the province of Buenos Aires. Pietrantonio learnt her trade from her older sister and eventually opened her own corset store. Among her customers were popular cinema and radio actresses such as Niní Marshall, Paulina Singerman, and Evita. Pietrantonio had been an employee at a corset maker's in Buenos Aires in 1935 when she first met Evita. In an interview, she recalled that Evita was pretty and quite shy. After Evita married **Juan Domingo Perón**, she asked Pietrantonio to continue making corsets for her. As Pietrantonio knew Evita's exact size, the first lady never had to try on a corset again.

The Pink House at 50 Balcarce Street, Buenos Aires. Also known as the Government House, it is currently the workplace of the president of Argentina.

PINK HOUSE. Also known as the Government House, the Pink House has historically been the residence of Argentine government authorities. Currently, however, it is the workplace and not the residence of the president of Argentina. It is located in the Montserrat neighborhood in Buenos Aires, at the eastern end of the **Plaza de Mayo**. Its name derives from the color of its façade, which is pink. The construction of the Pink House dates from the foundation of Buenos Aires in 1580, but the building of the present Pink House began in 1873. It was from the balconies of the Pink House that **Juan Domingo Perón** and Evita delivered their impassioned speeches to the crowds gathered in the Plaza de Mayo.

PINK ROOM. Owing its name to the pink décor, this meeting room (known in Spanish as Salón Rosado) was set up by Evita in the Argentine Congress to mark the insertion of Argentine women in political life. Evita's intention was to have a room where women could meet and discuss politics without men's interference. The stylish room was used by the first six Argentine female senators who were elected to Congress in 1952. See also FEMALE SUFFRAGE; LARRAURI, JUANITA.

PLAZA DE MAYO. This square is located in the Montserrat neighborhood in Buenos Aires. It is surrounded by several major buildings, such as the Cabildo, the **Pink House**, the Metropolitan Cathedral, and the National Bank of Argentina. In Argentine culture and society, the Plaza the Mayo has a strong symbolic value connected to nationalism, freedom, and justice as it was where the May Revolution of 1810, which started the process toward the country's independence from Spain in 1816, took place. Since then, many historically and politically significant events have taken place there—one of them being the 17 October 1945 demonstration. See also PERONIST LOYALTY DAY.

POLICLÍNICO PRESIDENTE PERÓN. Located in the city of Sarandí in Avellaneda County, Buenos Aires Province, this hospital was built as part of an ambitious public health scheme launched by the Ministry of Health in collaboration with the **Fundación Eva Perón**. It opened its doors on 24 February 1951. The opening ceremony was attended by Minister of Health **Ramón Carrillo**, President **Juan Domingo Perón**, the director of the polyclinic Dr. **Ricardo Finochietto**, and Evita, who was in charge of delivering the opening speech. Evita was to return to the polyclinic to undergo a hysterectomy on 6 November 1951. While recovering from surgery, she cast her vote for president from her hospital bed on 11 November. Currently known as Presidente Perón

Hospital of Avellaneda, this polyclinic has kept the original furniture—bed, bedside table, desk, and pictures—in the en suite room where Evita recovered from surgery.

POLITICAL MYTH. According to the German scholar Heidi Hein-Kircher, a political myth is an ideologically marked narrative that intends to provide an account of past, present, or predicted political events and which is accepted as valid in its essentials by a sociopolitically defined group. A political myth stresses the significance of the individual's actions, and in doing so, some facts in the telling of their story are underlined while others are overlooked. Hence, a political myth is a flexible construction of meaning with legitimizing, integrating, and identifying functions. The mythological narrative is usually conveyed through narration (for instance, biographies, historical books, and schoolbooks), visualization (through posters and photomontages), and ritualization (in the form of political rallies). Hein-Kircher asserts that the myth of Evita is still present in Argentine society because Peronist leaders continue to appeal to Evita's memory. Hein-Kircher notes that the fact that the myth of Evita is still used by political leaders as a tool to legitimize their practice in Argentina proves that it has not lost its powerful efficacy. *See also* TRANSNATIONAL ICONIC IMAGE OF EVITA.

POLO Y MARTÍNEZ-VALDÉS, MARÍA DEL CARMEN (1900–1988). Commonly referred to as Carmen Polo, this Spanish aristocrat was the wife of the Spanish dictator **Francisco Franco Bahamonde**. She came from a wealthy family in Oviedo, Spain, and met her future husband at the age of 17. At first, her family did not accept their relationship. However, Polo managed to get her family's approval to accept Franco two years later. She married Franco in 1923, and they had their only child, **María del Carmen Franco y Polo**, in 1926. The **Royal Palace of El Pardo** became the residence of Franco and his family in 1940. They lived there for 35 years. Polo met Evita on 8 June 1947. As part of her **Rainbow Tour**, Evita landed in **Madrid**, where she was welcomed by Polo, Franco, and their daughter, among others. During her stay in Madrid, Evita was always accompanied by Polo. Together they visited the city's neighborhoods, hospitals, factories, institutions, historical sites, and places of interest. In addition, they traveled together to **Ávila**, **Medina del Campo**, **Segovia**, and **Toledo**. Rumor had it that Polo could not stand Evita's personality and ideals. Reportedly, their relationship was so tense that Polo decided that future diplomatic visitors would not stay at El Pardo.

POPE PIUS XII (1876–1958). Born Eugenio Maria Giuseppe Giovanni Pacelli, Pope Pius XII headed the Catholic Church from 2 March 1939 until his death. He went down in history as the most controversial pontiff of the 20th century for failing to publicly condemn the Holocaust during his papacy. While he encouraged convents and Catholic churches to hide Jews during World War II, he also urged clemency for convicted Nazi criminals in the name of Christian forgiveness. Some of these Nazi criminals used forged documents issued by the **Vatican** to enter and settle in Argentina during the administration of **Juan Domingo Perón**. Whether the pope was aware of the Vatican's involvement in aiding Nazi criminals in escaping Europe remains an unanswered question. In June 1947, Pius XII met Evita in an audience at the Vatican during her European tour. The following day at the Argentine Embassy in **Rome**, he awarded her the Order of the Grand Cross of Pope Pius IX on behalf of Perón. The award was given in recognition of the help Perón had offered to the peoples of Europe through Vatican organizations. Years later, when Perón called for the separation between the church and the state in Argentina, Pius XII excommunicated him. Once Perón was toppled, the government of President **Pedro Eugenio Aramburu** had Evita's remains buried in Italy, allegedly with the complicity of the Vatican. The pope reportedly gave his consent for the burial of Evita in the Maggiore Cemetery in Milan. *See also* BODY OF EVITA; CABANILLAS, HÉCTOR EDUARDO.

POR QUÉ SOY PERONISTA POR EVA PERÓN. See ESCRIBE EVA PERÓN.

PRADO MUSEUM. Located in central **Madrid**, Spain, this museum opened to the public in November 1819. Comprising 8,600 paintings and more than 700 sculptures, its collection is one of the finest in the world. During Evita's stay in Madrid in 1947, she visited the Prado Museum with **María del Carmen Polo y Martínez-Valdés**. They arrived at around 2 p.m. and were given a brief tour. Evita expressed extreme admiration for different pieces of art and regretted not having enough time to enjoy the collection in detail. *See also* RAINBOW TOUR.

PRESIDENT JUAN DOMINGO PERÓN STUDENT CITY. *See* CIUDAD ESTUDIANTIL PRESIDENTE JUAN PERÓN.

PRESIDENT PERÓN POLYCLINIC. *See* POLICLÍNICO PRESIDENTE PERÓN

PRESIDENT PERÓN UNIVERSITY CITY. *See* CIUDAD UNIVERSITARIA ESTUDIANTIL PRESIDENTE PERÓN.

PRIMATE CATHEDRAL OF ST. MARY OF TOLEDO. One of the three 13th-century Gothic cathedrals in Spain, this must-see place was included on Evita's tour during her visit to **Toledo** in 1947. The first lady of Argentina and **María del Carmen Polo y Martínez-Valdés** arrived at the cathedral on 13 June at around 4 p.m. After touring the cathedral, the two guests prayed before the image of the Virgin of the Tabernacle, the patron saint of the city. *See also* RAINBOW TOUR.

PRINCE, NELLY (1925–2021). Nélida Cuoto, better known as Nelly Prince, was an Argentine singer, radio presenter, and actress. She had a long and prolific career, which started in 1932. Coming from a family of musicians, Prince's artistic debut was in *La pandilla de Marilyn* (Marilyn's Gang) at **Radio Belgrano** when she was six years old. She made her stage debut in *Cumbres borrascosas* (*Wuthering Heights*) in 1936. Prince worked with Evita in 1944 at Radio Belgrano. In an interview with the writer Noemí Castiñeiras, Prince narrated how one day she was told her salary was to be reduced. The artistic director, Samuel Yankelevich, had explained to her that the radio station needed to cut costs. Prince was devastated, as her father was very ill and her salary was of great help to her family. In the middle of the rehearsals, Prince started crying. Evita approached her and asked her what was wrong. After listening to Prince's story, Evita stopped the rehearsal and went to talk to Yankelevich. Prince was outside Yankelevich's office and could hear Evita arguing with him. When Evita came out of the office, she told Prince that her salary was not going to be cut. Instead, Prince got a pay rise. They never worked together again, but Prince never forgot Evita's kind gesture. Prince continued developing as an actress and reached the zenith of her career in television and film in the 1950s. In addition, she collaborated with several singers and recorded a tango album in 2007.

PRODIGAL WOMAN, THE. *See LA PRÓDIGA*.

PROVEEDURÍAS. The **Fundación Eva Perón** opened its own chain of stores or *proveedurías* in 1950. They were painted in an easily recognizable light blue color. These stores offered subsidized food and other consumer goods at affordable prices. Although the plan was to open 6,000 stores across the country, the foundation managed to open 181 *proveedurías* before they were sold in 1953.

PUBLIC HEALTH CARE. While public health in Argentina had been administered by the **Society of Beneficence of Buenos Aires** until 1946, the government of **Juan Domingo Perón** ushered in new health policies. These would be carried out by a newly set up Secretariat of Health—transformed into the Ministry of Health in 1949—in tandem with the **Fundación Eva Perón**. The close collaboration between the ministry and the foundation changed the delivery of public health services in Argentina. As part of an ambitious public health scheme devised by Minister of Health **Ramón Carrillo**, the foundation built polyclinics that could provide health care to a large number of people.

These polyclinics were built in the counties of Avellaneda, Ezeiza, Lanús, and San Martín, all of them located in the province of Buenos Aires, as well as in the provinces of Salta, Jujuy, Santiago del Estero, Catamarca, Corrientes, Entre Ríos, Santa Fe, **Mendoza**, San Juan, San Luis, and Tucumán. Evita herself underwent surgery in one of these polyclinics, the **Policlínico Presidente Perón** in Avellaneda County. Aside from the polyclinics, the foundation set up a children's sanatorium in **Termas de Reyes** in the province of Jujuy, a Buenos Aires burn center, and a hospital specializing in chest surgery in Ramos Mejía County, Buenos Aires Province. Perhaps one of the most innovative ways of bringing health care to remote regions of Argentina was the establishment of a **hospital train** in 1951.

PUEBLO. With the advent of historical revisionism in Argentina in the second half of the 19th century, the language and terminology employed to describe historical facts and views were subject to significant changes. In other words, new terms were coined and existing words acquired new connotations. This is the case of the term *pueblo*, defined by revisionists as those sectors in society that produced and reproduced national traditions and earned their daily living by working. According to the revisionists, these people had been marginalized and excluded from historical accounts authored by the *oligarquía*. The revisionists' concept of *pueblo* was widely employed in Peronist discourse. For **Juan Domingo Perón**, the *pueblo* consisted of those coming from a disadvantaged background, workers, or simply those he called the ***descamisados***. In the **Twenty Peronist Tenets**, Perón summarized the ideals of **Peronism** and his intention to address the needs of the *pueblo* and follow its will. Moreover, Perón believed that a politically organized *pueblo* had a social conscience and made up the "collective soul" of the nation. The *pueblo* formed the basis for the building of a socially just, economically free, and politically independent nation that would serve popular interests and not those of the *oligarquía*. During 1951, Evita delivered a series of lectures at the **Escuela Superior Peronista**. She addressed the concepts of *pueblo* and *oligarquía* in one of them. *See also* ANTIPUEBLO; CIPAYO; JAURETCHE, ARTURO MARTÍN; VENDEPATRIA.

PURCHASE OF WEAPONS BY EVITA. On 29 September 1951, Evita reportedly purchased 5,000 automatic pistols, 1,500 machine guns, and a huge quantity of ammunition from Prince Bernhardt of the Netherlands. To this end, she allegedly used funds of the **Fundación Eva Perón**. As she was undergoing intravaginal radium brachytherapy in those days, she carried out the purchase from her sickbed. Apparently, the purpose of this purchase was to protect President **Juan Domingo Perón**, who had fallen victim to an attempted military coup d'état the day before. The weapons were to be distributed to workers, and the plan was to set up workers' militias as a defense against any possible rebellion. Whether these militias were ever set up or not is a question that remains unanswered. Peronist accounts state that a group of officers of unquestionable loyalty started training the workers in northern Argentina. Other sources claim that following Evita's death Perón instructed that the weapons should be placed in the Esteban de Luca military arsenal for use by the Argentine National Gendarmerie.

QUARTUCCI, PEDRO (1905–1983). After partaking in the 1924 Summer Olympic Games in the featherweight division and winning a bronze medal, Pedro Quartucci pursued an acting career in film and TV. He met Evita in 1937 while they were filming *¡Segundos afuera!* (Seconds Out!). Reportedly, Evita had an affair with Quartucci. Their paths would cross again in 1941 while shooting *Una novia en apuros* (A Bride in Trouble), a film in which both had bit parts. In the late 1990s, Quartucci's daughter, Nilda Quartucci, claimed to be Evita's daughter. However, because exhumation of Evita's remains was not an option, her version has never been confirmed.

QUIJANO, JUAN HORTENSIO (1884–1952). This Argentine lawyer and statesman was one of the leading men of the **Unión Cívica Radical (UCR)** and a fervent supporter of President Hipólito Yrigoyen. During the **Revolution of 1943**, he headed a group of UCR members who supported **Juan Domingo Perón**. He was appointed minister of interior for a brief period of time in 1945. In the same year, he fully embraced **Peronism** and founded the UCR–Junta Renovadora, one of the three parties that backed Perón's presidential candidacy. This earned him Perón's invitation to join his ticket, thus serving as vice president of Argentina from 1946 to 1952. Due to his failing health, he requested his exclusion from the 1951 Perón ticket. However, following Evita's renunciation from running for the position of vice president, Quijano was once again Perón's running mate, but he died before his reinauguration. *See also* CABILDO ABIERTO; CANDIDACY FOR VICE PRESIDENT.

QUILMES. Located 17 kilometers (11 miles) south of Buenos Aires, the city of Quilmes derives its name from the Quilmes or Kilmes people of Tucumán Province. The Spanish colonizers, who had defeated the Quilmes in Tucumán by the 17th century, deported the survivors to a *reducción* (a settlement for indigenous people) called Exaltación de la Santa Cruz de los Kilmes near Buenos Aires. Eventually, the *reduccción* evolved into an industrial city known for its eponymous beer. The company that produced Quilmes beer was expropriated and nationalized during the government of **Juan Domingo Perón**. Once the company was in the hands of the state, it made a generous donation to the **Fundación Eva Perón**. In 1949, the Quilmes Atlético Club conferred honorary membership on Evita and Perón. After Evita passed away, the city of Quilmes, wishing to honor her memory, sent a petition to the government of Buenos Aires Province to change its name to Eva Perón, but that was not granted.

QUIROGA, CAMILA (1891–1948). Camila Quiroga (née Camila Josefa Ramona Passera) was one of the greatest Argentine actresses of the first half of the 20th century. She made her stage debut with the Compañia Nacional de Aficionados in 1906. Two years later, she joined the touring company of the Spanish

José Tavallí and remained part of the troupe for four years. After setting up her own theater company, **Compañía de Camila Quiroga**, with her husband Héctor Quiroga in 1918, she toured the Americas and Europe, gaining international acclaim. Committed to improving the working conditions of actors, she spearheaded the establishment of the **Asociación Argentina de Actores** in 1919. In 1939, Evita joined Quiroga's company, performing in the play *Mercado de amor en Argelia* (Market of Love in Algeria), directed by **Edmundo Guibourg**.

R

RACIOPPI, PABLO (?–1981). This Argentine theater, film, and radio actor worked with Evita in 1942. Racioppi and Evita were the leading actors in the **Compañía Candilejas**, which performed a series of *radioteatros* at **Radio El Mundo**. Allegedly, Racioppi and Evita had a brief love affair.

RADICAL SOAP. *See* GUEREÑO RODRÍGUEZ, JUAN.

RADÍO, PEDRO (1894–?). This Argentine physician served as Argentine ambassador to Spain between 1947 and 1950. He had a key role in strengthening the diplomatic relations between Spain and Argentina and was actively involved in organizing Evita's official visit to this European country. During her visit, Radío escorted Evita and participated in official banquets in her honor. He held a welcome reception for her at the Argentine Embassy in **Madrid** on 14 June 1947. Apparently, Evita's visit to Spain caused trouble for Radío as she did not always follow the procedures of diplomatic protocol and etiquette. *See also* RAINBOW TOUR.

RADIO ARGENTINA. The first radio station in Argentina and the first Spanish-speaking radio station in the world, Radio Argentina was created by Enrique Susini, Miguel Mujica, César Guerrico, and Luis Carranza. On 27 August 1920, approximately 50 homes with radio receiver devices were able to listen to Richard Wagner's *Parsifal*, played at the Coliseo Theater in Buenos Aires. Over the years, Radio Argentina changed its name several times. It was first introduced as Sociedad Radio Argentina, and it became LOR Broadcasting de Crítica while being in partnership with the newspaper *Crítica* in 1925. However, a year and a half later the radio station returned to its original owners, who then sold it to **Radio Prieto**. Evita allegedly worked at Radio Argentina in the *radioteatro* La hora de las sorpresas (The Hour of Surprises) in 1941. *See also* COMPAÑÍA JUVENIL DE RADIOTEATRO.

RADIO BELGRANO. Initially known as Radio Nacional, this Argentine radio station was sold to **Jaime Yankelevich** on 5 February 1927. Yankelevich considerably reduced the practice of playing recorded music over the air, which was common at the time. Instead, he introduced live on-air performances in order to make Radio Nacional stand out. Furthermore, to attract good performers he paid them a fee. As its offerings broadened, Radio Nacional changed location several times in order to find a suitable venue. In 1933, the government issued a decree ordering private businesses not to include the term *nacional* (national) in their names. Listeners of Radio Nacional were then asked to come up with alternatives, and the radio changed its name to Radio Belgrano. Among the most popular artists of the 1930s who featured on the listings of this radio station were Carlos Gardel, Ignacio Corsini, Mercedes Simone, Ada Falcón, Charlo, Ramón Novarro, and Jorge Negrete. Aside from live music, Radio Belgrano broadcast other types of shows such as religious, sports, and news

Evita and Narciso Ibáñez Menta in a Christmas Eve special show at Radio Belgrano in 1944.

programs as well as serialized dramas. The station was incredibly successful, and Yankelevich was constantly devising ways to interact with the audience. Evita worked for Radio Belgrano in 1937 and came back to the station in 1943 with her own radio theater company after obtaining the approval of the Secretariat of Communications for dramatizations of historical figures. She was particularly known for her voice portrayal of the Polish Countess Maria Walewska, Napoleon Bonaparte's mistress. A few days after the January 1944 gala benefit for the victims of the **San Juan earthquake**, **Juan Domingo Perón** and **Domingo Alfredo Mercante** paid a visit to the station to attend one of Evita's performances. At that time, Evita was doing three radio programs a day at Radio Belgrano. Under the Perón administration, however, mass media came under scrutiny. The president's control of the media exerted so much pressure on Yankelevich that he sold his radio station to the government on 18 August 1947. *See also* ALEA S.A.; ANTI-ARGENTINE ACTIVITIES CONGRESSIONAL COMMITTEE; *HEROÍNAS DE LA HISTORIA*; *RADIOTEATRO*.

RADIO BELGRANO Y LA PRIMERA CADENA ARGENTINA DE BROADCASTING. The first and most important private radio station network in Argentina, **Radio Belgrano** y la Primera Cadena Argentina de Broadcasting was set up by **Jaime Yankelevich** in the late 1930s. Evita started working for Radio Belgrano and its affiliated network in 1937. She eventually became one of the network's biggest stars. Under the government's pressure, Yankelevich sold the network to the state in October 1947.

See also RED ARGENTINA DE EMISORAS SPLENDID; RED AZUL Y BLANCA DE EMISORAS ARGENTINAS.

RADIO CULTURA. Founded in the early 1920s by brothers Federico and Enrique del Ponte and Alberto de Bary, this was the first Argentine radio station to finance operations by commercial advertisement. It advertised perfumes, stockings, cars, and jewelry. It broadcast from the Plaza Hotel in Buenos Aires, but after a few months it moved to the Palermo neighborhood in the same city. Radio Cultura's programming targeted female audiences. Listeners could enjoy *radioteatros* as well as music and cooking shows. Reportedly, Evita made her radio debut at this station in October 1934. Radio Cultura was eventually bought by the businessman **Jaime Yankelevich**. *See also* RADIO DEBUT OF EVITA.

RADIO DEBUT OF EVITA. The precise circumstances of Evita's radio debut are unclear. According to *El Amigo del Pueblo*—a newspaper from **Junín**—Evita made her radio debut at the Buenos Aires radio station Radio La Nación on either 28 or 29 April 1934. On that occasion, she stepped in for someone called Miss Kelly. In her book *Mi hermana Evita* (My Sister Evita), Erminda claims that Evita made her radio debut on 1 October 1934, when **Radio Cultura** in Buenos Aires broadcast a program dedicated to the city of San Carlos de Bolívar in the province of Buenos Aires. As part of the program, Evita recited a poem by the Mexican poet Amado Nervo, "¿Adónde van los muertos?" (Where Do the Dead Go?). *See also* RADIO MITRE.

RADIO DEL ESTADO. In 1935, the Argentine government issued a public tender for a broadcasting license—the future concessionaire would have to provide a radio station for the exclusive use of the government. After winning the tender, **Haynes Publishing** announced the creation of Radio del Estado on 6 July 1937 in Buenos Aires. Officially referred to as Estación de Radiodifusión del Estado, it was eventually known as Radio del Estado. In 1957, it changed its name to Radio Nacional. Its programming was devoted to government information, culture, and education. Indeed, Radio del Estado allowed the government to promote and establish educational radio. One of the educational programs was *Escuela del aire* (School on Air), which was broadcast by Radio del Estado in the late 1930s and early 1940s. Even though it was initially aimed at adults who had not completed primary education, radio receivers were also placed in schools so that children could listen to the program. In June 1944, *Hacia un futuro mejor* (Toward a Better Future), starring Evita, was broadcast by Radio del Estado and **Radio Belgrano**.

RADIO EL MUNDO. This radio station went on the air on 29 November 1935. Radio El Mundo was the main radio station of the **Red Azul y Blanca de Emisoras Argentinas**, owned by **Haynes Publishing**. The radio studio, located at 555 Maipú Street in Buenos Aires, was built in the image and likeness of the London BBC. Thanks to its modern facilities and equipment, Radio El Mundo was the first Argentine radio station to broadcast to other countries. Its wide-ranging programming, which included live musicals, opinion programs, children's shows, and *radioteatros*, usually listed prominent national and international artists. In May 1942, the **Compañía Candilejas** performed a series of *radioteatros* at Radio El Mundo with Evita as the leading actress.

RADIO MITRE. One of the most renowned and oldest radio stations in Argentina, Radio Mitre was set up by the company Sociedad ABC under the name of LOZ Broadcasting La Nación in 1925. The station was located in the Flores neighborhood in Buenos Aires. Three years later, LOZ Broadcasting La Nación was transferred to La Nación S.A., a business owned by the Mitre family and devoted to print media. Changing its name to Radio Mitre, this radio station was the first to belong to a newspaper, a fact that made the Mitre company a pioneer in the multimedia industry. Radio Mitre provided a variety of programs, such as the daily reading of news from *La Nación*, which was considered innovative at the time. Eventually, the station became part of the **Red Azul y Blanca de Emisoras Argentinas**, owned by **Haynes Publishing**. In the early stages of her radio career, Evita got a starring role in *Una sombra en la recova* (A Shadow in the Arcade), one of the many *radioteatros* broadcast by Radio Mitre in 1937.

RADIO NACIONAL DE ESPAÑA. This radio station was founded during the Spanish Civil War (1936–1939) by the Nationalist general José Millán-Astray y Terreros. It went on the air in Salamanca, Spain, on 19 January 1937. Upon the Nationalists' victory in 1939, **Francisco Franco Bahamonde** issued a decree granting Radio Nacional de España the exclusive rights to transmit news. As a result, all public and private stations were forced to broadcast the same news reports as Radio Nacional de España. These news reports were known as *el parte* (the report), a term reminiscent of war reports. During her visit to Spain in June 1947, Evita delivered several radio speeches on Radio Nacional de España. *See also* RAINBOW TOUR.

RADIO PARÍS. Originally named Radio Cine París, this radio station was located at 860 Cangallo Street in Buenos Aires. The station was set up in the late 1920s, and its offering included operettas, zarzuelas, and programs promoting national and international folklore themes. Evita started working at Radio París in 1935. She had brief appearances in different *radioteatros*, including *La vida de Fray Mamerto Esquiú* (The Life of Friar Mamerto Esquiú).

RADIO PORTEÑA. This radio station was set up by Gregorio González Speroni in the late 1920s. Located in Buenos Aires, Radio Porteña offered diverse programming, including popular and classical music, children's programs, and *radioteatros*. Reportedly, Evita was part of the cast of a *radioteatro* series titled *Los caminos de la historia* (The Paths of History), which was broadcast by Radio Porteña in October and November 1937.

RADIO PRIETO. Founded by Teodoro Prieto, this radio station went on the air in 1925. Radio Prieto marked the Argentine soundscape by introducing advertising spots based on jingles. Furthermore, Prieto's was one of the first radio stations to broadcast directly from theaters, soccer and boxing stadiums, and running tracks. In May 1939, the theater company **Compañía de Teatro del Aire**, headed by **Pascual Pellicciotta** and Evita, joined Radio Prieto and **Radio Mitre** to broadcast a series of *radioteatros*. The first *radioteatro* in the series was *Los jazmines del 80* (The Jasmines of 1880), with Evita as the star of the show.

RADIOLANDIA. Julio Korn created this weekly show-business magazine in 1928 under the name *La Canción Moderna*. At first, the magazine offered the transcription of popular tango lyrics and included *Radiolandia* as a supplement. However, the boom in the radio industry made Korn change the title of the magazine to *Radiolandia* in 1934. As with the rest of his publications, Korn aimed at creating a simple and low-cost magazine of wide circulation to entertain the general public. *Radiolandia* included general information, interviews with artists, as well as gossip, radio, and cinema sections, among others. In contrast with **Sintonía** and **Antena**, *Radiolandia* focused mainly on the national show business. Its pages were in black and white, except for the front and back covers. The front cover usually featured the portrait of a famous artist. The drawn pictures were later replaced by photographs taken by **Annemarie Heinrich**. To appear on the cover of magazines like *Radiolandia* was an important step in any artist's career, and Evita's turn was on 3 June 1944. She graced the cover of *Radiolandia* with a color portrait by the cartoonist Vitucho based on a photograph taken by Heinrich. The picture shows a smiling Evita with long, brown hair. *Radiolandia* had published a short interview with Evita along with five photographs of the rising star in January 1940.

RADIOTEATRO. *Radioteatro* or radio drama refers to acoustic performances broadcast on radio or released in audio file formats. As such, they depend on sound effects, music, and dialogue to help listeners imagine the story. These performances can be plays, novels, or melodramas written specifically for radio, but they can also be adapted works. Radio drama was extremely trendy between the 1920s and 1940s. However, it gradually lost popularity once television emerged. In Argentina, the term *radioteatro* is used as a synonym for *radionovela*, which is a type of radio drama. *Radionovelas* are defined as serial radio dramas; that is, soap operas or melodramas broadcast in episodes. Their golden age in Argentina was during the 1940s. Evita performed in several *radioteatros*, eventually becoming a well-established radio drama actress. *See also* COMPAÑÍA CANDILEJAS; COMPAÑÍA DE TEATRO DEL AIRE; COMPAÑÍA JUVENIL DE RADIOTEATRO.

RAINBOW TOUR. On 6 June 1947, Evita embarked on an official visit to Europe that was called the "Rainbow Tour," a name that highlights the link between the Old and the New World. Initially, the purpose of this diplomatic mission was to strengthen the links between Argentina and Spain. The visit to Spain, which was suggested to **Juan Domingo Perón** by General **Francisco Franco Bahamonde**, was a way of maintaining the excellent diplomatic relations established between the two countries. Spain found itself diplomatically and economically isolated after World War II, but Argentina signed a contract with Spain in 1946 by which the European country got a loan to buy Argentine wheat and meat. Nevertheless, while Perón was helping Franco's Spain, Argentina was finally improving its relations with the United States and taking its place within the United Nations. A visit by Perón himself to a fascist country would have been too diplomatically provocative if Argentina wanted to keep its improved position. As a result, Evita traveled to Spain instead of Perón, and other countries were added to the tour as a way of making the visit to Spain less obviously political. Apart from Spain, Evita visited Italy, **Vatican City**, Portugal, France, **Monaco**, and **Switzerland**. She was accompanied by an entourage of 15 people, including her brother Juancito, **Alberto Dodero**, **Lillian Lagomarsino de Guardo, Francisco Muñoz Azpiri, Emilio Abras, Julio Alcaraz**, Francisco Aisina, Captain Adolfo Gutiérrez, her aide-de-camp Colonel Jorge Ballofet, and two dressmakers who looked after Evita's wardrobe. *See also* ADOLFO SUÁREZ MADRID–BARAJAS AIRPORT; ALCÁZAR DE TOLEDO; ALHAMBRA; ALHAMBRA PALACE HOTEL; AREILZA Y MARTÍNEZ DE RODAS, JOSÉ MARÍA DE; ARMILLA AIR BASE; AUGUSTO SEVERO INTERNATIONAL AIRPORT; ÁVILA; BARCELONA; BASILICA OF OUR LADY OF SORROWS; DAKHLA; DUARTE, JUAN "JUANCITO" RAMÓN; FOXÁ Y TORROBA, AGUSTÍN DE; FRANCO SALGADO-ARAUJO, FRANCISCO; FRANCO Y POLO, MARÍA DEL CARMEN "NENUCA"; FREIRE, JOSÉ MARÍA; GANDO AIRPORT; GARCÍA-ESCÁMEZ INIESTA, FRANCISCO; GENERALIFE; GRANADA; GRANADA CITY HALL; LA GRANJA DE SAN ILDEFONSO; LAS PALMAS DE GRAN CANARIA; LAS VENTAS BULLRING; LISBON; MADRID; MADRID CITY HALL; MARTÍN-ARTAJO ÁLVAREZ, ALBERTO; MEDINA DEL CAMPO; MORÓN AIRPORT; PARIS; POLO Y MARTÍNEZ-VALDÉS, MARÍA DEL CARMEN; POPE PIUS XII; PRIMATE CATHEDRAL OF ST. MARY OF TOLEDO; RADÍO, PEDRO; RAPALLO; RIO DE JANEIRO; ROME; ROYAL PALACE OF EL PARDO; ROYAL PALACE OF MADRID; SANTA MARÍA DEL BUEN AIRE NATIONAL CAMP; SANTIAGO DE COMPOSTELA; SEGOVIA; SEVILLE; TOLEDO; UNIVERSITY CITY OF MADRID; VIGO; ZARAGOZA.

RAMÍREZ, PEDRO PABLO (1884–1962). This Argentine military officer served as president of Argentina from 7 June 1943 to 25 February 1944. Before becoming president, he had been sent to Germany to train with the Prussian army. Back in Argentina, he participated in the coup d'état that toppled President Hipólito Yrigoyen in 1930. In 1942, he was appointed minister of war during the **Ramón Antonio Castillo** administration. The following year, the **Unión Cívica Radical (UCR)** offered Ramírez the presidential candidacy because they thought he would not let himself be beaten by vote rigging. When his acceptance as the UCR's presidential nominee came to President Castillo's knowledge, Ramírez was forced to resign and withdraw his nomination. As a result, the Campo de Mayo military base rose up in arms. Together with General **Arturo Franklin Rawson**, Ramírez led the **Revolution of 1943** to overthrow President Castillo. Rawson became president of Argentina, but he was soon replaced by Ramírez. During his mandate, he revealed his authoritarian tendencies by establishing mandatory religious instruction in public schools, banning political parties, and controlling the press. Under pressure from the United States, he broke off relations with the Axis powers, a move that was not approved by the new leaders of the country. Consequently, he was replaced by his vice president, General **Edelmiro Julián Farrell**.

RAPALLO. Located on the Italian Riviera coastline, the town of Rapallo became a seaside resort in the 1920s. Its mild winters coupled with its poetic and nostalgic air had made it a vacation spot for Italians and foreigners alike long before Evita set foot there on 6 July 1947. During her **Rainbow Tour**, Evita took a 10-day vacation in Rapallo, enjoying the same experiences as an ordinary visitor. She went shopping, had meals at restaurants, walked along the beach, and took day trips to San Remo and Portofino. However, Evita did not stay at a hotel but at **Alberto Dodero**'s sumptuous mansion, which he made available for her. Since she was in Rapallo on 9 July—Argentina's Independence Day—she attended a reception hosted by the Argentine consul.

RAWSON, ARTURO FRANKLIN (1885–1952). This general was the commanding officer of cavalry at the Campo de Mayo military base in the province of Buenos Aires. On 3 June 1943, he was contacted by the **Grupo de Oficiales Unidos** to help them carry out the coup d'état against President **Ramón Antonio Castillo**. The following day, Rawson commanded the troops that took possession of the Pink House and proclaimed himself president of Argentina. However, when he attempted to fill his cabinet with civilians and promised that he would break relations with the Axis powers, he was forced to resign. On 7 June, he was replaced by **Pedro Pablo Ramírez**. Rawson died of a heart attack a year after he had attempted to topple President **Juan Domingo Perón**. Like Evita, Rawson is buried in the Recoleta Cemetery in Buenos Aires. *See also* REVOLUTION OF 1943.

RED ARGENTINA DE EMISORAS SPLENDID. The third most important Argentine private radio network, Red Argentina de Emisoras Splendid (RADES) was set up by the directors of Radio Splendid and **Jaime Yankelevich** in 1940. RADES owned Radio Splendid and 15 provincial radio stations. Under the auspices of **Miguel Miranda** and with funds from the **Argentine Institute for the Promotion of Trade**, RADES was bought by the state during the Peronist government. *See also* ALEA S.A.; *LA RAZÓN*; LA RAZÓN S.A.; RADIO BELGRANO Y LA PRIMERA CADENA ARGENTINA DE BROADCASTING; RED AZUL Y BLANCA DE EMISORAS ARGENTINAS.

RED AZUL Y BLANCA DE EMISORAS ARGENTINAS. The origin of this radio network—also known as Cadena Azul y Blanca—dates back to the late 1930s. Owned by **Haynes Publishing**, the Red Azul y Blanca de Emisoras Argentinas was the second most important private radio network in Argentina. It included, among others, **Radio El Mundo**, **Radio Mitre**, Radio Libertad, and Radio Antártida. Evita first worked at Radio Mitre in 1937 and at Radio El Mundo in 1942. *See also* ALEA S.A.; *EL MUNDO*; RADIO BELGRANO Y LA PRIMERA CADENA ARGENTINA DE BROADCASTING; RED ARGENTINA DE EMISORAS SPLENDID.

REGIONAL PERONIST SCHOOLS. As part of the **Escuela Superior Peronista**, **Juan Domingo Perón** organized the opening of regional Peronist schools that would disseminate his doctrine in each province and national territory of Argentina. Hence, the Escuela Superior Peronista designed a course to train political cadres. These would become the Peronist leaders in charge of opening the regional schools. Titled "Provinces and Territories," the course was delivered in 1953 and attended by delegates from national territories and provinces picked by the **Partido Peronista**, the **Partido Peronista Femenino**, and the **Confederación General del Trabajo**. Those who completed the "Provinces and Territories" course oversaw the opening of 18 regional Peronist schools. Those who enrolled in the regional schools had to submit a brief reflection on one of the **Twenty Peronist Tenets** and a phrase said by either Perón or Evita. Candidates were accepted or rejected based on their reflections. At the end of the course, students had to submit a research project and pass all final exams. The modules included topics such as political leadership, history of **Peronism**, national doctrine, Peronist philosophy, Peronist sociology, Peronist politics, Peronist economics, Peronist organization, Peronist achievements, and Peronist indoctrination theory. The graduates from the regional schools went back to their ordinary lives with the mission to spread the Peronist doctrine. Some of them, however, were sent to the Escuela Superior Peronista to take part in a more advanced course. Following the **Liberating Revolution**, the schools ceased functioning.

RENZI, ATILIO. A former military man, Atilio Renzi was in charge of supervising the garage of the Argentine Ministry of War when he met **Juan Domingo Perón**. After Perón became president of Argentina in 1946, Evita hired Renzi as the butler of the **Olivos Presidential Residence**, where he and his family took up their abode. Renzi reorganized and improved the working conditions of the residence's employees. His reliability and morale led him to become Evita's private secretary and the steward of the **Unzué Palace**. In that capacity, he assisted Evita in every possible way. He drove her to poor neighborhoods and hospitals to give out food, clothes, and toys. When Evita was given in-kind donations, Renzi recorded, stored, packed, and dispatched the items to those in need. He was always by Evita's side even when the Peróns went to their **San Vicente country house**. After the **Fundación Eva Perón** was created, Renzi became very involved in the daily pursuits of the foundation.

REPETTI, PALMIRA. She was Evita's sixth-grade teacher at **Catalina Larralt de Estrugamou School**. In an interview, Repetti said that having noticed Evita's interest in reciting poetry, she encouraged her to pursue her passion. She would therefore let Evita go to other classrooms and recite poems for younger pupils on rainy days, when many children missed school due to bad weather.

REPÚBLICA DE LOS NIÑOS. This miniature city, which is home to 35 buildings and institutions proportionally sized for children, is located in Manuel Gonnet City, Buenos Aires Province. It consists of three main areas spread over approximately 50 hectares (123.5 acres): a civic center, a rural area, and a sports area. It also features an airport and an internal railway network. It was opened on 26 November 1951 by President **Juan Domingo Perón**. Under the auspices of the Buenos Aires governor, **Domingo Alfredo Mercante**, the republic aimed at both recreating and educating children in republican ethics. After the 1955 coup d'état that toppled Perón, the republic lost its original purpose and became a theme park. Only in 1983 did the republic begin to carry out a policy more in line with its original values. New activities included, for example, the running of educational workshops for primary school children. In 2017, the Argentine government started renovating more than 20 buildings in the republic, which was declared a national historical monument in 2001.

REVOLUTION OF 1943. On 4 June 1943, a military coup d'état put an end to the **Infamous Decade** in Argentina. This event was allegedly orchestrated by the **Grupo de Oficiales Unidos (GOU)**. The 1930s had been years characterized by a corrupt, fraudulent, and conservative government that was closely allied with the United Kingdom. The different governments of the Infamous Decade represented the landowning class and the Buenos Aires bourgeoisie, which was in turn associated with foreign capital. Its last ruler was President **Ramón Antonio Castillo**. In 1942, Castillo announced that Robustiano Patrón Costas—a successful businessman from the sugar industry—was going to be his successor. As Patrón Costas's candidacy meant the continuity of the conservative and fraudulent government, the GOU members decided to take action. Led by General **Arturo Franklin Rawson**, they ousted President Castillo and seized power. Subsequently, a process of nationalist, statist, and populist change emerged and was supported not only by the pro-Axis and anti-American GOU but also by a growing working class and a new nationalist business sector. Soon after Rawson became the de facto president, the GOU members discovered that the new president had decided, in collusion with the oligarchy that had supported the previous government, to include civilians in his cabinet and exclude the GOU officers. Moreover, Rawson favored the Allies, whereas the GOU mostly wished to remain neutral during World War II. As a result, he was replaced by **Pedro Pablo Ramírez** on 7 June 1943. With President Ramírez, Argentina remained officially neutral—a stance that was backed by the national right-wing and fascist sympathizers. Nevertheless, under pressure from the United States, Ramírez broke off diplomatic relations with Germany. Because his action was not well received by the Argentine military, he was removed and replaced by General **Edelmiro Julián Farrell** on 25 February 1944. With the victory of the Allies in March 1945, an opposition sector made up of a growing middle class, the oligarchy, and liberal and pro-Allied military demanded Farrell hold a position less ambiguous toward the Allies and the immediate holding of democratic elections. After finally declaring war on the Axis powers on 27 March 1945, Farrell called for presidential elections for February 1946.

REYES, CIPRIANO (1906–2001). This Argentine union leader participated in the massive labor demonstration in support of **Juan Domingo Perón**'s liberation on 17 October 1945. Although Reyes and Evita apparently disliked each other, they reportedly visited factories, docks, and union headquarters together to mobilize workers. After Perón was liberated, Reyes, in tandem with other union leaders, founded the **Partido Laborista (PL)** to back Perón's presidential bid for the 1946 general election. While Perón became president of Argentina on 4 June 1946, Reyes was elected to Congress. After his inauguration, Perón dissolved the PL to create the Partido Único de la Revolución. As Reyes was not in favor of this move, he became a member of the opposition and was critical of Perón, which made him a victim of government repression. When an attempt was made on Evita's and Perón's life in 1948, Reyes was arrested on charges of plotting against the president and his wife, remaining in prison until the end of the Perón administration. *See also* HUMAN RIGHTS IN ARGENTINA; PERONIST LOYALTY DAY.

RIGHTS OF THE ELDERLY PARK. *See* PEREYRA IRAOLA PARK.

RIO DE JANEIRO. After her European tour, Evita visited this Brazilian city to attend the Inter-American Conference for Peace and Security. She flew from Geneva via **Lisbon** to Dakar, where she boarded the *Buenos Aires*—one of **Alberto Dodero**'s ships—which took her to Brazil. On 15 August 1947, she disembarked in the Brazilian city of Recife, where she was warmly welcomed, and the following day she flew to Rio. Once there, she joined the Argentine delegation that had come from Buenos Aires equipped with posters bearing the likeness of Evita. The posters, which covered the walls of the city, bore the words, "To the Brazilian woman who, like the Argentine woman, is fighting for justice, work, and peace." During her five-day stay in Rio, Evita made a speech on Rádio Nacional, attended numerous banquets, dined with President Eurico Gaspar Dutra, was honored by the Chamber of Deputies, and listened attentively when the U.S. secretary of state, George Marshall, gave his speech at the Inter-American Conference for Peace and Security. The way she tackled the press was remarkable, as her answers were concise and politically correct. Her visit to Brazil proved to be successful. *See also* RAINBOW TOUR.

RIVAS, NÉLIDA "NELLY" HAYDEÉ (1939–2012). Nélida Haydeé Rivas, better known as Nelly Rivas, came from a working-class family from Buenos Aires. In her teenage years, Rivas became a member of the Peronist **Unión de Estudiantes Secundarios (UES)**. It was customary for the UES female branch members to visit the **Olivos Presidential Residence**, as they could avail of sports facilities there. During these visits in 1953, Rivas became acquainted with President **Juan Domingo Perón**. Soon they started a romantic relationship that lasted until Perón was toppled in 1955. At the time, Rivas was 14 years old and Perón 58. Following the **Liberating Revolution**, Rivas was placed in the youth care center Asilo San José. In the meantime, the new military government charged Perón with rape of a minor. Rivas's parents were also accused of child abuse since they consented to Rivas and Perón's relationship and were eventually sent to prison. While being physically apart, Rivas and Perón engaged in correspondence. These letters were published by an American newspaper in 1957. Rivas got married in 1958 and reunited with Perón in 1973.

ROJAS, ISAAC FRANCISCO DEL ÁNGEL (1906–1993). This navy officer and politician was Evita's naval aide-de-camp until her death in 1952. In the remaining three years of **Juan Domingo Perón**'s government, Rojas became commander of naval operations at Río Santiago. In August 1955, Admiral Rojas was persuaded to take part in the military coup d'état that would eventually topple Perón. As a result, he established a blockade around Buenos Aires and **La Plata**, but loyalist air force units attacked his ships on 16 September 1955. Two days later, additional vessels joined the rebellion and Rojas threatened to shell the oil distillery in the city of La Plata, south of Buenos Aires, if Perón did not resign. On the morning of 19 September, several oil storage tanks were bombed in another city, Mar del Plata. In the afternoon on the same day, Perón resigned and Rojas sailed into the port of Buenos Aires on ARA *General Belgrano*. He served as vice president of Argentina during the presidencies of **Eduardo Ernesto Lonardi** and **Pedro Eugenio Aramburu**. *See also* LIBERATING REVOLUTION.

ROME. As part of her **Rainbow Tour**, Evita visited the Italian capital from 25 June to 6 July 1947. During her stay, she attended official luncheons and receptions, was granted an audience with **Pope Pius XII**, paid tribute to the Tomb of the Unknown Soldier, saw a performance of the opera *Aida* at the Baths of Carcalla, visited an orphanage and the League of Women Voters, and took a short trip to Milan. She also held a press conference at the Argentine Embassy, during which she claimed that she did not understand anything about politics and that she was not in favor of the legalization of divorce. Evita's presence in Rome caused disturbances. Since the Communists were trying to dislodge the coalition of Socialists and Christian Democrats that ruled Italy, they gathered in front of the Argentine Embassy and shouted, "Down with fascism!," in reference to **Juan Domingo Perón**'s government and Evita's visit to Francoist Spain. The Communists' intention was to jeopardize the purpose of Evita's trip to Italy, which was the granting of loans and the increase in the number of European immigrants entering Argentina. By the end of her visit to Rome, Evita was exhausted and took a 10-day break in **Rapallo**.

ROSARIO. Located 300 kilometers (186 miles) northwest of Buenos Aires, Rosario is the largest city in the province of Santa Fe and the third most populous in Argentina. In 1936, Evita was on a tour of Rosario, **Córdoba**, and **Mendoza** with the **Compañia de Comedias Muñoz-Franco-Álvarez**. In Rosario, she performed at the Odeón Theater, and her performance did not escape the local newspaper *La Capital*, which published the first photo of Evita to appear in the print media. Evita returned to Rosario during the presidential campaign of 1945–1946. She was accompanying her husband **Juan Domingo Perón** on board the *Descamisado* Train. In her role as first lady, Evita visited Rosario together with Perón on 11 January 1947 to lay the foundation stone for a power plant in the neighborhood of Roque Sáenz Peña. On

30 September 1948, she attended a railroad workers' event held at the port of Rosario, where she delivered an impassioned speech. When the Fifth National Eucharistic Congress was celebrated in Rosario in 1950, Evita and Perón attended the closing session. They both knelt and kissed the ring of the papal legate Cardinal Ernesto Ruffini.

ROTH, SILVANA (1924–2010). Born Silvana Rota, Silvana Roth was an Argentine stage and film actress who appeared in more than 20 films between 1939 and 1971. She became a famous actress in Argentina during the 1940s and 1950s. Like Evita, she performed in *radioteatros*, enjoying great popularity. Roth met Evita at **Radio Belgrano**, and they became close friends. She was among the artists who collected money for the victims of the **San Juan earthquake** in 1944. With the rise of **Juan Domingo Perón** to power, Roth became a staunch **Peronist**. She was appointed vice president of the **Ateneo Cultural Eva Perón** in 1950.

ROYAL PALACE OF EL PARDO. Located in the district of Fuencarral-El Pardo in the city of **Madrid**, the Royal Palace of El Pardo was built in the 16th century. It was traditionally one of the Spanish royal family's residences. Between 1940 and 1975, however, the palace became the official residence of the dictator **Francisco Franco Bahamonde** and his family. During her stay in Madrid as part of the **Rainbow Tour**, Evita stayed in the palace for seven nights. Since 1982, the palace has served as a residence for visiting heads of state. In more recent years, it has also been the place chosen by the Spanish royal family to hold different official and social events. *See also* POLO Y MARTÍNEZ-VALDÉS, MARÍA DEL CARMEN.

ROYAL PALACE OF MADRID. Located in western **Madrid**, Spain, this palace is currently used for state ceremonies and events only. Although it is the official residence of the Spanish royal family, no aristocrat has lived there since 1931. With the proclamation of the Second Republic, the Spanish royal family fled the country and lived in exile for years. It was at this palace that Evita was decorated with the Great Cross of Isabella the Catholic by **Francisco Franco Bahamonde** on 9 June 1947. Both Franco and Evita delivered speeches on that day. After the ceremony, Evita appeared on the balcony of the palace to greet the thousands of people who had gathered in the Plaza de Oriente. *See also* RAINBOW TOUR.

ROYAL SITE OF SAN LORENZO DE EL ESCORIAL. Located in the town of San Lorenzo de El Escorial, 45 kilometers (28 miles) northwest of **Madrid**, this palace complex consists of a palace, a monastery, a basilica, a pantheon, a school, and a library. The palace was once the residence of the Spanish royal family, and the basilica is the burial site of the Spanish monarchs. On 10 June 1947, Evita paid a visit to the Royal Site of San Lorenzo de El Escorial as part of the **Rainbow Tour**. Evita and **María del Carmen Polo y Martínez-Valdés** arrived at 12:45 p.m. and were welcomed by the local authorities and members of the clergy. Their first stop was the basilica, where they prayed and visited the Pantheon of the Kings. Later, Evita had lunch at the palace.

S

SAINTHOOD OF EVITA. *See* CANONIZATION OF EVITA; ICON.

SAN JUAN EARTHQUAKE. This earthquake that affected San Juan Province in western Argentina on 15 January 1944 served as a catalyst for bringing **Juan Domingo Perón** and Evita together. Located in the Andes region, the city of San Juan is prone to seismic activity, and the devastating 1944 earthquake reduced the provincial capital to rubble in less than a minute. Almost 10,000 people lost their lives and 90 percent of the buildings were destroyed. As secretary of labor and social welfare, Perón acted quickly. Two days after the disaster, he organized and coordinated a national relief campaign to help the victims of the earthquake. Evita was among the volunteers who asked for cash donations in the central Florida Street of Buenos Aires. There are various accounts describing Evita and Perón's first encounter. One of them maintains that Evita met Perón at the **Secretariat of Labor and Social Welfare**, where she took the money collected. The official version, however, claims that Perón and Evita met during a fund-raising festival for the earthquake at the **Luna Park Stadium** on 22 January 1944. Perón attended the festival together with President **Pedro Pablo Ramírez** and his wife, while Evita went along with a friend of hers, Rita Molina. Once President Ramírez and his wife had left, Evita and Molina approached Perón and the three of them engaged in conversation. At the end of the festival, Evita and Perón left together, and a few days later they made their first public appearance as a couple at **Radio Belgrano**.

SAN MARTÍN, JOSÉ DE (1778–1850). Born to Spanish parents in the northeastern province of Corrientes, José Francisco de San Martín y Matorras—commonly known as José de San Martín—is considered one of the founding fathers of Argentina and a national hero. After serving in the Spanish army for 20 years, he switched sides and joined the Spanish American wars of independence against Spain in 1812. General San Martín was instrumental in the fight for the independence of Argentina, Chile, and Peru as he led his troops to victory. To honor his memory, the government of General **Pedro Pablo Ramírez** passed a decree on 17 August 1943 establishing the Order of the Liberator General San Martín, a national decoration to be awarded to foreign chiefs of state and military officers for distinguished service to Argentina and to humanity. Nine years later, when Evita was bedridden due to her illness, she was presented with the collar of the order—a magnificent piece of jewelry that she never had a chance to wear.

SAN VICENTE COUNTRY HOUSE. Before becoming president of Argentina, **Juan Domingo Perón** bought a country house in San Vicente, a town in Buenos Aires Province. After meeting Evita, he spent his weekends there with her and, later in his life, with his third wife, **Isabel Martínez de Perón**. The house, which dates from the 1940s, is approximately

400 square meters (4,300 square feet) and is currently home to the **Historical Museum 17 October**. Apart from the museum, visitors have access to the Torreón, a building in the shape of a tower from which Perón used to broadcast his speeches and Christmas greetings, and to a mausoleum that has held Perón's remains since 2006. The transfer of Perón's remains from the Chacarita Cemetery in Buenos Aires, where he was buried, to the mausoleum in San Vicente was supported by President **Eduardo Alberto Duhalde**. The most striking feature of this historical property is the display of two enormous marble statues that were originally intended to be part of Evita's resting place, the **Monument of the *Descamisado***. One of the statues depicts Perón and a *descamisado* holding the **Bill of Rights of the Workers** and the other, Evita holding her book *La razón de mi vida* (*My Mission in Life*). The monument was never built, and the statues were decapitated—except for the *descamisado* one—and thrown into the Río de la Matanza after Perón was toppled in 1955. It is said that the *descamisado*'s head was spared the same fate so as not to offend the working class. In 1996, the statues were recovered from the river and taken to San Vicente. *See also* LIBERATING REVOLUTION; TOMASSI, LEONE.

***SANTA EVITA* NOVEL.** Translated into more than 30 languages, *Santa Evita* is one of the best-selling books of all time. Published in 1995, this postmodern novel written by the Argentine writer **Tomás Eloy Martínez** explores the bizarre wandering of Evita's corpse—the novel's main character—without neglecting the inclusion of significant events in Evita's life. Set chiefly in Buenos Aires, *Santa Evita* begins with the last hours of Evita's life in July 1952 and then traces the peregrination of her corpse. The story narrates how her body becomes the object of obsession for the Spanish embalmer Dr. **Pedro Ara** and the various parties seeking to control Argentina after **Juan Domingo Perón**'s downfall in 1955. While narrating the odyssey of her body, the novel also employs flashbacks to tell the story of her life, starting with her death and finishing with her childhood. The penultimate chapter of the book deals with her infancy and another corpse, namely her father's. Martínez reconstructs the life and death of Evita through interviews, documents, screenplays, and testimonies. Challenging the borders between fiction and nonfiction, the novel incorporates excerpts from Evita's life based on interviews with, among others, her butler **Atilio Renzi** and her hairdresser **Julio Alcaraz**. The author appears in the novel as a fictional character and narrator who tells the reader about the book he is writing. He cites sources, describes interviews, ponders over the nature of his own project, and confesses that his novel is the result of many years of research and interviews. Drawing on magical realism, this fact-based novel blends biography, history, and myth. *Santa Evita* has become the foundation for an eponymous TV series directed by the Colombian filmmaker Rodrigo García. *See also* BODY OF EVITA; LIBERATING REVOLUTION; *SANTA EVITA* SERIES.

***SANTA EVITA* SERIES.** This seven-episode series produced by the Mexican actress Salma Hayek and directed by the Colombian filmmaker Rodrigo García is based on the eponymous best seller by the Argentine writer **Tomás Eloy Martínez**. The series, which portrays the odyssey of Evita's embalmed body after her death in 1952, is narrated from a contemporary feminist perspective. Starring Natalia Oreiro, Ernesto Alterio, and Darío Grandinetti, *Santa Evita* is currently in production. *See also* BODY OF EVITA; *SANTA EVITA* NOVEL.

SANTA MARÍA DEL BUEN AIRE NATIONAL CAMP. Located next to the **Royal Site of San Lorenzo de El Escorial** and named in honor of Argentina, the Santa María del Buen Aire National Camp was one of the many camps managed by the National Delegation of the Youth Front. Evita, **María del Carmen Polo y Martínez-Valdés**, and their entourage arrived at this camp on 10 June 1947 at 3:30 p.m. Following a welcoming ceremony, the guests took part in a tour of the grounds, received gifts, attended a puppet show, and enjoyed the performances of the camp's choir. *See also* MADRID; RAINBOW TOUR.

SANTIAGO DE COMPOSTELA. Worldwide known as the destination of the Camino de Santiago or the Way of St. James, Santiago de Compostela is the capital city of the autonomous community of Galicia in northwestern Spain. As part of her official visit to Spain, Evita visited the city on 19 June 1947. She arrived by plane at Lavacolla Airport, situated 11 kilometers (6.8 miles) from the city center, and was welcomed by the Spanish navy minister, Admiral Francisco Regalado Fernández, his wife, and local and regional authorities who had come from all over Galicia to greet her. Thousands of people lined the road from the airport to the city, cheering and gaping in awe as Evita drove past. Her arrival in the central Plaza de España was not less spectacular. People had descended on Santiago to see her, and the plaza was packed. When Evita arrived, the joyous crowd would not stop cheering. After a reception at the Pazo de Raxoi, where she received numerous gifts, Evita took part in the enthronement of Our Lady of Luján's image at the Santiago de Compostela Cathedral. Before leaving the city, Evita planted a Nordmann fir dubbed **La Perona** in the Alameda Park. The tree, which is 20 meters (72 feet) high, can still be seen today. *See also* RAINBOW TOUR.

SANTORO, DANIEL (1954–). This controversial Argentine visual artist studied at the Argentine Academy of Fine Arts. A trip to Singapore in the 1980s awakened his interest in the Chinese language, Chinese calligraphy, and Eastern philosophy—elements that he incorporated into his art. However, Santoro made a name for himself by fusing Peronist iconography with religious symbolism. Evita, the work of the **Fundación Eva Perón**, and **Juan Domingo Perón** feature prominently in many of his paintings. He collaborated with the sculptor **Alejandro Marmo** in crafting the **murals of Evita** that currently hang from the Ministry of Social Development Building in Buenos Aires.

SCHÖNFELD, NICOLÁS (1901–1977). Born in Hungary, this renowned photographer arrived in Argentina in 1930. His brother Luis, who also lived in Argentina, reportedly suggested that Schönfeld should become a photographer since he could not speak Spanish. Two years later, Schönfeld opened his studio in Buenos Aires. Like **Annemarie Heinrich** and **Sivul Wilenski**, Schönfeld specialized in portraits. He collaborated with such magazines as *El Hogar* and *Caras y Caretas* and photographed Evita in the late 1930s. In an interview with *Así* magazine in 1975, Schönfeld stated that Evita was a kind young woman, deeply sensitive, attentive, and very elegant. He added that the negatives of her portraits had been archived in his studio for many years. These portraits had been requested and paid for by the actor **Tomás Simari**. *See also* COMPAÑÍA CÓMICA SIMARI-SIMARI.

SECOND INAUGURATION OF JUAN DOMINGO PERÓN. On 4 June 1952—a few weeks before Evita died—**Raúl Alejandro Apold** arrived at the **Unzué Palace** to show her some propaganda work. Because Evita was feeble from her long illness, **Juan Domingo Perón** asked Apold to persuade her not to attend his second inauguration as president of Argentina, which was due on the same day. Apold used the cold weather as an excuse to prevent her from going, but she became furious, saying that only her death would keep her in bed. As she was too weak to stand up, one of the employees of the presidential residence put together a frame made of plaster and wire to support her frail limbs. Donning a fur coat too large for her and standing inside the contraption, Evita was able to ride next to Perón in the back of an open car from the Argentine National Congress to the **Pink House**. She waved and smiled to the crowds. To endure the inaugural ceremony, she took extra painkillers. At the time, she weighed less than 40 kilograms (88 pounds).

SECRETARIAT OF INFORMATION AND PRESS. This secretariat was created in 1943 by President **Pedro Pablo Ramírez**. Between 1947 and 1955, **Raúl Alejandro Apold**, the secretary of information and press, transformed it into a Peronist propaganda office. Not only did he promote **Peronism**, he also made sure that the press, broadcasting, and film industries followed the official line. Those artists and journalists who did not comply with the Peronist government regulations usually lost their jobs, were imprisoned, or had to go into exile. Furthermore, the secretariat also imposed strict restrictions on the distribution of press paper based unofficially on favoritism. The secretariat was part of the Peronist government's strategy to monopolize the mass media in Argentina. *See also* ALEA S.A.; ANTI-ARGENTINE ACTIVITIES CONGRESSIONAL COMMITTEE.

SECRETARIAT OF LABOR AND SOCIAL WELFARE. Since 1907, the former National Department of Labor, which was located in the current Palace of the Buenos Aires City Legislature, had been responsible for all labor issues in Argentina. In 1943, the military government that seized power carried out a reorganization of the state agencies, and this department became the Secretariat of Labor and Social Welfare. When Colonel **Juan Domingo Perón** became secretary of labor and social welfare, the secretariat changed radically the government's labor policy. Improvements for workers included higher wages, better working conditions, and paid vacation days, among others. Perón's pro-labor policy managed not only to organize the workers' unions but also to keep them under control and to guarantee their support. However, most employers, such as owners of factories and businesses, voiced their discontent with Perón's concessions to workers as they implied more problems and expenses. Evita had an office at the secretariat where she worked as an adviser and mediator between workers' unions and Perón, and as the head of her **Fundación Eva Perón**. With the amendment to the **Argentine Constitution of 1949**, the secretariat became the Ministry of Labor and Social Welfare and in 1958 the Ministry of Labor and Social Security. In 2002, the ministry changed its name once more to Ministry of Labor, Employment, and Social Security. In 2018, President Mauricio Macri announced a reduction in the number of ministries in the Argentine government. As a result, the ministry became the Secretariat of Labor under the Ministry of Labor and Production, currently located at 650 Leandro N. Alem Avenue in Buenos Aires. *See also* KIRCHNER CULTURAL CENTER; REVOLUTION OF 1943.

SEGOVIA. Located in the autonomous community of Castile and León, Spain, this is one of the cities that Evita visited together with **María del Carmen Polo y Martínez-Valdés** during her tour of Spain in 1947. The local authorities and hundreds of people welcomed the ladies at the Plaza del Azoguejo on 11 June at 8 p.m. After a brief stopover, the distinguished guests continued their journey to **La Granja de San Ildefonso**. *See also* RAINBOW TOUR.

¡SEGUNDOS AFUERA! Directed by Israel Chas de Cruz and Alberto Etchebehere, *¡Segundos afuera!* (Seconds Out!) was produced by **Argentina Sono Film** and released on 4 August 1937. This boxing comedy movie was Evita's debut film. It depicts the conflict between two identical twins with very distinctive personalities and professions—one is a boxer and the other an office clerk. The rivalry between the bold boxer and the clumsy office clerk is resolved by the latter taking the former's place in the boxing ring. These two characters are played by the same actor, **Pedro Quartucci**. Evita has a minimal participation in the film, and her role adds very little to driving the actual plot. She played a ship passenger who prevents a boxing manager from committing suicide. The boxing manager is on his way to Argentina to partake in a boxing fight, and his opponent is none other than the office clerk. Rumors had it that Evita and Quartucci were lovers, but this has never been confirmed.

SENIOR RESIDENCES. Upon the proclamation of the **Decalogue of the Rights of Seniors**, the **Fundación Eva Perón** inaugurated the Hogar para Ancianos Coronel Perón (Colonel Perón Senior Residence) on 17 October 1948 in Burzaco, Buenos Aires Province. This was one of the four residences for seniors opened by the foundation. It is currently the only one that remains in operation and that retains its distinct architectural style. The other residences were opened in the provinces of **Córdoba**, Santa Fe, and Tucumán. The residence—which formerly belonged to the German Society of Beneficence—originally included dormitories for 200 people, a dining room, medical and dental centers, recreation rooms, a library, a social room, workshops, a launderette, and a sewing room. During the day, the elderly could carry out recreational and occupational therapy activities, for example, in basketry, broom making, printing, or gardening. The elderly were cared for by personnel of the foundation, which in turn was assisted by nuns living on the premises.

SEVILLE. Seville is the capital city of the autonomous community of Andalusia in Spain. As part of her official visit to Spain, Evita and her entourage stayed in this city from 16 to 19 June 1947. Upon arriving in Seville by plane, she was greeted by, among others, the mayor of Seville, Rafael de Medina y Villalonga, who escorted her to the luxurious Alfonso XIII Hotel, where she would be staying during her visit. Later that day, she attended a welcoming ceremony at the Seville City Hall and a gala function at the Mudejar Pavilion together with the mayor of Seville and the Argentine ambassador to Spain, **Pedro Radío**, among other authorities. The grand finale of the eventful day was a folk music and dance show in her honor. The following day, Evita visited the impressive Seville Cathedral and the Church of St. Giles, where she was named Chamber Maid of Honor for the Brotherhood of Hope. She also paid a visit to the Royal Tobacco Factory and the Torre Pavadel Estate. On 18 June, she traveled to Huelva and returned to Seville late in the evening. During her visit, Evita received countless gifts, and wherever she went people crowded around her, cheering, waving, and holding Argentine and Spanish flags. *See also* RAINBOW TOUR.

SHIRTLESS ONES, THE. *See* DESCAMISADOS.

SIMARI, TOMÁS (1897–1981). This Argentine theater, radio, film, and television actor made his debut in film with Arturo Mom's *Loco lindo* (Crazy Dandy) in 1936. During his acting career, he was cast in 11 movies. He set up his own theater company with his bother Leopoldo. Evita was hired by the Simari brothers in 1940 and performed with them in three unsuccessful plays. Reportedly, she was photographed around this time by **Nicolás Schönfeld** at Simari's request. Simari continued working in theater until 1946, the year he launched his radio career. He became an established television actor in the 1950s and 1960s together with his wife, the famous Argentine actress Adelaida Soler. *See also* COMPAÑÍA CÓMICA SIMARI-SIMARI.

SINTONÍA. A show-business magazine, *Sintonía* was first published by **Haynes Publishing** in 1933 and served as **Radio El Mundo**'s supplement from 1935. *Sintonía* was issued monthly and was approximately 70 pages long. Its cover usually featured portraits of popular artists. The magazine focused on general information as well as the programming of the main radio stations in Buenos Aires. It also included ballet, folklore, music, gossip, fashion, and national and international cinema sections. Evita met the editor-in-chief of *Sintonía*, **Emilio Kartulovich**, in 1938 thanks to her involvement in a radio contest sponsored by the magazine. The winner of the contest would be one of the singers in *La gruta de la fortuna* (The Grotto of Fortune), a play to be performed by the **Compañía Argentina de Espectáculos Cómicos**. On 19 October of the same year, Evita had her first interview published in *Sintonía* with three photographs by **Sivul Wilenski**. The article was titled "El credo amoroso de una adolescente. Eva Duarte afirma que el amor solo llega una vez en la vida de una mujer" (A Teenager's Love Creed. Eva Duarte Says Love Only Comes Once in a Woman's Life). Evita appeared on the cover of *Sintonía* for the first time on 25 October 1939. The color picture shows Evita and Alberto Vila as the stars of **Radio Prieto**, which was celebrating its 14th anniversary. Although she appeared on the cover, Evita was barely mentioned in the cover article. Nevertheless, this was a significant step for the rising star.

SOCIETY OF BENEFICENCE OF BUENOS AIRES. By the time **Juan Domingo Perón**

became president of Argentina in 1946, this charitable organization, which had been created back in 1823, was run by 87 wealthy ladies who managed and inspected schools for girls, homes for orphans and the elderly, hospitals for women, and a sanatorium. Although the charity was funded mainly by the state, the ladies ran it as if the organization belonged to them. Their management was heavily criticized by Congress in 1946, to the extent that the charity's existence was at stake. On 26 July 1946, the Society of Beneficence of Buenos Aires ceased to exist. Evita's involvement in the dissolution of the charity has brought about at least two versions of the facts. The first claims that Evita took revenge when the ladies did not accept her as their honorary president, a role that was normally assigned to the country's first lady, who had usually come from an upper-class family. Seeking revenge, Evita closed the charity and handed it to the state. The second version posits that when there was very little to be done to save the charity, the ladies invited Evita as a last recourse and asked her to be their honorary president. Instead of accepting, Evita informed them that the government policy was to replace charity with social justice. Regardless of what took place, the charity was handed to the state, and two years later Evita created the Fundación de Ayuda Social María Eva Duarte de Perón. *See also* FUNDACIÓN EVA PERÓN.

ST. EVITA'S DAY. *See* ST. PERÓN'S DAY.

ST. PERÓN'S DAY. On 17 October 1945, thousands of Argentines flocked to the **Plaza de Mayo**, forcing the government to release **Juan Domingo Perón**, who had been taken to prison on **Martín García Island**. Late in the evening when Perón finally appeared on the balcony of the **Pink House**, the crowd cheered for 15 minutes before Perón could speak. He asked them to sing the national anthem, delivered an impromptu speech, and requested they disperse peacefully. As the following day had been scheduled as a general strike, Perón told them that they should spend the day celebrating their achievement and not actively protesting. Immediately after this, the crowd started chanting, "Tomorrow is St. Perón's Day, let the boss work." The next day, the general strike brought the country to a standstill, and people were indeed celebrating their victory instead of protesting. St. Perón's Day was thereafter celebrated every 18 October up to 1950. Perón himself declared 18 October 1951 St. Evita's Day in honor of his wife, who was terminally ill. *See also* CANONIZATION OF EVITA; ICON; PERONIST LOYALTY DAY.

STATE FUNERAL OF EVITA. Evita passed away on 26 July 1952. News of her death was broadcast throughout Argentina as soon as she died, and hundreds of thousands of Argentines made their way to the **Unzué Palace** and the Ministry of Labor and Social Welfare to mourn her. The grief was so deep that the whole country came to a standstill. Flags on government buildings were flown at half-mast for 10 days. All members of the **Confederación Genral del Trabajo (CGT)** were asked to wear a black tie or ribbon for a month. Tributes poured in from such world dignitaries as Britain's Queen Elizabeth and President Harry S. Truman. The day after her death, her embalmed body was taken to the Ministry of Labor and Social Welfare, where she lay in state for 13 days. Reportedly, 3,000,000 people attended her funeral and religious service. While some people just touched the coffin, others cried uncontrollably. On 9 August, the coffin was taken to the Argentine Congress, where she was given the honors due to a head of state. The following day an impressive cortège escorted the coffin to the headquarters of the CGT. Thousands of people lined the streets of Buenos Aires, and flowers rained down onto the cortège from the nearby balconies. The coffin was placed on the second floor of the building, where it remained until 1955, when a military coup d'état toppled **Juan Domingo Perón**'s government. *See also* ARA, PEDRO; BODY OF EVITA; LIBERATING REVOLUTION; MOORI KOENIG, CARLOS EUGENIO DE; SECRETARIAT OF LABOR AND SOCIAL WELFARE; TIME OF EVITA'S DEATH.

SU PALABRA, SU PENSAMIENTO Y SU ACCIÓN. *See* LA PALABRA, EL PENSAMIENTO Y LA ACCIÓN.

SUERO SIERO, PABLO "EL SAPO" (1898–1943). Born in Gijón, Spain, Pablo Suero Siero migrated with his family to Argentina when he was a child. On 15 June 1936, El Sapo, as he was known, married Delia Díaz Vélez, and they had two children—Pablo and Delia. Even though his passion was to write poetry and literature, he started working as a journalist to support his family. Suero worked for *Crítica* and later collaborated with other papers and magazines in Buenos Aires and Montevideo, Uruguay. He eventually became the editor-in-chief of the prestigious Argentine newspaper *Noticias Gráficas*. During his career, he interviewed many politicians and celebrities in Buenos Aires, Montevideo, **Madrid**, and **Paris**. In addition, his work as a writer, songwriter, playwright, and theater director allowed him to become acquainted with many artists. Suero met Evita in 1935. The young actress was hired to be part of his theater company, which performed *Las inocentes* (*The Children's Hour*) in Buenos Aires and Montevideo between December 1935 and January 1936. Reportedly, Evita and Suero became lovers, but their relationship was over as soon as the play stopped running. Suero apparently passed away after being knocked down by a car on 3 February 1943.

SWITZERLAND. This country was Evita's last stop during her **Rainbow Tour**. She and her entourage traveled by train from **Monaco** to Geneva in Switzerland, where they arrived on 3 August 1947. It was not made clear why Evita went to Switzerland since it was not part of the original itinerary and was only added to the list of countries while she was already in Europe. This lack of clarity gave rise to speculation. Whereas some opposing voices in Argentina claimed that she went there to deposit money in a Swiss bank account, others asserted that the purpose of her visit was to meet with Nazi collaborators and sympathizers. Regarding the former, **Lillian Lagomarsino de Guardo**, who was always by Evita's side on her European tour, denied it. Concerning the latter, there are several publications that argue in favor of this hypothesis. What is certain is that the Argentine ambassador to the country, **Benito Pedro Llambí**, had organized her visit, but, contrary to the warm welcome she received in Spain, she was met with hostility in Switzerland. While visiting Bern, Evita and the Swiss foreign minister, Max Petitpierre, were pelted with tomatoes. In Lucerne, her chauffeur was injured as a result of a flying rock that hit the windscreen of her car. Despite these incidents, Evita was composed. When one of the members of her entourage asked her if she was afraid, she replied, "One cannot be afraid when one represents a state." On 10 August, she left Switzerland, flying from Geneva first to **Lisbon** and then to Dakar, where she boarded the *Buenos Aires*—one of **Alberto Dodero**'s ships—for the return journey to South America. *See also* RIO DE JANEIRO.

T

TAIANA, JORGE ALBERTO (1911–2001). Together with Dr. Alberto Taquini, this Argentine physician issued Evita's death certificate on 26 July 1952.

TAILLEUR. A *tailleur* is a woman's tailor-made suit. Evita's iconic *tailleur* was originally designed by **Francisco "Paco" Vicente Jamandreu**. *See also* FERNÁNDEZ, MARÍA ASUNCIÓN "ASUNTA"; PALMOU, JUANA.

TECUARA. This presidential yacht was used by Evita on various occasions. One of her first trips on board the yacht was from Puerto de Barranqueras in the province of Chaco to Itatí in the province of Corrientes on 27 October 1947. She also sailed on the *Tecuara* from Buenos Aires to Santa Fe to partake in the celebrations commemorating the Battle of San Lorenzo on 3 February 1950. Her last trip outside of Buenos Aires was on the *Tecuara*. Despite being very ill, she sailed to Campana in the province of Buenos Aires on 10 January 1952 to attend the opening of a factory, but once she arrived at her destination, she did not leave the yacht. On each of these occasions, she was accompanying **Juan Domingo Perón**.

TEMPORARY HOMES. The **Fundación Eva Perón** opened three temporary residences in Buenos Aires in 1948. They were located very near each other: the first one, at 102 Carlos Calvo Street; the second one, at 2988 Lafinur Street; and the third one, at 2561 Austria Street. Soon after its opening, the first home had to be closed and reopened at a different location—1773 Las Heras Avenue—due to the poor condition of the building. Their main purpose was to provide temporary assistance and protection to people in need of medical treatment, employment, or housing. Their priority, however, was to aid (single) women (with children) who arrived in the capital city and had no place to stay. People usually stayed in the homes for approximately a week or until their issues were solved. The services provided, which included food and accommodation, were free, and upon leaving the premises people got additional assistance such as medical equipment, money, clothes, transport tickets, working tools, scholarships, or access to permanent accommodation. Each home had between 70 and 90 beds plus baby cots and a medical clinic. They offered luxury accommodation and amenities such as patios, libraries, and dining rooms with separate tables so that families could eat together. The home on Lafinur Street even had a chapel, often used for baptisms. Apart from this, women could train as secretaries or seamstresses, skills that would increase their chances to get a job in the future. After the 1955 military coup d'état, the homes were closed. However, in the 1990s, the one located on Lafinur Street eventually became the headquarters of the **Instituto Nacional de Investigaciones Históricas Eva Perón** and, in 2002, the **Evita Museum**, both still in operation. *See also* HOGAR DE LA EMPLEADA GENERAL SAN MARTÍN; LIBERATING REVOLUTION.

TEQUARA. *See TECUARA.*

TERMAS DE REYES. This spa is situated 19 kilometers (11.8 miles) from the city of San Salvador de Jujuy in the northern province of Jujuy. Termas de Reyes is currently a resort spa, but its history dates back to the times of the Incas, who believed in the healing properties of its waters. To promote tourism in the region, the government of Jujuy opened a hotel at this site in 1938. However, the hotel was expropriated by the Perón administration in 1946 and handed over to the **Fundación Eva Perón**. The hotel was then repurposed with the aim of turning it into a school, a home, and a sanatorium for children with special needs and those from disadvantaged backgrounds. Evita visited the place on 5 June 1950 as part of a tour in northern Argentina. She arrived in San Salvador de Jujuy by train and was warmly welcomed by crowds waving the Argentine flag and holding portraits of **Juan Domingo Perón** and Evita. With the overthrow of Perón in 1955, the place was closed. *See also* LIBERATING REVOLUTION.

THIRD POSITION. *See JUSTICIALISMO.*

THOUSAND SCHOOLS SCHEME. During **Juan Domingo Perón**'s second term (1952–1955), a great number of national primary schools and **home-schools** were built across Argentina. The delivery of this ambitious program, which was called the Thousand Schools Scheme, was overseen by the **Fun-**

School Number 165 in Puerto Piray (Guaraní for "river of fish"), Misiones Province, built in 1952 as part of the Thousand Schools Scheme.

Teacher's residence adjacent to School Number 165 in Puerto Piray, Misiones Province, built in 1952 as part of the Thousand Schools Scheme.

School Number 241 in Colonia Yabebiry (Guaraní for "river of frogs"), Misiones Province, built in 1952 as part of the Thousand Schools Scheme. The Fundación Eva Perón brought education to remote and rural areas of Argentina.

dación Eva Perón. In this way, education was provided to those children living in remote and rural areas of the country. By July 1952, the foundation had built 120 schools and 190 were under construction.

TIME. This weekly American magazine published several articles on Evita. The first article appeared in the 26 August 1946 issue and compared her busy public life with that of Eleanor Roosevelt. Dated 23 June 1947, "Dashing Blonde" was an article devoted to Evita's arrival in **Madrid**. The 14 July 1947 issue of *Time* displayed a portrait of Evita by the Russian-born artist Boris Chaliapin. Her portrait appears on a yellow sun partially surrounded by a blue background—an image that clearly alludes to the Argentine flag. The caption that accompanied the portrait read, "Between two worlds, an Argentine rainbow," which made reference to Evita's **Rainbow Tour**. Indeed, this issue of

Time reported on Evita's visit to Europe in a four-page feature article that also included an unsympathetic biography of her. The Argentine government reacted to the unpleasant article by banning the sale of the weekly in Argentina during the months of August and September 1947. Evita landed the cover of *Time* for a second time on 21 May 1951, sharing it with her husband, President **Juan Domingo Perón**. They were both portrayed by the American artist Ernest Baker, and the caption accompanying the illustration read, "Argentina's Peróns: Without fanaticism one cannot accomplish anything." While Perón appears as the dominant figure, exuding anger, Evita's smile and serenity counteracts his rage. The article of the 21 May 1951 issue was a critical view of the Peronist government, comparing Perón with the Italian fascist Benito Mussolini and criticizing his administration. Half of the article was devoted to Evita, who was also heavily criticized for her involvement in the government. Indeed, her involvement was unprecedented for Argentine women. The article concluded that the Peróns constituted an unstoppable tandem. On 5 March 2020 and as part of a revisionist project called "100 Women of the Year," *Time* selected a woman or group of women to represent each year between 1920 and 2020. Evita was chosen for the 1946 cover. The essay that accounts for the selection of Evita hinged on her social programs and her support to the passage of female suffrage in Argentina in 1947. The caption that accompanied the photo of Evita read, "Woman of the people."

TIME OF EVITA'S DEATH. Even though Evita died on 26 July 1952 at 8:23 p.m., the time of her death was officially listed as 8:25 p.m. Reportedly, Secretary of Information and Press **Raúl Alejandro Apold** modified the time of Evita's death by two minutes to achieve a more memorable number. From the day of Evita's death until the fall of **Peronism**, the news was interrupted each evening with the message, "It is 8:25 p.m., the time when Eva Perón entered immortality."

TIZÓN, AURELIA GABRIELA (1902–1938). The first wife of **Juan Domingo Perón**, Aurelia Gabriela Tizón came from a respectable middle-class Buenos Aires family. She was a schoolteacher who liked to draw and paint. As she could also read English, she reportedly translated a few English military textbooks for Perón. She married Perón on 5 January 1929 at Our Lady of Luján Church in the neighborhood of Belgrano, Buenos Aires, and the marriage lasted until her death. Like Evita, she died of cervical cancer.

TOLEDO. Toledo is the capital city of the eponymous province in the autonomous community of Castile-La Mancha, Spain. This ancient city is located approximately 67 kilometers (42 miles) southwest of **Madrid** on the banks of the Río Tagus. Toledo was part of Evita's itinerary during her visit to Spain in 1947. Shortly after 2:30 p.m. on 13 June, Evita and **María del Carmen Polo y Martínez-Valdés** were welcomed by Toledo's local authorities at the Plaza de Zocodover. After enjoying a dance and music show and receiving several gifts, Evita had lunch at the Toledo City Hall. She finished her tour of the city by visiting the **Primate Cathedral of St. Mary of Toledo** and the **Alcázar**. *See also* RAINBOW TOUR.

TOMASSI, LEONE (1903–1965). This famous Italian painter and sculptor lived most of his life in Pietrasanta, Italy, but from 1950 to 1954 he traveled back and forth between Italy and Argentina to carry out a series of projects that would exalt **Peronism**. Initially, **Juan Domingo Perón** and Evita had commissioned Tomassi to do two projects. The first one was to craft 10 statues six meters (19.6 feet) high for the frontispiece of the neoclassical building located at 850 Avenue Paseo Colón in Buenos Aires that would house the **Fundación Eva Perón**. The statues decorated the impressive building only until 1955, when the leaders of the **Liberating Revolution** got rid of them. The second project consisted of making statues of Perón and Evita, but this project was never completed. Instead, in 1951, Evita commissioned him to design a monument in honor of the *descamisados*. When Tomassi presented the model of the **Monument of the Descamisado** to Evita in December 1951, she was extremely pleased with the result. With her death, however, Tomassi was asked to redesign the monument, presenting a new model to Perón and the **National Commission for the Eva Perón Monument**. Tomassi managed to sculpt some of the figures that would decorate the monument before the Liberating Revolution seized power and threw them into the Río de la Matanza. *See also* FACULTY OF ENGINEERING BUILDING.

TOURNAMENTS. The **Fundación Eva Perón**, in collaboration with the Secretariat of Health, started to organize annual soccer tournaments for children and teenagers in 1948. Known as Campeonatos Infantiles Evita (Evita Children Tournaments), these championships were part of a state program that not only promoted sports among the less privileged but also assessed the health of the young participants. Before the children were allowed to take part in the games, they underwent a rigorous medical health screening. Attended by approximately 20,000 participants, the first of these tournaments featured a soccer championship targeted at boys and teenagers from the city and the province of Buenos Aires. This championship opened with a song titled "Marcha del Primer Campeonato de Fútbol Infantil Evita" (March of the First Children's Soccer Championship Evita), which praised Evita's work for children and underscored the function of sports as a socializing tool. The following tournaments included participants from the rest of the provinces and national territories. After 1951, other sports such as swimming, track and field, boxing, rope climbing, and water polo were included. From 1952, the Campeonatos welcomed girls into the tournaments for most sports. The success of these tournaments led to the creation of the Campeonatos Juveniles Deportivos **Juan Domingo Perón** (Juan Domingo Perón Youth Sports Tournaments) for teenagers in 1953. The biggest reward for the winning team was a new state-of-the-art soccer field in their neighborhood and a state-issued grant to improve other sports and recreation facilities in the winner's local area. Until 1951, Evita would be present at the opening ceremony of these tournaments, but her poor health prevented her from attending the 1952 tournament.

TRANSNATIONAL ICONIC IMAGE OF EVITA. Evita's image captivated worldwide attention through Alan Parker's 1996 film *Evita*, starring yet another popular **icon**, the American singer Madonna. This film took the image of Evita to another level due to the combination of Evita's and Madonna's public images. However, the global iconic force that Evita gained through this film was the result of a complex historical, political, and cultural process that started in the 1940s and culminated in 1996 with the release of Parker's film. Throughout that period, the image of Evita was re-iconized as a saint, a martyr, and a revolutionary. This in turn generated the creation of ideologically influenced cultural forms that increased the existing profusion of different images of Evita. A case in point is the narrative of the *Evita muerta*. This narrative, which encompasses Evita's death, funeral, quasi-holiness, and body, has developed at both national and transnational levels. An example of this narrative is **Tomás Eloy Martínez**'s best-selling novel *Santa Evita*. The revolutionary side of the re-iconized image of Evita, which emerged in the 1960s and 1970s with guerrilla groups such as the **Montoneros**, did not experience the same proliferation abroad as it did in Argentina. The remembrance of the political Evita, as encouraged by former president **Cristina Fernández de Kirchner**, might not refer specifically to the revolutionary figure but, to some extent, kept the image of Evita as a political symbol present in Argentina. Outside of Argentina, the image of Evita seems to have been denuded of the political associations that it acquired before and after her death to regain force as a more commercial transnational icon. In other words, at the time when Evita reached transnational iconic status in the 1990s, the images that were given prominence were not those that emerged in Argentina in the 1960s and 1970s but those that she had acquired prior to her death. *See also* BODY OF EVITA; CANONIZATION OF EVITA; CICCONE, MADONNA LOUISE; STATE FUNERAL OF EVITA.

TRIBUNA. This nationalist daily was founded in 1946 by Lautaro Ludañona y Vedia. *Tribuna* was one of the few papers that supported the **Juan Domingo Perón–Juan Hortensio Quijano** ticket during the 1945–1946 presidential campaign. *See also* DEMOCRACIA; *EL LABORISTA*; *LA ÉPOCA*.

TRIPLE A. The Argentine Anti-Communist Alliance, better known as the Triple A, was a far-right secret organization set up during **Juan Domingo Perón**'s third mandate by Minister of Social Welfare **José López Rega**. Police officers, military men, labor union leaders, and right-wing **Peronists** were among its members. The Triple A, whose modus operandi included kidnappings, torture, and executions of leftist Peronist militants and sympathizers, started its operations in 1973 and carried out hundreds of attacks, killing approximately 500 people. Whether the organization operated with Perón's consent remains an unanswered question, but it is certain that he did nothing to stop it. The Triple A was dismantled by the military government that seized power in 1976. Many Triple A members fled to Spain, where they became involved in assassinations of Spanish leftists during the transition to democracy in that country. *See also* DIRTY WAR; EZEIZA MASSACRE; HUMAN RIGHTS IN ARGENTINA; MONTONEROS.

TURISMO SOCIAL. Under the umbrella term *social justice*, the **Peronist** government introduced a series of policies to create the **New Argentina**—that is, a more just and equal society. As a result, leisure became a civic right, hitherto unattainable for most working-class people. One of the policies linked to leisure was the implementation of *turismo social* (social tourism), the aim of which was to make vacations and recreational activities accessible to all. To this end, the government promoted affordable vacation and excursion packages to national parks and popular destinations such as the Iguazú Falls in northern Argentina. The scheme also advertised (long) weekend breaks at camping sites managed by governmental institutions such as the **Fundación Eva Perón**. The most popular vacation destinations of the scheme were the Chapadmalal, Embalse Río Tercero, and Uspallata resorts in the provinces of Buenos Aires, **Córdoba**, and **Mendoza**, respectively. Sponsored by the government, the *turismo social* project was considered a public priority. It was initially managed by the **Confederación General del Trabajo** through the Workers' Tourism Council. Eventually, the organization and administration of social tourism was also the responsibility of the Fundación Eva Perón.

TWENTY PERONIST TENETS. On 17 October 1950, Peronist supporters gathered at the **Plaza de Mayo** in Buenos Aires to commemorate the **Peronist Loyalty Day**. During his speech, **Juan Domingo Perón** introduced the Twenty Peronist Tenets, which represented the essence of his political philosophy. From the balcony of the **Pink House**, Perón stated, "These are the twenty tenets of the Peronist *justicialismo*. I have put them together in this way so that each one of you may engrave them on your minds and on your hearts, spread them as a message of love and justice everywhere, live happily according to them, and willingly give your lives in their defense if necessary."

The tenets were the following: (1) True democracy is when the government does only what the people want and defends only one interest: that of the people. (2) **Peronism** is essentially popular. Every political clique is opposed to the popular interest and for that reason not Peronist. (3) A **Peronist** must be at the service of the cause. Whoever invokes the name of this cause is really at the service of a political clique or a **caudillo** and therefore only a Peronist in name. (4) For Peronism there exists only one class of men: workers. (5) In the **New Argentina**, work is a right and a duty because it is fair that everyone produces at least what he consumes. (6) For a Peronist, there is nothing better than another Peronist. (7) No Peronist should feel that he is more than he is, or less than he should be. When a Peronist begins to feel that he is more than he is, he begins to change into an **oligarch**. (8) In political action, the scale of value of each Peronist is the following: first the fatherland, later the movement, and then men. (9) For Peronism, politics is not the end, only the means for the good of the fatherland, which is the happiness of its people and national greatness. (10) The two arms of Peronism are social justice and social welfare. With these, Peronism embraces the people in justice and love. (11) Peronism wants national unity and not strife. It wants heroes and not martyrs. (12) In the New Argentina, the only privileged ones are the children. (13) A government without a doctrine is a body without a soul. For this reason, Peronism has its own political, economic, and social doctrine, *justicialismo*. (14) *Justicialismo* is a new life philosophy. It is simple, practical, popular, profoundly Christian, and profoundly humanist. (15) As a political doctrine, *justicialismo* establishes a fair balance between the rights of the individual and those of the community. (16) As an economic doctrine, *justicialismo* develops a true social economy, putting capital at the service of the economy and this at the service of social welfare. (17) As a social doctrine, *justicialismo* achieves social justice, which gives people the social rights they are entitled to. (18) Peronism wants a socially just, economically free, and politically sovereign Argentina. (19) Peronism constitutes a central government, an organized state, and a free people. (20) The best part of Argentina is its people.

TWENTY TRUTHS OF *JUSTICIALISMO*. *See* TWENTY PERONIST TENENTS.

UNA NOVIA EN APUROS. Directed by the American filmmaker John Reinhardt and produced by **Estudios Baires**, *Una novia en apuros* (A Bride in Trouble) was released on 10 March 1942. This film is a comedy of errors in which a newlywed bride embarks on a quest to find out who her secret admirer is. Evita had a bit part in this film, representing a young lady who is mistakenly thought to be the bride.

UNHAPPIEST MAN IN TOWN, THE. *See EL MÁS INFELIZ DEL PUEBLO.*

UNIDAD BÁSICA CULTURAL EVA PERÓN. In 1953, the **Ateneo Cultural Eva Perón** was transformed into the Unidad Básica Cultural Eva Perón. This new undertaking became part of the **Partido Peronista Femenino**, and its leader was **Delia Parodi**. While the Ateneo was a women-only institution, the Unidad Básica was a training center that offered classes in film, folklore, music, singing, and performing arts to both men and women. The classes were free of charge and delivered by male and female tutors. With the ousting of **Juan Domingo Perón** in 1955, it ceased to exist. *See also* LIBERATING REVOLUTION.

UNIDADES BÁSICAS. The structural organization of **Peronism** is still based on a network of local party-sponsored branches or *unidades básicas*. These branches serve as places where **Peronists** gather to organize political, social, charity, and educational activities and events. Initially, there were two types of *unidades básicas*, labor union and "ordinary" branches. The only difference between them was that the members of the labor union branches had to share the same trade or profession. In the late 1940s, the *unidades básicas* played a key role in affiliating thousands of middle- and working-class men and women with both the **Partido Peronista (PP)** and the **Partido Peronista Femenino (PPF)**. Even though all branches were engaged in political activism, the *unidades básicas* of the PPF focused more on domestic life and social work. After the PPF was established, Evita organized a national census of Peronist women. She appointed a delegate and subdelegates to each province and national territory. Their job was not only to carry out the census, but also to open *unidades básicas*. The first one was opened in Buenos Aires Province by **María Elena Caporale de Mercante**. By 1951, the PPF had opened 3,600 *unidades básicas* across the country, offering a wide range of free services, such as access to doctors and lawyers and classes in Peronist doctrine, literacy, hairdressing, typing, sewing, and painting. Furthermore, the branches functioned as social meeting places for women outside of their homes and as day-care centers. Under the leadership of Evita, the *unidades básicas* worked in close collaboration with the **Fundación Eva Perón** to address any domestic, work, or financial difficulties PPF members were going through. *See also* FEMALE SUFFRAGE; LIBERATING REVOLUTION.

UNIÓN CÍVICA RADICAL (UCR)/RADICAL CIVIC UNION. Founded in 1891 by Leandro N.

Alem, this centrist political party is still active in Argentina. The party's advocacy of universal male suffrage appealed to a wide range of social actors. Thus, members of aristocratic families, urban workers, country laborers, and ranch owners formed its electoral base. With the death of Alem in 1896, his nephew Hipólito Yrigoyen took over the leadership, leaving an indelible nationalistic mark that dominated the UCR party politics until 1935. With the emergence of **Peronism**, the UCR became the primary opposition party. However, a splinter group from the UCR composed of civil servants and dubbed UCR–Junta Renovadora built a coalition with the **Partido Laborista** and **Centros Independientes** in 1945 to support **Juan Domingo Perón**'s bid for the presidency. In the 1950s, the UCR went through another internal split. While **Arturo Frondizi** spearheaded the UCR Intransigente, Ricardo Balbín led the UCR del Pueblo. The UCR played a pivotal role in the transition to democratic rule in Argentina in 1983.

UNIÓN DE ESTUDIANTES SECUNDARIOS (UES)/SECONDARY SCHOOL STUDENTS' UNION. On 20 April 1953, Minister of Education **Armando Méndez de San Martín** founded the Unión de Estudiantes Secundarios (UES), a Peronist secondary school students' organization. Divided into two branches, male and female, the UES was funded and run by the state. The headquarters of the UES male and female branches were located in Buenos Aires. In addition, members of the female branch had access to a sports area at the **Olivos Presidential Residence**. President **Juan Domingo Perón** allegedly asked Méndez de San Martín to open this area to the female branch only. The presence of young women at the residence and the fact that they shared activities with Perón generated heated debate among Peronist opponents. They claimed that the UES was simply a way of procuring young women for the president. While it is not possible to confirm this, it is true that Perón started dating 14-year-old UES delegate **Nélida Haydeé Rivas** in 1953. This was not the first time Perón's name was romantically associated with a young woman. Seemingly, he was living with 20-year-old **María Cecilia Yurbel** when he met Evita. Although the UES ceased to function following the military coup d'état of 1955, it resumed its activities in 1973. See also LIBERATING REVOLUTION.

UNIÓN RANCH. See ESTANCIA LA UNIÓN.

UNIVERSIDAD TECNOLÓGICA NACIONAL. First known as the Universidad Nacional Obrera (National University of Workers), it was created on 19 August 1948 by government decree 13,229. It consisted of nine regional universities. The first students were admitted to the universities located in the cities of Buenos Aires, Santa Fe, **Rosario**, and **Córdoba** on 17 March 1953. The **Mendoza** regional university was inaugurated on 16 June 1953. In subsequent years, regional universities opened in Bahía Blanca, Tucumán, Avellaneda, and **La Plata**. The one in La Plata was named Universidad Nacional de Eva Perón (Eva Perón National University) between 1952 and 1954. The creation of these third-level institutions was part of the Peronist government's plan to build a complete educational system for working-class children. The aim was to supply highly skilled personnel to the national industry. The students could qualify as either industrial technicians (a three-year degree) or industrial engineers (a five-year degree). Following the **Liberating Revolution**, the university changed its name to Technological National University in 1959.

UNIVERSITY CAMPUSES. As part of the **Peronist** educational planning, the government, together with the **Fundación Eva Perón**, organized the construction of university campuses in the provinces of **Mendoza** and **Córdoba**. The aim was to make third-level education accessible to all Argentine citizens. As regards the structural plan, the colleges included a main building, featuring classrooms and dining rooms, surrounded by student and teaching staff accommodation. With the military coup d'état of 1955, the construction of these campuses was brought to a halt. The university campus in Córdoba was almost completed and was to be opened in 1956. *See also* CIUDAD UNIVERSITARIA ESTUDIANTIL PRESIDENTE PERÓN; LIBERATING REVOLUTION.

UNIVERSITY CITY OF MADRID. Located in the Moncloa-Aravaca district in **Madrid**, this university campus houses the Complutense University of Madrid and the Technical University of Madrid. Following the Spanish Civil War (1936–1939), the campus was refurbished and new buildings were added. On 14 June 1947, thousands of students gathered on the university campus to welcome Evita and **María del Carmen Polo y Martínez-Valdés**. The distinguished guests arrived at 12:30 p.m. After receiving flowers, the two ladies were given a detailed tour of the Government Pavilion. They admired the sports grounds, the Mayor Ximénez de Cisneros College, and the School of Philosophy and Literature, where an event in honor of Evita was held. *See also* RAINBOW TOUR.

UNZUÉ PALACE. This was a turn-of-the-century building of 283 rooms located in Recoleta, an upmarket suburb in Buenos Aires. Built in 1887, the mansion was the Unzué family's vacation home, but it was rebuilt when the family decided to live there on a permanent basis. In 1937, however, the palace was expropriated by the government due to tax debts, and from 1942 it became the official residence of the president of Argentina. While his predecessors preferred to use it as a place of relaxation, **Juan Domingo Perón** made the palace his home. He and Evita lived there and refurbished it according to their needs. On 26 July 1952, Evita passed away at the Unzué Palace. After Evita's demise, **Peronists** would flock to the palace to leave offerings such as candles, messages, and flowers. Because the military government that ousted Perón in 1955 wanted to erase all memory of Evita and take revenge against the Perón administration, the palace was demolished in 1958. The building of the National Library of the Argentine Republic opened its door on the same site of the former Unzué Palace in 1992. A statue honoring the memory of Evita stands in the gardens of the library. *See also* LIBERATING REVOLUTION; STATE FUNERAL OF EVITA.

Monument located at the Plaza del Lector in the gardens of the National Library, Buenos Aires. Featuring Evita, Juan Domingo Perón, and their dog, this monument was inaugurated in 2014 as a tribute to the Unzué Palace, Evita and Perón's residence between 1946 and 1952. Before being demolished by the Liberating Revolution government in 1958, the palace used to sit on the site where the library is currently located.

V

VALLE, PABLO OSVALDO (1905–1992). This renowned Argentine songwriter, radio pioneer, host, and artistic director founded Radio Nacional in 1924. Even though Valle sold his radio station to **Jaime Yankelevich** in 1927, he worked as Radio Nacional's artistic director for eight more years, developing the future **Radio Belgrano y la Primera Cadena Argentina de Broadcasting**. Valle most likely met Evita in October 1934 at **Radio Cultura**. At the time, Valle was the artistic director of this radio station, which was hosting a program in honor of the city of San Carlos de Bolívar in the province of Buenos Aires. The program offered a variety of performances, including the reciting of a poem by Evita. Between 1935 and 1943, Valle was **Radio El Mundo** artistic director. In May 1942, Evita's theater company **Compañía Juvenil de Radioteatro** joined the **Compañía Candilejas** to work at Radio El Mundo in a series of *radioteatros*. See also RADIO DEBUT OF EVITA.

VATICAN CITY. Evita visited Vatican City on 27 June 1947 as part of her **Rainbow Tour**. She was granted a 20-minute private audience with **Pope Pius XII**, for which she complied with Vatican protocol for women in diplomatic circumstances. She was therefore dressed in a long black gown and a black mantilla. The pope received her in the papal library, blessed the Argentine delegation that accompanied her, presented her with a rosary, and made her an honorary member of a Franciscan religious order, but no other honors were bestowed upon her. Following the audience, Evita walked around the Apostolic Palace, the Borgia Apartments, the Sistine Chapel, and St. Peter's Square, escorted by elderly members of the Vatican nobility and Swiss guards. See also BENÍTEZ, HERNÁN.

VENDEPATRIA. This term was popularized first by the Argentine revisionist **Arturo Martín Jauretche** and later borrowed and employed in Peronist discourse. Both **Juan Domingo Perón** and Evita used *vendepatria* to refer to a political figure despised by the *pueblo* for handing over the country's resources to foreign powers. A *vendepatria* would do this without considering the plunder of national resources. See also *ANTIPUEBLO*; *CIPAYO*; *OLIGARQUÍA*.

VENTURINI, AURORA (1922–2015). This renowned Argentine writer, poet, and translator married Judge Eduardo Varela. Following her husband's death, she married the writer and historian **Benito Enrique "Fermín" Chávez**. During **Domingo Alfredo Mercante**'s term as governor of Buenos Aires Province, Venturini used to write the speeches of Mercante's wife, **María Elena Caporale de Mercante**. Venturini had long wanted to meet Evita and asked Caporale to introduce her to the first lady. Eventually, Venturini became a Peronist supporter and one of Evita's close friends. Shortly after graduating with a degree in philosophy and educational sciences from the National University of **La Plata**, Venturini began working as an adviser at the Child Psychology and Reeducation Institute in Buenos Aires. With Evita's support, Venturini developed a school reentry program for children. To put it simply, those children who showed potential were taken out of the institution and sent to school. Many of them reentered society successfully thanks to Venturini's undertaking. At the end of Evita's life, Venturini was by her side. During her life, Venturini often recalled how much Evita liked the dirty jokes she told the first lady. Following the **Liberating Revolution**, the writer went into exile in **Paris** and remained there for 25 years. In the French capital, she studied psychology and mingled with intellectuals such as Jean-Paul Sartre, Simone de Beauvoir, Albert Camus, Eugène Ionesco, Juliette Gréco, and Violette Leduc. She also went to Sicily, where she became acquainted with Salvatore Quasimodo.

VIDELA, JORGE RAFAEL (1925–2013). This army general became president of Argentina after leading a military coup d'état that toppled President **Isabel Martínez de Perón** on 24 March 1976. Two days after the coup, Videla formally assumed the presidency as head of a military junta made up of himself, representing the army; General **Emilio Eduardo Massera**, representing the navy; and General Orlando Agosti, representing the air force. During Videla's military government, **human rights** violations became commonplace as the military illegally detained, tortured, and killed suspected terrorists and political opponents. In October 1976, he had the **body of Evita** removed from the **Olivos Presidential Residence** and agreed to have it entombed in the Duarte family mausoleum in the Recoleta Cemetery in Buenos Aires. Videla retired in 1981 and was succeeded by General Roberto Viola. With the restoration of democracy in Argentina in 1983, Videla was put on trial and found guilty of, among other crimes, disappearances, homicide, and torture. After being imprisoned for five years, he was pardoned by President **Carlos Saúl Menem** in 1990. Following a new trial, Videla received a 50-year sentence in 2012. He died on 17 May 2013 while serving his sentence. *See also* DIRTY WAR; DUARTE FAMILY TOMB; KIRCHNER, NÉSTOR.

VIGO. Located in the autonomous community of Galicia in northwestern Spain, Vigo is the capital city of the province of Pontevedra and one of the major fishing ports in Europe. During the time of mass immigration to Argentina (1880–1930), the port of Vigo was the main point of embarkation for Galician immigrants to Argentina. They chose to migrate to the South American nation for its economic growth and its favorable immigration policies. During Evita's official visit to the city from 19 to 21 June 1947, Vigo celebrated and reinforced its links to Argentina through a mass gathering held in honor of the workers of Argentina. The event took place at the fishing port in the evening of 20 June. Thousands of people had descended on Vigo to catch a glimpse of Evita and attend the celebration. The speeches delivered at the event, the Argentine and Spanish flags that decorated the city, and the cheering crowd recalled the strong bonds between Vigo and Argentina. *See also* RAINBOW TOUR.

VILLA CISNEROS. *See* DAKHLA.

VISCA–DECKER COMMISSION. *See* ANTI-ARGENTINE ACTIVITIES CONGRESSIONAL COMMITTEE.

WEB.MUSEOEVITA.ORG.AR. This is the official website of the **Evita Museum**. It features PDF versions of *La razón de mi vida* (*My Mission in Life*) as well as books on Evita's biography, the **Fundación Eva Perón**, and Evita's legacy. It includes a virtual tour of the museum, images, and videos related to Evita's personal life and her work. One of the most salient sections of the website is the celebration of the 100th anniversary of Evita's birth, which lists many of the events prompted by the commemoration. The website offers its contents in Spanish.

WEDDING OF EVITA. Evita and **Juan Domingo Perón** met in January 1944 and moved in together shortly after. By mid-1944, they were sharing two adjoining apartments on Posadas Street, Buenos Aires. While one was used by Perón to hold political gatherings, the other was the couple's private living quarters. However, it was not common for unmarried couples to live together at the time. Their cohabitation, in tandem with Evita's acting career, was frowned upon by those union leaders and military officers who worked closely with Perón. To make matters worse, Evita would accompany Perón to official events and be present at his meetings. All of these were activities in which women did not normally partake. In early spring 1945, Perón's supporters reportedly gathered outside of their home on Posadas Street and shouted, "Get married, get married." It is likely that Perón and Evita had talked about marriage plans before the memorable 17 October 1945, but his proposal materialized while he was imprisoned on **Martín García Island**. He wrote two letters to Evita from Martín García. In one of them, he promised her that as soon as he was released, he would marry her. Perón fulfilled his promise. The couple held a secret civil wedding in their apartment in the presence of two witnesses, **Domingo Alfredo Mercante** and Juancito, Evita's brother, on 22 October 1945. Although this is the date that appears on their marriage certificate, it may not be correct as the document shows several inaccuracies, stating that Perón was a bachelor, asserting that the wedding ceremony took place in **Junín**, and claiming that Evita was born María Eva Duarte on 7 May 1922 in Junín. On 10 December, they had a secret Catholic wedding at San Francisco de Asís Church in **La Plata**. This time the witnesses were Mercante and **Juana Ibarguren**, Evita's mother. After the wedding, the couple spent their honeymoon at Perón's **San Vicente country house**. Evita's marriage to Perón was a turning point in her life. As she was officially the wife of a presidential candidate, she abandoned her artistic career and made every effort to bury her past as an actress. Her contract with **Radio Belgrano** was annulled, publicity stills and negatives were handed over to her, and her last film, *La pródiga* (The Prodigal Woman), was not released until 1984. As Evita herself asserted several times, she was "born" on 17 October 1945, an assertion that in turn contributed to the construction of her myth. *See also* BIRTH CERTIFICATE OF EVITA; DUARTE, JUAN "JUANCITO" RAMÓN; LOS TOLDOS; PERONIST LOYALTY DAY; POLITICAL MYTH; WHITE AND BLACK MYTHS.

WHITE AND BLACK MYTHS. Essentially, white and black myths can be regarded as synonyms for **Peronist and anti-Peronist myths.** The origin of the use of the terms *white myth* and *black myth* in the context of Evita is not clear. However, these concepts have been employed mainly by early scholars of **Peronism.** One of those who employed the term was the Austrian-born psychoanalyst Marie Langer, who utilized the phrase *mito oficial de Evita* (Evita's official myth) to refer to the Peronist mythological narrative in her 1957 work *Fantasías eternas a la luz del psicoanálisis* (Eternal Fantasies through the Prism of Psychoanalysis). Another early researcher in this area, the American anthropologist Julie M. Taylor, employed the term *black myth* to refer to the narrative of the anti-Peronist mythology in her 1979 book *Eva Perón: The Myths of a Woman.*

WILENSKI, SIVUL (1897–1952). Born in Poland, the photographer Sivul Wilenski arrived in Argentina as a member of a theater company in 1920. He opened his own studio in Buenos Aires in the 1930s. Renowned for his touched-up and stylized portraits, Wilenski specialized in the use of lightning and the retouching of prints. Such style and techniques were shared and developed by Wilenski's assistant and student **Annemarie Heinrich.** Although he collaborated with numerous newspapers and magazines, Wilenski worked as an exclusive photographer for **Sintonía**, and his portraits of popular radio artists usually appeared on the magazine's front cover. One of the earliest photographs of Evita by Wilenski appeared on the cover of **Antena** on 20 May 1939. Wilenski's portraits of Evita graced the front covers of *Sintonía* on 25 October 1939 and of **Damas y Damitas** on 13 December 1939.

WOMAN WITH THE WHIP: EVA PERÓN, THE. This biography of Evita was written by **Mary Main** and published on 16 October 1952 by Doubleday in New York. The author of the book first appeared under the pseudonym of María Flores as a precaution for fear of Peronist reprisals. By 1956, 26,000 copies had been published. In her book, Main portrays Evita as a woman who was the leader of a totalitarian government disguised as a democracy. She did, however, attempt to show a positive side of Evita in the epilogue, added to the 1977 edition of the book, when she stated that "to Eva's credit lays the liberation of the Argentine women. During the Perón regime women were given the vote for the first time and divorce was legalized: but it was Eva herself who was the flamboyant challenge to the tradition of women's inferiority." The renowned scholar Marysa Navarro has stated that *The Woman with the Whip: Eva Perón* has been the most influential text in the development of the "anti-Evita" mythology. In the same light, the scholar Lucila Carzolio has pointed out that the publication of **La razón de mi vida** (*My Mission in Life*) in 1951 and *The Woman with the Whip: Eva Perón* in 1952 marked the genesis of the **white and black myths** of Evita in text. *The Woman with the Whip: Eva Perón* was translated into Spanish and published in Buenos Aires by La Reja in December 1955 under the title *La mujer del látigo: Eva Perón* shortly after **Juan Domingo Perón** fled the country. The release of both Andrew Lloyd Webber and Tim Rice's rock opera *Evita* in 1976 and the film *Evita* in 1996 revived interest in the *The Woman with the Whip: Eva Perón.* As a result, it was republished several times both in Great Britain and the United States. *See also* EVITA CONCEPT ALBUM; EVITA FILM; EVITA MUSICAL: AMERICAN STAGE PRODUCTION; EVITA MUSICAL: BRITISH STAGE PRODUCTION; FEMALE SUFFRAGE.

WRITINGS OF EVA PERÓN, THE. See *ESCRIBE EVA PERÓN.*

Y

YANKELEVICH, JAIME (1896–1952). This Bulgarian-born businessman pioneered radio and television broadcasting in Argentina. His interest in broadcasting led him to purchase a radio station in 1927. In order to promote his station and reach a wider audience, he shifted from the transmission of recorded music to live shows and introduced the payment of a fee to performers, a practice that was later replicated by other radio stations in the country. As such, **Radio Belgrano** became one of the most coveted stations among Argentine artists. By 1937, Yankelevich had acquired several radio stations across Argentina and created **Radio Belgrano y la Primera Cadena Argentina de Broadcasting**. When Evita, who had worked at Radio Belgrano, married **Juan Domingo Perón**, Yankelevich was asked to annul her contract, and in order to erase her artistic past, she requested all the publicity photos of her held by the radio station. In 1949, Yankelevich lost his son Miguel, who was fascinated with the growth of television in the United States. A grieving Yankelevich approached Minister of Communications **Oscar Lorenzo Nicolini** to obtain permission to import the necessary equipment for the introduction of television in Argentina. Permission was granted on condition that the 1951 commemoration of the **Peronist Loyalty Day** was televised. The act became the first television broadcast in Argentina, and Evita's face was the first image to be emitted.

YURBEL, MARÍA CECILIA "LA PIRAÑA" (1924–1989). Allegedly **Juan Domingo Perón**'s mistress between 1941 and 1944. Perón reportedly met Yurbel upon his return from Europe in the province of **Mendoza**, where he served as an army skiing instructor. The circumstances in which they met, however, are not clear. Reportedly, the colonel needed a maid and offered the job to the young girl. Yurbel's father, a farm laborer and widower, welcomed Perón's offer without hesitation. By 1943, Yurbel had moved with Perón to Buenos Aires. The colonel nicknamed Yurbel La Piraña, supposedly referring to her big appetite. In December of the same year, Perón was invited to be a guest on a program at **Radio Belgrano**. He arrived at the radio station with Yurbel and introduced her as his daughter—she was 30 years younger than him. When Evita moved in with Perón in 1944, Yurbel returned to Mendoza.

Z

ZARAGOZA. Located in the autonomous community of Aragon in northeastern Spain, Zaragoza is the capital city of the eponymous province. The city is known for its impressive basilica, the Cathedral-Basilica of Our Lady of the Pillar, where Evita attended a religious ceremony in her honor and offered her earrings to Our Lady of the Pillar as a sign of gratefulness during her official visit to the city. She visited Zaragoza on 21 and 22 June 1947 and, as in all other Spanish cities she stopped at, was warmly welcomed by authorities and people alike. *See also* RAINBOW TOUR.

ZUCKER, MARCOS (1921–2003). This Argentine stage, TV, and film actor and comedian was the son of Polish Jewish immigrants who had arrived in Argentina at the beginning of the 20th century. He made his stage debut when he was six years of age in the play *Rosa de Oro* (Golden Rose) by the Argentine author Arturo Capdevila. In 1938, he met Evita when they shared the stage in *La gruta de la fortuna* (The Grotto of Fortune). Their paths crossed again in *El cura de Santa Clara* (Santa Clara's Priest). The two young artists became good friends and would go out for a quick meal at one of the cheap eats on Montevideo Street in Buenos Aires after their performances. When Evita became a radio actress, she invited Zucker to work with her in *Los jazmines del 80* (The Jasmines of 1880) and *Las rosas de Caseros* (Caseros's Roses). He was a highly esteemed actor. In 1997, he was declared Honorary Citizen of Buenos Aires.

Bibliography

CONTENTS

Introduction	153
I. Published Works by Eva Perón	155
II. Published Works about Eva Perón	156
1. Biographies	156
A. Longer	156
B. Shorter	157
C. Juvenile	157
D. Comics	157
2. Her Contemporaries	157
3. Culture	158
A. Plays	158
B. Musicals	158
C. Novels	158
D. Short Stories	158
E. Publications on Cultural Productions	159
4. Politics	161
A. Her Political Life	161
B. Juan Domingo Perón	161
C. Peronism	161
5. Society	163
A. Welfare	163
B. Lifestyle	163
C. Education	163
D. Mass Media	163
E. Gender	164
6. Illness, Death, and Myth	164

INTRODUCTION

Although Evita was an outstanding orator, she was not a woman of letters. The rabble-rousing and impassioned speeches she delivered to the crowds from the balcony of the Pink House and at public events were penned by others or improvised on the spur of the moment. In spite of this fact, five books have been attributed to her: *Escribe Eva Perón* (*The Writings of Eva Perón*), *Historia del peronismo* (*History of Peronism*), *La palabra, el pensamiento y la acción* (*The Word, the Thought, and the Action*), *La razón de mi vida* (*My Mission in Life*), and *Mi mensaje* (*In My Own Words*). All of these works are listed in the first section of this bibliography. *Escribe Eva Perón* is a compilation of articles authored by Evita and published in the Peronist newspaper *Democracia* in the second half of 1948. In these articles, Evita addresses topics ranging from her own political position to Argentine politics more generally. In 1951, Evita lectured on Peronist history and ideals at the newly founded Escuela Superior Peronista. These lectures were compiled and published under the title *Historia del peronismo*. The volume *La palabra, el pensamiento y la acción* is a collection of quotes that outlines Evita's beliefs and ideas about such topics as women, social justice, and education. Of the few works identified as being authored by her, *La razón de mi vida* is arguably the most important contribution to the construction of her iconic image. Ghostwritten by the Spanish writer and journalist Manuel Penella de Silva, the book was published in Argentina in 1951 with an initial run of 300,000 copies. The volume, which consists of 59 chapters, is a first-person account of Evita's relationship with Peronism. It addresses Evita's view on the magnificence of the Peronist doctrine and its values, while the greatness of Juan Domingo Perón is underscored in every chapter. Employed as reading material in Argentine schools, *La razón de mi vida* was the first of Evita's books to be officially launched, becoming a best seller after her death in 1952. *Mi mensaje* was written between 1951 and 1952, but the manuscript seemed to have disappeared until the Argentine newspaper *La Nación* announced its auction in 1987. The second edition of *Mi mensaje* was edited by the Peronist militant Alberto Schprejer. Curiously, Evita's sisters Blanca and Erminda initiated legal proceedings against Schprejer since they believed that Evita had not authored the volume. In 2006, however, a judge ruled that the sisters were wrong, confirming that Evita was indeed the author of *Mi mensaje*.

Aside from including the aforementioned titles, the first section of the bibliography also lists *Discursos completos* (Complete Speeches), *Eva Perón habla a las mujeres* (Eva Perón Talks to Women), and *Evita: su legado de puño y letra* (Evita: Her Legacy). While the first two are compilations of Evita's speeches, the third publication contains two of Evita's works, *La palabra, el pensamiento y la acción* and *Escribe Eva Perón*. The publication of these works was prompted by two significant events that drew renewed attention to Evita. The first one was the resurgence of Peronism in Argentina in the 1970s after years of proscription, whereas the second was the commemoration of the 60th anniversary of Evita's death in 2012. This section of the bibliography includes the first and the latest Spanish edition of the works listed as well as their translations, provided of course they have been translated.

In the second section of the bibliography, which encompasses works about Evita, we have only included the latest reprint or edition of the publications listed. As in the first section, if an English translation of a Spanish publication exists, it has also been added. Moreover, books and articles have been interfiled under the same subject headings.

One of the most challenging tasks has been the compilation of English-language literature about Evita given that most of the works that examine her life and legacy have been written in Spanish. Considering this, we have opted for putting together a bibliography that not only does justice to the abundance of literature in Spanish but also reflects the burgeoning interest in Evita outside of her native Argentina. As a consequence, half of the bibliographic entries listed in the second section are publications in Spanish, while the other half includes literature published in English. Furthermore, since our intention is to offer a panoramic view of recent works about Evita, the section lists only literature that has been published since 1990. Nevertheless, if a work was published before 1990 but a new edition or reprint has come out since, it has also been included.

The first part of the second section opens with biographies of Evita. One of the pioneers in the academic scholarship on Evita is the Spanish historian Marysa Navarro. Together with Alicia Dujovne Ortiz's *Eva Perón*, Navarro's *Evita* is one of the most compelling texts about Evita's life to this day. As our intention has been to cater to a wide audience, we have also incorporated biographies for juvenile readers. The second part, "Her Contemporaries," lists biographies and autobiographies of people who were personally acquainted with Evita. Among the titles listed, Carolyn A. Becker's *Domingo A. Mercante: A Democrat in the Shadow of Perón and Evita* stands out as an insightful account of one of the closest associates of the presidential couple. The third part, "Culture," reflects the interest Evita has piqued in the cultural world. From the renowned novel *Santa Evita* by Tomás Eloy Martínez to the much-celebrated musical *Evita* by Tim Rice and Andrew Lloyd Webber, Evita's protean image has surfaced in practically every cultural form. This in turn has had a profound bearing on the number of books and articles that critically examine these cultural manifestations. The fourth and fifth parts, "Politics" and "Society," comprise literature devoted to the exploration of Evita's political and social work as well as her influence on education, the mass media, and gender issues. The literature listed in these two parts testifies to the fact that Evita has left an indelible mark on many aspects of Argentine society. Finally, "Illness, Death, and Myth" provides a list of illuminating titles unveiling details about the last years of

Evita's life, her demise, and the construction of the myths surrounding her.

The bibliography is by no means exhaustive but provides further information about Evita and offers a solid starting point for specialists and newcomers interested in studying this extraordinary woman. For those readers who wish to consult bibliographies that include works previous to 1990, we recommend Gabriela Sonntag's *Eva Perón Books, Articles, and Other Sources of Study: An Annotated Bibliography* from 1983, Roberto Baschetti's *Eva Perón: registros bibliográficos* (Eva Perón: Bibliographic Records) from 2013, and the website "El peronismo en sus fuentes" at http://www.peronlibros.com.ar/. The last two items are targeted at a Spanish-speaking audience.

I. PUBLISHED WORKS BY EVA PERÓN

a. *Discursos completos*

Spanish Editions

Perón, Eva. *Discursos completos*. 3 vols. San Isidro, Buenos Aires: Megafón, 1985–1987.

———. *Discursos completos*. Edited by Aníbal Fernández. 2 vols. Vol. 1, *1946–1948*. Vol. 2, *1949–1952*. Buenos Aires: Planeta, 2012.

b. *Escribe Eva Perón*

Spanish Editions

Perón, Eva. *Escribe Eva Perón*. Buenos Aires: Subsecretaría de Informaciones de la Presidencia de la Nación, 1950.

———. *Escribe Eva Perón*. Buenos Aires: Fabro, 2015.

English Edition

Perón, Eva. *The Writings of Eva Perón*. Buenos Aires: Subsecretaría de Informaciones de la Presidencia de la Nación, 1950.

French Edition

Perón, Eva. *Eva Perón ecrit*. Buenos Aires: Subsecretaría de Informaciones de la Presidencia de la Nación, 1950.

c. *Eva Perón habla a las mujeres*

Spanish Editions

Perón, Eva. *Eva Perón habla a las mujeres*. Buenos Aires: Editorial de la Reconstrucción, 1975.

———. *Eva Perón habla a las mujeres*. Buenos Aires: CS Ediciones, 1996.

d. *Evita: su legado de puño y letra*

Spanish Edition

Perón, Eva. *Evita: su legado de puño y letra*. Buenos Aires: Fabro, 2010.

———. *Evita: su legado de puño y letra*. Buenos Aires: Gustavo R. Ciraolo, 2013.

e. *Historia del peronismo*

Spanish Editions

Perón, Eva. *Historia del peronismo*. Buenos Aires: Escuela Superior Peronista, 1951.

———. *Historia del peronismo*. Buenos Aires: Fabro, 2012.

English Edition

Perón, Eva. *History of Peronism*. Buenos Aires: Servicio Internacional de Publicaciones Argentinas, 1952.

f. *La palabra, el pensamiento y la acción*

Spanish Editions

Perón, Eva. *La palabra, el pensamiento y la acción*. Buenos Aires: Subsecretaría de Informaciones de la Presidencia de la Nación, 1949.

———. *La palabra, el pensamiento y la acción*. Buenos Aires: Fabro, 2015.

g. *La razón de mi vida*

Spanish Editions

Perón, Eva. *La razón de mi vida*. Buenos Aires: Peuser, 1951.

———. *La razón de mi vida*. Buenos Aires: Fabro, 2013.

English Editions

Perón, Eva. *My Mission in Life.* Translated by Ethel Cherry. New York: Vantage Press, 1953.

———. *My Mission in Life.* Translated by Ethel Cherry. Ann Arbor, MI: University Microfilms International, 1982.

Italian Editions

Perón, Eva. *La ragione della mia vita.* Milan: Fratelli Bocca, 1953.

———. *La ragione della mia vita: Evita racconta se stessa.* Translated by Vanni Blengino. Rome: Editori Riuniti, 1996.

German Edition

Perón, Eva. *Der Sinn meines Lebens.* Zürich: Thomas-Verlag, 1952.

French Edition

Perón, Eva. *La raison de ma vie.* Paris: Raoul Solar, 1952.

h. *Mi mensaje*

Spanish Editions

Perón, Eva. *Mi mensaje: el libro desaparecido durante 32 años.* Buenos Aires: Del Mundo, 1987.

———. *Mi mensaje.* 3rd ed. Buenos Aires: Fabro, 2013.

English Editions

Perón, Eva. *In My Own Words.* Translated by Laura Dail. New York: New Press, 1996.

———. *In My Own Words.* Translated by Laura Dail. 2nd ed. New York: New Press, 2005.

Italian Edition

Perón, Eva. *Il mio messagio.* Translated by Stefano Tummolini. Rome: Fazi, 1996.

German Edition

Perón, Eva. *Mein Vermächtnis Evita: das kontrovers diskutierte "Sterbebett-Manuskript," das Eva Perón zugeschrieben wird.* Translated by Vivian A. Puhlmann. Bergisch Gladbach, Germany: Bastei-Lübbe, 1997.

II. PUBLISHED WORKS ABOUT EVA PERÓN

1. Biographies

A. Longer

Barnes, John. *Evita, First Lady: A Biography of Eva Perón.* New York: Grove, 1996.

Bellotta, Araceli. *Eva y Cristina: la razón de sus vidas.* Barcelona: Vergara, 2012.

Castiñeiras, Noemí. *El ajedrez de la gloria: Evita Duarte actriz.* Buenos Aires: Catálogos, 2003.

Chávez, Fermín. *Eva Perón: sin mitos.* Buenos Aires: Ediciones Theoría, 1996.

Dujovne Ortiz, Alicia. *Eva Perón.* Translated by Shawn Fields. London: Warner Books, 1997.

———. *Eva Perón: la biografía.* Translated by Alicia Dujovne Ortiz. Buenos Aires: Punto de Lectura, 2008.

Fraser, Nicholas, and Marysa Navarro. *Evita: The Real Lives of Eva Perón.* Richmond, BC: ReadHowYouWant, 2012.

Galasso, Norberto. *La compañera Evita.* Buenos Aires: Colihue, 2012.

Guzmán Suárez, M. Silvina. *Evita: la pasión de su vida.* 2nd ed. Buenos Aires: Dunken, 2011.

Hedges, Jill. *Evita: The Life of Eva Perón.* London: I. B. Tauris, 2017.

Main, Mary. *Evita: The Woman with the Whip.* London: Transworld, 2012.

Maranghello, César. *Eva Duarte: más allá de tanta pena.* Buenos Aires, Eudeba, 2016.

Navarro, Marysa. *Evita.* Buenos Aires: Edhasa, 2018.

Pigna, Felipe. *Evita, la biografía: jirones de su vida.* Buenos Aires: Planeta, 2012.

———. *Evita, realidad y mito: la biografía definitiva de la mujer más amada y más odiada de Argentina.* Barcelona: Destino, 2013.

Seoane, María, and Víctor Santa María. *Evita: esa mujer.* Buenos Aires: Caras y Caretas, 2007.

Sucarrat, María. *Vida sentimental de Eva Perón*. Buenos Aires: Editorial Sudamericana, 2006.

Taylor, Julie M. *Eva Perón: The Myths of a Woman*. Chicago: University of Chicago Press, 1996.

Taylor, William C. *Evita*. Barcelona: Ultramar Editores, 1997.

Vecchioni, Domenico. *Evita: Argentina's Heart*. Translated by Ellen Bain Prior. Chicago: Babelcube, 2020.

Zanatta, Loris. *Eva Perón: una biografía política*. Translated by Carlos Catroppi. Buenos Aires: Sudamericana, 2011.

B. Shorter

Castiñeiras, Noemí. *Ser Evita: síntesis biográfica*. Buenos Aires: Instituto Nacional de Investigaciones Históricas Eva Perón, 2007.

———. *To Be Evita: Biography*. Translated by Dolane Larson. Buenos Aires: Instituto Nacional de Investigaciones Históricas Eva Perón, 2003.

Montero, Rosa. *Pasiones: Amores y desamores que han cambiado la historia*. Barcelona: Debolsillo, 2016.

Queiroz, Juan Pablo, and Tomás de Elia. *Evita: An Intimate Portrait of Eva Perón*. London: Thames and Hudson, 1997.

C. Juvenile

Favor, Lesli J. *Eva Perón*. New York: Marshall Cavendish, 2011.

Gulotta, Charles. *Extraordinary Women in Politics*. New York: Children's Press, 1998.

Larson, Dolane J. *Evita's World: The Defining Years 1919–1947*. Scotts Valley, CA: CreateSpace, 2017.

Mattern, Joanne. *Eva Perón*. New York: Chelsea House, 2013.

Parker, Janice. *Political Leaders*. New York: Crabtree, 1998.

Spengler, Kremena. *Eva Perón: First Lady of the People*. Mankato, MN: Capstone, 2007.

Stille, Darlene R. *Eva Perón: First Lady of Argentina*. Minneapolis: Compass Point Books, 2006.

D. Comics

Cristaldo, Macarena. *El amor de Evita*. Paraná, Argentina: Museo Provincial Hogar Escuela Eva Perón, 2020.

Oesterheld, Héctor, and Alberto Breccia. *Evita: vida y obra de Eva Perón*. Buenos Aires: Doedytores, 2002.

2. Her Contemporaries

Álvarez, María Eugenia. *La enfermera de Evita*. Buenos Aires: Instituto Nacional de Investigaciones Históricas Eva Perón, 2010.

Alzugaray, Rodolfo A. *Ramón Carrillo: el fundador del sanitarismo nacional*. Buenos Aires: Colihue, 2008.

Becker, Carolyn A. *Domingo A. Mercante: A Democrat in the Shadow of Perón and Evita*. Philadelphia: Xlibris, 2005.

Duarte, Erminda. *Mi hermana Evita*. 4th ed. Buenos Aires: Ediciones Asociación Museo Evita, 2014.

Galasso, Norberto. *Yo fui el confesor de Evita: conversaciones con el padre Hernán Benítez*. Rosario, Argentina: Homo Sapiens Ediciones, 1999.

Gil, Clementina Florencia. *Memorias*. Buenos Aires: Instituto de Investigaciones Históricas Eva Perón, 2004.

Guerrero García, Pablo. *Areilza y Eva Perón: la tormentosa relación del embajador español en Argentina*. Castellón, Spain: Sar Alejandría Ediciones, 2020.

Jamandreu, Paco. *Evita fuera del balcón*. Córdoba, Argentina: Caballo Negro Editora, 2019.

Lagomarsino de Guardo, Lillian. *Y ahora . . . hablo yo*. 2nd ed. Buenos Aires: Editorial Sudamericana, 1996.

Lardone, Lilia. *20.25: quince mujeres hablan de Eva Perón*. Buenos Aires: Editorial Sudamericana, 2012.

Llambí, Benito. *Medio siglo de política y diplomacia*. Buenos Aires: Corregidor, 1997.

Macri, Ana Carmen. *Mi biografía política*. Buenos Aires: Instituto de Investigaciones Históricas Eva Perón, 2006.

Mercado, Silvia D. *El inventor del peronismo: Raúl Apold, el cerebro oculto que cambió la política argentina. Buenos Aires: Planeta, 2013.

Penella, Manuel. *Evita y yo: la verdadera historia del libro de Eva Perón*. Buenos Aires: Emecé, 2019.

Rein, Raanan. *In the shadow of Perón: Juan Atilio Bramuglia and the Second Line of Argentina's Populist Movement*. Translated by Martha Grenzeback. Stanford, CA: Stanford University Press, 2008.

Venturini, Aurora. *Eva alfa y omega*. Buenos Aires: Sudamericana, 2014.

3. Culture

A. Plays

Copi. *Eva Perón*. In *Four Plays*. Translated by Anni Lee Taylor. This new edition was first published by Alma Classics, 2012. Richmond, UK: Calder, 2019.

Guglielmino, Osvaldo César. *Eva de América: Teatro*. Buenos Aires: Corregidor, 1995.

Ottino, Mónica. *Evita y Victoria: comedia patriótica en 3 actos*. Buenos Aires: Grupo Editor Latinoamericano, 1990.

Pérez Pardella, Agustín. *Evita: la mujer del siglo*. In *Teatro*. Buenos Aires: Corregidor, 2001.

Perlongher, Néstor. *Evita lives*. In *Plebeian Prose*. Translated by Frances Riddle. Cambridge, UK: Polity Press, 2019.

———. *Evita vive*. In *Prosa plebeya: ensayos 1980–1992*. Buenos Aires: Colihue, 2016.

Suárez, Patricia, and Leonel Giacometto. *Trilogía peronista: Las 20 y 25; Puerta de hierro; La eterna*. Buenos Aires: Teatro Vivo, 2005.

B. Musicals

Guevara, Nacha. *Eva, el gran musical argentino*. Libretto by Pedro Orgambide and Nacha Guevara and music by Alberto Favero. Recorded 1986. Sony Music Entertainment Argentina, Spotify.

Rice, Tim, and Andrew Lloyd Webber. *Evita: 2006 London Cast Recording*. Simon Lee. With Elena Roger, Matt Rawle, Philip Quat, et al. Recorded 2006. Polydor, Spotify.

———. *Evita: New Broadway Cast Recording*. Kristen Blodgette. With Elena Roger, Ricky Martin, Michael Cerveris, et al. Recorded 2012. Sony Music Entertainment, Spotify.

C. Novels

Aguinis, Marcos. *La furia de Evita*. Buenos Aires: Sudamericana, 2013.

Alfieri, Annamaria. *Blood Tango: A Mystery*. New York: Minotaur, 2013.

Blanco, Ángeles. *Los dos viajes de Evita*. 2nd ed. Madrid: La Esfera de los Libros, 2019.

Coscia, Jorge. *Juan y Eva: el amor, el odio y la revolución; La historia de amor jamás contada*. Buenos Aires: Sudamericana, 2011.

Davis, Helen. *Evita: una vida apasionada*. Madrid: Calíope, 2017.

Gamerro, Carlos. *Adventures of the Busts of Eva Perón*. Translated by Ian Barnett. London: And Other Stories, 2015.

———. *La aventura de los bustos de Eva*. Buenos Aires: Edhasa, 2012.

Guebel, Daniel. *La carne de Evita*. Buenos Aires: Mondadori, 2012.

Ivker, Estelle J. *Elegance and Ecstasy: Evita Perón and Anya*. Mustang, OK: Tate Publishing & Enterprises, 2014.

Martínez, Tomás Eloy. *Santa Evita*. Translated by Helen Lane. London: Black Swan, 2012.

Martini, Juan. *Cine*. 3 vols. Buenos Aires: Eterna Cadencia, 2009–2011.

Posse, Abel. *La pasión según Eva*. Seville, Spain: Samarcanda, 2018.

Pridgen, William. *Night of the Dragon's Blood*. Palatka, FL: Hodge & Braddock, 1997.

Widen, Gregory. *Blood Makes Noise*. Las Vegas: Thomas & Mercer, 2013.

D. Short Stories

Aira, César. "Las dos muñecas." In *La trompeta de mimbre*. Rosario, Argentina: Beatriz Viterbo, 1998.

Borges, Jorge Luis. "El simulacro." In *El hacedor*. Mexico City: Castillo, 2018.

———. "The Sham." In *Dreamtigers*. Translated by Mildred Boyer and Harold Morland. Austin, TX: University of Texas Press, 2017.

Cortázar, Julio. "Las puertas del cielo." In *Bestiario*. Barcelona: Alfaguara, 2017.
———. "The Gates of Heaven." In *Bestiary: Selected Stories*. Translated by Alberto Manguel. London: Vintage, 2020.
Cozarinsky, Edgardo. "(Star Quality)." In *Urban Voodoo*. New York: Lumen Books, 1992.
———. "(Star Quality)." In *Vudú urbano*. 2nd ed. Buenos Aires: Emecé, 2007.
Martínez, Tomás Eloy. "Volveré y seré Madonna." In *Argentina y otras crónicas*. Buenos Aires: Alfaguara, 2016.
Onetti, Juan Carlos. "Ella." In *Cuentos completos*. Barcelona: Delbolsillo, 2017.
———. "She." In *A Dream Come True: The Collected Stories of Juan Carlos Onetti*. Translated by Katherine Silver. New York: Archipelago Books, 2019.
Viñas, David. "La señora muerta." In *Las malas costumbres*. Buenos Aires: Peón Negro, 2007.
Walsh, Rodolfo. "Esa mujer." Buenos Aires: Eloísa Cartonera, 2010.
———. "That Woman." Translated by Rosalie Knecht. Buenos Aires: Eloísa Cartonera, 2010.

E. Publications on Cultural Productions

Bollig, Ben. "¡Evitá hablar de la política! Multiple Critical Readings of Néstor Perlongher's *Evita vive (en cada hotel organizado).*" *Journal of Iberian and Latin American Studies* 9, no. 1 (2003): 3–18.
Bowsher, Kerstin. "Eva Perón and Argentine Postmodernity Reconsidered: Abel Posse's *La pasión según Eva*." *Bulletin of Hispanic Studies* 79 (2002): 225–40.
Burgos, Nidia. "Los textos literarios sobre Eva Perón: apropiaciones, representaciones y desplazamientos del imaginario popular." *Imaginario* 13 (2007): 67–83.
Chumo, Peter N., II "The Greatest Social Climber since Cinderella: Evita and the American Success Story." *Literature/Film Quarterly* 29, no. 1 (2001): 32–36.
Cortés Rocca, Paola, and Martín Kohan. *Imágenes de vida, relatos de muerte; Eva Perón: cuerpo y política*. Rosario, Argentina: Beatriz Viterbo, 2002.
Davies, Lloyd Hughes. "Portraits of a Lady: Postmodern Readings of Tomás Eloy Martínez 'Santa Evita.'" *Modern Language Review* 95 (2000): 415–23.
———. *Projections of Peronism in Argentine Autobiography, Biography and Fiction*. Cardiff: University of Wales Press, 2007.
De Grandis, Rita. "*Evita/Eva Perón*: Between the Global and the Local." *Canadian Journal of Latin American and Caribbean Studies* 34, no. 48 (1999): 245–58.
Dunstan, Inés. "The Lowest Kitchen Maid: Evita as an Evil *Mucama* (1946–2005)." *Hispanofila* 173 (2015): 303–17.
Ellison, Michael, and Lesa Lockford. "Power and Personality as Commodity in *Evita*." *Theatre Annual* 54 (2004): 69–94.
Foster, David William. "El escenario de 'Eva Perón' de Copi como caja negra." *Hispanic Journal* 30, no. 1/2 (2009): 205–11.
Fridman, Viviana. "Dos muertes y la construcción de una identidad argentina." *Canadian Journal of Latin American and Caribbean Studies* 34, no. 48 (1999): 233–44.
Graham-Jones, Jean. "Eva/Nacha/Cristina and the Argentine Trinity of Local, National, and Global Urban Politics." In *Performance and the Global City*, edited by D. J. Hopkins and Kim Solga, 61–77. New York: Palgrave Macmillan, 2013.
———. *Evita Inevitably*. Ann Arbor, MI: University of Michigan Press, 2014.
———. "'The Truth Is . . . My Soul Is with You': Documenting the Tale of Two Evitas." *Theatre Survey* 46, no. 1 (2005): 67–78.
Guevara, Omar, II, and Diane Waryas. "(Media)ting Competing Recollections: Argentine Expatriates Respond to Popular Depictions of Eva Perón." *Journal of the Northwest Communication Association* 31 (2002): 40–67.
Harbinson, W. A. *Evita: Saint or Sinner?* London: Boxtree, 1996.
Lagos, María Inés. "Género y representación literaria en la construcción de Eva Perón: Narraciones de Abel Posse, Alicia Dujov-

ne Ortiz y Tomás Eloy Martínez." *Revista Chilena de Literatura* 68 (2006): 73–103.

Lavery, Jane E. "Postmodern Interpretations of the Iconic Self: *Tinísima* by Elena Poniatowska and *Santa Evita* by Tomás Eloy Martínez." *Romance Studies* 25, no. 3 (2007): 227–40.

Leigh, Courtney. "Goodnight and Thank You, Evita: The Sexualization of Eva Perón in Popular Culture and Its Implications." *Articulãte: A Journal of Literary and Cultural Criticism* 15 (2010): 15–27.

Martin, Gerald. "Tomás Eloy Martínez, Biography and the Boom: *La novela de Perón* (1985) and *Santa Evita* (1995)." *Bulletin of Latin American Research* 31, no. 4 (2012): 460–72.

Mesa Gancedo, Daniel. "Perón, Eva." In *Temas literarios hispánicos*, edited by Leonardo Romero Tobar, vol. 1, 219–42. Zaragoza, Spain: Prensas Universitarias de Zaragoza, 2013.

Misemer, Sarah M. *Secular Saints: Performing Frida Kahlo, Carlos Gardel, Eva Perón, and Selena*. Woodbridge, UK: Tamesis, 2008.

Moore, J. Robert. "Don't Cry for Us, Richard Wagner: The Artwork of the Future and Evita." *International Journal of Music and Performing Arts* 3, no. 2 (2015): 1–6.

Nasi, Kristina. "Eva Perón in the Twenty-First Century: The Power of the Image in Argentina." *International Journal of the Image* 2, no. 1 (2012): 99–106.

Navarro, Marysa. "Of Sparrows and Condors: The Autobiography of Eva Perón." In *The Female Autograph*, edited by Domna C. Stanton, 180–86. Chicago: University of Chicago Press, 1995.

Parker, Alan. *The Making of Evita*. London: Boxtree, 1998.

Patruno, Luigi. "The City Evita Built: Cinematic Childhood and Peronism in Luis César Amadori's *Soñemos* (1951)." *Journal of Latin American Cultural Studies* 29 (2020): 63–84.

Rea, Lauren. "'Que al fin todas somos Eva': Nacha Guevara, Cristina Fernández and *Eva, el gran musical argentino*." *Journal of Iberian and Latin American Studies* 17, no. 1 (2011): 77–99.

Rice, Tim. *Oh, What a Circus: The Autobiography*. London: Hodder & Stoughton, 2000.

Rosano, Susana. "Eva Perón es un travesti: sobre Copi, entre el mito y la blasfemia." *Badebec: Revista del Centro de Estudios de Teoría y Crítica Literaria* 2, no. 4 (2013): 163–80.

———. *Rostros y máscaras de Eva Perón*. Rosario, Argentina: Beatriz Viterbo, 2006.

Sacca, Zulma. *Eva Perón: de figura política a heroína de novela*. Quito: Ediciones Abya Yala, 2003.

Savigliano, Marta E. "The Globalization of a National Myth." *Latin American Perspectives* 24, no. 6 (1997): 156–72.

Sillato, María del Carmen. "*La razón de mi vida* de Eva Perón: el texto como espacio de auto-representación melodramática." *Canadian Journal of Latin American and Caribbean Studies* 34, no. 48 (1999): 177–93.

Taylor, Julie M. *Eva Perón: The Myths of a Woman*. Chicago: University of Chicago Press, 1996.

Thompson, Currie K. *Picturing Argentina: Myths, Movies, and the Peronist Vision*. Amherst, NY: Cambria Press, 2014.

Trombetta, Jimena. "El cuerpo de las actrices al encarnar a Eva Perón desde 1983–2014 en Buenos Aires." *Culturales* 1, no. 2 (2017): 189–237.

———. "La representación de Eva Perón en el cine argentino." In *Una historia del cine político y social en Argentina (1969–2009)*, edited by Ana Laura Lusnich and Pablo Piedras, 675–91. Buenos Aires: Nueva Librería, 2011.

Young, Richard A. "Textualizing Evita: 'Oh, What a Circus! Oh, What a Show!'" *Canadian Journal of Latin American and Caribbean Studies* 34, no. 48 (1999): 215–32.

Zabaleta, Marta Raquel. "Eva Perón and Diana Spencer: Victims or Accomplices of Cultural Uniformity?" *Canadian Journal of Latin American and Caribbean Studies* 34, no. 48 (1999): 259–76.

Zangrandi, Marcos. "Escribir sobre Evita: Victoria Ocampo y el ejemplar anotado de Eva Perón, ¿aventurera o militante?" *Mora* 24 (2018): 5–22.

4. Politics

A. Her Political Life

Auyero, Javier. "Performing Evita: A Tale of Two Peronist Women." *Journal of Contemporary Ethnography* 27, no. 4 (1999): 461–93.

———. *Poor People's Politics: Peronist Survival Network and the Legacy of Evita*. Durham, NC: Duke University Press, 2002.

Barry, Carolina. *Evita capitana: el Partido Peronista Femenino 1949–1955*. 2nd. ed. Caseros, Argentina: Editorial Eduntref, 2016.

Castiñeiras, Noemí, *Sufragio femenino: algo más que un trámite legal*. Buenos Aires: Instituto Nacional de Investigaciones Históricas Eva Perón, 2007.

D'Arino Aringoli, Guillermo E. *Evita en Europa: un viaje iniciático; La construcción del mito*. 2nd ed. Barcelona: Caligrama, 2018.

Deleis, Mónica, Ricardo de Titto, and Diego L. Arguindeguy. *Mujeres de la política argentina*. Buenos Aires: Aguilar, 2001.

Diez Puertas, Emeterio. "Evita en España: máscaras de una primera dama." *Comunicación y Sociedad* 27, no. 3 (2014): 107–26.

Foss, Clive. *Juan and Eva Perón*. Stroud, UK: Sutton, 2006.

Patroni, Viviana. "A Discourse of Love and Hate: Eva Perón and the Labour Movement (1940s–1950s)." *Canadian Journal of Latin American and Caribbean Studies* 34, no. 48 (1999): 153–75.

Pellarolo, Silvia. "The Melodramatic Seductions of Eva Perón." In *Corpus Delecti: Performance Art of the Americas*, edited by Coco Fusco, 23–40. New York: Routledge, 2000.

Sánchez Hernández, María F. *Eva Perón y la política argentina*. Madrid: Dykinson, 2013.

Widmann-Miguel, Enrique F. *Eva Perón en España*. Buenos Aires: Iberinfo, 2014.

B. Juan Domingo Perón

Alexander, Robert J. *Juan Domingo Perón: A History*. New York: Routledge, 2018.

Bellotta, Araceli. *Las mujeres de Perón*. Buenos Aires: Planeta, 2005.

Blaquier, Carlos Pedro. *Juan Domingo Perón*. Buenos Aires: Dunken, 2008.

Gambini, Hugo, and Ariel Kocik. *Crímenes y mentiras: las prácticas oscuras de Perón*. Buenos Aires: Sudamericana, 2017.

———. *Las traiciones de Perón*. Buenos Aires: Sudamericana, 2019.

Luna, Félix. *Perón y su tiempo*. 3 vols. Vol. 1, *La Argentina era una fiesta (1946–1949)*. Vol. 2, *La comunidad organizada (1950–1952)*. Vol. 3, *El régimen exhausto (1953–1955)*. Buenos Aires: Sudamericana, 2013.

Rein, Raanan. *The Franco-Perón Alliance: Relations between Spain and Argentina, 1946–1955*. Pittsburgh: University of Pittsburgh Press, 1993.

———. "Turning the Country into an 'Immense and Clamorous Stadium': Perón, the New Argentina, and the 1951 Pan-American Games." *International Journal of the History of Sport* 33, no. 1/2 (2016): 29–43.

C. Peronism

Alexander, Robert. *A History of Organized Labor in Argentina*. Westport, CT: Praeger, 2003.

Allison, Victoria. "White Evil: Peronist Argentina in the USA Popular Imagination since 1955." *American Studies International* 42, no. 1 (2004): 4–48.

Barrios, Miguel Ángel. *Perón y el peronismo en el sistema-mundo del siglo XXI*. Buenos Aires: Editorial Biblos, 2008.

Brennan, John. *Peronism and Argentina*. Wilmington, DE: Scholarly Resources, 1998.

Brinkerhoff, Thomas J. "The Experience of Children in Perón's Argentina: Recent Interventions and Future Directions." *History Compass* 12, no. 11 (2014): 833–42.

Cepero, Iliana. "Photographic Propaganda under Peronism, 1946–55: Selections from the Archivo General de la Nación Argentina." *History of Photography* 40 (2016): 193–214.

Cosse, Isabella. *Estigmas de nacimiento: peronismo y orden familiar, 1946–1955*. Buenos Aires: Fondo de Cultura Económica, Universidad de San Andrés, 2006.

De Jorge, Carlos. "La visión del peronismo en el interior del país a través de los diarios capitalinos." Paper presented at the Segundo Congreso de Estudios sobre el Peronismo, Red de Estudios sobre el Peronismo, 2010. http://redesperonismo.org/articulo/la-vision-del-peronismo-en-el-interior-del-pais-a-traves-de-los-diarios-capitalinos/.

Edwards, Rodolfo. *Con el bombo y la palabra: El peronismo en las letras argentinas; Una historia de odios y lealtades.* Buenos Aires: Seix Barral, 2014.

Elena, Eduardo. *Dignifying Argentina: Peronism, Citizenship and Mass Consumption.* Pittsburgh: University of Pittsburgh Press, 2011.

Feinmann, José P. *Peronismo: filosofía política de una persistencia argentina.* 5th ed. Buenos Aires: Planeta, 2011.

Gambini, Hugo. *Historia del Peronismo.* 3 vols. Vol. 1, *El poder total (1943–1951).* Vol. 2, *La obsecuencia (1952–1955).* Vol. 3, *La violencia (1953–1983).* Buenos Aires: Ediciones B Argentina, 2016.

García, Marcelo. *La agente nazi Eva Perón y el tesoro de Hitler: los archivos desclasificados del FBI de Hoover; La trama de acuerdos y traiciones entre la Alemania nazi y la Argentina de Juan Domingo Perón.* Buenos Aires: Sudamericana, 2017.

Gay, Luis. *El partido laborista en Argentina.* Buenos Aires: Biblos, 1999.

Goldwert, Marvin. *Democracy, Militarism and Nationalism in Argentina 1930–1966: An Interpretation.* 2nd ed. Austin, TX: University of Texas Press, 2014.

Guy, Donna. *Creating Charismatic Bonds: Letters to Juan and Eva Perón.* Albuquerque: University of New Mexico Press, 2016.

Halperín, Jorge, and Diego Tomasi. *Las muchachas peronistas: Eva, Isabel y Cristina; ¿por qué desatan odios las mujeres en el poder?* Buenos Aires: Aguilar, 2009.

Healey, Mark Alan. *The Ruins of the New Argentina: Peronism and the Remaking of San Juan after the 1944 Earthquake.* Durham, NC: Duke University Press, 2011.

James, Daniel. *Resistance and Integration: Peronism and the Argentine Working Class, 1946–1979.* Cambridge: Cambridge University Press, 1988.

Jiménez Ruiz, Laura. "Peronism and Anti-imperialism in the Argentine Press: 'Braden or Perón' Was Also 'Perón Is Roosevelt.'" *Journal of Latin American Studies* 30, no. 3 (1998): 551–71.

Karush, Matthew B., and Oscar Chamosa, eds. *The New Cultural History of Peronism: Power and Identity in Mid-Twentieth-Century Argentina.* Durham, NC: Duke University Press, 2010.

Klich, Ignacio. "Towards an Arab–Latin American Bloc? The Genesis of Argentine–Middle East Relations: Jordan, 1945–54." *Middle Eastern Studies* 31, no. 3 (1995): 550–72.

Luna, Félix. *A Short History of the Argentinians.* 4th ed. Translated by Cynthia Mansfield and Ian Barnett. Buenos Aires: Planeta, 2011.

McGuire, James W. *Peronism without Perón: Unions, Parties, and Democracy in Argentina.* Stanford, CA: Stanford University Press, 1999.

Pappas, Takis S. *Populism and Liberal Democracy: A Comparative and Theoretical Analysis.* Oxford: Oxford University Press, 2019.

Pelazas, Myriam. "*Democracia en los albores peronistas.*" Paper presented at the 11th Jornadas Interescuelas/Departamentos de Historia, September 2007. http://historiapolitica.com/datos/biblioteca/pelazas.pdf.

Plotkin, Mariano B. *El día que se inventó el Peronismo: la construcción del 17 de octubre.* Buenos Aires: Sudamericana, 2007.

Quiroga, Nicolás. "Las unidades básicas durante el primer peronismo: cuatro notas sobre el Partido Peronista a nivel local." *Nuevo Mundo Mundos Nuevos,* 2008. http://journals.openedition.org/nuevomundo/30565.

Ramacciotti, Karina. *La política sanitaria del peronismo.* Buenos Aires: Biblos, 2009.

Rein, Raanan. *La salvación de una dictadura: la alianza Franco-Perón 1946–1955.* Madrid: Consejo Superior de Investigaciones Científicas, 1995.

Sáenz Quesada, María. *1943: el fin de la Argentina liberal; El surgimiento del Peronismo.* Buenos Aires: Sudamericana, 2019.

———. *La Libertadora: de Perón a Frondizi 1955–1958; Historia pública y secreta.* Buenos Aires: Sudamericana, 2011.

Turner, Frederick, and José Enrique Miguens, eds. *Juan Perón and the Reshaping of Argentina.* Pittsburgh: University of Pittsburgh Press, 2009.

5. Society

A. Welfare

Barry, Carolina. "Las monjas peronistas: política y religión en la ayuda social, 1946–1955." *Revista Cultura & Religión* 5, no. 1 (2011): 117–34.

Barry, Carolina, Karina Ramacciotti, and Adriana Valobra, eds. *La Fundación Eva Perón y las mujeres: entre la provocación y la inclusión.* Buenos Aires: Editorial Biblos, 2008.

Ferioli, Néstor. *La Fundación Eva Perón.* 2 vols. Buenos Aires: Centro Editor de América Latina, 1990.

Guy, Donna. *Women Build the Welfare State: Performing Charity and Creating Rights in Argentina, 1880–1955.* Durham, NC: Duke University Press, 2009.

Moreno, José Luis. *Éramos tan pobres: de la caridad colonial a la Fundación Eva Perón.* Buenos Aires: Sudamericana, 2009.

Viladrich, Anahí, and Andrés A. Thompson. "Women and Philanthropy in Argentina: From the Society of Beneficence to Eva Perón." *Voluntas: International Journal of Voluntary and Nonprofit Organizations* 7 (1996): 336–49.

B. Lifestyle

André, María Claudia. "New Look, melodrama y poder: Eva Perón y la moda." In *Pasado de moda, expresiones culturales y consumo en la Argentina*, edited by Regina Root and Susan Halstead, 202–13. Buenos Aires: Ampersand, 2017.

Ballent, Anahí. "Faces of Modernity in the Architecture of the Peronist State, 1943–1955." *Fascism* 7, no. 1 (2018): 80–108.

Betti, María del Rosario. "Architecture as the Built Message of Power: Buenos Aires under Evita's Spell." *Journal of Architecture* 11, no. 2 (2006): 225–39.

Milanesio, Natalia. "'The Guardian Angels of the Domestic Economy': Housewives' Responsible Consumption in Peronist Argentina." *Journal of Women's History* 18, no. 3 (2006): 91–117.

Pite, Rebekah E. *Creating a Common Table in Twentieth-Century Argentina: Doña Petrona, Women and Food.* Chapel Hill: University of North Carolina Press, 2013.

C. Education

Cucuzza, Héctor Rubén, ed. *Estudios de historia de la educación durante el primer peronismo (1943–1955).* Buenos Aires: Los Libros del Riel, 1997.

———. "Ruptura hegemónica ruptura pedagógica: *La razón de mi vida* como texto escolar durante el primer peronismo." *Sarmiento* 2 (1998): 153–79.

Galak, Eduardo Lautaro, and Iván Pablo Orbuch. "La educación de los sentidos en la Argentina de Perón: el caso de la revista *Noticioso* y la cinematografía escolar." *Paedagogica Histórica* 55 (2019): 137–51.

Glozman, Mara. "Debate parlamentario e imaginarios pedagógicos durante el primer peronismo: *La razón de mi vida* como objeto de disputa." *De signos y sentidos* 13 (2012): 27–51.

Gvirtz, Silvina, and Mariano Narodowski. "The Micro-Politics of School Resistance: The Case of Argentine Teachers versus the Educational Policies of Perón and Evita." *Discourse: Studies in the Cultural Politics of Education* 19, no. 2 (1998): 233–41.

Puiggrós, Adriana, and Jorge Luis Bernetti. *Cultura política y educación (1945–1955).* Buenos Aires: Editorial Galerna, 1993.

Rein, Mónica Esti. *Politics and Education in Argentina, 1946–1962.* Translated by Martha Grenzeback. London: Routledge, 2016.

D. Mass Media

Cane, James. *The Fourth Enemy: Journalism and Power in the Making of Peronist*

Argentina, 1930–1955. University Park: Pennsylvania State University Press, 2012.

Carnevale, Susana. *La patria periodística*. Buenos Aires: Colihue, 1999.

Ehrlich, Laura, and Sandra Gayol. "Las vidas post mortem de Eva Perón: cuerpo, ausencia y biografías en las revistas de masas de Argentina." *Historia Crítica* 70 (2018): 111–31.

Lindenboim, Federico M. "Radio y peronismo: la construcción de una narración nacional." Paper presented at the 16th Jornadas Interescuelas/Departamentos de Historia, 2013. http://cdsa.aacademica.org/000-010/993.

Miranda, Lida. "Prensa católica, sociedad y política de masas: el caso del diario *El Pueblo* en la ciudad de Buenos Aires (1920–1946)." *Revista Electrónica de Fuentes y Archivos* 7, no. 7 (2016): 41–66. https://refa.org.ar/file.php?tipo=Contenido&id=151.

Rein, Raanan, and Claudio Panella, eds. *Peronismo y prensa escrita: abordajes, miradas e interpretaciones nacionales y extranjeras*. La Plata, Argentina: Editorial de la Universidad de La Plata, 2008.

Ruiz, Fernando J. *Guerras mediáticas: las grandes batallas periodísticas desde la Revolución de Mayo hasta la actualidad*. Buenos Aires: Sudamericana, 2014.

Sirvén, Pablo Martín. *Perón y los medios de comunicación, 1943–1955*. Buenos Aires: Sudamericana, 2014.

Varela, Mirta. "Peronismo y medios: control político, industria nacional y gusto popular." Rehime, 2012. http://www.rehime.com.ar/escritos/documentos/idexalfa/v/varelam.php#articulos.

E. Gender

Carlson, Marifran. *¡Feminismo! The Woman's Movement in Argentina from Its Beginnings to Eva Perón*. Chicago: Chicago Review Press, 2005.

Davies, Lloyd Hughes. "Eva in the Shadows: The Partial Revenge of Dr Pedro Ara." *Hispanic Research Journal* 8, no. 2 (2007): 123–40.

Foster, David William. "Evita Perón, Juan José Sebreli, and Gender." In *Sexual Textualities: Essays on Queer/ing Latin American Writing*, edited by David William Foster, 22–38. Austin: University of Texas Press, 1997.

Hammond, Gregory. *The Women's Suffrage Movement and Feminism in Argentina from Roca to Perón*. Albuquerque: University of New Mexico Press, 2011.

Kraus, Carolyn. "Power, Resistance, and the Writings of Female Illegitimacy: Eva Perón, Clare Boothe Luce, and Flora Tristan." *Journal of Research in Gender Studies* 1, no. 1 (2011): 9–42.

Lavrin, Asunción. *Women, Feminism, and Social Change in Argentina, Chile, and Uruguay 1890–1940*. Lincoln: University of Nebraska Press, 1995.

Macón, Cecilia. "'Santa Evita Montonera': Envious, Therefore Empowered." *Journal of Romance Studies* 15, no. 1 (2015): 1–28.

Mengo, Renée Isabel. "Eva Perón, entre el discurso y la acción/Eva Perón, Speeches and Action." *Historia y Comunicación Social* 12 (2007): 111–33.

Navarro, Marysa, and Virginia Sánchez Korrol. *Women in Latin America and the Caribbean: Restoring Women to History*. Bloomington: Indiana University Press, 1999.

Rosano, Susana. "Imaginario femenino en el populismo argentino: género y nación en *La razón de mi vida*, de Eva Perón." *Iberoamericana* 5, no. 19 (2014): 51–63.

Sanville, Jean B. "Transcending Gender Stereotypes: Eluding the Eva Perónista Position." *Gender and Psychoanalysis* 3, no. 2 (1998): 175–95.

Zabaleta, Marta Raquel. *Feminine Stereotypes and Roles in Theory and Practice in Argentina before and after the First Lady Eva Perón*. Lewiston, NY: Edwin Mellen Press, 2001.

6. Illness, Death, and Myth

Albertelli, Jorge. *Los "cien días" de Eva Perón*. Buenos Aires: Cesarini, 1994.

Baumgartner, Juana M. "Eva Perón: The Myth and Cult of the Anti-virgin." *Michigan Discussions in Anthropology* 9 (1990): 31–56.

Bosca, Roberto. "Evita: A Case of Political Canonization." In *The Making of Saints: Contesting Sacred Ground*, edited by James F. Hopgood, 59–74. Tuscaloosa: University of Alabama Press, 2005.

Castro, Nelson. *Los últimos días de Eva: historia de un engaño*. 2nd ed. Buenos Aires: Sudamericana, 2015.

Díaz, Gwendolyn. "Making the Myth of Evita Perón: Saint, Martyr, Prostitute." *Studies in Latin American Popular Culture* 22 (2003): 181–92.

Gerassi-Navarro, Nina. "Las tres Evas: de la historia al mito en cinemascope." In *Evita: mitos y representaciones*, edited by Marysa Navarro, 65–100. Buenos Aires: Fondo de Cultura Económica, 2002.

Hall, Linda B. "Evita and María: Religious Reverence and Political Resonance in Argentina." In *Mary, Mother and Warrior: The Virgin in Spain and the Americas*, 207–42. Austin: University of Texas Press, 2004.

———. "Evita Perón: Beauty, Resonance, and Heroism." In *Heroes and Hero Cults in Latin America*, edited by Samuel Brunk and Ben Fallaw, 229–63. Austin: University of Texas Press, 2006.

Hein-Kircher, Heidi. "Social Master Narratives: Romanticization and Functionalization of Personalities and Events through Political Myths." In *Evita Vive*, edited by Anne-Berenike Rothstein and Pere Joan Tous, 13–32. Berlin: Verlag Walter Frey, 2013.

Lerner, Barron H. "The Illness and Death of Eva Perón: Cancer, Politics and Secrecy." *Lancet* 355 (2000): 1988–91.

Navarro, Marysa. "Evita: historia y mitología." *Caravelle* 98 (2012): 113–33. https://journals.openedition.org/caravelle/1185.

———. "Wonder Woman Was Argentine and Her Real Name Was Evita." *Canadian Journal of Latin American and Caribbean Studies* 34, no. 48 (1999): 133–52.

Nijensohn, Daniel E. "Prefrontal Lobotomy on Evita Was Done for Behavior/Personality Modification, not Just for Pain Control." *Neurosurgical Focus* 39 (2015): 1–6.

Rodriguez, Anne O. "Eva Perón: Cervical Cancer and the Effect on a Nation." *Current Opinions in Gynecology and Obstetrics* 21, no. 1 (2009): 1–3.

Santos, Lidia. "Eva Perón: One Woman, Several Masks." In *Contemporary Latin American Cultural Studies*, edited by Stephen Hart and Richard A. Young, 102–15. New York: Routledge, 2014.

———. "Los hijos bastardos de Evita, o la literatura bajo el manto de estrellas de la cultura de masas." *Canadian Journal of Latin American and Caribbean Studies* 34, no. 48 (1999): 195–213.

Santos Lepera, Lucía. "Las manifestaciones colectivas de duelo frente a la muerte de Eva Perón (Tucumán, 1952)." *Boletín Americanista* 64 (2012): 161–80.

Schwartz, Margaret. "Proper Corruption: Index and Metaphor in Photographs of the Embalmed Corpse of Eva Perón." *Framework* 51, no. 1 (2010): 7–32.

Young, Grace J., Wenya Linda Bi, Timothy R. Smith, Ryan Brewster, William B. Gormley, Ian F. Dunn, Edward R. Laws, and Daniel E. Nijensohn. "Evita's Lobotomy." *Journal of Clinical Neuroscience* 22 (2015): 1883–88.

Filmography

CONTENTS

Introduction	167
1. Movie Appearances of Evita	168
2. Films and Series on Evita	168
A. Documentaries	168
B. Feature Films	169
C. TV Series	169

INTRODUCTION

When it comes to compiling a filmography on Evita, it is necessary to draw a distinction between her movie appearances and the cinematic and TV representations about her that never seem to stop surfacing. Mirroring that distinction, we have divided this filmography into two sections. In the first section, we have listed all the films in which Evita made an appearance. Evita's role in the cinema of Argentina can be considered modest given that she landed chiefly small roles during her acting career. The exception to this was the leading role she played in *La pródiga* (The Prodigal Woman), the pinnacle of her movie career. This film bridges the gap between Evita the actress and Evita the politician for, while *La pródiga* was her last movie, it also foreshadowed part of her crucial role in mid-20th century Argentine politics. In the movie, her concerns for the welfare of the villagers typify the monumental social work she carried out during her political career.

In the second section of the filmography, we have included Argentine and international films as well as TV series in an attempt to capture as many productions as possible. The on-screen portrayals of Evita started to crop up the moment she passed away on 26 July 1952, with two documentaries depicting her impressive funeral, *Y la Argentina detuvo su corazón* (And Argentina's Heart Stopped) and *Eva Perón inmortal* (Immortal Eva Perón). Apart from these two, the many titles appearing in the "Documentaries" subsection tap into Evita's life, the work of the Fundación Eva Perón, the Partido Peronista Femenino, her legacy, her death, and the odyssey of her corpse. The panoramic view offered in this subsection stems from an ever-growing fascination with Evita.

Much shorter than "Documentaries," the "Feature Films" subsection showcases movies made since 1996, with the exception of the 1993 film *Gatica "el mono."* Centering on the life of the renowned Argentine boxer José María Gatica, *Gatica "el mono"* offers a peripheral portrayal of Evita. Only in 1996 did the depiction of Evita take center stage. Two movies from that year focus on her life, Alan Parker's musical film *Evita* and its Argentine counterpart Juan Carlos Desanzo's drama *Eva Perón: la verdadera historia* (Eva Perón: The True Story). It was by virtue of the former that the image of Evita exploded onto the global stage. If Parker's movie had a bearing on the internationalization of Evita, the Argentine bicentennial celebration of 2010 was the event that reinforced her image in Argentina. In 2010, Argentina commemorated the May

Revolution of 1810, a pivotal event that led to the declaration of the country's independence from Spain in 1816. Evita was named the Woman of the Bicentennial, an acknowledgment that spawned numerous cultural expressions. Among these were two Argentine films, *Juan y Eva* (Juan and Eva), a romantic drama, and *Eva de la Argentina* (Eva from Argentina), an animated biopic.

The subsection "TV Series" rounds off this filmography. It is our contention that a filmography on Evita would not be complete without the inclusion of the noteworthy TV series and episodes that have portrayed her. Their ease of access makes them arguably one of the best ways of disseminating the image of Evita, and they are thereby worthy of inclusion in this filmography. The most successful of the series listed here is the Spanish award-winning miniseries *Carta a Eva* (Letter to Eva), which revolves around Evita's official visit to Spain in 1947 and her confrontation with the Spanish first lady, María del Carmen Polo y Martínez-Valdés. The other miniseries included in this subsection is the American *Evita Perón*, which conveys a negative portrayal of Evita. Undoubtedly, Evita's Cinderella story, her marriage to Juan Domingo Perón, her rise to power, her rejection of the upper classes, her death, and the disappearance of her body are some aspects of her intriguing persona that have greatly contributed to inspiring the film and TV industry.

1. MOVIE APPEARENCES OF EVITA

Bayón Herrera, Luis, dir. *El más infeliz del pueblo*. 1941. Buenos Aires: Beverly Hills Video Home Producciones, 1994. VHS.

Boneo, Eduardo, and Mario Soffici, dir. *La cabalgata del circo*. 1945. Buenos Aires: Arte Video, 2012. DVD.

Chas de Cruz, Israel, and Alberto Etchebehere, dir. *¡Segundos afuera!* 1937.

Migliar, Adelqui, dir. *La carga de los valientes*. 1940.

Reinhardt, John, dir. *Una novia en apuros*. 1942.

Soffici, Mario, dir. *La pródiga*. 1945. Released on 16 August 1984. Buenos Aires: Arte Video, 2012. DVD.

2. FILMS AND SERIES ON EVITA

A. Documentaries

Amadori, Luis César, dir. *Eva Perón inmortal*. Buenos Aires: Secretaría de Prensa y Difusión de la Presidencia de la Nación, 1952. https://www.youtube.com/watch?v=HBF8URKQ8gs.

Bauer, Tristán, dir. *Evita: la tumba sin paz*. 1997. Buenos Aires: South Productions, 1997. VHS.

Blanco, Martín, and Daniel Soria, dir. *Los ojos que miraron a Evita*. 2002.

Bluth, Richard, dir. *Eva Perón: The Life of Eva Perón*. Chatsworth, CA: Bluth Enterprises in association with Aims Multimedia, 2003. DVD.

Borcosque, Carlos, dir. *Su obra de amor*. Buenos Aires: Noticiario Panamericano, 1953.

Ciudad estudiantil: el sueño de Eva Perón. La Matanza: Instituto de Medios de Comunicación de la Universidad Nacional de La Matanza, 2016. Filmstrip, 45 min.

Cronjager, Edward, dir. *Y la Argentina detuvo su corazón*. Aired on 17 October 1952 on Canal 7. https://www.youtube.com/watch?v=iWhfXVGcsr8.

Demicheli, Tulio, dir. *El misterio Eva Perón*. 1987. New York: First Run Features, 2008. DVD.

Favio, Leonardo, dir. *Perón: sinfonía del sentimiento*. 1999. Buenos Aires: Página/12, 2009. DVD.

Gassió, Xavier, dir. *La sombra de Evita: volveré y seré millones*. 2011. Barcelona: Cameo, 2013. DVD.

Getino, Octavio, and Fernanado Solanas, dir. *La hora de los hornos*. 1968. Buenos Aires: Cine Sur, 2008. DVD.

Gómez, José Manuel, and María Teresa Mazzorotolo, dir. *Evita: la otra mirada*. 2005.

Goyeneche, Marcelo, dir. *Las enfermeras de Evita*. 2015. Buenos Aires: MG Documentales 2016. DVD.

Horas inolvidables. Buenos Aires: Secretaría de Prensa y Difusión, 1953.

Ladd, Martín, dir. *Eva, trazos de una infancia*. Aired on 26 July 2020 on Canal Encuentro. https://www.abratv.com.ar/serie/312-Eva-trazos-de-una-infancia.

Las compañeras de Eva Perón. Buenos Aires: Partido Justicialista, 1996. https://www.youtube.com/watch?v=cCRmZnxeDz8.

Malowicki, Nicolás, dir. *Evita capitana*. 2000.

Marino, Alejandra, dir. *Las muchachas*. 2011.

Meilij, Eduardo, dir. *Permiso para pensar*. 1989. https://www.youtube.com/watch?v=__m4E7rFGx4.

Mignogna, Eduardo, dir. *Evita: quien quiera oír que oiga*. 1984. Buenos Aires: All Video, 1984. VHS.

Montes-Bradley, Eduardo, dir. *Evita*. 2007. Charlottesville, VA: Heritage Film Project, 2013. eVideo.

Pasini Hansen, Carlos, dir. *Queen of Hearts*. Aired on 24 October 1972 on Thames Television. https://vimeo.com/64517710.

Pigna, Felipe, dir. *Eva Perón: jirones de su vida*. Buenos Aires: Federación de Docentes de las Universidades, 2019. https://www.youtube.com/watch?v=Fm5OOFi7zKQ.

Rotondaro, Fernanda, dir. *Eva Perón: 100 años*. Aired on 5 December 2019 on Canal Encuentro. https://www.youtube.com/watch?reload=9&v=ASQbo7pxeeM.

Serrano, Carlos Luis, dir. *Una mujer, un pueblo*. Aired on 28 February 1974 on Televisión Argentina.

Schroeder, Juan, dir. *Evita*. 1974.

Solanas, Fernando, and Octavio Getino, dir. *Perón, la revolución justicialista*. 1971. Parts of it were aired in 1973 on Canal 9. https://www.youtube.com/watch?v=r2VK2YSOpxI.

Tosín, Armando, dir. *Evita: una vida*. 1985.

Walger, Eduardo Félix, dir. *Evita: una bandera*. 1995.

B. Feature Films

Agüero, Pablo, dir. *Eva no duerme*. 2015. San Francisco: Kanopy, 2018. Streaming.

Desanzo, Juan Carlos, dir. *Eva Perón: la verdadera historia*. 1996. Buenos Aires: SBP, 2007. DVD.

Favio, Leonardo, dir. *Gatica "el mono."* 1993. Barcelona: DeAPlaneta: SAVOR, 2009. DVD.

Luque, Paula de, dir. *Juan y Eva*. 2011. Buenos Aires: SBP, 2013. DVD.

Metzger, Radley, dir. *Don't Cry for Me Little Mother*. 1972. New York: First Run Features, 2005. DVD.

Olivera, Héctor, dir. *Ay, Juancito*. 2004. Buenos Aires: Perfil, 2011. DVD.

Parker, Alan, dir. *Evita*. 1996. San Francisco: Kanopy, 2017. Streaming.

Seoane, María, dir. *Eva de la Argentina*. 2011. Buenos Aires: Emerald, 2012. DVD.

C. TV Series

Caetano, Israel Adrián, dir. *Lo que el tiempo nos dejó*. Episode 1, "Mi mensaje." Aired on 1 September 2010 on Telefé.

Chomsky, Marvin, dir. *Evita Perón*. 2 episodes. Aired on 23 and 24 February 1981 on NBC.

Intimate Portrait. Episode "Eva Perón." Narrated by Jill St. John and aired on 22 December 1996. https://www.youtube.com/watch?v=DdPzp6KcQhl.

Saban, Martín, and Sebastián Pivotto, dir. *Padre coraje*. Episode 34. Aired on El Trece.

Villaronga, Agustí, dir. *Carta a Eva*. 2 episodes, 2012. Barcelona: a contracorriente films, 2013. DVD.

Index

Abras, Emilio, xvii, 11, 121
Acevedo Pérez, María Georgina Cecilia, 11, 24
Acosta, Clotilde, 11, 59
Acosta Machado, Américo, 11
Adolfo Suárez Madrid–Barajas Airport, xviii, 11
"¿Adónde van los muertos?" (poem), xiii, 2, 119
Agosti, Orlando, 146
Agüero, Pablo, 43
Agusti, José, 100
Aisina, Francisco, xvii, 121
"Alabanza" (poem), 107
Albertelli, Jorge, xxii, 11–12, 35, 52
Alcaraz, Julio, xvii, 12, 121, 128
Alcázar of Toledo, xviii, 12, 137
Aldrey, Florencio, 80
Alea Building, 12–13, 35
Alem, Leandro N., 141–142
Alfonsín, Raúl, 64
Alhambra, xviii, 13, 58
Alhambra Palace Hotel, xviii, 13, 58
Allen, Amanda, 28
Allies, 124
Aloé, Carlos Vicente, 12–13, 34, 61
Alterio, Ernesto, 128
Álvarez, Eloy, xiv, 30
Álvarez, María Eugenia, 13
Álvarez Rodríguez, Justo, 36, 87
Amanda Allen Children's City, Argentina, 13
American wars of independence, 127
anarchist ideas, 83
anti-American group, 124
anti-Argentine behavior, 14, 80
Anti-Argentine Activities Congressional Committee, 14

anti-Peronist campaign, 25
anti-Peronist civic and military groups, 85, 110
anti-Peronist government, 21
anti-Peronist ideology, 85
anti-Peronist militants, 49
anti-Peronist myths. *See* Peronist and anti-Peronist myths
anti-Peronist policy, 85
anti-Peronists, 23, 46, 96
antipueblo, 14, 28, 101
Apold, Raúl Alejandro, 7, 14–15, 34, 129, 137
Ara, Pedro, xxii–xxiii, 8, 15, 21, 24, 43, 93, 128
ARA *General Belgrano*, 125
Arab–Israeli War, 92
Aramburu, Pedro Eugenio, xxiii, 15–17, 21, 23–24, 26–27, 43, 85–86, 95–96, 105, 112, 125
Areilza y Martínez de Rodas, José María de, xvii, 16
Ares, Roberto, 95
Argentine Academy of Fine Arts, 129
Argentine Antarctic Institute, 93
Argentine Anti-Communist Alliance, 17, 35, 87, 96, 139. *See also* Triple A
Argentine Atomic Energy Commission, 93
Argentine Constitution of 1949, 6, 17, 20, 33, 41, 54, 70, 93, 130
Argentine Council of Scientific Research, 93
Argentine Football Association, 100
Argentine Institute for the Promotion of Trade, 17, 95, 122
Argentine Military Academy, 94
Argentine Pampas, 47, 72, 77

Argentine Patagonia, 96, 107
Armilla Air Base, xviii, 17
Army of the Andes, 93
Arrieta, Alfredo, 36, 37
Artagnan Petit, Carlos, 110
Asociación Argentina de Actores (AAA), xiv, 17, 53, 116
Asociación Radial Argentina (ARA), xvi, 2, 17
Ateneo Cultural Eva Perón, 17, 33, 99, 126, 141
Augusto Severo International Airport, xvii, 18
Auriol, Vincent, xx, 104
Avellaneda (city), Argentina, 142
Ávila, Spain, xviii, 18, 89, 112
Axis powers, 4, 71, 122, 124
Ayrinhac, Numa, 18, 97

Bahía Blanca, Argentina, xvii, xxi, 142
Baker, Ernest, 137
Balbín, Ricardo, 142
Ballofet, Jorge, xvii, 121
Barberá, Manuel, 31
Barcelona, Spain, xix, 19, 57
Bary, Alberto de, 119
Basilica of Our Lady of Luján, xv, 87
Basilica of Our Lady of Sorrows, xviii, 19, 58
battle of Carmen de Patagones, 78
Battle of San Lorenzo, 135
Baty, Gaston, 30
Bauer, Tristán, 23
Bayón Herrera, Luis, 39
Beauvoir, Simone de, 146
Bedoya, Eduardo, 42
Benítez, Hernán, 19–20, 25
Berlin, Germany, 106
Bern, Switzerland, xx, 133
Bernarda (fashion house), 59
Bernhardt, Prince of the Netherlands, xxii, 114
Bidault, Georges, xx, 104
Bill of Rights of the Workers, 17, 20, 128
Birabent, Mauricio, 34
Blomberg, Héctor, 20, 30
Blomberg, Pedro, 20
Boneo, Eduardo, 77
books:
    Escribe Eva Perón, 40, 44
    Eva Perón: The Myths of a Woman, 148
    Evita: su legado de puño y letra, 44
    Evita fuera del balcón, 71
    Evita íntima, 110
    Evita y yo: la verdadera historia del libro de Eva Perón, 107
    Fantasías eternas a la luz del psicoanálisis, 148
    Historia del peronismo, 62–63
    History of Peronism, 63
    In My Own Words, 68
    La enfermera de Evita, 13
    La mujer del látigo: Eva Perón, 79, 148
    La novela de Perón, 91
    La palabra, el pensamiento y la acción, 44, 79
    La razón de mi vida, xxii, 18, 26, 82, 93, 98, 101, 106, 110, 128, 147, 148
    Los "cien días" de Eva Perón, 12
    Mi hermana Evita, 2, 36, 119
    Mi mensaje, xxii, xiii, 94–95
    My Mission in Life, 98
    Por qué soy peronista por Eva Perón, 40, 112
    Santa Evita, 23, 91, 128, 138
    Su palabra, su pensamiento y su acción, 79, 132
    The Woman with the Whip: Eva Perón, 90, 148
    The Writings of Eva Perón, 148
Borlenghi, Ángel Gabriel, 21–22, 39, 57
Botana, Natalio, 32, 42
Botta, Antonio, 29
Bramuglia, Juan Atilio, 22
Broadway, United States, 46
Buenos Aires (ship), xx, 124, 133
Buenos Aires Central Post Office, xvii, 55, 75
bunker of Juan Domingo Perón, 12–13, 22

Cabanillas, Héctor Eduardo, 23
Cabildo, Buenos Aires, 111
Cabildo, Montevideo, xx
Cabildo Abierto, xxii, 18, 23, 41, 97
Cabrera de Ferrari, Irma, 23–24, 84
Camino de Santiago, 129
Campo de Mayo military base, 122
Cámpora, Héctor José, 7, 11, 24, 47, 54–55, 59, 64, 83, 84, 105, 108
Camus, Albert, 146
Canónico, Abel, 12, 24, 103
Cantilo, José, 78
capitalism, 108
Caporale de Mercante, María Elena, 11, 25, 94, 141, 145
Cárcova, Ernesto de la, 18

Carmona, António Óscar Fragoso, xx, 85
Carranza, Luis, 117
Carrasco, Eudoro, 78
Carril, Hugo del, 42, 90, 110
Carrillo, Ramón, 25–26, 40–41, 111, 113
Carzolio, Lucila, 148
Castillo, Cátulo, 110
Castillo, Ramón Antonio, 3, 26, 50, 59, 108–109, 121–122, 124
Castiñeira de Dios, José, 26, 107
Castiñeiras, Noemí, 32, 113
Catalina Larralt de Estrugamou School, xiii, 1, 26, 123
Catamarca, Argentina, 114
Catholic Church, 8, 25, 40, 64, 85, 91, 112
Catholic education, 107
Catholic ideology, 95
Catholic social teaching, 72
Catholicism, 40, 72
caudillismo, 27, 108
caudillo, 27, 139
Central Bank of Argentina, 17, 34, 61, 91, 95
Centros Independientes, 27, 105, 142
Cereijo, Ramón Antonio, 27
Chacarita Cemetery, 96, 128
Chaco, Argentina, xxi–xxii, 135
Chaliapin, Boris, 136
Charlo, 117
Charmiello, Francisco, xiv, 30
Chas de Cruz, Israel, 130
Chávez, Benito Enrique "Fermín," 27, 145
Che, 46
Cherry, Ethel, 98
Child Psychology and Reeducation Institute, 145
The Children's Republic, Argentina, 27
Chivilcoy, Argentina, xiii, 1, 36, 67
Chomsky, Marvin J., 47
Christian Democrats, 125
Ciccone, Madonna Louise, 27–28
cipayo, 14, 28, 71, 101
Ciudad Estudiantil Presidente Juan Domingo Perón, Argentina, 28
Ciudad Eva Perón, Argentina, 79
Ciudad Infantil Amanda Allen, Argentina, 16, 28
Ciudad Universitaria Estudiantil Presidente Perón, Argentina, 29
Colom, Eduardo, 78
Colonia Yabebiry, Argentina, *136*

Comisión Nacional sobre la Desaparición de Personas (CONADEP), 64
Comodoro Rivadavia, Argentina, 96
communism, 54, 108
Communists, 125
Communist Party, 104
Concordancia, 68
Confederación General del Trabajo (CGT), xxi–xxiii, 7, 8, 15, 20–21, 23–25, 27, 31, 41–43, 54, 57, 76, 80, 85, 96, 106, 108, 123, 132, 139
Congress, xvii, xxii, 6, 15, 25, 50– 51, 89, 104, 111, 124, 129, 132
Copi, 32, 44
Córdoba (city), Argentina, 30, 32, 35, 90, 125, 142
Córdoba (province), Argentina, xvii, xxi, xxiii, 29, 32, 85, 94, 130, 139, 142
Córdoba, Irma, 32
Corrientes, Argentina, 32, 94, 114, 127, 135
Corsini, Ignacio, 117
Cortejarena, José, 81
Coscia, Jorge, 72
Covington, Julie, 36
Cuban Revolution, 73
Cultural Athenaeum Eva Perón, 32

Dakar, Senegal, xx, 124, 133
Dakhla, Western Sahara, xvii, 18, 33, 53, 55, 91
Damonte Botana, Raúl, 33, 44
Dealessi, Pierina, xiv, 29, 33
Decalogue of the Rights of Seniors, 17, 22, 33–34, 107, 130
Decker, Rodolfo, 14
de-Peronization, xxiii, 21, 34, 85
Descamisado Train, xvi, 32, 34, 93, 125
descamisados, xxii, 24, 25, 34, 40, 43, 58, 96, 99, 108, 114, 128, 137
Díaz, Julieta, 34, 72
Dionisi, Humberto, xxii, 11–12, 34–35, 52, 85
Dior, Christian, 104
Directorate General for Architecture, 49
Directorate General for Information Distribution, 15
Directorate General for Labor and Women's Assistance, 50
Directorate General for Social Assistance, 52, 89, 93

Dirty War, xxiii, 35, 47, 64. *See also* military dictatorship (1976–1983)
the disappeared, 35, 64
Discépolo, Armando, xiv, 30, 35, 71
Discépolo, Enrique Santos, 35
Discépolo, Santos, 35
Dodero, Alberto, xvii, 35, 95, 121–122, 124, 133
Dodero, Alberto Nicolás, 12, 35
Doña, Juana, 26
Duarte, Blanca, xv, 7, 36, 87, 95, 154
Duarte, Elisa, 1, 7, 20, 36–37, 67, 72, 100
Duarte, Erminda, 1–2, 7, 27, 36, 67, 95, 119, 154
Duarte, Juan, xiii, 1, 20, 36–37, 42, 67
Duarte, Juan "Juancito" Ramón, xvii, 2–4, 7, 18, 27, 36–37, 59, 99, 121, 147
Duarte family tomb, xxiii, 8, 21, 37
Duhalde, Eduardo Alberto, 37, 75, 109, 128
Dunaway, Faye, 46
Dutra, Eurico Gaspar, xx, 124

educational radio, 119
Ejército Peronista de Liberación Nacional, 73
Ejército Revolucionario del Pueblo, 95
Elizabeth (queen), 8, 132
Entre Ríos, Argentina, 62, 84, 114
Ernst, Isabel, xvii, 40, 94, 100
Escuela de Enfermeras Eva Perón, 13, 16, 40–41, 52
Escuela del aire, 119
Escuela Superior Peronista, xxii, 41, 62, 93, 101, 114, 122–123
Espejo, José, 23, 41–42, 57
Esperanza, Argentina, 93
Estancia La Unión, Argentina, xiii, 1, 36, 42, 87
Esteban de Luca military arsenal, 114
Estrada, Fernando, 34
Etchebehere, Alberto, 130
European tour, xx, 5, 42, 67, 97, 112, 124, 133. *See also* Rainbow Tour
"Eva Perón" (poem), 26
Eva Perón Foundation, 44
Eva Perón Home/Museum, 44
Eva Perón Nursing School, 44
Eva Perón Province, Argentina, 79
Eva Perón Room, 44, 75
Evita:
　artistic life, 2–3
　audience at the Vatican, 112, 125, 145

awards, titles and honors, xviii, xx–xxii, 15, 16, 24–25, 41, 51, 53, 95, 112, 126–127, 131–132, 145
bid for vice president, xxiii, 20, 43
biographies, 86, 90, 110, 128, 137, 147–148
birth anniversary, 44, 147
birth certificate, 3, 20, 55
birthplace, 42, 87
body, xxiii, 8, 15–16, 20–21, 23, 36–37, 43, 84–85, 96, 101–103, 112, 115, 128, 132, 138, 146
illegitimacy, 1, 3, 20, 55
illness, xxi, xxii, 7, 11, 35, 43, 52, 70–71, 80, 85–86, 94, 100, 103, 108, 111–112, 114, 127, 129, 132, 135, 137
candidacy for vice president and renunciation, xxii, 15, 18, 20, 23–24, 86, 97, 115
canonization and sainthood, 24–25, 127, 132, 138
Catholic sacraments, 26–27
childhood, 1–2, 36, 43, 44, 82, 128
close collaborators and friends, xvii, 3, 25, 30, 33, 35, 54, 59–60, 71, 83–84, 92–94, 99–100, 106, 110, 123, 126, 145, 151
death, xxii–xxiii, 7, 15, 18, 20–24, 42–43, 45, 51, 79, 82, 84, 86, 95–96, 101–104, 106, 108, 110, 115, 128, 132, 135, 137–138, 143
death certificate, 135
death mask, 103
death time, xxii, 15, 97, 137
debut film, 17, 130
embalming, xxii, 8, 12, 15, 20–21, 40
first lady, xvii, xx, 4, 5, 32, 43, 51, 54–55, 58, 70, 81, 92, 94, 110, 113, 125, 132, 145–146
first published interview, 131
first solo picture in a paper, 78
formal education, xiii, 1–2, 52, 123
Great Cross of Isabella the Catholic, xviii, 16, 58, 126
hairstyle, 12
hometown, 36, 45, 72, 87, 89
images, 5, 51, 76, 95, 98, 109, 138, 147, 149
lectures on history of Peronism, xxii, 41, 62–63, 101, 114

letters, 55, 63, 75, 84
love letters, 3, 92, 147
labor mediation, 31
labor unions, xvii, 17, 27, 40–41, 54–55
lobotomy, 86
magazine covers, xv–xvi, xx, 14, 28, 33, 60, 96, 102, 120, 131, 136–137, 148
monument, 21, 84, 96, 99, 128, 137–138
murals, xxiii, 51, 90, *97*, 129
myths, 98, 109, 112, 128, 147–148
name, 1, 3, 20, 27, 52 147
office, 130
portraits, *18*, 40, *97*, 102, 129, 131, 136–137, 148
purchase of weapons, xxii, 114
radio debut, xiii, 1–2, 119
residences, xvi–xvii, xxi–xxii, 3, 7, 12, 51, 55, 87, 127, *143*
resting place, xxiii, 8, 15, 16, 21, 23, 99, 112, 122, 128, 146. See also Duarte family tomb
scripts and speeches, xvii–xxii, 6, 23–24, 41, 50, 79, 97, 99–100, 111, 120, 126
social assistance, xxi, 5–6, 25, 55. See also Fundación Eva Perón
St. Evita's Day, 25, 132
stage debut, xiv, 2, 29
state funeral, xxii, 7–8, 15, 21, 132, 138
statues, 99, 128, 137, 143
transnational iconic image, 5, 138
wardrobe, xvi, 5, 46, 51, 71, 103–104, 110, 121, 135
wedding, xvi, 3–4, 20, 79–81, 110, 147, 149
youth, 1–2, 24, 82
Evita Children Tournaments, 27, 44, 138
Evita City, Argentina, 44
Evita Museum, 45–*46*, 68–*69*, 135, 147
evitaperon.org, 47
Ezeiza International Airport, xxiii, 47, 96, 108
Ezeiza massacre, xxiii, 47, 64, 96, 108

Faculty of Engineering Building, *49*
Fain, Jordana, 30
Falange Española, 52
Falcón, Ada, 117
Falla, Manuel de, 15
Farentino, James, 46
Farrell, Edelmiro Julián, 50, 94, 108–110, 122, 124
fascism, 50, 53, 58–59, 107, 125

fascists, 53, 83, 109, 137
fascist behavior, 110
fascist country, 4, 121
fascist events, 87
fascist government, 46
fascist paper, 83
fascist principles, 59
fascist sympathizers, 124
Favero, Alberto, 43
Favre, Lucienne, 30
female suffrage, xvii, xx, 5–7, 22, 39, 50, 84, 105, 137, 148
Fernández, Alberto Ángel, 50–51, 54, 105, 109
Fernández, María Asunción "Asunta," 51
Fernández Alvariño, Próspero, 99
Fernández de Kirchner, Cristina, xxiii, 43, 50–51, 54, 60, 65, 75–76, 97, 102, 105, 109, 138
Ferradás Campos, Manuel, 31
Ferrario, Florindo, 11, 51, 62
Fifth National Eucharistic Congress (1950), 126
film production companies:
    Argentina Sono Film, 2, 14, 16–17, 130
    Establecimientos Filmadores Argentinos, 39, 42
    Estudios Baires, 42, 141
    Estudios San Miguel, xvi, 2, 42, 80
    Pampa Film, 12, 78, 104
    Rayton Cinematográfica Argentina, 75
    Warner Bros., 104
films and TV series:
    Argentina de hoy, 16, 100
    A Bride in Trouble, 22
    Carta a Eva, 26
    Circus Cavalcade, 28
    El más infeliz del pueblo, xv, 2, 39, 42
    Eva de la Argentina, 43
    Eva no duerme, 43
    Eva Perón, 46–47
    Eva Perón: la verdadera historia, 43–44
    Eva Perón: The True Story, 44
    Evita, xxiii, 27, 44–45, 148
    Evita: la tumba sin paz, 23
    Evita, quien quiera oír que oiga, 106
    Juan and Eva, 72
    Juan y Eva, 34, 72
    La cabalgata del circo, xvi, 2–3, 12, 42, 77–78, 83

La carga de los valientes, xv, 2, 12, 71, 78, 104
La luna de miel de Inés, 85
La pródiga, xvi, 2, 42, *80–81*, 147
Letter to Eva, 85
Only the Valiant, 102
The Prodigal Woman, 113
Santa Evita, 128
¡Segundos afuera!, xiv, 2, 17, 115, 130
Una novia en apuros, xv, 2, 42, 115, 141
The Unhappiest Man in Town, 141
Y la Argentina detuvo su corazón, xxii, 15
Finochietto, Ricardo, 51–52, 111
Fiora, Teresa Adelina, 11, 41, 52
Firtuoso, Rafael, 29
Flores, María, 52, 90, 148
Foxá y Torroba, Agustín de, xvii, 52
Franco, Eva, xiv, 29, 32, 52–53
Franco, Herminia, 53
Franco, José, xiv, 29, 30, 52, 53
Franco, Nélida, 53
Franco Bahamonde, Francisco, xvii–xix, 4, 11, 19, 26, 33, 53, 85, 89, 91, 112, 120–121, 126
Franco Salgado-Araujo, Francisco, xvii, 33, 53
Franco y Polo, María del Carmen "Nenuca," xviii, 19, 53, 85, 89, 112
Francoist dictatorship, 106
Francoist secret service, 106
Freire, José María, xvii, 53–54
French–Argentine Treaty of Commerce, 104
Frente de Todos, 51, 54
Frente Justicialista de Liberación (FREJULI), 54, 105
Frente Justicialista de Unidad Popular (FREJUPO), 54
Frente para la Victoria (FPV), 54, 75
Freude, Ludwig, 54
Freude, Rodolfo "Rudi" Ludovico, 54–55
Frondizi, Arturo, 16, 42, 54–55, 85, 91, 104, 142
Fuerza de Orientación Radical de la Joven Argentina (FORJA), 71
Fuerzas Armadas Revolucionarias, 95
Fundación de Ayuda Social María Eva Duarte de Perón, xxi, 5, 55, 132. *See also* Fundación Eva Perón
Fundación Eva Perón, xxi, 5–6, 11, 13, 16, 20, 26–29, 33, 40–42, 45, 47, 49, 52, 54–56, 63–64, 75, 84, 92, 99, 103, 111, 113–115, 123, 129–130, 135–139, 141–142, 147

Gainza Paz, Alberto, 79
Gando Airport, xviii, 57, 84
Gandulla, Bernardo, xv, 28
García, Rodrigo, 128
García-Escámez Iniesta, Francisco, xviii, 57
García Ibañez, Rafael, 31
García Lorca, Federico, 52
Gardel, Carlos, 117
gaucho, 78
Gay, Luis, 57, 105
Generalife, xviii, 57
Geneva, Switzerland, xx, 124, 133
German Society of Beneficence, 131
Ghioldi, Américo, 83
Gijón, Spain, 133
Gil, Roberto "Erregé," xv, 31, 58, 90
Giménez, Antonio, 61
Gómez Morales, Alfredo, 95
González Speroni, Gregorio, 120
Goris, Esther, 43
Granada, Spain, xviii, 11, 13, 17, 19, 57–58
Granada City Hall, xviii, 13, 58
Grandinetti, Darío, 128
grasa, 58
Gréco, Juliette, 146
Grierson, Cecilia, 6, 26
Grisolía, Estela, 36, 67
Grupo de Oficiales Unidos (GOU), 19, 58–59, 68, 71, 86, 94, 107, 122–123
Guardo, Ricardo César, 59, 83
Guereño Rodríguez, Juan, xiv–xv, 37, 59
Guerrico, César, 117
guerrilla groups, xxiii, 16, 21, 47, 73, 92, 95, 108, 138
Guevara, Che, 45
Guevara, Nacha, 43, 59–60
Guibourg, Edmundo "Pucho," 30, 60, 116
Gutiérrez, Adolfo, xvii, 121

Hacia un futuro mejor, xvi, 2–3, 61, 97, 119
Hayek, Salma, 128
Haynes, Albert, 39, 61
Hein-Kircher, Heidi, 112
Heinrich, Annemarie, 60–62, 120, 129, 148
Hellman, Lillian, 30
Helú, Antonio, 110

Henriette (fashion house), 51
Hernández, Aurelio, 57
Heroínas de la historia, xvi, 2, 51, 62, 97
Hicken, Ricardo, 29
Historical Museum 17 October, 63, 127–128
historical revisionists, 27–28, 71, 101, 114, 145
Hogar de la Empleada General San Martín, xxi, 63, 107
Hogar para Ancianos Coronel Perón, 34, 130
Holocaust, 112
Home for the Employed Women General San Martín, 63
home-schools, xxi, 28–29, 63–64, 136
hospital train, 64, 114
Huelva, Spain, xix, 131
human rights in Argentina, 25, 35, 64–65, 75, 92, 96, 146

Ibañez Menta, Narciso, xvi, 67, *118*
Ibañez Salvador, Narciso, 67
Ibarguren, Eva María, xiii, 1, 20, 27, 52, 67. *See also* Evita
Ibarguren, Joaquín, 67
Ibarguren, Juana, xiii, 1, 4, 7, 20, 27, 36–37, 42, 67, 147
icon, 45, 68, 138
iconic image of Evita, 5, *18*, 25, 68, 138
Iguazú Falls, Argentina, 139
Imbert, Aníbal Francisco, 68, 100
Incas, 136
Infamous Decade, 26, 59, 68, 123–124
Inspectorate of Mountain Troops, 50, 94
Instituto Nacional de Investigaciones Históricas Eva Perón, 46, 68–70, 135
Insúa, Alberto, 62, 97
Inter-American Conference for Peace and Security, 124
interior of Argentina, 28, 31, 34, 68, 70, 84, 93
International Labor Organization, 57
Ionesco, Eugène, 146
Italiano Hospital of Buenos Aires, 85
Itatí, Argentina, 135
Ivanissevich, Oscar, xxi, 52, 70, 90, 93

Jamandreu, Francisco "Paco" Vicente, xvi, 71, 135
Jauretche, Arturo Martín, 28, 71, 101, 145
Joly, Julio, 42

Jordán, Anita, xvii, 30, 71–72
Juan de Borbón, Prince of Spain, xx, 85
Juancito. *See* Duarte, Juan "Juancito" Ramón
Jujuy, Argentina, xxi, 114, 136
Junín, Argentina, xiii, xv–xvii, 1, 2, 20, 26, 36–37, 39, 42, 45, 52, 55, 67, 72, 87, 89–90, 100, 110, 119, 147
justicialismo, 41, 72, 108, 139–140
Justo, Juan B., 83
Juventud Peronista (JP), 47, 72–73, 75, 94

Kartulovich "Kartulo", Emilio, 75, 131
Kirchner, Néstor, 50, 51, 54, 65, 75–76, 105, 109
Kirchner Cultural Center, 75
Kirchnerism, 54, 76
Korn, Julio, 14, 120

La Granja de San Ildefonso, Spain, xviii, 78–79, 89, 130
La Pampa, Argentina, xxii, 79
La Perona, xix, 79, 129
La Plata, Argentina, xvi, 4, 43, 51, 60, 79, 107, 125, 142, 147
La Rioja (city), Argentina, 91
La Rioja (province), Argentina, 91, 94
Lagomarsino de Guardo, Lillian, xvii, 59, 83, 85, 104, 121, 133
Lagos, Ovidio, 78
Lamarque Bouza, Libertad, 42, 77–78, 83
Lang, Melita, 62
Langer, Marie, 148
Lanusse, Alejandro Agustín, 21, 23, 47, 84
Larrauri, Juanita, 84, 99
Las Delicias, 84
Las Palmas de Gran Canaria, Spain, xviii, 33, 57, 84
Las Ventas Bullring, xviii, 84–85
Lascano González, Julio, 85
Lavacolla Airport, xix, 129
Leduc, Violette, 146
Legrand, Mirtha, 104
León Suárez massacre, 96
Levín, Anita, 60
liberalism, 94, 101
Liberating Revolution (1955), xxiii, 13, 17–18, 23, 26, 28, 40, 61, 63–64, 78, 82–83, 85–86, 95–96, 123, 125, 132, 135, 137–138, 142–*143*, 146
Linter Publicidad, xiv, xvi, 31, 85

Lisbon, Portugal, xx, 85, 124, 133
Llambí, Benito Pedro, 86, 106, 133
Lloyd Webber, Andrew, xxiii, 36, 42, 44–46, 60, 148
Lobos, Argentina, 107
local branches of the PPF, 6, 25, 31, 52, 89, 104. See also unidades básicas
Lococo, Clemente, 42
Lonardi, Eduardo Ernesto, xxiii, 16, 85–86, 125
López, Ercilia, 20
López Rega, José, 86–87, 91–92, 96, 139
Los Angeles, United States, xxiii, 45–46
Los Toldos, Argentina, xiii, 1, 20, 26–27, 36–37, 42, 44, 52, 67, 87
Lucchi, Luisa de, 35
Lucerne, Switzerland, xx, 133
Ludañona y Vedia, Lautaro, 139
Luján, Argentina, xv, xvii, 87
Luna Park Stadium, xvi–xvii, xxi, 3, 87, 127
Luque, Paula de, 34, 72

Machinandiarena, Miguel, 42
Machinandiarena, Narciso, 42
Macri, Ana Carmen, 89
Macri, Mauricio, 65, 130
Madonna, xxiii, 27–28, 45, 89, 138
Madrid, Spain, xvii–xix, 8, 11, 15, 19, 21, 23, 26, 33, 36, 52–53, 59, 83–85, 89, 91, 101, 112–113, 117, 126, 133, 136–137, 143
Madrid City Hall, xviii, 89
Magaldi, Agustín, 2, 89–90
magazines:
  Antena, xiv–xvi, 14, 30–31, 62, 120, 148
  Así, 129
  Caras y Caretas, 20, 61, 129
  Cine Argentino, xv, 28
  Damas y Damitas, xv, 33, 110, 148
  El Hogar, 61, 129
  Guión, xv, 60, 62
  La Canción Moderna, 120
  Mundo Agrario, 61
  Mundo Argentino, xv, 61, 96
  Mundo Atómico, 61
  Mundo Deportivo, 61
  Mundo Infantil, 61
  Mundo Peronista, 41, 61
  Mundo Radial, 61
  Ondanía, xv–xvi, 102
  PBT, 61
  Radiolandia, xvi, 62, 120
  Radiolandia 2000, 32, 52
  Selecta, 61
  Sintonía, xiv–xv, 30, 58, 61–62, 75, 120, 131, 148
  Time, xx, 136–137
Maggi de Magistris, Maria, xxiii, 8, 21, 90
Maggiore Cemetery, xxiii, 8, 15, 21, 23, 112
Main, James, 90
Main, Mary, 90, 148
Malcom family, 36, 42
Manuel Gonnet City, Argentina, 123
Manzi, Homero, 110
Mapuche community, 42
Mar del Plata, Argentina, 37, 53, 125
Mariño, César, 31, 58, 90
Marmo, Alejandro, 90, 97, 129
Maroglio, Domingo Orlando, 61, 91
Maroni, Enrique, 110
Marshall, George, 124
Marshall, Niní, 110
Martín García Island, Argentina, 3, 55, 72, 91–92, 110, 132, 147
Martín-Artajo Álvarez, Alberto, xvii, 33, 91
Martinelli Massa, Félix, 29
Martínez, Tomás Eloy, 23, 91, 128, 138
Martínez de Perón, Isabel "Isabelita," xxiii, 8, 21, 64, 70, 86–87, 91–92, 94, 101, 108–109, 127, 146
Martínez-Bordiú y Ortega, Cristóbal, 53
Martino, Claudio, 85
Mary, Felisa, 32
Massera, Emilio Eduardo, 43, 92, 146
May Revolution of 1810, xvii, xxi, 51, 111
Mazza, Miguel Ángel, 92
media groups:
  Alea S.A., 12–13, 15, 32, 34, 39, 78, 95
  Democracia S.A., 34, 100
  Haynes Publishing, 39, 61, 91, 96, 119–120, 122, 131
  La Capital, 80
  La Nación S.A., 119
  La Razón S.A., 82
Medina del Campo, Spain, xviii, 89, 92, 112
Medina Onrubia de Botana, Salvadora, 32
Medina y Villalonga, Rafael de, 131
Meir, Golda, xxii, 92
Mendé, Raúl, 11, 24, 35, 41, 82, 92–93, 106
Méndez de San Martín, Armando, 52, 89, 93, 106, 142

Mendoza (city), Argentina, xxi, 30, 32, 54, 93, 125, 142
Mendoza (province), Argentina, xvii, 50, 72, 93, 114, 139, 142, 149
Menem, Carlos Saúl, 13, 26, 37, 45, 51, 54, 64, 92, 94, 105, 109, 146
Mentasti, Ángel, 16
Mercado, Silvia, 15
Mercante, Domingo Alfredo, xvi, 3–4, 25, 40, 94, 107, 110, 118, 123, 145, 147
Mercante, Hugo, 40
Metropolitan Cathedral, 111
Michotorena, Paz, 27
Mignogna, Eduardo, 106
Milan, Italy, xx, xxiii, 8, 15, 21, 23, 112, 125
military coup d'état (1951), 21, 43, 114
military dictatorship (1976–1983), xxiii, 8, 35, 43, 54, 64, 75, 92, 96, 146
Military Hospital, 92, 110
Millán-Astray y Terreros, José, 120
Millar, Adelqui, 78
Miller, Edward Gr., Jr., xxi
Milwaukee Labor Zionist Party, 92
Ministry of Health, 64, 111, 113
Ministry of Labor, 70
Ministry of Labor and Production, 130
Ministry of Labor and Social Security, 130
Ministry of Labor and Social Welfare, xxii, 8, 21, 99, 130, 132
Ministry of Labor, Employment, and Social Security, 130
Ministry of Social Development Building, xxiii, 51, 90, 97, 129
Miranda, Miguel, 17, 34, 61, 82, 95, 122
Misemer, Sarah, 68
Mitre, Bartolomé, 79
Mitre, Jorge, 100
Mitre family, 79, 119
Moglia Barth, Luis José, 16, 99
Molina, Rita, 3, 127
Molinari, Antonio, 34
Monaco, xx, 95, 121, 133
Montevideo, Uruguay, xiv, xx, 30, 35, 95, 133
Montoneros, xxiii, 16, 21, 47, 95–96, 108, 138
Monument of the *Descamisado*, 96, 128, 137
Moori Koenig, Carlos Eugenio de, xxiii, 21, 23, 96
Morales, Emilio, 81
Morandi, Ernesta, 52–53

Moreau de Justo, Alicia, 6
Morón Airport, xvii, 96
Moscardó Ituarte, José, 12
Mothers of the Plaza de Mayo, 35, 64
Movimiento de la Juventud Peronista, 72
Movimiento Nacional Justicialista (MNJ), 96, 105
Movimiento Peronista Femenino, 105
Mujica, Miguel, 117
Muñoz, Pepita, xiv, 30
Muñoz Azpiri, Francisco, xvii, 61–62, 96–97, 121
Mussolini, Benito, 137
Myerson, Morris, 92

National Bank of Argentina, 111
National Commission for the Eva Perón Monument, 84, 99, 138
National Delegation of the Youth Front, 128
National Department of Labor, 130
National Economic Council, 82, 95
national historical monuments, 28, 44, 123
National Library of the Argentine Republic, *143*
national right-wing sympathizers, 124
National Technological University, Argentina, 99
National University of Córdoba, Argentina, 24, 29, 34, 93–94
National University of La Plata, Argentina, 51, 75, 145
nationalism, 50, 58, 70, 76, 85, 95, 111, 124, 139
Nationalists, 11, 57, 120
Navarro, Fanny, 17, 99
Navarro, Marysa, 148
Navy Mechanics School, 92
Nazis, 5, 35, 83, 86, 112, 133
Nazism, 59, 87, 107
Negrete, Jorge, 117
neoliberalism, 76, 94
Nervo, Amado, 2, 119
Neuquén, Argentina, 94
Neuquén Convuco Center, 94
New Argentina, 16, 63, 100, 139–140
New York, United States, 45, 98, 103, 148
newspapers:
  Conquista, 31
  Crítica, xiv, 29–30, 32, 40, 42, 60, 79, 81, 100, 117, 133

Democracia, xvii, xxi, 15, 22, 25, 34, 40, 95
El Amigo del Pueblo, xiii–xiv, 39, 119
El Laborista, 34, 39, 40
El Mundo, 14, 32, 39, 61, 81, 100
El Pueblo, 34, 40
La Capital, xiv, 78, 125
La Época, 14, 78, 33
La Nación, 32, 60, 79, 81, 94, 100
La Prensa, 32, 40, 60, 79, 81, 100
La Razón, 20, 32, 40, 81–82, 100
La Vanguardia, 32, 60, 81, 83, 100
Noticias Gráficas, 32, 81, 100, 133
Tribuna, 60, 139
Nicolini, Emma, 11, 100
Nicolini, Oscar Lorenzo, 7, 100, 149
Nieves, Ana, 77
Nijensohn, Daniel, 86
Ninth Inter-American Conference of Women, 89
non-Marxist political parties, 84
non-Peronist intellectuals and artists, 109
Novarro, Ramón, 117
Núñez, Petronia, 67

Obra de Ayuda Social de la Gobernación de Buenos Aires, 25
Ochotorena, Antonio, 27
Olarra, José, 77
oligarca, 14, 28, 71, 101
oligarch, 101, 107, 139
oligarchy, 58, 95, 101, 124
oligarquía, 71, 101, 114
Olivos Presidential Residence, xxi, xxiii, 8, 21, 24, 43, 101–102, 123, 125, 142, 146
Omar, Nelly, 110
Onassis, Aristotle, 95
one-hundred-peso banknote, xxiii, 102
Onganía, Juan Carlos, 104
Oreiro, Natalia, 128
Orgambide, Pedro, 43
Ortega Sanz, Atilano, xv, 31
Ortíz, Mecha, 80
Ortíz, Roberto, 26
Ostende (cabin), 54

Pack, George, 7, 12, 24, 52, 93, 103
Palace of the Buenos Aires City Legislature, 130
Pallarols, Juan Carlos, 103
Pallarols Cuni, Carlos, 103
Pallarols Museum, 103
Palmou, Juana, 103
Paris, France, 23, 44, 51, 60, 95, 100, 103–104, 133, 146
Parker, Alan, xxiii, 27, 44–45, 138
Parodi, Delia, 18, 104, 141
Parodi, Juan Carlos, 104
Partido Justicialista (PJ), 50, 54, 76, 84, 96, 104–105, 109
Partido Laborista (PL), 21, 27, 39, 57, 105, 124, 142
Partido Peronista (PP), xxi, 6, 16, 37, 41, 47, 50, 55, 70, 79, 85–86, 94, 104–105, 108, 123, 141
Partido Peronista Femenino (PPF), xxi, 5–7, 17, 24–25, 31, 44, 50, 52, 84, 89, 99, 104–106, 108, 123, 141
Partido Socialista (PS), 83
Partido Único de la Revolución, 21, 105–106, 124
Patrón Costas, Robustiano, 124
Paula, Francisco de, 31
Paula Naletoff (fashion house), 103
Paz, Ezequiel, 79
Paz, José C., 79
Pelay, Ivo, 29
Pellicciotta, Pascual, xv, 20, 106, 120
Penella de Silva, Manuel, 82, 86, 106–107
Penella Heller, Manuel, 107
Peña Eva Perón, 26–27, 107
Peralta Ramos, Ricardo, 81–82
Peralta Ramos Hospital of Buenos Aires, 41, 52
Peralta Thorp de Leonard, María, 39
Pereyra Iraola Park, 107
Perón, Juan Domingo:
    close collaborators and friends, 3, 26, 54, 59, 86, 92–94
    control of the media, 13–15, 61, 118
    death and resting place, 21, 64, 91, 101–102, 108, 128
    exile, 8, 15, 27, 47, 84, 86, 91, 96, 104–105, 108
    first inauguration, xvii, 59, 124
    first term, 40, 55
    honorary membership, 115
    images, 76, 137
    imprisonment, 3, 21, 31, 34, 72, 91–92, 110, 132, 147

labor, social, and economic reforms, 17, 20, 31, 50, 58, 100, 108–109, 130
love affairs, 101, 125, 142, 149
love letters, 3, 92, 125, 147
magazine cover, 137
marriages, 2–4, 79–81, 91, 147
ousting (1955), xxiii, 15, 23, 27, 31, 41, 49, 72, 79, 84–86, 90, 99, 103–105, 107–109, 112, 123, 125, 132, 136, 141, 143
presidential election of 1946, 15, 21, 31–32, 34, 39, 59, 105, 109, 115, 124–125, 132, 139, 142
presidential election of 1952, xxi, xxii, 23, 41, 55, 97, 110, 115
residences, xvi–xvii, 3, 54, 86, 101, 127, 143, 147
return to Argentina, 21, 24, 45, 47, 64, 91, 96, 105
second inauguration, xxii, 7, 129
secretary of labor and social welfare, xvi, 3, 6, 20–21 50, 53, 86, 108–109, 127, 130
speeches, 34, 41, 61, 93, 97, 99, 108, 110–111, 128, 132
St. Perón's Day, 132
statues, 128, 137, 143
third inauguration, xxiii
third term, 24, 35, 47, 54, 108, 139
wives, xxiii, 64, 91–93, 107–108, 137, 147
Perón, Mario Tomás, 107
Peronism, 5, 14–17, 21, 25–26, 31, 34–35, 40–41, 46, 50–51, 53–54, 61, 63, 70, 72–73, 78–79, 82, 84–86, 90–91, 93–95, 97–99, 104–106, 108–110, 114–115, 123, 129, 137, 139–142, 148
Peronist ideology, 13–14, 28, 85, 101
Peronists, 40–41, 44, 51, 64, 89, 93, 109, 126, 139, 141, 143
Peronist achievements (module), 123
Peronist and anti-Peronist myths, 109, 148
Peronist beliefs, 95
Peronist candidates, 24, 55, 105, 109
Peronist collaborator, 24
Peronist discourse, 14, 101, 114, 145
Peronist doctrine, 82, 93, 123, 141
Peronist economics (module), 123
Peronist educational planning, 142
Peronist electoral body, 6, 50
Peronist electoral victory, 105
Peronist government, 13–15, 17, 21, 27, 34, 40, 44, 61, 78–80, 82–83, 90–91, 100, 109, 122, 130, 137, 139, 142
Peronist guerrilla groups, 21, 95
Peronist iconography, 18, 129
Peronist ideology, 13–14, 28, 67, 101
Peronist imagery, 15
Peronist indoctrination, 93
Peronist indoctrination theory (module), 123
Peronist institutions, 64, 85
Peronist leaders, 28, 86, 112, 123
Peronist leanings, 109
Peronist Loyalty Day, xvii, xxi–xxii, 3, 15, 27, 31, 34, 41, 57, 62, 72, 91–92, 94, 96, 108–111, 124, 130, 132, 139, 147, 149
Peronist media conglomerate, 32
Peronist militants, 27, 94, 96
Peronist movement, 25, 72, 91, 95, 108
Peronist opponents, 142
Peronist organization (module), 123
Peronist organizations, 14
Peronist philosophy (module), 123
Peronist politics (module), 123
Peronist politicians, 28
Peronist propaganda, 15, 24, 39, 100, 129
Peronist regime, 71
Peronist reprisals, 90, 148
Peronist resistance, 26
Peronist right, 96
Peronist right- and left-wing supporters, 96
Peronist right- and left-wing organizations, xxiii, 108
Peronist School, 110
Peronist shrine, 42
Peronist snipers, 96
Peronist sociology (module), 123
Peronist songs, 110. *See also* songs and musicals
Peronist supporters, xx, 24, 26, 28, 71, 85, 96, 106–107, 110, 139, 145
Peronist symbols, 16
Peronist terminology, 85
Peronist union leaders, 28
Peronist women, xxi, 6, 44, 106, 141
Peronization of school textbooks, 93
Petitpierre, Max, 133
Pichel, Vera, 33, 110
Pietrantonio, Angélica Clara, 110
Pietrasanta, Italy, 137

Pink House, xx–xxii, 11, 34, 44–45, 50, 59, 108, 110–*111*, 122, 129, 132, 139
Pink Room, 111
Pirandello, Luigi, 30
Pirovano, Estanislao, 45
plays:
  Baturros y más baturros, xiv, 93
  Cada casa es un mundo, xiv, 29
  Corazón de manteca, xv, 29
  El beso mortal, xiv, 30
  El cura de Santa Clara, xiv, 29, 151
  Eva Perón, 44
  La dama, el caballero y el ladrón, xiv, 29
  La fiesta de Juan Manuel, xiv, 31
  La gruta de la fortuna, xiv, 29, 131, 151
  La nueva colonia, xiv, 30, 35, 71
  ¡La plata hay que repartirla!, xv, 29
  La señora de los Pérez, xiv, 2, 29, 32, 60
  Las inocentes, xiv, 30, 133
  ¡Llegaron parientes de España!, xv, 29
  Madame Sans-Gêne, xiv, 29
  Mercado de amor en Argelia, xiv, 30, 60, 116
  Miente y serás feliz, xiv, 30
  No hay suegra como la mía, xiv, 30
  ¡Si los viejos levantaran la cabeza!, 29
  The Children's Hour, xiv, 30, 133
  Una noche en Viena, xiv, 29
Plaza de Mayo, xx, 6, 34–35, 64, 108, 110–111, 132, 139
Policlínico Presidente Perón, xxii, 52, 103, 111, 114
political myth, 112
Polo y Martínez-Valdés, María del Carmen, xviii, xix, 12, 18, 26, 53, 78–79, 85, 89, 92, 112–113, 126, 128, 130, 137, 143
Podestá, José, 51
Ponte, Enrique del, 119
Ponte, Federico del, 119
Pope Pius XII, xx, 20, 112, 125, 145
Poppen, James, 86
populism, 76
"Por qué soy peronista," xxi, 40
Portofino, Italy, 122
PPF delegates, 52, 84, 89, 104, 106, 141
Prado, Blanca del, 31
Prado Museum, xviii, 113
President Juan Domingo Perón Student City, Argentina, 113
President Perón Polyclinic, 113

President Perón University City, Argentina, 113
Presidente Perón Hospital Avellaneda, 111–112
press censorship, 79, 83, 98, 130
Prieto, Teodoro, 120
Primate Cathedral of St. Mary of Toledo, xviii, 113, 137
Primo de Rivera, José Antonio, 52
Primo de Rivera, Pilar, 92
Prince, Harold, 46
Prince, Nelly, 113
Process of National Reorganization. *See* Dirty War
proveedurías, 16, 113
public health care, 25–26, 40–41, 64, 113
pueblo, 14, 71, 101, 114, 145
Puerto de Barranqueras, Argentina, 135
Puerto Piray, Argentina, *136*
Pueyrredón, Prilidiano, 101

Quartucci, Nilda, 115
Quartucci, Pedro, 115, 130
Quasimodo, Salvatore, 146
Quijano, Juan Hortensio, xvi, 39, 115, 139
Quilmes, Argentina, 115
Quilmes (beer), 115
Quilmes Atlético Club, 115
Quintana, Elvira, 77
Quiroga, Camila, 30, 51, 115–116
Quiroga, Héctor, 116

Racioppi, Pablo, 11, 29, 117
Radical soap, xiv–xv, 29, 31, 59, 62, 90, 117
Radío, Pedro, xviii, 58, 117, 131
radio stations and networks:
  BBC Radio, 45, 119
  Cadena Azul y Blanca, 122
  Estación de Radio Difusión del Estado, 119
  LOR Broadcasting de Crítica, 117
  LOZ Broadcasting La Nación, 119
  Radio Antártida, 122
  Radio Argentina, xv, 31, 58–59, 90, 117
  Radio Belgrano (ex-Radio Nacional), xiv, xvi, 2–3, 11, 14, 19, 31, 51, 61–62, 67, 84, 97, 100, 113, 117–119, 126–127, 145, 147, 149
  Radio Belgrano y la Primera Cadena Argentina de Broadcasting, 14, 118, 145, 149

Radio Cine París, 120
Radio Cultura, xiii, 1, 119, 145
Radio del Estado (ex-Radio Nacional), xvi–xvii, 61, 119
Radio del Pueblo, 58, 84
Radio El Mundo, xv, 29, 31, 51, 58, 117, 119, 122, 131, 145
Radio La Voz del Aire, 75
Radio Libertad, 122
Radio Mitre, xiii–xv, 2, 30–31, 39, 119–120, 122
Rádio Nacional (Brazil), xx, 124
Radio Nacional de España, xviii–xix, 57, 120
Radio París, xiv, 2, 90, 120
Radio Porteña, xiv, 120
Radio Prieto, xv, 30, 58, 84, 117, 120, 131
Radio Rivadavia, 61, 84
Radio Splendid, 30, 58, 122
Red Argentina de Emisoras Splendid (RADES), 82, 122
Red Argentina de Radiodifusión, xvii
Red Azul y Blanca de Emisoras Argentinas, 61, 119–120, 122
Sociedad Radio Argentina, 117
radioteatros (synonym for *radionovela* in Argentina), xiv–xv, 2–3, 11, 14, 20, 29–31, 58–59, 62, 79, 90, 117–121, 126, 145. *See also* serial radio dramas
Rainbow Tour, xvii–xx, 4–5, 11–13, 16–18, 20–22, 33, 37, 50, 55, 63, 79, 83–86, 89, 95, 97, 112–113, 115, 120–122, 125–126, 130–131, 133, 136–137, 143, 145–146, 151
Ramírez, Emilio, 33
Ramírez, Pedro Pablo, 50, 68, 71, 109, 121–122, 124, 127, 129
Rapallo, Italy, xx, 122, 125
Rawson, Arturo Franklin, 122, 124
Rawson de Guayaquil, Juana, 42
Rawson Hospital of Buenos Aires, 51
Rearte, Gustavo, 72
Recife, Brazil, xx, 124
Recoleta Cemetery, xxiii, 8, 16, 21, 37, 43, 122, 146
Regalado Fernández, Francisco, 129
regional Peronist schools, 122–123
Reinhardt, John, 141
religious icon, 68
Renzi, Atilio, 7, 55, 84, 123, 128

Repetti, Palmira, 123
República de los Niños, Argentina, 123
Revolution of 1943, 2, 15, 19, 26, 59, 61, 107, 109, 115, 122–124, 130
Reyes, Cipriano, 39, 90, 105, 110, 124
Rice, Tim, xxiii, 36, 42, 44–46, 60, 148
Riccheri, Pablo, 14
Rif War, 57
right- and left-wing Peronists, 47, 108–109, 139. *See also* Peronists
rights of the elderly, 34, 40, 64
Rights of the Elderly Park, xxi, 107, 124
Rinaldi, Leonor, xiv, 30
Rio de Janeiro, Brazil, xx, 22, 124
Río de la Matanza, 49, 128, 138
Río de la Plata, 91
Río Gallegos, Argentina, 42, 51, 75
Río Santiago, 125
Rivadavia Hospital of Buenos Aires, 89
Rivas, Nélida "Nelly" Haydeé, 101, 125, 142
Rivera, Claudio, 31
Rojas, Isaac Francisco del Ángel, 85, 125
Rome, Italy, xix–xx, 20, 112, 125
Rosario, Argentina, xiv, xvii, xxi, 30, 32, 78, 83, 125–126, 142
Roosevelt, Eleanor, 136
Rotger, Francisco, 23
Roth, Silvana, 126
Royal Palace of El Pardo, xviii, 53, 89, 112, 126
Royal Palace of Madrid, xviii, 53, 126
Royal Site of San Lorenzo de El Escorial, xviii, 126, 128
Ruffini, Ernesto, 126
rural workers' statute, 109

Sabaté, Jorge, 29
Salamanca, Spain, 20, 84, 120
Salazar, Antonio Oliveira, 85
Salta, Argentina, 114
Salvador, Pepita, 67
San Carlos de Bolívar, Argentina, 2, 119, 145
San Francisco de Asís Church, 4, 79, 147
San Juan (city), Argentina, 54, 127
San Juan (province), Argentina, 3, 6, 93, 114, 127
San Juan earthquake, xvi, 3, 42, 104, 108, 118, 126–127
San Lorenzo de El Escorial, Spain, 126
San Luis, Argentina, 93, 104, 114
San Martín, José de, xxi, 14, 93, 127

INDEX

San Miguel de Tucumán, Argentina, xvii, 90, 142
San Remo, Italy, 122
San Salvador de Jujuy, Argentina, xxi, 136
San Vicente, Argentina, 4, 63, 83, 127
San Vicente country house, 4, 37, 63, 83, 123, 127–128, 147
Sandrini, Luis, 104
Santa Cruz, Argentina, 42, 51, 75
Santa Fe (city), Argentina, 142
Santa Fe (province), Argentina, xiv, xxi, 78, 89, 93, 107, 114, 125, 130, 135
Santa María del Buen Aire National Camp, xviii, 128
Santiago de Compostela, Spain, xix, 79, 129
Santiago del Estero, Argentina, 114
Santoro, Daniel, 97, 129
Sarandí, Argentina, 111
Sartre, Jean-Paul, 146
Satanowsky, Marcos, 82
Savigliano Marta E., 28
Schönfeld, Nicolás, 129, 131
Schprejer, Alberto, 95
Sciammarella, Rodolfo, 44, 90, 110
Scioli, Daniel, 43, 60
Scolatti Almeyda, Félix, 110
Secretariat of Communications, 68, 97, 100, 118
Secretariat of Health, 113, 138
Secretariat of Information and Press, xxi–xxii, 14–16, 97, 129–130
Secretariat of Labor, 130
Secretariat of Labor and Social Welfare, xvii, 16–17, 33, 40, 53–55, 104, 127, 130
secular icon, 67
Segovia, Spain, xviii, 78, 89, 112, 130
senior residences, 16, 29, 130–131
Seoane, María, 43
serial radio dramas:
    Amanecer, 31
    Así era mi casa, 31
    Cara sucia, 31
    El amor de una esposa, 31
    El pasado regresa, xvi
    El rostro y el aullido del lobo, xv, 29
    En el valle hay una sombra, xvi
    Infortunio, xv, 29
    La calandria ciega, xv, 31
    La carga de los valientes, xv
    La estrella del pirata, 30
    La hora de las sorpresas, xv, 59, 117
    La otra cara de la máscara, xv, 29
    La vengadora, xiv
    La vida de Fray Mamerto Esquiú, 120
    Las rosas de Caseros, 30, 151
    Llora una emperatriz, 11
    Los caminos de la historia, xiv, 120
    Los desesperados, 31
    Los jazmines del 80, xv, 14, 30, 120, 151
    Mi amor nace en ti, xv, 29
    Oro blanco, 31
    Tempestad, xvi
    Una promesa de amor, xv,
    Una rosa en el río, 11
    Una sombra en la recova, 120
Serrano, Enrique, 32
Severo de Albuquerque Maranhão, Augusto, 18
Seville, Spain, xviii–xix, 57, 131
Sforza, Carlo, xix–xx
the shirtless ones, xxii, 34, 131
Sicily, Italy, 146
Simari, Leopoldo, 29, 131
Simari, Tomás, xv, 29, 129, 131
Simone, Mercedes, 117
Singerman, Paulina, 110
social justice, 6, 17, 19, 63–64, 72, 79, 95, 108, 132, 139–140
socialism, 6, 35, 50, 54, 64, 95
Socialists, 125
Sociedad ABC, 119
Society of Beneficence of Buenos Aires, 13, 63, 93, 113, 131–132
Soffici, Mario, 77, 80
Solá, Luis, 31
Soler, Adelaida, 131
songs and musicals:
    "Don't Cry for Me Argentina," 28, 36, 45
    Eva, el gran musical argentino, 42–43, 59
    "Evita Capitana," 44, 84, 90, 110
    Evita musical, 42–43, 60, 148, 154
    Evita musical: American Stage Production, xxiii, 46
    Evita musical: British Stage Production, xxiii, 46
    Evita concept album, xxiii, 36, 44–46
    "La descamisada," 110
    "Los muchachos peronistas," 90
    "Madrecita de los pobres," 110
    "Marcha del primer campeonato de fútbol infantil Evita," 110, 138

"Marcha Peronista," 44, 70, 90, 110
"Serenata de la muerte de Eva," 110
"Versos de un payador a la señora Eva Perón," 110
Sosa Toledo, Juana, 107
Spanish Civil War, 12, 53, 57–58, 120, 143
Stigwood, Robert, 45
Stone, Oliver, 45
Storni, Alfonsina, 6
Suero Siero, Pablo "El Sapo," 30, 133
suffrage. *See* female suffrage
Sujo, Juana, 30
Sundmark, Betty, 35
Susini, Enrique, 117
Switzerland, xx, 4, 86, 106, 121, 133

Tagle Lara, Alfonso, 110
Taiana, Jorge Alberto, 135
Taquini, Alberto, 135
Taylor, Julie M., 148
Tecuara (presidential yacht), xxi, 135
television broadcasting, 100, 149
temporary homes, *69*, 89, 135
Tequara, 135
Termas de Reyes, Argentina, xxi, 114, 136
theater companies:
    Compañía Argentina de Comedias, xiv, 2, 29, 32, 52–53, 106
    Compañía Argentina de Espectáculos Cómicos, xiv, 29, 33, 106, 131
    Compañía Candilejas, xv, 11, 29, 31, 117, 119, 145
    Compañía Cómica Simari-Simari, xv, 29
    Compañía de Armando Discépolo, 30
    Compañía de Camila Quiroga, xiv, 30, 116
    Compañía de Comedias Muñoz-Franco-Álvarez, xiv, 30, 32, 53, 93, 125
    Compañía de Comedias y Sainetes Rinaldi-Charmiello, 30
    Compañía de Pablo Suero Siero, xiv, 30, 133
    Compañía Romances del Pueblo, 31
    Compañía de Teatro del Aire, xv, 20, 30, 106, 120
    Compañía del Padro-de Paula, 30–31
    Compañía Juvenil de Radioteatro, xv, 29, 31, 58, 145
    Compañía Remembranzas, xiv, 31
    Compañía Romances del Pueblo, xv, 31
theaters:
    Argentino Theater, 43, 60
    Astral Theater, 30, xiv
    Coliseo Theater, 117
    Colón Theater, xvi, xxi, 20, 83
    Comedia Theater, xiv, 29
    Cómico Theater, xiv
    Corrientes Theater, xiv, 30
    Cervantes Theater, 106
    Dorothy Chandler Pavilion, 46
    18 July Theater, xiv, 30
    L'Épée de Bois Theater, 44
    Liceo Theater, xiv, 29–30
    Lola Membrives Theater, 43
    Maipo Theater, 42, 59
    Municipal Theater, xiv, 93
    Odeón Theater, xiv, 30, 78, 125
    Orpheum Theater, 46
    Politeama Theater, xiv, 30, 35, 71
    Regent's Park Open Air Theater, 46
    Smart Theater, xv, 29
third position, 72, 108, 136
third way, 22
Thousand Schools Scheme, *136*
Tizón, Aurelia Gabriela, 19, 107, 137
Toledo, Spain, xviii, 12, 53, 57, 112–113, 137
Tomassi, Leone, 96, 137–138
Torres, José Luis, 68
Torreón (building), 128
tournaments, xxi, 27, 55, 110, 138
treaty of commerce between Spain and Argentina, 121
Triple A, 35, 59, 87, 92, 96, 139
Truman, Harry S., 8, 132
Tucumán, Argentina, xvii, 89, 114–115, 130
turismo social, 139
Twenty Peronist Tenets, 72, 114, 123, 139
Twenty Truths of *Justicialismo*, 72, 140

Umberto II (king of Italy), xx, 85
Unidad Básica Cultural Eva Perón, 18, 141
unidades básicas, 25, 106, 141
Unión Cívica Radical (UCR), xi, 50, 55, 71, 78, 85, 115, 122, 141
Unión Cívica Radical del Pueblo, 142
Unión Cívica Radical Intransigente, 85, 142
Unión Cívica Radical-Junta Renovadora, 27, 105, 115, 142
Unión de Estudiantes Secundarios (UES), ix, 93, 101, 125, 142
Unión Democrática, 79
Unión Ranch, Argentina, 142

United Nations (UN), 4, 22, 34, 53, 121
United States, xxiii, 4, 14–15, 22, 24, 45–46, 50, 57, 70, 90–91, 98, 109, 121–122, 124, 148–149
Universidad Nacional de Eva Perón, Argentina, 142
Universidad Nacional Obrera, Argentina, 93, 142
Universidad Tecnológica Nacional, Argentina, 142
university campuses, 142
University City of Madrid, Spain, xviii, 143
University of Buenos Aires, Argentina, xxi, 49–50, 55, 70, 100
University of Cuyo, Argentina, 72
Unzué Palace, xvii, xxi, 12, 84, 86, 123, 129, 132, *143*
Urquizo, Electo, 87

Vajna, Andrew G., 45
Valle, Pablo Osvaldo, 145
Varela, Eduardo, 145
Vatican (City), xix, 4, 20, 25, 112, 121, 145
Vázquez, Pablo Adrián, 44
Vedia, Joaquín de, xiv, 29
vendepatria, 14, 28, 71, 101, 145
Venturini, Aurora, 145–146
Versailles, France, xx, 78, 104
Vicone, Carmelo, 27
Victorica Roca, Julio, xx, 104
Videla, Jorge Rafael, 21, 54, 102, 146
Vigo, Spain, xix, 146
Vila, Alberto, 131

Villa Cisneros, Western Sahara, 146
Villaronga, Agustí, 26
Villate Olaguer, Carlos, 101
Viola, Roberto, 146
Visca, José, 14
Visca-Decker Commission, 14, 146
Vitucho, 120
Vuletich, Eduardo, 42

Walsh, Rodolfo, 43
wars of independence from Spain, 95
Way of St. James. *See* Camino de Santiago
web.museoevita.org.ar, 147
Western Sahara, xvii, 33
white and black myths, 5, 109, 148
Wilenski, Sivul, 14, 33, 62, 129, 131, 148
Wilson, Alfredo, 42
World War I, 35, 62
World War II, 4, 14, 71, 87, 98, 112, 121, 124
Workers' Tourism Council, 139

Yankelevich, Jaime, 13–14, 117–119, 122, 145, 149
Yankelevich, Samuel, 113
Yrigoyen, Hipólito, 68, 91, 115, 121, 142
Yurbel, María Cecilia "La Piraña," 142, 149

Zaragoza, Spain, xix, 151
Zipman, Boris, 31
Zucker, Marcos, 151
Zuluaga, Ángel María, 15
Zurich, Switzerland, 106

About the Authors

María Belén Rabadán Vega is a faculty member in the Department of Spanish and Latin American Studies at Maynooth University, where she teaches translation, Latin American literature, and Spanish language. She holds an MA in Hispanic and Lusophone studies and a PhD in Hispanic studies, both from University College Dublin. In her doctoral thesis, she analyzes the construction and reconstruction of the transnational iconic image of Evita, bringing together diverse fields such as cultural, translation, and film studies as well as literary criticism and history. Her research on the figure of Evita led her to interview people who were personally acquainted with Evita. She has presented her research findings at national and international academic conferences. In 2014, the Association of Hispanists of Great Britain and Ireland awarded her the Valentina Guevara Prize for her paper "Rewriting Evita: María Eva Duarte de Perón's Transformation into an International Icon." Together with her colleague and friend Mirna Vohnsen, she coauthored the article "100 Years of Eva Perón" in 2019.

Mirna Vohnsen is a faculty member in the Department of Languages at Technological University Dublin, where she teaches literary and critical theory, Latin American and Spanish literature and culture, Argentine cinema, as well as Spanish language. She holds a PhD in Hispanic studies from University College Dublin on the representation of Jewishness in contemporary Argentine cinema. Her PhD thesis was awarded a publication prize in 2017 and was published as a monograph titled *Portrayals of Jews in Contemporary Argentine Cinema: Rethinking Argentinidad* in 2019. Her interest in Argentine culture in tandem with her friendship with María Belén Rabadán Vega led her to coauthor the article "100 Years of Eva Perón," which attracted widespread attention. She is the conference secretary of the Association for Women in Spanish and Portuguese Studies and the contributing editor for the Latin American film section of *The Year's Work in Modern Language Studies*. She is currently coediting a collected volume on contemporary Argentine women filmmakers to be published in 2023. When not teaching or researching, she enjoys traveling around the world with her husband, Brian.

www.ingramcontent.com/pod-product-compliance
Lightning Source LLC
Chambersburg PA
CBHW081934240426
43669CB00050B/2782